The Editor

ALAN RYAN was Professor of Politics at Princeton University from 1988 to 1996 and is now Warden of New College, Oxford. He is the author of *John Dewey and the High Tide of American Liberalism, Bertrand Russell: A Political Life, J. S. Mill,* and *The Philosophy of John Stuart Mill.*

Norton Critical Editions in the History of Ideas

AQUINAS *St. Thomas Aquinas on Politics and Ethics* translated and edited by
   Paul E. Sigmund
DARWIN *Darwin* selected and edited by Philip Appleman *Third Edition*
ERASMUS *The Praise of Folly and Other Writings* translated and edited by Robert
   M. Adams
HERODOTUS *The Histories* translated by Walter Blanco edited by Walter Blanco
   and Jennifer Tolbert Roberts
HOBBES *Leviathan* edited by Richard E. Flathman and David Johnston
MACHIAVELLI *The Prince* translated and edited by Robert M. Adams *Second
   Edition*
MALTHUS *An Essay on the Principle of Population* edited by Philip Appleman
MARX *The Communist Manifesto* edited by Frederic L. Bender
MILL *Mill: The Spirit of the Age, On Liberty, The Subjection of Women* edited by Alan
   Ryan
MORE *Utopia* translated and edited by Robert M. Adams *Second Edition*
NEWMAN *Apologia pro Vita Sua* edited by David J. DeLaura *Second Edition*
NEWTON *Newton* selected and edited by I. Bernard Cohen and Richard S. Westfall
ROUSSEAU *Rousseau's Political Writings* translated by Julia Conaway Bondanella
   edited by Alan Ritter
ST. PAUL *The Writings of St. Paul* edited by Wayne A. Meeks
THOREAU *Walden and Resistance to Civil Government* edited by William Rossi
   Second Edition
THUCYDIDES *The Peloponnesian War* translated by Walter Blanco edited by
   Walter Blanco and Jennifer Tolbert Roberts
WATSON *The Double Helix: A Personal Account of the Discovery of the Structure of
   DNA* edited by Gunther S. Stent
WOLLSTONECRAFT *A Vindication of the Rights of Woman* edited by
   Carol H. Poston *Second Edition*

A NORTON CRITICAL EDITION

MILL

The Spirit of the Age, On Liberty, The Subjection of Women

TEXTS

COMMENTARIES

Selected and Edited by

ALAN RYAN

NEW COLLEGE, OXFORD

An expanded and revised edition based on the Norton Critical Edition
of John Stuart Mill's *On Liberty*, edited by David Spitz

W • W • NORTON & COMPANY • *New York* • *London*

The text of this book is composed in Electra
with the display set in Bernhard Modern.
Composition by PennSet, Inc.
Manufacturing by Courier Companies.
Cover illustration: Pierre Thomas Le Clerc, *La Liberté*, 1794,
Paris, Mus. Carnvalet. Reproduced by permission of Giraudon/Art Resource.

Library of Congress Cataloging-in-Publication Data
Mill, John Stuart, 1806–1873.
[Selections. 1996]
Mill : texts, commentaries / selected and edited by Alan Ryan.
p.   cm. — (A Norton critical edition)
"An expanded and revised edition based on the Norton critical
edition of John Stuart Mill's On liberty, edited by David Spitz."
Includes bibliographical references (p.   ) and index.
Partial Contents: The spirit of the age — On liberty — The
subjection of women.
1. Liberty. 2. Women's rights. 3. Equality. 4. Mill, John
Stuart, 1806–1873. I. Ryan, Alan. II. Mill, John Stuart,
1806–1873. On liberty. III. Mill, John Stuart, 1806–1873. Spirit
of the age. IV. Mill, John Stuart, 1806–1873. On liberty.
V. Mill, John Stuart, 1806–1873. Subjection of women. VI. Title.
JC585.M7425   1996   96-7642

ISBN 0-393-97009-4 (pbk.)

W. W. Norton & Company, Inc., 500 Fifth Avenue, New York, N.Y. 10110
http://www.wwnorton.com

W. W. Norton & Company Ltd., Castle House, 75/76 Wells Street, London W1T 3QT

4 5 6 7 8 9 0

Contents

Preface

The first edition of this Norton Critical Edition was published in 1975, edited by the late David Spitz. Two decades later, there has been a continued flow of critical work on Mill, while writers have become increasingly interested in the connections between *On Liberty* and Mill's other writings, whether early like "The Spirit of the Age" or late like *The Subjection of Women*. For this edition, I therefore have added "The Spirit of the Age" and *The Subjection of Women* to *On Liberty*. I have retained R. H. Hutton's review of *On Liberty* from the first edition, together with David Spitz's selections from Fitzjames Stephen's *Liberty, Equality, Fraternity*, but I have changed the later essays entirely. Isaiah Berlin's "John Stuart Mill and the Ends of Life" provides an overview of Mill's liberalism; an extract from Gertrude Himmelfarb's *On Liberty and Liberalism* provides reasons for preferring "The Spirit of the Age" to *On Liberty*; John Rees's "The Principle of Liberty" explains what "harms" Mill thought justified legal and other sanctions; Jeremy Waldron's "Mill and the Value of Moral Distress" explains what Mill refused to count as "harm"; and Susan Okin's "Mill's Feminist Egalitarianism" assesses the strengths and weaknesses of Mill's feminism. Because I have provided a substantial biographical and analytical introduction, I have reduced Professor Spitz's footnotes to the first edition; the notes now provide literary, historical, and biographical references and translate quotations. Mill's own notes are, of course, left intact. I was a good, though not a close, friend of David Spitz and an admirer of his work; I hope this new edition maintains intellectual standards he would have approved of. I am happy to end by thanking Sadie Ryan for her very considerable labors in helping to put this new edition together.

Introduction

Life

John Stuart Mill was born on May 20, 1806, in north London and died at Avignon on May 6, 1873. He was the oldest of the nine children of James Mill (1773–1836) and his wife, Harriet (née Burrow.) Mill left an extraordinary account of his life in his *Autobiography* (1873),[1] one extremely relevant to the essays in this volume, concerned as they are with self-creation, with the liberty of both men and women, and with authority in a secular society. Mill's *Autobiography* exerts a great emotional grip on everyone who reads it. Mill was at pains to treat his life with a detached scientific objectivity and to present it to his readers only as an example of what a well-designed education could achieve with what he claimed to be very ordinary raw material. In reality, Mill was unusually intelligent, unusually sensitive, and to a distressing degree the victim of tougher but less subtle people than himself; the *Autobiography* is engrossing because it reveals all this in spite of its author's best efforts. He felt emotionally deprived but morally obliged to transcend such feelings — and, of course, could not entirely do so.

A striking feature of the *Autobiography* is the complete absence of Mill's mother. "I was born in London," writes Mill, "on the 20th of May 1806, and was the eldest son of James Mill, the author of *The History of British India*."[2] Even in Victorian fairy tales children are not taken down from a bookshelf. In a draft of his opening chapter cut before publication, Mill devoted three sentences to his mother, notable both for their coldness and for what they suggest of the author's thwarted need for affection and encouragement.

> That rarity in England, a really warm-hearted mother, would in the first place have made my father a totally different being, and in the second would have made his children grow up loving and being loved. But my mother, with the very best of intentions, only

1. The *Autobiography* has been published in innumerable editions; the best is in *The Collected Works of John Stuart Mill* (CW), vol. 1, edited by John M. Robson and Jack Stillinger (Toronto, 1981). As with all the volumes in the Toronto edition, the introduction is an impressive work of scholarship in its own right. This edition also contains Mill's early drafts of the *Autobiography* as well as an engrossing few paragraphs on his father and mother and a lengthy panegyric on the mind and character of Mrs. Taylor that were cut out before publication.
2. CW, vol. 1, 4.

knew how to pass her life in drudging for them. Whatever she could do for them she did, and they liked her, because she was kind to them, but to make herself loved, looked up to, or even obeyed, required qualities which she unfortunately did not possess.[3]

Other observers agreed that Mill's mother was an attractive young woman, but without intellectual interests and unfit to be the companion of a hard-driving, clever, and ambitious man like James Mill. She became a *Hausfrau*, good natured but querulous — and as her son certainly felt, ground down by bearing nine children in as many years. J. S. Mill's unkindness was not just a matter of childhood miseries surfacing in later years. He was also bitterly resentful of what he fancied was a lack of respect on the part of his mother toward the woman he had married in 1851, a few years before he wrote these pages. The contrast between Harriet Mill, his mother, and Harriet Mill, his wife, will occupy us again below, but the author of *The Subjection of Women* knew something of what subjected and liberated women were. His mother was the victim of both her son's chief mentors.

James Mill, by contrast, was all willpower and self-confidence. He had been born in humble circumstances in the little Scottish town of Northwater Bridge but attracted the attention of a member of the local gentry, Sir John Stuart — after whom his eldest son was named. Sir John's assistance enabled Mill to attend Edinburgh University. It became clear that he could never practice the profession to which this naturally led, that of the ministry, so he made his way to London, where he edited *The Anti-Jacobin* and later made himself indispensable to Jeremy Bentham. His role in "philosophical radicalism" — the loose-knit reform movement of the early 1800s built around *The Westminster Review* — was that of publicist and propagandist. He had a great talent for the clear, almost brutally clear, exposition of complicated ideas. He once memorably offered to write an account of the human mind that would make its operations "as plain as the road from St. Paul's to Charing Cross"; and in 1820, he published *An Essay on Government* that advanced with breathtaking speed from the premise that each man pursues his own interests to the conclusion that the only valid form of government was democracy — in which the people would pursue their interests, not those of some group or section.[4] In the same spirit he exercised enormous power over the largest of British colonial possessions. Until 1858, the Indian subcontinent was governed by the East India Company, which by the early nineteenth century was an agency operating a "contracted-out" form of government rather than a trading company. James Mill was the chief civil servant in the company's Lon-

3. "Early Draft Rejected Leaves," CW, vol. 1, 612.
4. It was savaged by Macaulay in one of the funniest essays in political controversy ever penned; see John Rees and Jack Lively, eds., *Utilitarian Logic and Politics* (Oxford, 1983).

don office. The government of India wholly depended on the energy
and expertise of its civil servants — indeed the term *civil servant* was
coined to distinguish the East India Company's civilian employees and
administrators from its "military servants," the soldiers with whom it
preserved order. As the chief permanent official of the company, Mill's
authority was as great as that of a minister in any British government.

Education

James Mill passionately believed in education. He had risen from obscurity by taking advantage of educational opportunity, and philosophical radicalism rested on the assumptions that human nature was
malleable, that superstition and prejudice could be abolished by education, and that governments could be compelled to govern in the
interests of the common people once the common people had the vote
and the intelligence to use it to hold their rulers to account. Young
John was the beneficiary of his father's belief. Readers of the *Autobiography* have never been of one mind about the education he received
at his father's hands. The late-nineteenth-century intellectual historian
Leslie Stephen thought it was cram and that boys ought to play more
cricket. Mill faced that complaint in another of the "rejected leaves"
that he omitted from the *Autobiography* and dismissed it. As a radical
social critic of somewhat mystical leanings, Thomas Carlyle cared nothing for cricket but thought Mill's education had been an experiment
in "manufacturing" a soul, and deplored it accordingly. For some years
in his middle twenties, Mill was inclined to agree. Literary critics from
F. R. Leavis on have suggested that Charles Dickens's description of
the education handed out by Gradgrind in *Hard Times* was modeled
on what James Mill provided for John. This is at least partly mistaken;
whatever Dickens's inspiration may have been, John Mill's education
was utterly unlike Sissy Jupe's suffering from Gradgrind's emphasis on
facts.[5] James Mill cared for theory and analysis, rather than facts, and
although John Mill complained that his education had been lacking
in the poetic spirit, he read an astonishing quantity of poetry by the
time he was a teenager. Mill learned Greek at three, by the advanced
method of using "flash cards" with Greek and English equivalents on
them. He learned Latin at eight. As soon as he was fluent, he read
ancient history, Greek and Latin verse, and modern historians such as
Robertson and Millar. He became a competent mathematician and at
twelve learned logic, economics, and philosophy. At fourteen he went
to France for a year to stay with Jeremy Bentham's brother, Sir Samuel
Bentham, and become fluent in French.

Mill insisted that he was not made conceited by all this, though he

5. K. J. Fielding, "Mill and Gradgrind," *Nineteenth Century Fiction*, 11 (1953), 148–51.

confessed that many of his father's friends mistook his argumentative style for arrogance. His father insisted that he should argue through every idea he was offered, and he was too frightened of his father to refuse. His own sentiments were of the extreme inadequacy of his attainments. The account of his relations with his father that he offers in other "rejected leaves" of the *Autobiography* makes it all too credible that he felt as diffident as he says there. The chief characteristic of his father's treatment of him was its unkindness. Until he joined the East India Company in 1819, James Mill was anxious because he had no settled income, burdened by writing his *History* and cursed with an impatient temper. Since he had no idea just how intelligent his son was, he constantly criticized him and led him to think that he was dimmer than the average.[6] James Mill's younger children benefited from their brother's suffering and were treated more kindly. But in regard to the themes that dominate the essays in this volume, it is of interest that Mill complained that his father's ferocity tended to weaken, or even destroy, his will.

> To have been, through childhood, under the constant rule of a strong will, certainly is not favourable to strength of will. I was so much accustomed to expect to be told what to do, either in the form of direct command or of rebuke for not doing it, that I acquired a habit of leaving my responsibility as a moral agent to rest on my father, my conscience never speaking to me except by his voice. The things I ought *not* to do were mostly provided for by his precepts, rigorously enforced whenever violated, but the things I *ought* to do I hardly ever did of my own mere motion, but waited till he told me to do them; and if he forbore or forgot to tell me, they were generally left undone. I thus acquired a habit of backwardness, of waiting to follow the lead of others, an absence of moral spontaneity, an inactivity of the moral sense and even to a large extent, of the intellect, unless aroused by the appeal of some one else, — for which a large abatement must be made from the benefits, either moral or intellectual, which flowed from any other part of my education.[7]

By the age of fourteen, he was better educated than most men of forty and already a formidable intellectual figure, but emotionally insecure. It was not out of the question that he should go to Cambridge a year or two later, but it was clear that he would not learn very much from the ordinary course of undergraduate studies there. Accordingly, in 1823, at the age of seventeen, he joined the East India Company as a junior clerk — that is, as an apprentice administrator — in his father's department and started on a career that ended thirty-five years later

---

6. Psychologists who try to guess what the measured IQ of distinguished figures from the past might have been usually place Mill at the top of the chart with a guessed IQ of 192.
7. *CW*, vol. 1, 613.

when the company was dissolved and he refused an appointment to the India Council that succeeded it. The office did not consume all his energies, and he began at this point to write short essays for radical newspapers such as *The Examiner*, in which his "Spirit of the Age" essays later appeared, and for radical journals, especially the *Westminster Review*. These were written from the standpoint of his father and Bentham; they were utilitarian, radical, and reformist, and Mill rightly regarded them as a beginner's practice pieces.

Disillusionment

Less happily, he acted as ammanuensis to Jeremy Bentham while the latter was compiling his *Rationale of Judicial Evidence*. This was exhausting and tedious work. Bentham's attempt to bring order to the English Law was conducted in a very disorderly fashion. His notes were illegible, scattered hither and yon, even pinned to the drapes of his windows. Mill assembled the intended book after three years of unremitting effort, and at twenty he felt as exhausted as many men after a lifetime's work. Then he asked himself a fatal question. Having grown up to believe that his father's and Bentham's projects for the improvement of the lives of their fellow creatures were entirely rational, Mill paused: "I put the question distinctly to myself, 'Suppose that all your objects in life were realized, that all the changes in institutions and opinions which you are looking forward to, could be completely effected at this very instant; would this be a great joy and happiness to you?' and an irrepressible self-consciousness distinctly answered 'No!' "[8] It was a decisive moment. Utilitarianism, the doctrine that the only thing of ultimate value in the world is happiness and that all institutions, activities, and states of mind are valuable only to the extent that they promote happiness, stands or falls by the answer to the question whether utilitarians really will be happy. Mill's answer doomed— apparently—either himself or the doctrine or both. He fell into a depression from which he emerged only many months later.

Mill's account of what he called "a crisis in my mental life" is low-key. He says that he was in low spirits and overworked, as though it were the kind of late-adolescent depression that any hardworking and ambitious young man might suffer—and perhaps it partly was. Yet, it formed a hinge in his life, and he rightly devoted an entire chapter of his *Autobiography* to it: before it, he had been his father's child, the product of an education devised by somebody else, created not creative. His condition had been that to which many women are condemned all their lives, acted on, not acting, working out plans made for them by others. After he had analyzed to his own satisfaction what had been missing in his education and how he could replace it, he became his own man, the captain of his own fate. Two features of the experience bear directly on the essays in this volume. First, Mill's account of his experience applies to his individual case the view of the French Revolution that he learned from Carlyle and the St.-Simonian missionaries who came to London in the late 1820s with whom he made close friends. This view was that the revolution happened with the suddenness and completeness that it did because the *ancien régime* was a "sham," a fraud, an untruth.[9] Once the fraud was detected, the old regime collapsed.

The eighteenth century, represented both by the monarchical regime of Louis XVI and by the revolutionaries of 1789, had a thin and inadequate grasp of social and individual truth. Mill came to think that his father and Bentham were essentially eighteenth-century figures; they had a mechanical, overly rationalist and analytical picture of human nature and human society. Their reforming schemes were too simple to carry emotional conviction; they seemed logically compelling, but they had no purchase on the soul. Mill thus underwent a real revolution in his ideas and his feelings. After it, the truth about how we might improve society or the individual appeared much more complex than before. Now Mill took Goethe's motto — "manysidedness" — as his own. Indeed, the very idea of "truth" in human affairs acquired an emotional, or poetic, dimension it had lacked in the thought of Bentham and James Mill. In his almost absurdly calm way, Mill declared that poetry had saved him and that the poet who had done most for him was Wordsworth, "the poet of unpoetical natures"; this has led critics to scoff at Mill for treating poetry as a form of therapy, but wrongly. Mill's view may or may not be sound, but it had nothing to do with therapy. What he had in mind was the accessibility of the truths perceived by a particular writer. Wordsworth came closer than other Romantic poets to saying what he meant; unpoetical natures needed to make less of a leap of the imagination to understand him.

The second idea that Mill seized on was that human character was not formed once and for all, that it was not an inflexible carapace. Bentham and James Mill shared with Robert Owen the view that education should inculcate in malleable infants the habits that would make them useful to themselves and everyone else. Character once properly formed need not be reformed. It was assumed rather too readily that character could be formed by any more or less intelligent parent in such a way that everyone would find happiness in working for the general welfare — whence Mill's despair. But this view of character displayed little concern with freedom, not freedom in the sense of the usual political liberties and the rule of law, but freedom in the sense

9. R. D. Cumming, "John Stuart Mill's History of His Ideas," *Journal of the History of Ideas*, 25 (1968), 235–56.

of the individual's own consciousness of himself or herself as a free agent. Robert Owen denied outright that individuals possessed that sort of freedom; and Jeremy Bentham had scoffed at the thought that individuals could want the freedom to make themselves miserable. It is not surprising that Mill described the doctrine of determinism as "lying like an incubus" on his spirits during the months of his depression.

He came to see, dimly at first, but later quite clearly, that he must neither throw away a concern with character nor see character as Robert Owen had done. Intelligent beings needed some fixity of character; they needed both a compass and the motive power to move in the chosen direction. Yet it must always be possible for them to stand back, look at their existing habits, desires, beliefs, and the other psychic elements that made up their characters and decide to change them. This new view of truth and this understanding of character as something *self*-created, gave Mill the two central ideas of *On Liberty* and *The Subjection of Women*. It is not surprising that this should all emerge in the *Autobiography*. Mill wrote the first draft of the *Autobiography* at the time he was writing *On Liberty*; his account of his "mental crisis" was essentially crafted in the light of his later ideas. It is not a young man's spontaneous creation but a middle-aged man's reflection on what that young man's experience had meant.

The East India Company

None of Mill's friends noticed that he was in emotional turmoil. Neither did his employers at the East India Company. From his twenties onward, he was intermittently unwell, and in his early thirties he suffered some sort of brain trauma that left him with a nervous tic and a twitch in his left eye that stayed with him all his life. This and other mishaps necessitated occasional lengthy periods of leave and rest, but Mill rose steadily in the East India Company, writing dispatches and deciding policy on the so-called Princely States, the Indian states that governed themselves under the general supervision of the company while preserving a nominal independence. His work sheds little direct light on the subjects dealt with here. The converse is less true. Mill was unusual among nineteenth-century Indian administrators in looking forward to the day when the Indian subcontinent would be home to a modern, self-governing society and no longer in need of the tutelage of the British. For this to happen, the Indian people must acquire the character appropriate to self-government—far-sighted, provident, self-controlled, and eager for freedom. Like his father, Mill was to a twentieth-century eye too quick to dismiss Hinduism as a tissue of servile superstitions, but unlike his father he wanted to give something more than efficient administration to their subjects. Mill was sufficiently convinced of the virtues of the company as a provider of that education for liberty to undertake its defence when it was facing extinction in 1858. His defence contained a number of characteristic ideas; the most relevant here was his argument that the curious system whereby the company was not a branch of the British government but was nonetheless answerable to it for its management of Indian affairs provided what Mill and Tocqueville declared to be essential for progress—a way to create an "antagonism of opinions."[1] The company was unique among British institutions in the care with which it chose, trained, and promoted its administrators, but they were then checked up on by Parliament, so combining efficiency and accountability. If company rule was technically a "despotism," because it was not answerable to the Indian people, it was an "improving" government, dedicated to progress—and "progress" is one of two or three key concepts of *On Liberty*.[2]

Harriet Taylor

If Mill said too little about the effect on his mental development of his occupation at India House, he said perhaps too much about the greatest influence on his life—or perhaps the greatest after his father. He met Harriet Taylor in 1830; he was twenty-four and so was she. She had married young, found her husband dull, had found childbirth extremely unpleasant, and therefore found the rarified charms of Mill's intelligence irresistible. To judge by their letters, Mill would have pursued a more indiscreet and sensual liaison had it been offered; but it was not. For the next twenty-one years they pursued a chaste relationship that was at once touching, absurd, pure, high-minded, and scandalous. They went on holidays together but never went into society as a couple; Harriet Taylor's husband, John, behaved with astonishing self-restraint and forbearance. He insisted that Mill and Mrs. Taylor avoid anything that would make him look ridiculous and otherwise accepted their infatuation with each other as a *fait accompli*.

What Mrs. Taylor got from Mill was not only adulation; she was a very intelligent and attractive woman and might have had any amount of adulation had she sought it. What she valued was the intellectual respect she received. All commentators have thought Mill gave her a great deal more than her due;[3] the dedication of *On Liberty* gives a fair sample of Mill's estimate of her abilities and simultaneously suggests some grounds for scepticism about that estimate. A woman of no matter

---

1. See my "John Stuart Mill and Bureaucracy," in G. Sutherland, ed., *The Growth of Nineteenth Century Government* (London, 1973).
2. For Mill's references to "despotism" see pp. 48–49.
3. One qualification should be made: recent writers on Mill's feminism have thought well of Harriet Taylor; see, for example, pp. 345–47.

how much native wit could not, without much more education than
Harriet Taylor ever received, have been a match for Mill, let alone seen
so much further than he. It hardly needs saying that nobody other than
Mill has thought that she was superior in poetic sensibility to Carlyle
and intellectually his own superior in all but matters of technical detail.
Still, she gave him many valuable things, and we may be as grateful as
Mill that she did. On the equality of women's rights with those of men,
she was a simpler, bolder, and more unequivocal liberal than he. She,
not he, took the lead in arguing that whatever men were entitled to do,
women should be entitled to do too. Moreover, she was quicker than
he to accept that women would want to do more of what had formerly
been "men's work" than had hitherto been supposed. Mill too readily
dropped into thinking that men were "naturally" inclined to engage in
the world's work, in warfare, and in the hurly-burly of politics, while
women would "beautify" life. He also, as a good classical economist,
feared that encouraging women to go out to work would simply lower
the wages of the laboring poor. The classical theory of wages held that
wages were determined by the numbers of workers looking for work; if
we double the number of workers we halve the average wage. Harriet
Taylor's energy and perhaps also her economic ignorance—a happy
ignorance, since the classical theory of wages was wrong—put a stop
to such arguments.

   Where her influence was more equivocal was in strengthening Mill's
suspicious view of his own society. Once Harriet and he had become
deeply committed to one another, they ceased to go out into society.
They felt surrounded by a hostile, overrespectable society and returned
a joint condemnation of society's narrow-mindedness. It is worth emphasizing that what they deplored was a *middle-class* society; Mill makes
much of the connection between a tyrannical public opinion and the
rise of democratic government, but he was not thinking of the dangers
that would be posed by the working class when it got the vote. Mill
was frightened by the conformism of a middle-class society, not by the
dangers of proletarian insurrection. Since many of his anxieties about
a democratic society had been provoked by Tocqueville's *Democracy
in America* or had been reinforced by that work, it is worth noticing
that the epitome of middle-class society was the United States; he saw
Britain as a version of America and had no such fears about France or
Italy—though he deplored their illiberal governments as much as one
might expect. What made the United States "middle-class" was not that
the country was full of the sort of *bons bourgeois* that Balzac and other
nineteenth-century French novelists described—for there were few or
no such people to be found there. It was rather that outside the black
and American Indian population, there was no deep, persistent, and
inescapable poverty. Everyone could aspire to comfort and a reasonable
degree of economic security. The question was whether people whose
economic needs had been taken care of, and whose political rights were

secure, would use this foundation to launch into a new and lively civilization or would settle for a boring, sheeplike uniformity. Mill feared the latter. In exciting these fears, Harriet Taylor and their illicit relationship played a considerable role. *On Liberty* was conceived as a memorial to her, for she died in 1858, after a mere seven years of married life with Mill, and the book came out in the following year, dedicated to her memory. It would be a vulgar but not wholly inaccurate description of *On Liberty* to say that the substance of the fears it expresses was provided by Tocqueville, but the intensity of the emotion that went into that expression was provided by Harriet Mill.

Parliament

Although Mill maintained that the spring of his life was broken by Harriet's death, he was in fact a liberated man. In part, this was simply because the two of them had spent most of the previous decade contemplating their own extinction. She and Mill were consumptive, and all too likely Mill infected her, he having been infected by his own father many years before. But he recovered from the illness while she died. Freed after her death of the anxieties caused by their unorthodox relationship, Mill once more went into society, rediscovered old friendships, and took a vigorous role in public controversy. Not only did he write a great deal in the fifteen years remaining to him, he entered Parliament in 1865 as a Liberal MP, and although he lost his seat in the election of 1868, he was a surprisingly effective speaker and controversialist. Under his leadership, the advocates of votes for women came closer during the debates over the Reform Act of 1867 to passing the necessary legislation than anyone for fifty years thereafter. Only in 1918 did a British government finally see reason, bite the bullet, and give women the vote. Inside Parliament and out, Mill spoke in favor of female suffrage, a large measure of independence for Ireland, substantial reform of the system of land tenure, the need for an international system of security to replace war as presently instituted, and much else on the radical liberal agenda.

When Mill died on May 6, 1873, he was acknowledged as the outstanding intellectual figure of the day. Hyppolyte Taine observed that the British were an unphilosophical people but admitted that "they do have John Stuart Mill." He was not universally liked or admired, however. American critics disliked his free trade economics, feared his agnosticism in matters of religion, and found him glacially cold — "an intellectual iceberg," said Charles Eliot Norton. His British critics thought he was too prim, too aggressively liberal, unfeelingly intellectual, and out of touch with the coarse common sense of "the man on the Clapham omnibus." It was not only robust conservatives like James

Fitzjames Stephen who thought Mill's liberalism was foolish in itself
and at odds with the utilitarianism on which Mill claimed to have based
it. The liberal Walter Bagehot thought Mill's commitment to an abstract and high-principled liberalism reflected a misunderstanding of
the real liberalism embedded in the English political system. Bagehot
suggested that Mill was too readily carried away by his hatred of conservative stupidity; when he was not confronted by conservatives, he
was judicious, balanced, calm, and cautious, but when they appeared
in his sights a red veil came across his eyes, and the Voltairean desire
to *écraser l'infame* overcame him.[4] But nobody doubted that Mill was
the patron saint of advanced liberalism, and that is what he has remained for the past century and a quarter. His political reputation, as
distinct from his narrowly philosophical reputation, has risen and fallen
with that of the liberalism he stood for.

The *Autobiography* was an account of "an unusual education" and
a history of Mill's ideas. Before I summarize the argument of the essays
printed here, I should outline four elements in that history. The first
concerns Mill's reaction against Bentham and against what he saw as
the Benthamite spirit. Mill never doubted that Bentham's analytical
approach to legal and political reform was an essential weapon in the
progressive armory, but he thought Bentham's blindness to the deepest
springs of human well-being made him almost comically unsuited to
offer advice to a society that suffered from the moral and spiritual un-
certainties of early-nineteenth-century British society. In the essay
"Bentham," which he published in 1838,[5] Mill gave a considered judgment on its subject. It was harsh, but not dismissive. Bentham was a
"one-eyed" thinker; his gaze was penetrating but narrow. What he saw,
he saw clearly, but what he did not see clearly he did not see at all.
The most damning indictment against Bentham came when Mill discussed Bentham's attempt to classify human action and its motivation
in his "Table of the Springs of Action." It was defective because it
omitted the aesthetic dimension of life, not only in the usual sense of
a concern for beauty but in the more complex sense of an individual's
concern for the balance, harmony, consistency, and coherence of her
or his existence; it omitted the passion of honor that would lead someone to sacrifice his or her life before violating a promise; it omitted the
spirit of perfection that leads us to pursue excellence for its own sake.
Finding room for all these things is one purpose of the essay *On Liberty*.

Bentham's democratic inclinations attracted censure too. In the spirit
of *On Liberty*, Mill deplores the way Bentham's politics allows the

---

4. It is in Mill's *Considerations on Representative Government* that the famous phrase about the
(British) Conservatives being the "stupid party" first appears. Mill in fact described the Conservatives as "being by the law of their being the stupidest party"; it is a moot point whether
Conservatives should take comfort that other parties are presumably stupid as well or take
umbrage as being described as stupider than the rest (CW, vol. 19, 452n).
5. *London and Westminster Review*, Aug. 1838 (CW, vol. 10, 75–115).

numerical majority of a society to dictate its character in all respects. Mill was a radical who believed that in some way the majority must have the last word on who was to govern society and on the acceptability of legislation and regulation. But it was very much the *last* word to which it was entitled; the majority should not have every word. Mill invoked a thought that also occurs in "Coleridge," the essay that he wrote as a companion piece to the essay on Bentham.[6] Far from assuming that "the people" was entitled to govern as it chose, we must ask how it ought to choose; that is, we must ask, "to what authority is it good for the people that they should submit?" This question is more in the mood of "The Spirit of the Age" than in that of *On Liberty*. For in the latter essay, Mill seems to assume that society possesses rather too much authority over the individual and is looking for ways to reduce it; in the earlier essay, he thought that authority in general had decayed to nearly nothing. He shared Carlyle's sense that what was missing in British life was an authoritative sense of what held society together, a sense on which political authority could draw, and in the absence of which political leadership was doomed to be ineffective. It is worth remembering how far the late 1820s and early 1830s were years of public and political turmoil as well as of turmoil in Mill's bosom. Demands for political reform and economic relief were loud — demands that Catholics and Dissenters should be relieved of the various disabilities they still suffered; demands for the removal of agricultural tariffs that raised the price of food and threatened starvation to the poor; and demands for the extension of the suffrage, shorter parliaments, the ballot, and an end to rotten boroughs. Catholic Emancipation passed in 1829 in an atmosphere of near revolution, and the Reform Act of 1832 in an even more violent atmosphere. In such a climate, Mill's sense that *authority* rather than individuality was the subject at hand was not implausible. By the time he wrote *On Liberty*, he had a more nuanced view.

What Mill acquired from the various influences that he invoked to balance Bentham was a historical and sociological approach to the problem of authority and individuality. Although his first reaction against Bentham suggested that he might abandon his liberal allegiances altogether, this was a passing mood. The impact of the St.-Simonian missionaries and of Auguste Comte, who coined the word *sociology* — described by Mill as a "convenient barbarism" for its mixing of Latin and Greek roots — was less than that of Alexis de Tocqueville. Tocqueville's account of the American experiment in liberty and equality was the occasion for two of Mill's very best essays.[7] More to the

6. *London and Westminster Review*, Mar. 1840 (CW, vol. 10, 117–63).
7. "Tocqueville on Democracy in America (vol. I)," *London Review*, 1835 (CW, vol. 18, 47–90), and "Tocqueville on Democracy in America (vol. II)," *Edinburgh Review*, 1840 (CW, vol. 18, 153–204).

point, Tocqueville taught Mill to understand what it was that he feared about the nature of a mass society: the subtle and insidious threats to individuality that hid behind an apparently rampant individualism.

Second, then, it fell to Mill to explain in *A System of Logic* how there might be a social science that took proper account of both individuality and the workings of society and how liberalism might see society as a field for rational reform based on the findings of social science without slighting the insights of conservatives like Coleridge. This is not the place to do more than say dogmatically that *A System of Logic* occupies the central place in Mill's intellectual career. Its purpose was to show how there was room for liberal reform and how individual liberty was consistent with sufficient predictability in social life for the purposes of the scientific reformer. Thus it was essential for Mill to subvert what he denounced as

> The notion that truths external to the mind may be known by intuition or consciousness, independent of observation and experience, is, I am persuaded, in these times, the great intellectual supports of false doctrines and bad institutions. By the aid of this theory, every inveterate belief and every intense feeling, of which the origin is not remembered is enabled to dispense with the obligation of justifying itself by reason, and is erected into its own all-sufficient voucher and justification. There never was an instrument devised for consecrating all deep-seated prejudices.[8]

Social change depended on people coming to hold new views, and this included new views in morality as well as in physical and social science; if the truths of morality were simply "intuited," and if the intuitions so arrived at were, as they were usually said to be, infallible, then change would be impossible. So substantial portions of *A System of Logic* pursue intuitionism into the remote recesses of mathematics and logic, not only to give a rational account of these subject matters but because these were the strongholds of intuitionism; if it could be expelled from these, it could be expelled from ethics and politics. Many readers have wondered at the polemical tone of *A System of Logic*, but Mill's passion is understandable. Both *On Liberty* and *The Subjection of Women* complain that a besetting vice of human beings is to mistake the prejudices of second nature or custom for the deliverances of first nature and to suppose that what they believe firmly enough is certified as true. Intuitionism reinforced that vice; the point, however, was to curb it.

Third, the main works of Mill's middle years formed something like a repository of advanced liberal doctrine. *The Principles of Political Economy* summed up the agreed view of economic theory but carefully detached that theory from any commitment to the merits of capi-

8. CW, vol. 1, 233; cf. 269–70.

talism — Mill hoped that the workers would become their own masters and practice a form of cooperativism, because it was impossible for a free person to spend all his or her life taking orders from an employer. *Utilitarianism* explained how to lay the foundations of a rational secular morality in the search for human happiness; like his other works, it was obsessed with the idea of character and has kept critics happily occupied for 140 years as they have tried to make sense of Mill's claim that some sorts of happiness are intrinsically superior to others and that we should prefer to be Socrates dissatisfied rather than a fool satisfied. *Considerations on Representative Government* was a more sober and nuanced work than *On Liberty*, and has been less admired in consequence; but it, too, set out a case Mill made over and over again. The test of a good government is whether it leads to progress; the usual cant about the need for a party of order and a party of progress is foolish, since it is obvious that for there to be progress there must not be retrogression. What we need is a party of progress — with many competing views of just what progress involves. It is in *Representative Government* that Mill coined the famous — and much misquoted — phrase "the Conservative is from the law of its being the stupidest party" and dismissed opponents of votes for women with the observation that gender is as irrelevant to the suffrage as height or hair color.

Fourth is Mill's concern with the position of women in Victorian society. If it is wrong to suggest that this was Mill's chief preoccupation, he certainly treated the standing of women as a litmus test of a society's moral worth. It is said that as a youth he came across the abandoned body of a dead baby on his way to East India House and was appalled. He certainly was arrested at the age of sixteen for distributing birth control advice to working-class households; he was let off with a caution — it was felt that the women to whom the advice was tendered would be unable to understand it.[9] He wrote in the newspaper press to denounce the leniency with which courts treated husbands who violently abused their wives, and although a good deal of the discussion of population in *The Principles of Political Economy* was directed to the standard anxieties of the classical economists — mostly, the fear that whatever gains in wages the laboring classes might briefly make would instantly evaporate as the workers had more children or more of them survived — he struck a distinctive note in urging a check to population for the sake of women's welfare. He held strikingly sceptical views on marriage — his discussion of slavery in *On Liberty* is really aimed at marriage rather than slavery — and he was, perhaps sadly, inclined to

9. Whence the jingle: "Two Mills there are, whom those who like reading / What's vastly unreadable, call very clever. / But whereas Mill Senior makes war on good breeding / Mill Junior makes war on all breeding whatever." But the incident had repercussions sixty years afterwards; Gladstone hastily withdrew from the committee formed to see to the erection of a statue in Mill's memory when he learned of it.

dismiss sexuality as an "animal function."[1] But it is hard to deny the plausibility of Mill's view that a society's commitment to equality, justice, physical security, and self-development is best tested by what happens to its women members.

"The Spirit of the Age"

The essay "The Spirit of the Age" is not one of Mill's most elegant works; it was written in installments, and Mill was obviously groping toward new ideas that he had not fully mastered. Still, it is about one issue only and, therefore, has a certain clarity of purpose. The issue was progress, and the question was whether an age that was fertile in industrial and mechanical progress was likely to be fertile in intellectual and moral progress. Mill's recurrent questions about the nature of moral and spiritual authority in post–Napoleonic Wars Britain and his use of St.-Simonian ideas about social analysis are all subordinate to this main theme. The first significant feature of Mill's essay is its title. The concept of the spirit of the age — later and commonly called the *Zeitgeist* — was a recent importation into British social thinking. Mill himself observes, "the 'spirit of the age' is in some measure a novel expression. I do not believe that it is to be met with in any work exceeding fifty years in antiquity. The idea of comparing one's own age with former ages, or with our notion of those which are yet to come, had occurred to philosophers; but it never before was itself the dominant idea of any age."[2] William Hazlitt had published his wonderful essays on his contemporaries and their ideas under the title *The Spirit of the Age* in 1825, but it was the French Revolution that brought the idea into general consciousness. The revolution raised in the starkest possible way the question of why it had turned out to be impossible to replace the *ancien régime* with a timelessly incorruptible republic of virtuous citizens. The most plausible answer was that it was an anachronistic aspiration; painters like David might depict patriotic themes and fill canvases with toga-clad figures, but modern Frenchmen were not, and could not become, ancient Romans.

Anyone who hoped to write intelligently about social and political reform must do so in the light of a historical understanding of society. Social and political theory must be part of a theory of progress. "Progress" is a slippery idea, and Mill was aware of its slipperiness. Indeed, he employed it to his advantage. For Mill already wished to do what

---

1. Susan Okin complains of Mill's "refusal to question the traditional family and its demands on women" (see p. 347); but nothing could be further from the truth. Mill offers the thought that most women will wish to work at home rather than anywhere else as a concession to Conservatives. It is quite difficult to see how anything much like the traditional family could survive in a world where Mill's egalitarian liberalism had taken hold.
2. See p. 3.

he did at length in *A System of Logic*, that is, to distinguish sharply between progress in the sense of cumulative change and progress in the sense of improvement; and he wanted to distinguish, as he did in many places thereafter, between what he perceived as undeniable progress in technology and mechanical skill on the one hand and the mix of improvement and retrogression that characterized religion, ethics, and politics on the other.

The apparatus Mill employed was in part borrowed from the St.-Simonians. The disciples of the French philosopher and social theorist Henri de St.-Simon had dispatched two of their number to Britain a couple of years earlier, and they had made good friends with Mill.[3] Thinking as he did that Bentham was deaf to the lessons of history and blind to the "organic" quality of social existence — the qualities that made him Coleridge's opposite — Mill was very ready to hear the St.-Simonian message. What he acquired was a rather simple piece of analysis, but it seemed to him to shed a flood of light on social change. This was the distinction between "natural" and "transitional" periods of history — the "natural" was often termed the "organic," as it was in Comte's work. In natural or organic periods or epochs, society's structure was accepted by everyone, those who bore religious, political, and intellectual authority knew what they must do to earn it and keep it, and those who accepted that authority did so readily and in some confidence that it was founded on the truth about the world. In transitional periods there is no such consensus. Mill, of course, thought that his own age was preeminently an age of transition. It is hardly astonishing that Mill's picture of his own frame of mind in the aftermath of the crisis he endured at the age of twenty is so rich in allusions to its transitional quality and the pressure he felt to find a settled view of the world; "I found," he says, "the fabric of my old and taught opinions giving way in many fresh places, and I never allowed it to fall to pieces, but was incessantly occupied in weaving it anew. I never, in the course of my transition, was content to remain, for ever so short a time, confused and unsettled. When I had taken in any new idea, I could not rest till I had adjusted it to my old opinions, and ascertained exactly how far its effect ought to extend in modifying or superseding them."[4]

What makes Mill's account of all this richer than a mere translation of St.-Simonian concerns into English dress is the way he balanced the themes of liberty and authority. Many, probably most, writers who think in terms of such a contrast between the natural and transitional phases of social life have an essentially conservative cast of mind. They wish, generally, to cut short the transitional period and to reestablish authority. Mill was unusual in wanting to use conservative writers for radical ends and unusual in being willing to defer the arrival of the next or-

3. The story is well told in Michael St. J. Packe, *The Life of John Stuart Mill* (London, 1954), 90–98.
4. *CW*, vol. 1, 163–65.

ganic epoch to the very distant future. In his essay "Auguste Comte and Positivism" many years afterward, Mill mocked Comte's desire to inaugurate the next organic epoch in the immediate future; if the transitional period had thus far lasted six centuries according to Comte, why should it not go on a great deal longer?[5]

In "The Spirit of the Age" Mill did something not dissimilar. The essay is conservative to the degree that it laments the absence of authority — intellectual, religious, and political — but radical to the extent that it uses the exemplars of *true* authority beloved of the conservatives to mock the claims of contemporary intellectuals, aristocracy, and clergy to such an authority. Contemporary intellectuals were not true intellectuals, and the contemporary Church of England had no true spirituality. The radical Mill judges the institutions admired by the conservatives in terms of their own standards and finds them wanting. This was a characteristic Mill trope. Interestingly, the argumentative style of almost all his works is expressed in a distinctive literary and rhetorical manner, too. What one might call "rocking antitheses" play a large role in the discussion of everything from the philosophy of science to the standing of the Church of England. Argument takes the form, "*if* the clergy were virtuous and devout, the aristocracy bold and far-sighted, the intellectuals both rigorous and sensitive, then we should surely call on the ordinary man to be guided by them, *but . . .*"

There are two very different views that we might take about the relationship between "The Spirit of the Age" and the other two essays in this volume. On the one hand, we might follow Gertrude Himmelfarb's view that there were two John Stuart Mills, the one a cautious, subtle, sensitive conservative, not wholly unlike Lord Acton, the other a simpleminded radical, led astray by Harriet Taylor, who was always ready to revert to a Benthamite simplemindedness.[6] Ms. Himmelfarb, therefore, says of *On Liberty* that "there is no doubt of its antagonism, in substance and in spirit, to the early essays of Mill."[7] On the other hand, we might take a somewhat more complicated view of their relationship. We might think that there is some tension between the spirit of "The Spirit of the Age" and the spirit of *On Liberty* but go on to deny that there is so much difference of substance. It is in "The Spirit of the Age" that Mill says firmly that in the absence of a consensus on the basis of social and moral authority we must accept absolute freedom of thought and inquiry; and it is in *On Liberty* that Mill readily concedes that in most matters the ordinary man must needs be governed by the authority of the better informed.

"The Spirit of the Age" is apprentice work in Mill's new vein. Mill

---

5. CW, vol. 1, 325–26.
6. See, for instance, "The Other John Stuart Mill," in *Victorian Minds* (New York, 1968); her introduction to her *Essays on Politics and Culture* (New York, 1963), and the essay here (p. 279).
7. *Politics and Culture*, xx.

himself broke off the sequence of short essays that made up the whole piece as the agitation over the Reform Act stirred up the *Examiner*'s readers and himself. His later essays in the same vein ("Civilisation," the two essays on Tocqueville, and the essays on Bentham and Coleridge) are less excitable and more accomplished. More is later made of another of his favorite dichotomies, the tendency of masses to prevail over individuals, and only the very attentive reader would wonder whether Mill thinks bad forms of democracy—majority tyranny, the despotism of the mass, the elevation of public opinion to unchallengeable authority—are aberrations that mark a transitional age, to be replaced in a more organic age by a society in which each person has achieved the level of cultivation of which she or he is capable, so that a true equality of authority has been attained. "The Spirit of the Age" remains fascinating because it is there that Mill himself raises most of the anxieties that readers of *On Liberty* have had: is *everyone* to lead the examined life; does constant questioning undermine authority; is there room for moral, political, and intellectual authority in a classless, democratic society? Just as *The Subjection of Women* completes *On Liberty* by showing what its implications are for relations between the sexes, so "The Spirit of the Age" provides an intellectual and political context for both later essays.

On Liberty

On Liberty is Mill's best-known work. Unusual among his works, it is a manifesto for a single idea: "The object of this Essay is to assert one very simple principle as entitled to govern absolutely the dealings of society with the individual in the way of compulsion and control, whether the means used by physical force in the form of legal penalties, or the moral coercion of public opinion. That principle is, that the sole end for which mankind are warranted, individually or collectively, in interfering with the liberty of any of their number, is self-protection."[8] It was written with a degree of passion unusual in Mill's other writings, and it has aroused passionate responses in its readers; some have felt it to be a noble piece of work but too demanding for ordinary mortals, others have felt it to be out of touch with the society it depicts, a work that pours kerosene on a bonfire, one whose influence has mostly been for the worse.[9] Those academic commentators who have restrained their political emotions while keeping their critical capacities intact have generally been very puzzled by the connection between *On Liberty* and *Utilitarianism*. On the face of it, a Utilitarian should favor

8. See p. 48.
9. R. H. Hutton's review (see p. 225) and the extracts from Fitzjames Stephen's *Liberty, Equality, Fraternity* (see p. 243). give an idea of the hostility of his contemporaries.

whatever interference with liberty does the most good; certainly, he should not favor an "absolute" prohibition on certain sorts of interference in advance of any inquiry into the good they might do. That Mill presumably knew this as well as anyone else makes their relationship all the more puzzling.[1] Mill was in no doubt that *On Liberty* was to be a major part of his intellectual legacy. Exactly what sparked off the idea of writing it is slightly mysterious, however. This is a pity because it would be interesting to have a more precise knowledge of Mill's target. The essay itself has echoes of almost everything that Mill cared for: it attacks the hold of custom on human thinking as *A System of Logic* did; it urges reformers not to allow their benevolence to lead them to create a "nanny" society and thus sacrifice individuality and spontaneity, as the essays "Bentham" and "Coleridge," and the essays on Tocqueville's *Democracy in America* had done; it espouses a doctrine of progress that appears once more in *Representative Government*; and Tocqueville's fear that a democracy might become a society of "industrious sheep" animates the whole work and provides its coda. A thinker who is mentioned only once in the text, but who seems to have been present in Mill's mind throughout was Auguste Comte; Mill's attack on the "liberticide" implications of Comte's plans for the Positivist utopia culminated in his *Auguste Comte and Positivism* in 1865, but it was in his mind from the early 1850s. *On Liberty* was thus an essay attacking not only conservatives but misguided progressives. It was also addressed to himself. Mill, too, wanted social, political, and economic reform for the sake of human happiness and had the intellectual's usual conviction that he knew what would promote that happiness. So it was to himself as well as others that he addressed the demand that they recognize their fallibility, that they acknowledge the autonomy of other persons and their right to conduct their own lives in their own way.

More than any other of his major works, *On Liberty* was influenced throughout by Harriet Taylor. When they discovered that they were both likely to die of consumption in the near future, they set about preparing what they—with a dismaying lack of modesty—referred to as "a sort of mental pemmican for thinkers—if there are any—who come after us."[2] The image seems especially inapt when applied to a literary gem like this. Pemmican was a rather disgusting form of preserved food relied on by arctic explorers, mostly composed of dried bear meat and biscuit; it could be dried, compressed, and rehydrated when needed, but nobody thought it an attractive substance. Still, it is hardly to be wondered at that Mill and his new wife felt bitter and beleaguered when they discovered that the happiness they had waited twenty years to enjoy was to be snatched away so soon. Harriet read the drafts of the

---

1. This is discussed at length in John Gray, *Mill on Liberty: A Defence* (London, 1983).
2. Mill to Harriet Mill, *Later Letters*, CW, vol. 14, 141–42.

essay, made suggestions that Mill always accepted, and died just as it was finished. It went to the printer with not a comma altered from the last draft that she had approved. Critics who dislike both Harriet Taylor and *On Liberty* emphasize her role in its composition.[3] They think the essay is narrow, oversimple, implausible, and mischievous in its effects, that it has encouraged an unwomanly form of feminism and an anti-social individualism that together have made late-twentieth-century America an increasingly unlikeable society. They are not numerous; Professor Himmelfarb has secured rather few converts over the past twenty-five years. More numerous are critics who dislike Mrs. Taylor but like the essay. They have some difficulty in reconciling her effect on the work with their estimation of it.

There is one plausible way of allowing her influence its full weight while arguing that the essay is neither simpleminded nor malign in its implications and subsequent impact. This is to acknowledge that it is more anxious about the actual condition of Britain in the late 1850s than there was any need to be — that it was foolish to think that intellectual genius had dried up when 1859 saw the publication of *The Origin of Species* as well as *On Liberty* and James Clerk Maxwell was closing in on the fundamental laws of thermodynamics and electrodynamics. That is not to say that Harriet alone was responsible for this exaggeration; Mill was always ready to believe that mental and moral progress was about to come to a halt — it was an affliction of many liberals, including Walter Bagehot and Henry Maine. But here and elsewhere, we may suspect that Mill's deference to Harriet's wishes went along with an irrepressible intellectual honesty and a (perhaps somewhat evasive) insistence on his own ideas. Given the echoes of so much else in his work that we hear in the essay, it would be more foolish to exaggerate Harriet's role than to deny it.

On Liberty has always been a difficult work to construe. Like much else of Mill's work it has a deceptive clarity; the transparency and simplicity of the prose gives no clue to the complexities lurking in the depths of the argument. Structurally, it seems to present no problems. It begins with a statement of the essay's purpose and devotes the opening, introductory chapter to a statement of the principle to whose defence the essay is devoted and an explication of its nature, its intellectual basis, and its historical importance. "That principle is, that the sole end for which mankind are warranted, individually or collectively, in interfering with the liberty of action of any of their number, is self-protection." It is a principle that Mill argues is more important in the nineteenth century than in earlier ages when the most important task was to prevent royal and aristocratic rulers from oppressing the ordinary people. The second chapter discusses what is usually referred

---

3. Indeed, much of Gertrude Himmelfarb's *On Liberty and Liberalism* (New York, 1974) is devoted to assailing Harriet's role in the work.

to as freedom of thought; Mill argues for an almost absolute freedom to say what we please outside those situations where we would cause immediate, unjustifiable damage. In American law, this is often referred to as the rule that we should not shout "fire" in a crowded theater—unless there really is a fire, and the damage done by the ensuing panic is less than the damage that would be done by the fire. Mill insists that causing offense to others does not justify the suppression of free speech; nor does an opinion's contradiction of religious beliefs or of the unanimous opinion of everyone other than the speaker. What holds for speech holds for publication. The grounds for proposing this regime of almost absolute free speech are twofold: first, that truth is promoted by the conflict of ideas, and second, that ideas are held vividly and honestly only if we hold them after knowing what can be said against them.

Thus far, Mill's argument for the most part proceeds negatively: that is, people may be coerced only to prevent harm to others, and where they cause no harm they may not be prevented from doing what they choose. Already, however, he has broached the positive defence of liberty, by arguing that a belief is not vitally held unless it is held with full self-consciousness. In essence, he has begun to argue that a belief is not *ours* until it is held in that way. Chapter III spells out Mill's view of the individuality that the essay is defending. The argument is simple enough: Mill fears that too many people take their plans of life from those around them. Their ideas of what is worth knowing, worth pursuing, and worth doing with one's life are taken from the commonplaces they hear every day. Mill argues against this passive and conformist view of life on two grounds. First, individuals vary and will not be happy unless they find a way of life that suits them individually. Second, society will stagnate unless individuals wish to strike out on their own. Of course, most of us will have to follow the lead of more talented and original individuals than ourselves, but we can at least choose intelligently and for ourselves which leads to follow, and there will always be some people who strike out the trail that we must follow. We now have much of Mill's case before us; we must fetter individual initiative as little as possible, for the sake of lively belief, so that life shall be lived to the full and so that moral and intellectual stagnation shall not be our lot.

Chapter IV then recurs to first principles and asks the question, "How far shall society's authority over the individual extend?" The answer is that it can extend only to the extent of preventing individuals from making themselves a nuisance to others. Some positive good, we can be compelled to do—such as giving evidence in a trial—but the presumption is that we can be prevented from doing harm and can only be exhorted, urged, or cajoled into doing good. Mill draws a sharp line between what one might call *direct* harm to others, such as is caused by assault or fraud and the *indirect* harm of, for instance, the distress they may feel at seeing us behaving badly or the failure of their hopes for some good we might have done them. It is in this chapter that Mill attacks temperance movements, Sabbatarian movements (the Sunday observance movement that prevented shops from opening on Sundays), and restrictions on behavior that offends the religious sensibilities of other groups in society. Finally, in Chapter V, Mill works his way through a number of "applications." These are what one might call "hard cases for the harm principle." Thus, Mill says, somewhat surprisingly, that compulsory education is justified, since it is a way of making parents do their duty to their children; by the same token, it is right for a government to insist that a couple has the resources to bring up children before it allows them to marry. One of Mill's complaints is that because people had a very poor grasp of when they ought *not* to interfere, they had an equally poor grasp of when they *ought*. Mill takes several other examples of difficult cases, such as the sale of poisons and noxious drugs, running a gambling house, or acting as a pimp. These present rather different problems: dangerous drugs present the problem of reconciling the demand for liberty with the risk of misuse and murder, while the pimp presents the difficulty that we punish the accessory without punishing the prostitute. And Mill ends with Tocqueville's plea that we should not turn society into a flock of sheep — even with the best of intentions.

The problems of the essay begin at once. In the introductory chapter, Mill writes of a very simple principle that is entitled to govern "absolutely" the dealings of society with the individual by way of compulsion and control. Yet, Mill was a utilitarian; the only principle allowed to govern "absolutely" anything at all in human life was the principle of utility. Just what this utility requires has always been hotly debated; but it certainly requires that we ask of all lesser principles the question whether it will promote the welfare of all sentient creatures to follow them rather than other principles or none. What, then, is "absolute" about the principle of liberty, as we may call it? Before we answer that question, we must recognize that Mill himself makes it as hard as possible to do so. For he insists that his defence of a maximum of individual liberty is a Utilitarian defence. "It is proper to state that I forego any advantage that could be derived to my argument from the idea of abstract right, as a thing independent of utility."[4] He repudiated the idea, found in almost all recent liberal theories, that the limits of legitimate coercion are set by the natural, or human, or fundamental or basic *rights* of individuals. Where recent writers have overwhelmingly started from the thought that there is an insurmountable tension between Utilitarian and rights-based considerations, Mill offers to reduce rights-based arguments to Utilitarian ones. As the contemporary near-consensus suggests, his discussion has not carried conviction.[5]

---

4. See p. 49.
5. The *locus classicus* for the past twenty-five years has been John Rawls, A *Theory of Justice* (Cambridge, Mass., 1971).

Mill claims that the principle of liberty rests on "utility in the largest sense, the utility of man as a progressive being."[6] This helps a little, for it allows us to say that it is good to leave someone to make their own mistakes, say, and not interfere on paternalistic grounds, since *self-education* is a better route to self-improvement than being forced into a particular mold. But this is not enough. It may generally be true, but where it is not, the Utilitarian emphasis on achieving good results implies that we should do what works better, even if this involves paternalism. An "absolute" principle must not be vulnerable to being overridden in this way. Mill's next addition achieves something more. The utility that Mill has in mind, the utility "of a man as a progressive being," embraces components that connect more directly to a right to be left alone, except when one is a threat to other people or violates their rights. One of these components is autonomy, the power of self-creation and self-direction that Mill made so much of in other writings. If its exercise is indispensable to utility so conceived, we have something close to an absolute principle. A person cannot be autonomous under compulsion.

This, however, raises new problems. Is it true that self-direction or autonomy is vital to the happiness of a progressive being? There is much to be said for the thought that it is, or at any rate that once people have experienced the life of free agency, they will not give it up. That is, freedom becomes a centrally important part of happiness once it is experienced. Mill argues for this view only indirectly in the essay *On Liberty*. In his essay "Bentham" and in *A System of Logic* Mill gave a more elaborate account of how different his conception of Utilitarianism was from Bentham's. There Mill distinguished between *prudential*, *aesthetic*, and *moral* evaluation. Prudential evaluation concerns the assessment of action so far as it bears on our own happiness; morality, its assessment so far as it bears on the effect of our behavior on nonconsenting others. Aesthetic evaluation is the realm of the "fine," or "noble." A man who grudgingly repays a loan does what is morally right, may do what is prudent—it may do him good by inspiring confidence in his creditors—but he does not do what is fine or noble, since he acts grudgingly and mean-spiritedly. One goal of the essay is to persuade his readers that such aesthetic goals give meaning to life and that people can be urged, coaxed, perhaps even nagged into taking them seriously, but that coercion is not the route.

Mill's critics have thought it was as rash to announce that the object of the essay was to defend one "very simple principle," as it was to announce that it was an absolute principle. A proper treatment of this objection would take us into very thorny territory; what constitutes simplicity is far from being a simple matter, and one that has much exer-

---

6. This hotly debated issue is the subject of the essays by Rees (see p. 294) and Waldron (see p. 311). In essence, Rees explains what Mill counted as interests and Waldron explains what Mill refused to count as interests, damage to which counted as "harm."

cised philosophers. For our immediate purposes, there is no need to go very far afield. The only reply to the critics is that a principle may itself be simple without it being simple to decide on its application. Teachers have great difficulty judging the merit of their students, but the principle that they should rank their students in order of merit is a simple principle. In the same way Mill's principle that we cannot interfere with other persons in the way of compulsion and control save to prevent harm to others is a simple principle but requires a complicated understanding of such ideas as "harm" and a careful attempt to distinguish between compulsion and other ways of influencing someone's behavior—what Mill calls "exhortation and entreaty," among other things.

Mill says that coercion may be employed to make people do what they otherwise would not to prevent harm to others. He somewhat rashly offers several near-equivalent accounts of what distinction he proposes here; one that has caused much trouble is the distinction between "what concerns others" and "what concerns only himself." This distinction between the "self-regarding" and "other-regarding" aspects of action has drawn criticism from antiindividualist and anti-Utilitarian thinkers who have wanted to say that we are so implicated in society and social relations that there is no such distinction to be drawn. Mill was well aware that he would attract this objection and was careful to explain what kind of harm he had in mind.[7] In short, he equated "harm" with "damage to our interests," and our "interests" he understood as those things that we needed for our long-term flourishing; as progressive beings, what we needed was, roughly, protection from physical harm, the benefits of a stable legal order, and plenty of room for "experiments in living." What we did not need was protection from the mere fact of difference. However unhappy we may be that others have different tastes, sexual allegiances, religious beliefs, and the like from ourselves, that unhappiness is not a "harm."

I cannot complain that your homosexual conduct harms me if all I mean is that I dislike the thought of your engaging in it; Mill's complaint that people too often allow "the likings and mislikings" of society to determine the law addresses just that point. If you are flying an aircraft in which I am a passenger and endanger my life by engaging in homosexual activity with your copilot, I have every right to stop you, but that is because I may stop you flying recklessly, *whatever the cause.* Mill's notion of harm is largely uncontroversial. Contentiously, however, it excludes all the discomforts of disagreement. Indeed, Mill regards such discomfort as positively good for us. One complexity lies in Mill's suggestion that where society sets up procedures and organizational arrangements to make social and economic life safe and prosperous, we harm others by not doing our part in sustaining those

7. See p. 99.

arrangements. This thought occurs both in the introductory chapter and in Chapter IV. I can harm you by not giving evidence in a court of law or by not paying my taxes as much as by throwing a rock at you. Society is a system of collective security; each is thus under an obligation to do his or her part in keeping the system of collective security working. So Mill's simple principle essentially says that people may be forced only to (1) refrain from physically damaging or threatening to damage others; (2) meet the obligations they have contracted with others, whether these are commercial, marital, parental, or whatever; and (3) perform their share of the common work of preserving society's arrangements for ensuring that 1 and 2 happen. All else must be a matter of entreaty, exhortation, encouragement, reproach, and whatever noncoercive interaction is appropriate.

We may now move very rapidly through Mill's account of why it is so important to hold the line at this point. First, Mill argued for absolute freedom of thought and expression within the limits of the harm principle. It should be noticed that Mill has nothing to say about at least one of the subjects that most vex late-twentieth-century Americans. Obscenity and questions of decency Mill declared not to be questions of liberty at all. Why may we not copulate in the street? It cannot be because all copulation is wicked; a husband and wife copulating in the street are not copulating outside marriage, but they are performing an indecent act. Readers of Mill find it hard to believe that they will not find answers to First Amendment questions about indecency, but the truth is that they will not. In Chapter V, Mill says firmly that questions of decency are outside the scope of his discussion.

On the other hand, Mill has much to say that is relevant to the question of speech that will be found offensive by some of those who hear it. In general, he stands by the principle that we must not silence people because what they say is offensive; a university lecture on psychology cannot be shut down because the lecturer's view that Irishmen are genetically doomed to be bad at mathematics upsets Irish students in the audience. On the other hand, there is much speech that may in context amount to an incitement to riot, and it is not privileged. A man who writes "Corn Dealers Are Thieves" on a placard waved before an angry mob in front of a corn dealer's house is inciting a riot; an economics text that argues that corn dealers make grossly excessive profits is not, so the first is restricted and the second is not. For all his talk of absolute principles, it is likely that Mill would allow much less freedom of speech to, say, antiabortion protesters parading up and down outside an abortion doctor's house than the U.S. Supreme Court has done.

Mill does not pay much attention to the right of political self-expression, largely because his concern is with *social* restraints on freedom and partly because he was soon to write *Considerations on Representative Government*. In this essay, free speech is considered a condition of the search for truth. It is almost *logically* required in such a search, for Mill argues that nobody truly understands a doctrine that he or she cannot defend against criticism and that even in the most advanced sciences there must be room for dissenters. Indeed, he suggests that we might do well to have an *advocatus diaboli* handy to remind us of the grounds for believing the truths we do take for granted. Mill's emphasis on the controvertibility of received views in science has been taken up in the twentieth century by Karl Popper[8] and his disciples. It has also been attacked by several schools in the history and sociology of science that have argued that scientific progress is a much more authoritarian business than Mill thought. Scientists who try to work outside the prevailing "paradigm"—the assumptions that define science as practiced—will be shut out of the profession.[9] Those who work inside the paradigm will solve the puzzles the paradigm suggests as interesting and solvable. Every so often there will be an irrational move to another all-embracing vision of what chemistry or physics or biology is about, and the process will go on.

The point is partly epistemological and partly sociological. Epistemologically, the thought is that setting up hypotheses about the world and testing them against evidence and criticism would not rule out lunatic or incompetent criticism and would not rule in a narrow enough vision of the world to explore in the way science does explore its theories. Sociologically the thought is that science needs authority; someone must set a program for experimenters and observers to follow. None of this implies that if we wish to denounce the inverse square law or the Second Law of Thermodynamics we should be thrown in jail, and it may be that this is enough for Mill's purposes. It distinguishes science and religion well enough. Many people who denied the divinity of Christ or the doctrine of the Trinity in medieval and early-modern Europe encountered the stake, the executioner, and the gibbet, let alone lesser social and legal sanctions. The contrast between scientists' willingness to let people think what they like—so long as they stay out of the laboratory—and the churches' unwillingness to do so, is sharp and very much to Mill's purpose. But that may be too optimistic. For Mill's argument for free speech and expression is instrumental; he justifies freedom of thought and speech because they lead to the truth. The critics retort that they have a better recipe: some free speech together with a lot of control of what speech is listened to.

Mill's concern with truth, however, was not a concern for scientific truth. It was more like the concern he broached in "Bentham" and "Coleridge," that is, with a true picture of human existence. It is truth in ethics and religion that most concerns him, and here one might reasonably say that the connection between freedom of speech and

---

8. For instance, K. R. Popper, *The Logic of Scientific Discovery* (London, 1957) and *Conjectures and Refutations* (Oxford, 1974).
9. The most famous argument to this effect is T. S. Kuhn, *The Structure of Scientific Revolutions* (Chicago, 1962).

what we could call "living" truth is very close. Mill's concern with religious truth in the essay is easy to see if we look at the number of instances he offers of religious persecution, at his constant references to the self-abnegation required by Calvinism, the references to persons denied justice in British courts because they would not swear on the Bible when giving evidence, and so on. Mill's religious views were complicated, but two things were not. He was not a Christian of any sort; he had been brought up agnostic and had no attachment to any of the Christian churches. Second, he was inclined to place pagan societies and pagan ethics higher than Christian societies and Christian ethics in the moral scale; they had a higher ideal of human individuality and human greatness than the Christian tradition had. He was not strictly an atheist; he thought it more likely than not that some sort of intelligent force operated in the world. And he was not hostile to the thought that some sort of post-Christian religion would be socially valuable, in encouraging individual effort, providing the comfort that comes from believing that the universe is on our side, and in giving us images of good and productive lives on which we might model our own. Still, the main point remains that his defense of freedom of thought is a defense of what one might call unbridled speculation on the terrain of religious debate, and much more nearly that than of unbridled debate in science.

The contrast is simple enough. Many students have a clear but far from lively grasp of inorganic chemistry; a professor who marked down their papers because they lacked inner conviction would be thought very eccentric. (It would be another matter if a Nobel Prize was at stake.) A preacher whose audience said only "I suppose that's right" after forty minutes of his best efforts would despair of his skills. It is clear what Mill was doing. He was setting out an ideal of the examined life. Almost the first of his youthful philosophical exercises had been to translate several of Plato's Dialogues, and Mill was deeply imbued with the passion that had animated Plato. "The unexamined life is not worth living," said Socrates; and Mill wrote *On Liberty* to repeat the lesson to a Victorian audience.

Mill departed dramatically from his classical predecessor in explaining the values to which the examined life tended. Socrates as presented by Plato held one individualistic belief: he believed that he possessed a *daemon*, an inner voice that told him whether he was doing right or wrong and which he was ready to follow even to the extent of refusing to obey the Athenian court that ordered him to stop practicing philosophy on pain of death. Otherwise, he was not in the modern sense an individualist. He thought that the universe possessed a fixed, almost mathematical, harmony and order, to which individuals ought to conform their lives. The ideal was to find one's place in the universe and fit in to it. Mill was a modern. Individuality was a matter of creating our own lives as something interesting, original, progressive, and suited to us in particular. It was not a selfish individualism; selfishness is a bad bargain for the individual, and only people who have other people's welfare at heart are happy. But it was a doctrine that looked to the particular person for its goals; each of us should look for what made the most of *our* life.

The way Mill combined a belief in individuality and a strong sense of social duty appears in two of the many illustrations that he offers. Mill was fiercely opposed to the temperance movement that was a prominent feature of Victorian Britain. He agreed that drunkenness was a social evil, he deplored the readiness of public opinion to tolerate the drunken brutality of husbands toward their wives, and he urged that intoxication should be treated as an aggravating feature of crimes of violence. What he did not think was that alcoholic drink should be banned because it was abused. Nor did he think that it should be taxed to discourage its consumption. The way he argued was instructive. A person who drinks need not, and ordinarily does not, become a drunkard. To that extent, drinking is a harmless indulgence and falls squarely within the liberty principle. Suppose, though, that a man spends money on drink that he ought to spend on his family; then he is answerable for their neglect. But he is no more answerable than if he had spent the housekeeping money on rearing exotic birds or on a political campaign. What he is answerable for is the *neglect*, not the habits that led to it. A train driver can be jailed for drinking on duty; but the example itself presupposes that we can distinguish between being on duty and off duty. The temperance campaigner might retort that the person who drinks to excess without doing anyone else a direct injury nonetheless does two other injuries, one to the society that receives from him less than he could contribute and the other to himself. This is the terrain on which Mill wished to stand and fight. Society, he said, was better off tolerating the shortfall for the sake of freedom than trying to extort more by coercion; in any case, it was intolerable that a person might have his or her liberty circumscribed by other people unilaterally declaring that they had an indefinite right to her or his services and might, therefore, dictate the pattern of her or his life to exact them. So far as the individual's own life was concerned, Mill drew a careful line between illicit coercion on the one hand and legitimate exhortation and reproach on the other. What we might not do was penalize the person who was degraded by drink. We could not threaten him with dismissal from employment *unless* he failed to perform his duties properly; we ought not to encourage other people to gang up against him or isolate and ostracize him. What we might do was tell such people plainly and squarely that drunkenness was disgusting; we might tell them how boring they were, how their friends had come to dislike their company, how far below their better selves they had fallen. All this would be painful to say and painful to hear; but it was not coercion. It was indeed the performance of "good offices."

Many readers find Mill's views on the duties of parents toward their children even more alarming. Mill claimed that the muddled state of social thinking meant that society failed to interfere with people's behavior when it ought to interfere almost as often as it interfered when it ought not. It was proper for the state to insist that people could not marry until they had the resources needed to rear a family, to charge the upkeep of children against the labor of their parents, and to defend the rights of children against the incompetence and idleness of parents to almost any degree. Education was not a sphere of parents' rights but parents' duties. They must see that their children went to school, and the state should compel them to do it, even though the state should not provide the education. If parents were too poor to pay for the education of their children, the state should provide the fees. If children failed to learn, parents should be held to account. The reason is simple enough; parental incompetence is a crime against two groups of people. In the first place it violates the rights of the children who are harmed by being sent into the world unable to earn a living and deprived of the chance to become free, self-creating persons. In the second place, it violates the rights of everyone else, for they have to devote resources to supporting the incompetent children of incompetent parents. Mill had no tenderness to the thought that familial relations are private or intimate in any sense that entitles them to particular respect or to be treated with particular sensitivity. He asks only one question: When is it legitimate for society to compel people to act in a way they otherwise would not? And he sticks to principle, for the answer is always: when that is necessary to prevent them harming others.

Some last observations may be helpful to new readers. The first is that nothing separates Mill from his twentieth-century readers so sharply as his commitment to progress. Mill did not believe that progress was automatic: "deterioration is the law of being," he once observed. He did believe that we could with the necessary effort and intelligence make progress, not only technically and scientifically but morally and spiritually. It is this belief that twentieth-century readers find difficult to sympathize with. On the one hand, they look at the twentieth century's dismal record of two world wars, famine, genocide, and the like and argue that the doctrine of original sin captures the realities of human nature rather better than talk of progress. On the other, they hold a variety of philosophical positions that suggest that moralities may change, but not in any unequivocal way "improve"; what one ethical theory calls improvement another will decry as deterioration, and there is no neutral arbiter to decide between them.

A second important issue is the extent to which *On Liberty* was meant by Mill to make a difference to a specific society that differs drastically from our own. Mill meant the essay for the Victorian English middle classes. He told his Italian friend Pasquale Villari that the book had no value except in England, where political liberty was secure and social liberty under threat. In Europe, political liberty was a rare commodity, social liberty was less threatened. Europeans who faced tyrannical governments were more inclined to stand up for themselves against all bullying than were the English — and the Americans. Mill's view of what we had to fear was drawn in part from Tocqueville's account of the lack of intellectual liberty in the United States, and what he made much of was something that became a matter of intense discussion in the 1950s with the publication of David Riesman's *The Lonely Crowd*. The social oppressiveness of a democratic society was particularly difficult to fight because individuals sided with their oppressors against themselves; as Riesman put it, they were "other-directed" rather than autonomous. They wanted to know what other people thought so as to think like them. Curiously, this links Mill not only with Tocqueville but with a much more bitter critic of the nineteenth century, Friedrich Nietzsche, whose diatribes against herd mentality far outdid Mill's. This is why critics of Mill who point to the diversity of tastes and lifestyles in twentieth-century Britain and America miss the point; it is not whether we do or do not decide to be like other people that matters, but whether *we decide*. To the extent that we follow a trend set by others without reflecting on whether we wish to make it *our own* way of life, we are enslaved, and we have conspired in our own enslavement; the fact that the trend is toward a vacuous variety is irrelevant.

Last, there should be no blinking at the fierceness of the demands that *On Liberty* makes on us. Mill did not urge us to do our own thing. Mill urged us to find the best and make that our own thing. It is, as has often been said, a defence of "aristocratic liberalism."[1] It defends the right of the ordinary person to do as he or she chooses so long as nobody is harmed thereby, but the ultimate goal is less happiness than a life lived to the full. That is why it is so difficult to attach the usual labels to the essay; Mill is not quite a defender of classical ideals or quite a romantic, he is hostile to self-abnegation but not to self-discipline, he is hostile to those aspects of Christianity that encourage resignation but not to those that encourage the ambition to perfect our characters. He is as distinctive as the author of such a work should be.

The Subjection of Women

The Subjection of Women was Mill's last book. It was in some respects his least successful book, not in the sense that it was commercially a failure but in the sense that after his death it was the least discussed of his works. All Mill's philosophical works continued to provoke discussion in some form or other, even if that was the contemptuous dismissal

---

1. Most recently in Alan Kahan, *Aristocratic Liberalism* (New York, 1992).

that G. E. Moore's *Principia Ethica* directed at *Utilitarianism. On Liberty* was acknowledged as a classic statement of the liberal cause, and *A System of Logic* was acknowledged as the classic statement of an empiricist philosophy of science. *The Subjection of Women* was treated as a polemic with no lasting interest. Only in the last quarter of a century has it received extended treatment again. The reason is curious. On the one hand, many progressives thought that Mill's goals had been realized in the more advanced and prosperous societies: Britain and the United States had by 1930 given women the vote, removed barriers to their becoming doctors or lawyers or professors, and eased their subordinate position in the law of marriage and divorce. Meanwhile, other issues, such as war and depression, seemed more urgent. Thirty years later, the dictators' threat to liberal democracy had been crushed and post-1945 prosperity was in full flood. Yet women were underrepresented in politics, in the ranks of senior management, in the better universities, in the learned professions, and many places besides. Their incomes were lower, they chronically did worse than their husbands in divorce settlements, and within marriage they still did 95 percent of the domestic work without compensation. So Mill's doubts about the disparity between male power and female subordination were again taken seriously, as was the question whether there was something in male and female *nature* that led to this disparity.

As usual, Mill sets out the argument with extreme lucidity. His first chapter raises the central issue: Is women's nature different from that of men? As always, he affects to believe his task to be extremely hard: customary relations corrupt our intellects, so that people believe that social relations are the result of natural differences whether or not there is any real evidence to that effect.[2] The chapter does not set out to argue that women are by nature the equals of men, only that there is absolutely no reason to suppose that they are not. Rhetorically, it works by simply adducing numerous cases in which writers have argued from a *social* inferiority to a *natural* incapacity; since Mill's readers can see the folly of those who have argued thus in these cases, they can draw the obvious inference about their own beliefs. Mill's point is that he need do no more; outside slavery, there are no modern institutions in which people are assigned to a subordinate role merely in virtue of their birth — other than women vis à vis marriage, politics, and access to the professions.

Chapter 2 applies the same rhetorical strategy to marriage. Mill points out that English marriage law placed wives in a position not very different from that of a slave under Roman law. Her property passed to her husband on marriage, and short of expensive and complicated proceedings for divorce that few women could afford, she had no recourse if he was a wastrel and a drunkard. Her position was as bad if he turned

---

2. See pp. 133–34.

out to be a bully and a thug. The law treated domestic violence with excessive indulgence, and it was notoriously true that a wife could not resist the sexual assaults of her husband, either. Mill was cagey about just what he thought about divorce; his strategy was to suggest that this was a matter that should be left until women had enough political power to set the terms of a new divorce law. It is clear enough, however, that his view was the usual liberal view — unbreakable and permanent contracts offend the principle of liberty.

Chapter 3 turns to occupational opportunity. The interest of this chapter is less in seeing that Mill argued for complete equality of access as between men and women, as we should expect. More interesting is Mill's rhetorical strategy. Essentially, he held that *if* there were such differences in men and women's natural aptitudes that women were incapable of succeeding in occupations now barred to them — medicine, law, politics, for instance — there would be no reason to stop them attempting to become lawyers, doctors, and Members of Parliament, since competition would stop them succeeding when they tried. People who maintained that they were incompetent and yet wanted to throw up extra barriers were not strong on credibility.

The most elegant stroke against his opponents is Chapter 4. Mill saw perfectly well that what he had to aim at was the hearts and minds of his male readers. They, after all, were going to vote and decide who joined the professions and who could attend university. So he raised the crucial question: What would men gain from the equality of women? The answer was very pure Mill. No self-regarding man could prefer the company of a semislave to that of an intelligent person. Men did not want to have the services of a drudge or odalisque, but a common life with an equal.

The Subjection of Women looks simpler than it is. It purports to raise the question of the equality of women in marriage and employment, against the background of the simple question whether there is anything in the nature of women that dictates the inegalitarian structure of marriage and occupation that actually exists in Britain in 1869. Mill does something rhetorically cleverer and less obvious than that suggests. Essentially, he sets out from the assumption that marriage is legally on a par with slavery: the view of the English common law that husband and wife are one person and that person the husband amounts to saying that the husband owns his wife, her person, her property, her sexual services, and her domestic labor.[3] Mill disarmingly acknowledges that most husbands do not take advantage of every power that the law in principle offers them. But that does not settle the matter. To say that many masters treat their slaves decently does not make slavery legitimate.

---

3. He does the same in the essay *On Liberty*; almost whenever he discusses irrevocable contracts or "literal" slavery, it is marriage that he has in mind.

Once the argument has been turned into an argument about power even more than an argument about equal opportunity, Mill has placed himself in a strong position. He assumes without argument that the exercise of power demands justification. It is a distinctively modern assumption that it is not enough just to say "I am a man" or "I am her husband," but Mill's opponents shared it with him. All agreed that neither tradition nor divine right nor the mere intuition of a natural right to rule will do. The question is then simple: Is there any reason to suppose that merely in virtue of being a woman, a woman should always be in a subordinate role? Does her *nature* subordinate her?

Behind this lurks a difficult methodological question. Does behavior tell us what we need to know about "nature"? The issue is not unlike that of the relationship between measured performance on tests and claims about the innate or natural differences in intelligence between men and women or members of different races. Mill essentially argues that there is no reason to suppose that women are naturally fitted for subordination; a priori, there is no reason to suppose that their physical or psychic construction makes subordination somehow suitable for them, and empirically, it is fallacious to argue from women's present subordinate position and often deferential opinions to what is "natural" to them. People who habitually occupy subordinate positions often come to think it proper that they should do so; this is one of the ways in which human beings make subordination more tolerable. That tells us nothing about what they would feel and do if they grew up under egalitarian conditions.[4]

Once the thought that subordination is natural to women has been defused, Mill's meritocratic and egalitarian principles have a clear run. Access to education should be gender blind, all occupations and professions should be open to women on the same terms as men. Mill was not an advocate of quotas, the reservation of a proportion of positions for members of one sex or another, or an advocate of programs of affirmative action. He supported the pure liberal position of competition on merit. If women were incompetent for some particular occupations or especially suited to others, that would emerge in an environment of genuinely free and equal competition, and absent such competition there was nothing more we could say. There is much one might say about meritocracy and the difficulty of deciding what "merit" is, as also about the difficulty of deciding whether the competition is really free and equal. But Mill was writing well before the past century of women's entry into higher education and into occupations previously barred to them.

More interesting, Mill never raised the question whether women's perspectives may alter our view of the occupations they enter. Years

---

4. This is not to say that Mill is always perfectly fair; he is sometimes ready to say more about women's nature on his own side than he will allow to his opponents on theirs. See Stefan Collini, "Introduction," *Essays on Equality, Law and Education*, CW, vol. 21, xxxiii–iv.

before, Mary Wollstonecraft explored the question of the impact that equal rights for women would have on political life and political leadership. Mill was interested in something else. This was the corrupting effect of power, especially in domestic relations. Inequality of power he thought bad for all parties; the less powerful became subservient and got their way by wheedling or curtailed their ambitions; the more powerful became self-deceiving bullies. To put it differently, Mill thought equality was good for the character and inequality bad for it. This was not an argument with implications for one sex alone: unchecked power would corrupt a woman as readily as it would corrupt a man. But in most human societies, it was men who had such power, even if they had it only at home.[5]

Two final features of *The Subjection of Women* are worth noticing. The first is Mill's invitation to men to learn the pleasures of living with women who are free agents and their moral and intellectual equals. It is, one might say, a slightly reckless argument, or at any rate one that not all men will swallow. Yet, much as with *On Liberty*, Mill is undaunted. The contented drunk lives a dreary life, and we should not flinch from saying so; the husband who treats his wife like a piece of furniture lives a dreary life, and we should not flinch from saying so. Men who live with persons who are their inferiors are getting less out of life than they might and could. Second and last, Mill employs an argument in favor of women's emancipation that fills out the arguments of *On Liberty* in a fashion that *On Liberty* itself does not. Mill contemplates the person who says that women are happier in traditional, deferential roles than they would be if they were free. But what adult, he asks, so seriously believes that his schooldays were the happiest days of his life that he wants to go back to school; what country is willing to sell its independence for the sake of prosperity; what grown person would return under his parents' roof once he had left home? Surely, women are in the same boat. Once free, they would not wish to relinquish their liberty. That being so, men who pretend to believe that women are better off unliberated are either ignorant or hypocritical.

The three essays printed here form a connected set of reflections on freedom, authority, and equality. They show Mill reversing the usual order of things and becoming more radical rather than more conservative as he gets older. They show him constantly concerned with the relation of social orders and social regulation to the dictates of nature and especially with our fondness for reading social habit into nature. They are written from within a liberal perspective on the world — they take ideas and arguments absolutely seriously and are innocent of the more subversive forms of critique that late-twentieth-century writers enjoy playing with; they are not naive about the importance of material

5. Susan Okin (see pp. 334–35) takes up these arguments in more detail than I do here.

interests, but they think them less important than moral and political principle; they focus continuously on the fate of the individual. Since we live in a world in which these are still live options, they are not only classical expressions of that perspective but contributions to contemporary argument too.

Still, it is worth asking once more, exactly what Mill means to a late-twentieth-century reader. "The Spirit of the Age," now almost one and three-quarters centuries old, raises a question to which we still have no real answer. What is the source of moral and intellectual authority in a free and pluralist society? The answer that we might perhaps extract from *On Liberty*, that each of us must look within ourselves to find our own ideals and then try to live up to them, does not seem quite adequate. It is certainly better than what readers have too often extracted from Mill, the injunction to "do your own thing." Mill's injunction is "find the best you are capable of, then make it your own." The continued attraction of religious faith — 94 percent of Americans claim to believe in a personal deity — suggests that most Americans have less trust in their inner resources than Mill supposed we should have.

This, though, is to pitch the matter at a very high level of abstraction. What of particular issues? Here, Mill is an interesting figure to wrestle with. Consider education, where Mill insisted that the state was entitled to make parents send children to some school, or at any rate to get an education, but insisted as firmly that the state must not provide the education itself. The opponents of public education today are usually people who are hostile to compulsory education in any shape or form; what Mill gives them by thinking that the state should not itself provide schools, he promptly takes back by insisting that the state may legitimately require that children pass a state examination, and their parents be fined if they fail. Of course, Mill wanted the state to keep out of the business of providing schools because he feared a uniform education; today's opponents often have reasons with which Mill would not have sympathized in the least, namely a fear of secular education. But they and he might have allied over one issue: the examinations he thought children could rightly be compelled to pass were to be rigidly factual and raise no questions of religious allegiance or moral outlook. We might decently demand that children give an account of what different faiths have believed, but not that they profess allegiance to one or other of them.

Consider, again, Mill's view of legislation against the use of dangerous drugs. Mill did not to any great extent have the problems of drug abuse in mind. Victorian England certainly abused opiates on a considerable scale, but few observers thought this a matter of anything but a personal failing. Mill's response to the question of controlling poisons that had a legitimate use but could be used to kill people was essentially regulatory: it was not an infringement of liberty to require people to sign a register of poisons at the pharmacy. Mill does not compare poisons and firearms; in Victorian Britain, there was no general prohibition on owning firearms. To a late-twentieth-century American, however, the analogy between Mill's view of the purchase of poisons and modern views on the purchase of firearms is hard to escape. On drug legislation in the modern sense, the implications of Mill's position are obvious but to many people quite alarming. So-called recreational drugs would fall squarely within the arena of what harmed only the agent and harmed others only to the extent that they were connected with him or her. Mill's denunciation of temperance movements extends inevitably to an attack on the legitimacy of laws against recreational drug use. No doubt, narcotics make us less competent to drive a car; if so, driving under the influence of narcotics should attract the same penalties as driving while intoxicated. Any case where a person forseeably renders himself or herself a danger to others should attract severe penalties. The mere use of an intoxicant or narcotic should attract none.

In these areas, Mill resembles late-twentieth-century libertarians. It is a plausible inference that he does so in one area of sexual conduct, that of prostitution. To the degree that prostitution is a victimless crime, it falls within the area covered by Mill's principle that coercion may be employed only to prevent harm to others. It is worth observing, however, that Mill is not interested in sex in the way we are. He says, for instance, nothing about the right of individuals to engage in unconventional forms of sexual self-expression. Advocates of gay liberation, or even of a regime of basic nondiscrimination against people of minority sexual persuasions, can find nothing to their purpose in Mill beyond the general principle of not repressing what does no harm. They frequently employ just such a principle, but then the argument focuses on the question of what we should count as "harm." What there is nothing of in Mill is the suggestion that sexual allegiances matter because sex matters in some deep or special way. By the same token, Mill has nothing to say about protecting the family as an arena of intimate relationships; when he insists that parents have only those rights *over* their children that they have to be able to exercise in order to do their duty *to* their children, he sweeps aside the idea that blood ties matter in some deep or special way and ignores any suggestion that parents have rights over children stemming from the intimacy and personal importance of family ties.

This is part and parcel of what I observed before, that Mill's discussion of the nature and purpose of freedom of speech never touched on the issue that obsesses us — pornographic displays. To mount a convincing argument against pornography, one must either find a harm that Mill was blind to — perhaps that it encourages men to ill-treat women — or tell a story about decency that he never tried to tell. One might, for instance, argue that particularly blatant displays violate our concern for what we try to keep intimate and protected from the public gaze, or that we — or most of us — have to partition our lives in such a way that we are not bombarded with sexual invitations and evocations while going about our everyday business. To go far down this track, however, raises some very large questions about the boundaries of Mill's antipaternalist principles. *Ought* we to ask the law to protect us against these distractions and temptations when we do not ask for its aid against others?

Recent feminist critics of pornography as well as recent feminist advocates of unbridled liberty for pornography and other forms of expression raise some interesting questions about the difference between the feminism of *The Subjection of Women* and that of our own day. Mill's individualism meant that he was straightforwardly hostile to anything more than the removal of legal disabilities that created something other than a level playing field. Demands for a supportive environment he would have thought fair enough if addressed to people who could provide it or not as they chose, but not acceptable as a demand for coercive measures by government or other bodies. The equality he aimed at did not suggest that women had special or different needs from those of men; raised no questions about different cognitive, emotional, or moral styles; and assumed that liberals were committed to feminism only in the sense that they were committed to equal justice for all. Whether this is a virtue of Mill's position or simple naïveté is not a question to be settled quickly.

In short, Mill is neither a remote and unapproachable Victorian nor someone who is deeply and constantly embroiled in our contemporary debates. We cannot turn to him for answers to most of our anxieties, and would anyway be violating the spirit of his work if we were to try to do so. There are some issues, such as legislation against "hate speech" for instance, where it is not hard to see what he would say: roughly, that we should distinguish between offense and incitement, suppress the second and leave the first to free discussion. There are many more where a much greater exercise of the imagination would be needed, and where, indeed, the more fruitful approach is to consider what it is about his world and ours that made some issues salient for him and others salient for us. It was, after all, his great achievement after his mental crisis to insist that good philosophy unites imagination with analysis, and the least we can do is take that discovery seriously.

The Texts of
"THE SPIRIT OF THE AGE,"
ON LIBERTY, AND
*THE SUBJECTION OF
WOMEN*

"The Spirit of the Age"

I

The "spirit of the age" is in some measure a novel expression. I do not believe that it is to be met with in any work exceeding fifty years in antiquity. The idea of comparing one's own age with former ages, or with our notion of those which are yet to come, had occurred to philosophers; but it never before was itself the dominant idea of any age.

It is an idea essentially belonging to an age of change. Before men begin to think much and long on the peculiarities of their own times, they must have begun to think that those times are, or are destined to be, distinguished in a very remarkable manner from the times which preceded them. Mankind are then divided, into those who are still what they were, and those who have changed: into the men of the present age, and the men of the past. To the former, the spirit of the age is a subject of exultation; to the latter, of terror; to both, of eager and anxious interest. The wisdom of ancestors, and the march of intellect, are bandied from mouth to mouth; each phrase originally an expression of respect and homage, each ultimately usurped by the partisans of the opposite catch-word, and in the bitterness of their spirit, turned into the sarcastic jibe of hatred and insult.

The present times possess this character. A change has taken place in the human mind; a change which, being effected by insensible gradations, and without noise, had already proceeded far before it was generally perceived. When the fact disclosed itself, thousands awoke as from a dream. They knew not what processes had been going on in the minds of others, or even in their own, until the change began to invade outward objects; and it became clear that those were indeed new men, who insisted upon being governed in a new way.

But mankind are now conscious of their new position. The conviction is already not far from being universal, that the times are pregnant with change; and that the nineteenth century will be known to posterity as the era of one of the greatest revolutions of which history has preserved the remembrance, in the human mind, and in the whole constitution of human society. Even the religious world teems with new interpretations of the Prophecies, foreboding mighty changes near at hand. It is felt that men are henceforth to be held together by new ties, and separated by new barriers; for the ancient bonds will now no longer unite, nor the ancient boundaries confine. Those men who carry their eyes in the back of their heads and can see no other portion of the destined track of humanity than that which it has already travelled, imagine that because the old ties are severed mankind henceforth are

3

not to be connected by any ties at all; and hence their affliction, and their awful warnings. For proof of this assertion, I may refer to the gloomiest book ever written by a cheerful man — Southey's[1] "Colloquies on the Progress and Prospects of Society"; a very curious and not uninstructive exhibition of one of the points of view from which the spirit of the age may be contemplated. They who prefer the ravings of a party politician to the musings of a recluse, may consult a late article in Blackwood's Magazine, under the same title which I have prefixed to this paper.[2] For the reverse of the picture, we have only to look into any popular newspaper or review.

Amidst all this indiscriminate eulogy and abuse, these undistinguishing hopes and fears, it seems to be a very fit subject for philosophical inquiry, what the spirit of the age really is; and how or wherein it differs from the spirit of any other age. The subject is deeply important: for, whatever we may think or affect to think of the present age, we cannot get out of it; we must suffer with its sufferings, and enjoy with its enjoyments; we must share in its lot, and, to be either useful or at ease, we must even partake its character. No man whose good qualities were mainly those of another age, ever had much influence on his own. And since every age contains in itself the germ of all future ages as surely as the acorn contains the future forest, a knowledge of our own age is the fountain of prophecy — the only key to the history of posterity. It is only in the present that we can know the future; it is only through the present that it is in our power to influence that which is to come.

Yet, because our own age is *familiar* to us, we are presumed, if I may judge from appearances, to know it by nature. A statesman, for example, if it be required of him to have studied any thing at all (which, however, is more than I would venture to affirm) is supposed to have studied history — which is at best the spirit of ages long past, and more often the mere inanimate carcass without the spirit: but is it ever asked (or to whom does the question ever occur?) whether he understands his own age? Yet that also is history, and the most important part of history, and the only part which a man may know and understand, with absolute certainty, by using the proper means. He may learn in a morning's walk through London more of the history of England during the nineteenth century, than all the professed English histories in existence will tell him concerning the other eighteen: for, the obvious and universal facts, which every one sees and no one is astonished at, it seldom occurs to any one to place upon record; and posterity, if it learn the rule, learns it, generally, from the notice bestowed by contemporaries on some accidental exception. Yet are politicians and philosophers perpetually exhorted to judge of the present by the past, when the present

---

1. Robert Southey (1774–1843), once a radical, later a Tory poet and author. Appointed poet laureate, 1813.
2. David Robinson, "Letter to Christopher North, Esq., on the Spirit of the Age," *Blackwood's* (Dec. 1830).

alone affords a fund of materials for judging, richer than the whole stores of the past, and far more accessible.

But it is unadvisable to dwell longer on this topic, lest we should be deemed studiously to exaggerate that want, which we desire that the reader should think ourselves qualified to supply. It were better, without further preamble, to enter upon the subject, and be tried by our ideas themselves, rather than by the need of them.

The first of the leading peculiarities of the present age is, that it is an age of transition. Mankind have outgrown old institutions and old doctrines, and have not yet acquired new ones. When we say outgrown, we intend to prejudge nothing. A man may not be either better or happier at six-and-twenty, than he was at six years of age: but the same jacket which fitted him then, will not fit him now.

The prominent trait just indicated in the character of the present age, was obvious a few years ago only to the more discerning: at present it forces itself upon the most inobservant. Much might be said, and shall be said on a fitting occasion, of the mode in which the old order of things has become unsuited to the state of society and of the human mind. But when almost every nation on the continent of Europe has achieved, or is in the course of rapidly achieving, a change in its form of government; when our own country, at all former times the most attached in Europe to its old institutions, proclaims almost with one voice that they are vicious both in the outline and in the details, and that they *shall* be renovated, and purified, and made fit for civilized man, we may assume that a part of the effects of the cause just now pointed out, speak sufficiently loudly for themselves. To him who can reflect, even these are but indications which tell of a more vital and radical change. Not only, in the conviction of almost all men, things as they are, are wrong — but, according to that same conviction, it is not by remaining in the old ways that they can be set right. Society demands, and anticipates, not merely a new machine, but a machine constructed in another manner. Mankind will not be led by their old maxims, nor by their old guides; and they will not choose either their opinions or their guides as they have done heretofore. The ancient constitutional texts were formerly spells which would call forth or allay the spirit of the English people at pleasure: what has become of the charm? Who can hope to sway the minds of the public by the old maxims of law, or commerce, or foreign policy, or ecclesiastical policy? Whose feelings are now roused by the mottoes and watch-words of Whig and Tory? And what Whig or Tory could command ten followers in the warfare of politics by the weight of his own personal authority? Nay, what landlord could call forth his tenants, or what manufacturer his men? Do the poor respect the rich, or adopt their sentiments? Do the young respect the old, or adopt their sentiments? Of the feelings of our ancestors it may almost be said that we retain only such as are the natural and necessary growth of a state of human society, however constituted; and I only adopt the energetic expression of a member of the House of Commons, less than two years ago, in saying of the young men, even of that rank in society, that they are ready to advertise for opinions.

Since the facts are so manifest, there is the more chance that a few reflections on their causes, and on their probable consequences, will receive whatever portion of the reader's attention they may happen to deserve.

With respect, then, to the discredit into which old institutions and old doctrines have fallen, I may premise, that this discredit is, in my opinion, perfectly deserved. Having said this, I may perhaps hope, that no perverse interpretation will be put upon the remainder of my observations, in case some of them should not be quite so conformable to the sentiments of the day as my commencement might give reason to expect. The best guide is not he who, when people are in the right path, merely praises it, but he who shows them the pitfalls and the precipices by which it is endangered; and of which, as long as they were in the wrong road, it was not so necessary that they should be warned.

There is one very easy, and very pleasant way of accounting for this general departure from the modes of thinking of our ancestors: so easy, indeed, and so pleasant, especially to the hearer, as to be very convenient to such writers for hire or for applause, as address themselves not to the men of the age that is gone by, but to the men of the age which has commenced. This explanation is that which ascribes the altered state of opinion and feeling to the growth of the human understanding. According to this doctrine, we reject the sophisms and prejudices which misled the uncultivated minds of our ancestors, because we have learnt too much, and have become too wise, to be imposed upon by such sophisms and such prejudices. It is our knowledge and our sagacity which keep us free from these gross errors. We have now risen to the capacity of perceiving our true interests; and it is no longer in the power of impostors and charlatans to deceive us.

I am unable to adopt this theory. Though a firm believer in the improvement of the age, I do not believe that its improvement has been of this kind. The grand achievement of the present age is the *diffusion* of *superficial* knowledge; and that surely is no trifle, to have been accomplished by a single generation. The persons who are in possession of knowledge adequate to the formation of sound opinions by their own lights, form also a constantly increasing number, but hitherto at all times a small one. It would be carrying the notion of the march of intellect too far, to suppose that an average man of the present day is superior to the greatest men of the beginning of the eighteenth century; yet they *held* many opinions which we are fast renouncing. The intellect of the age, therefore, is not the cause which we are in search of. I do not perceive that, in the mental training which has been received by the immense majority of the reading and thinking part of my coun-trymen, or in the kind of knowledge and other intellectual aliment which has been supplied to them, there is any thing likely to render them much less accessible to the influence of imposture and charla-tanerie than there ever was. The Dr. Eadys still dupe the lower classes, the St. John Longs[3] the higher: and it would not be difficult to produce the political and literary antitypes of both. Neither do I see, in such observations as I am able to make upon my cotemporaries, evidence that they have any principle within them which renders them much less liable now than at any former period to be misled by sophisms and prejudices. All I see is, that the opinions which have been transmitted to them from their ancestors, are not the kind of sophisms and preju-dices which are fitted to possess any considerable ascendancy in their altered frame of mind. And I am rather inclined to account for this fact in a manner not reflecting such extraordinarily great honour upon the times we live in, as would result from the theory by which all is ascribed to the superior expansion of our understandings.

The intellectual tendencies of the age, considered both on the fa-vourable and on the unfavourable side, it will be necessary, in the prosecution of the present design, to review and analyse in some detail. For the present it may be enough to remark, that it is seldom safe to ground a positive estimate of a character upon mere negatives: and that the faults or the prejudices, which a person, or an age, or a nation *has not*, go but a very little way with a wise man towards forming a high opinion of them. A person may be without a single prejudice, and yet utterly unfit for every purpose in nature. To have erroneous convictions is one evil; but to have no strong or deep-rooted convictions at all, is an enormous one. Before I compliment either a man or a generation upon having got rid of their prejudices, I require to know what they have substituted in lieu of them.

Now, it is self-evident that no fixed opinions have yet generally es-tablished themselves in the place of those which we have abandoned; that no new doctrines, philosophical or social, as yet command, or appear likely soon to command, an assent at all comparable in unanim-ity to that which the ancient doctrines could boast of while they con-tinued in vogue. So long as this intellectual anarchy shall endure, we may be warranted in believing that we are in a fair way to become wiser than our forefathers; but it would be premature to affirm that we are already wiser. We have not yet advanced beyond the unsettled state, in which the mind is, when it has recently found itself out in a grievous error, and has not yet satisfied itself of the truth. The men of the present day rather incline to an opinion than embrace it; few, except the very penetrating, or the very presumptuous, have full confidence in their

3. John St. John Long was a Harley Street practitioner and a notorious charlatan of the day. "Dr." Eady was a provincial draper who practiced as a quack doctor.

own convictions. This is not a state of health, but, at the best, of convalescence. It is a necessary stage in the progress of civilization, but it
is attended with numerous evils; as one part of a road may be rougher
or more dangerous than another, although every step brings the traveller
nearer to his desired end.

Not increase of wisdom, but a cause of the reality of which we are
better assured, may serve to account for the decay of prejudices; and
this is, increase of discussion. Men may not reason, better, concerning
the great questions in which human nature is interested, but they reason more. Large subjects are discussed more, and longer, and by more
minds. Discussion has penetrated deeper into society; and if no greater
numbers than before have attained the higher degrees of intelligence,
fewer grovel in that state of abject stupidity, which can only co-exist
with utter apathy and sluggishness.

The progress which we have made, is precisely that sort of progress
which increase of discussion suffices to produce, whether it be attended
with increase of wisdom or no. To discuss, and to question established
opinions, are merely two phrases for the same thing. When all opinions
are questioned, it is in time found out what are those which will not
bear a close examination. Ancient doctrines are then put upon their
proofs; and those which were originally errors, or have become so by
change of circumstances, are thrown aside. Discussion does this. It is
by discussion, also, that true opinions are discovered and diffused. But
this is not so certain a consequence of it as the weakening of error. To
be rationally assured that a given doctrine is *true*, it is often necessary
to examine and weigh an immense variety of facts. One single well-
established fact, clearly irreconcilable with a doctrine, is sufficient to
prove that it is *false*. Nay, opinions often upset themselves by their own
incoherence; and the impossibility of their being well-founded may
admit of being brought home to a mind not possessed of so much as
one positive truth. All the inconsistencies of an opinion with itself, with
obvious facts, or even with other prejudices, discussion evolves and
makes manifest: and indeed this mode of refutation, requiring less study
and less real knowledge than any other, is better suited to the inclination of most disputants. But the moment, and the mood of mind, in
which men break loose from an error, is not, except in natures very
happily constituted, the most favourable to those mental processes
which are necessary to the investigation of truth. What led them wrong
at first, was generally nothing else but the incapacity of seeing more
than one thing at a time; and that incapacity is apt to stick to them
when they have turned their eyes in an altered direction. They usually
resolve that the new light which has broken in upon them shall be the
sole light; and they wilfully and passionately blew out the ancient lamp,
which, though it did not show them what they now see, served very
well to enlighten the objects in its immediate neighbourhood. Whether
men adhere to old opinions or adopt new ones, they have in general

an invincible propensity to split the truth, and take half, or less than half of it; and a habit of erecting their quills and bristling up like a porcupine against any one who brings them the other half, as if he were attempting to deprive them of the portion which they have.

I am far from denying, that, besides getting rid of error, we are also continually enlarging the stock of positive truth. In physical science and art, this is too manifest to be called in question; and in the moral and social sciences, I believe it to be as undeniably true. The wisest men in every age generally surpass in wisdom the wisest of any preceding age, because the wisest men possess and profit by the constantly increasing accumulation of the ideas of all ages: but the multitude (by which I mean the majority of all ranks) have the ideas of their own age, and no others: and if the multitude of one age are nearer to the truth than the multitude of another, it is only in so far as they are guided and influenced by the authority of the wisest among them.

This is connected with certain points which, as it appears to me, have not been sufficiently adverted to by many of those who hold, in common with me, the doctrine of the indefinite progressiveness of the human mind; but which must be understood, in order correctly to appreciate the character of the present age, as an age of moral and political transition. These, therefore, I shall attempt to enforce and illustrate in the next paper.

II

I have said that the present age is an age of transition: I shall now attempt to point out one of the most important consequences of this fact. In all other conditions of mankind, the uninstructed have faith in the instructed. In an age of transition, the divisions among the instructed nullify their authority, and the uninstructed lose their faith in them. The multitude are without a guide; and society is exposed to all the errors and dangers which are to be expected when persons who have never studied any branch of knowledge comprehensively and as a whole attempt to judge for themselves upon particular parts of it.

That this is the condition we are really in, I may spare myself the trouble of attempting to prove: it has become so habitual, that the only difficulty to be anticipated is in persuading any one that this is not our natural state, and that it is consistent with any good wishes towards the human species, to pray that we may come safely out of it. The longer any one observes and meditates, the more clearly he will see, that even wise men are apt to mistake the almanack of the year for a treatise on chronology; and as in an age of transition the source of all improvement is the exercise of private judgment, no wonder that mankind should attach themselves to that, as to the ultimate refuge, the last and only resource of humanity. In like manner, if a caravan of travellers had long been journeying in an unknown country under a blind guide,

with what earnestness would the wiser among them exhort the remainder to use their own eyes, and with what disfavour would any one be
listened to who should insist upon the difficulty of finding their way,
and the necessity of procuring a guide after all. He would be told with
warmth, that they had hitherto missed their way solely from the fatal
weakness of allowing themselves to be guided, and that they never
should reach their journey's end until each man dared to think and
see for himself. And it would perhaps be added (with a smile of contempt), that if he were sincere in doubting the capacity of his fellow-
travellers to see their way, he might prove his sincerity by presenting
each person with a pair of spectacles, by means whereof their powers
of vision might be strengthened, and, all indistinctness removed.

The men of the past, are those who continue to insist upon our still
adhering to the blind guide. The men of the present, are those who
bid each man look about for himself, with or without the promise of
spectacles to assist him.

While these two contending parties are measuring their sophistries
against one another, the man who is capable of other ideas than those
of his age, has an example in the present state of physical science, and
in the manner in which men shape their thoughts and their actions
within its sphere, of what is to be hoped for and laboured for in all
other departments of human knowledge; and what, beyond all possibility of doubt, will one day be attained.

We never hear of the right of private judgment in physical science;
yet it exists; for what is there to prevent any one from denying every
proposition in natural philosophy, if he be so minded? The physical
sciences however have been brought to so advanced a stage of improvement by a series of great men, and the methods by which they are
cultivated so entirely preclude the possibility of material error when
due pains are taken to arrive at the truth, that all persons who have
studied those subjects have come to a nearly unanimous agreement
upon them. Some minor differences doubtless exist; there are points
on which the opinion of the scientific world is not finally made up.
But these are mostly questions rather of curiosity than of use, and it is
seldom attempted to thrust them into undue importance, nor to remove
them, by way of appeal from the tribunal of the specially instructed to
that of the public at large. The compact mass of authority thus created
over-awes the minds of the uninformed: and if here and there a wrong-
headed individual, like Sir Richard Phillips, impugns Newton's discoveries, and revives the long-forgotten sophisms of the Cartesians,[4] he is
not regarded. Yet the fallacies which at one time enthralled the subtlest
understandings, might find, we suspect, in the present day, some intellects scarcely strong enough to resist them: but no one dares to stand

4. Followers of the French philosopher René Descartes (1596–1650). Phillips (1767–1840), a
   bookseller and not a scientist, published several anti-Newtonian treatises.

up against the scientific world, until he too has qualified himself to be named as a man of science: and no one does this without being forced, by irresistible evidence, to adopt the received opinion. The physical sciences, therefore, (speaking of them generally) are continually *growing*, but never *changing*: in every age they receive indeed mighty improvements, but for them the age of transition is past.

It is almost unnecessary to remark in how very different a condition from this, are the sciences which are conversant with the moral nature and social condition of man. In those sciences, this imposing unanimity among all who have studied the subject does not exist; and every dabbler, consequently, thinks his opinion as good as another's. Any man who has eyes and ears shall be judge whether, in point of fact, a person who has never studied politics, for instance, or political economy systematically, regards himself as any-way precluded thereby from promulgating with the most unbounded assurance the crudest opinions, and taxing men who have made those sciences the occupation of a laborious life, with the most contemptible ignorance and imbecility. It is rather the person who *has* studied the subject systematically that is regarded as disqualified. He is a *theorist*: and the word which expresses the highest and noblest effort of human intelligence is turned into a bye-word of derision. People pride themselves upon taking a "plain, matter-of-fact" view of a subject. I once heard of a book entitled "Plain Politics for Plain People." I well remember the remark of an able man on that occasion: "What would be thought of a work with such a title as this, Plain Mathematics for Plain People?" The parallel is most accurate. The nature of the evidence on which these two sciences rest, is different, but both are systems of connected truth: there are very few of the practical questions of either, which can be discussed with profit unless the parties are agreed on a great number of preliminary questions: and accordingly, most of the political discussions which one hears and reads are not unlike what one would expect if the binomial theorem were propounded for argument in a debating society none of whose members had completely made up their minds upon the Rule of Three. Men enter upon a subject with minds in no degree fitted, by previous acquirements, to understand and appreciate the true arguments: yet they lay the blame on the arguments, not on themselves: truth, they think, is under a peremptory obligation of being intelligible to them, whether they take the right means of understanding it or no. Every mode of judging, except from first appearances, is scouted as false refinement. If there were a party among philosophers who still held to the opinion that the sun moves round the earth, can any one doubt on which side of the question the vulgar would be? What terms could express their contempt for those who maintained the contrary! Men form their opinions according to natural shrewdness, without any of the advantages of study. Here and there a hardheaded man, who sees farther into a mill-stone than his neighbours, and takes it into his head that thinking on a subject is one way of understanding it, excogitates an entire science, and publishes his volume; in utter unconsciousness of the fact, that a tithe of his discoveries were known a century ago, and the remainder (supposing them not too absurd to have occurred to anybody before) have been refuted in any year which you can mention, from that time to the present.

This is the state we are in; and the question is, how we are to get out of it. As I am unable to take the view of this matter which will probably occur to most persons as being the most simple and natural, I shall state in the first instance what this is, and my reasons for dissenting from it.

A large portion of the talking and writing common in the present day, respecting the instruction of the people, and the diffusion of knowledge, appears to me to conceal, under loose and vague generalities, notions at bottom altogether fallacious and visionary.

I go, perhaps, still further than most of those to whose language I so strongly object, in the expectations which I entertain of vast improvements in the social condition of man, from the growth of intelligence among the body of the people; and I yield to no one in the degree of intelligence of which I believe them to be capable. But I do not believe that, along with this intelligence, they will ever have sufficient opportunities of study and experience, to become themselves familiarly conversant with all the inquiries which lead to the truths by which it is good that they should regulate their conduct, and to receive into their own minds the whole of the evidence from which those truths have been collected, and which is necessary for their establishment. If I thought all this indispensable, I should despair of human nature. As long as the day consists but of twenty-four hours, and the age of man extends but to threescore and ten, so long (unless we expect improvements in the arts of production sufficient to restore the golden age) the great majority of mankind will need the far greater part of their time and exertions for procuring their daily bread. Some few remarkable individuals will attain great eminence under every conceivable disadvantage; but for men in general, the principal field for the exercise and display of their intellectual faculties is, and ever will be, no other than their own particular calling or occupation. This does not place any limit to their possible intelligence; since the mode of learning, and the mode of practising, that occupation itself, might be made one of the most valuable of all exercises of intelligence: especially when, in all the occupations in which man is a mere machine, his agency is so rapidly becoming superseded by real machinery. But what sets no limit to the *powers* of the mass of mankind, nevertheless limits greatly their possible *acquirements*. Those persons whom the circumstances of society, and their own position in it, permit to dedicate themselves to the investigation and study of physical, moral, and social truths, as their peculiar calling, can alone be expected to make the evidences of such truths a

subject of profound meditation, and to make themselves thorough masters of the philosophical grounds of those opinions of which it is desirable that all should be firmly *persuaded*, but which they alone can
entirely and philosophically *know*. The remainder of mankind must,
and, except in periods of transition like the present, always do, take the
far greater part of their opinions on all extensive subjects upon the
authority of those who have studied them.

It does not follow that all men are not to inquire and investigate.
The only complaint is, that most of them are precluded by the nature
of things from ever inquiring and investigating enough. It is right that
they should acquaint themselves with the evidence of the truths which
are presented to them, to the utmost extent of each man's intellects,
leisure, and inclination. Though a man may never be able to understand Laplace, that is no reason he should not read Euclid.[5] But it by
no means follows that Euclid is a blunderer, or an arrant knave, because
a man who begins at the forty-seventh proposition cannot understand
it: and even he who begins at the beginning, and is stopped by the
pons asinorum,[6] is very much in the wrong if he swears he will navigate
his vessel himself, and not trust to the nonsensical calculations of mathematical land-lubbers. Let him learn what he can, and as well as he
can — still however bearing in mind, that there are others who probably
know much with which he not only is unacquainted, but of the evidence of which, in the existing state of his knowledge, it is impossible
that he should be a competent judge.

It is no answer to what has just been observed, to say that the grounds
of the most important moral and political truths are simple and obvious,
intelligible to persons of the most limited faculties, with moderate study
and attention; that all mankind, therefore, may master the evidences,
and none need take the doctrines upon trust. The matter of fact upon
which this objection proceeds, is happily true. The proofs of the moral
and social truths of greatest importance to mankind, are few, brief, and
easily intelligible; and happy will be the day on which these shall begin
to be circulated among the people, instead of second-rate treatises on
the Polarization of Light, and on the Rigidity of Cordage.[7] But, in the
first place, it is not every one — and there is no one at a very early
period of life — who has had sufficient experience of mankind in general, and has sufficiently reflected upon what passes in his own mind,
to be able to appreciate the force of the reasons when laid before him.
There is, however, a great number of important truths, especially in
Political Economy, to which, from the particular nature of the evidence

5. Greek mathematician (c. 300 B.C.) famous for reducing geometry to a deductive system in
   his *Elements*. Pierre-Simon de Laplace (1749–1827), French astronomer, physicist, and
   mathematician.
6. Mill's readers would know that proposition forty-seven was Pythagoras' Theorem. The *pons
   asinorum* (bridge of asses) was proposition five, where beginners often stumbled.
7. Mill is attacking the Society for the Promotion of Useful Knowledge, founded by Lord
   Brougham in 1825.

on which they rest, this difficulty does not apply. The proofs of these truths may be brought down to the level of even the uninformed multitude, with the most complete success. But, when all is done, there still remains something which they must always and inevitably take upon trust: and this is, that the arguments really *are* as conclusive as they appear; that there exist no considerations relevant to the subject which have been kept back from them; that every objection which can suggest itself has been duly examined by competent judges, and found immaterial. It is easy to say that the truth of certain propositions is obvious to *common sense*. It may be so: but how am I assured that the conclusions of common sense are confirmed by accurate knowledge? Judging by common sense is merely another phrase for judging by first appearances; and every one who has mixed among mankind with any capacity for observing them, knows that the men who place implicit faith in their own common sense are, without any exception, the most wrong-headed, and impracticable persons with whom he has ever had to deal. The maxim of pursuing truth without being biassed by authority, does not state the question fairly; there is no person who does not prefer truth to authority—for authority is only appealed to as a voucher for truth. The real question, to be determined by each man's own judgment, is, whether most confidence is due in the particular case, to his own understanding, or to the opinion of his authority? It is therefore obvious, that there are some persons in whom disregard of authority is a virtue, and others in whom it is both an absurdity and a vice. The presumptuous man needs authority to restrain him from error: the modest man needs it to strengthen him in the right. What truths, for example, can be more obvious, or can rest upon considerations more simple and familiar, than the first principles of morality? Yet we know that extremely ingenious things may be said in opposition to the plainest of them—things which the most highly-instructed men, though never for a single moment misled by them, have had no small difficulty in satisfactorily answering. It is to be imagined that if these sophisms had been referred to the verdict of the half-instructed—and we cannot expect the majority of every class to be any thing more—the solution of the fallacy would always have been found and understood? notwithstanding which, the fallacy would not, it is most probable, have made the slightest impression upon them:—and why? Because the judgment of the multitude would have told them, that their own judgment was not a decision in the last resort; because the conviction of their understandings going along with the moral truth, was sanctioned by the authority of the best-informed; and the objection, though insoluble by their own understandings, was not supported but contradicted by the same imposing authority. But if you once persuade an ignorant or a half-instructed person, that he ought to assert his liberty of thought, discard all authority, and—I do not say *use* his own judgment, for that he never can do too much—but *trust* solely to his own judgment, and receive or reject opinions according to his own views of the evidence; — if, in short, you teach to all the lesson of *indifferency*, so earnestly, and with such admirable effect, inculcated by Locke[8] upon *students*, for whom alone that great man wrote, the merest trifle will suffice to unsettle and perplex their minds. There is not a truth in the whole range of human affairs, however obvious and simple, the evidence of which an ingenious and artful sophist may not succeed in rendering doubtful to minds not very highly cultivated, if those minds insist upon judging of all things exclusively by their own lights. The presumptuous man will dogmatize, and rush headlong into opinions, always shallow, and as often wrong as right; the man who sets only the just value upon his own moderate powers, will scarcely ever feel more than a half-conviction. You may prevail on them to repudiate the authority of the best-instructed, but each will full surely be a mere slave to the authority of the person next to him, who has greatest facilities for continually forcing upon his attention considerations favourable to the conclusion he himself wishes to be drawn.

It is, therefore, one of the necessary conditions of humanity, that the majority must either have wrong opinions, or no fixed opinions, or must place the degree of reliance warranted by reason, in the authority of those who have made moral and social philosophy their peculiar study. It is right that every man should attempt to understand his interest and his duty. It is right that he should follow his reason as far as his reason will carry him, and cultivate the faculty as highly as possible. But reason itself will teach most men that they must, in the last resort, fall back upon the authority of still more cultivated minds, as the ultimate sanction of the convictions of their reason itself.

But where is the authority which commands this confidence, or deserves it? Nowhere: and here we see the peculiar character, and at the same time the peculiar inconvenience, of a period of moral and social transition. At all other periods there exists a large body of received doctrine, covering nearly the whole field of the moral relations of man, and which no one thinks of questioning, backed as it is by the authority of all, or nearly all, persons, supposed to possess knowledge enough to qualify them for giving an opinion on the subject. This state of things does not now exist in the civilized world — except, indeed, to a certain limited extent in the United States of America. The progress of inquiry has brought to light the insufficiency of the ancient doctrines; but those who have made the investigation of social truths their occupation, have not yet sanctioned any new body of doctrine with their unanimous, or nearly unanimous, consent. The true opinion is recommended to the public by no greater weight of authority than hundreds of false opinions; and, even at this day, to find any thing like a united body of grave

---

8. John Locke (1632–1704) argued that we should suspend belief in matters where the evidence is uncertain.

and commanding authority, we must revert to the doctrines from which the progressiveness of the human mind, or, as it is more popularly called, the improvement of the age, has set us free.

In the mean time, as the old doctrines have gone out, and the new ones have not yet come in, every one must judge for himself as he best may. Learn, and think for yourself, is reasonable advice for the day: but let not the business of the day be so done as to prejudice the work of the morrow. "Les supériorités morales," to use the words of Fiévée,[9] "finiront par s'entendre"; the first men of the age will one day join hands and be agreed: and then there is no power in itself, on earth or in hell, capable of withstanding them.

But ere this can happen there must be a change in the whole framework of society, as at present constituted. Worldly power must pass from the hands of the stationary part of mankind into those of the progressive part. There must be a moral and social revolution, which shall, indeed, take away no men's lives or property, but which shall leave to no man one fraction of unearned distinction or unearned importance.

That man cannot achieve his destiny but through such a transformation, and that it will and *shall* be effected, is the conclusion of every man who can *feel the wants of his own age*, without hankering after past ages. Those who may read these papers, and in particular the next succeeding one, will find there an attempt, how far successful others must judge, to set forth the grounds of this belief.

For mankind to change their institutions while their minds are unsettled, without fixed principles, and unable to trust either themselves or other people, is, indeed, a fearful thing. But a bad way is often the best, to get out of a bad position. Let us place our trust for the future, not in the wisdom of mankind, but in something far surer — the force of circumstances — which makes men see that, when it is near at hand, which they could not foresee when it was at a distance, and which so often and so unexpectedly makes the right course, in a moment of emergency, at once the easiest and the most obvious.

III

The affairs of mankind, or of any of those smaller political societies which we call nations, are always either in one or the other of two states, one of them in its nature durable, the other essentially transitory. The former of these we may term the *natural* state, the latter the *transitional*.

Society may be said to be in its *natural* state, when worldly power, and moral influence, are habitually and undisputedly exercised by the fittest persons whom the existing state of society affords. Or, to be more explicit; when on the one hand, the temporal, or, as the French would

9. Joseph Fiévée (1767–1834), French author and political commentator. Mill provides a paraphrase of the French he quotes.

say, the *material* interests of the community, are managed by those of its members who possess the greatest capacity for such management; and on the other hand, those whose opinions the people follow, whose feelings they imbibe, and who practically and by common consent, perform, no matter under what original title, the office of thinking for the people, are persons better qualified than any others whom the civilization of the age and country affords, to think and judge rightly and usefully.

In these circumstances the people, although they may at times be unhappy and consequently discontented, habitually acquiesce in the laws and institutions which they live under, and seek for relief through those institutions and not in defiance of them. Individual ambition struggles to ascend by no other paths than those which the law recognizes and allows. The ruling powers have no immediate interest in counteracting the progress of civilization; society is either stationary, or moves onward solely in those directions in which its progress brings it into no collision with the established order of things.

Society may be said to be in its *transitional* state, when it contains other persons fitter for worldly power and moral influence than those who have hitherto enjoyed them: when worldly power, and the greatest existing capacity for worldly affairs, are no longer united but severed; and when the authority which sets the opinions and forms the feelings of those who are not accustomed to think for themselves, does not exist at all, or, existing, resides anywhere but in the most cultivated intellects, and the most exalted characters, of the age.

When this is the posture of affairs, society has either entered or is on the point of entering into a state in which there are no established doctrines; in which the world of opinions is a mere chaos; and in which, as to worldly affairs, whosoever is dissatisfied with any thing or for any reason, flies at once to an alteration in the conditions of worldly power, as a means for obtaining something which would remove what he deems the cause of his dissatisfaction. And this continues until a moral and social revolution (or it may be, a series of such) has replaced worldly power and moral influence in the hands of the most competent: when society is once more in its natural state, and resumes its onward progress, at the point where it was stopped before by the social system which it has shivered.

It is the object of the present paper, and of that by which it will be immediately followed, to demonstrate, that the changes in the visible structure of society which are manifestly approaching, and which so many anticipate with dread, and so many with hope of a nature far different from that which I feel, are the means by which we are to be carried through our present transitional state, and the human mind is to resume its quiet and regular onward course; a course as undisturbed by convulsions or anarchy, either in the political or in the moral world, as in the best times heretofore, but far more favoured than any former period in respect to the means of rapid advancement, and less impeded by the effect of counteracting forces.

To begin with the conditions of worldly power.

There are two states of society, differing in other respects, but agreeing in this, that worldly power is habitually exercised by the fittest men. One is, when the holders of power are purposely selected for their fitness. The other is, when the circumstances of society are such, that the possession of power of itself calls forth the qualifications for its exercise, in a greater degree than they can be acquired by any other persons in that state of society.

The former state was exemplified in the best constituted republics of antiquity, and is now realized in the United States of America: the latter prevailed throughout most of the nations of Europe in the middle ages.

In the best of the ancient republics all offices, political or military, which were supposed to require peculiar abilities, were conferred upon those who, in the opinion of the best judges, the educated gentlemen of the country (for such the free citizens of Athens, and, in its best times, of Rome, essentially were) possessed the greatest personal qualifications for administering the affairs of the state, and would administer them according to the best ideas of their age. With how much wisdom the choice was usually made, is evidenced in the case of Athens, by the extraordinary series of great men by whom the affairs of that little commonwealth were successively managed, and who made it the source of light and civilization to the world, and the most inspiring and elevating example which history has yet produced, of how much human nature is capable. In the case of Rome, the same fact is as certainly demonstrated, by the steady unintermitted progress of that community from the smallest beginnings to the highest prosperity and power.

In the United States, where those who are called to power, are so by the general voice of the whole people, experience equally testifies to the admirable good sense with which the highest offices have been bestowed. At every election of a President, without exception, the people's choice has fallen on the person whom, as all impartial observers must admit, every circumstance that the people knew, pointed out as the fittest; nor is it possible to name one person pre-eminently qualified for the office, who has not, if he was a candidate, obtained it. In the only two cases in which subsequent experience did not confirm the people's judgment, they corrected the error on the very first lawful opportunity.

But supposing that, in communities constituted like the United States, the holders of power were not really, as in fact they are, the most qualified persons; they are at least those whom the people imagine to be so. The people, consequently, are satisfied with their institutions, and with their rulers; and feel no disposition to lay the blame of their private ills upon the existing order of society, nor to seek the improve-

ment of their circumstances by any means which are repugnant to that
order.

In addition to these instances, where the management of the affairs
of the community is in the fittest hands because those hands are deliberately selected and put in charge of it there is another class of cases,
in which power is not assigned to him who is already the fittest, but
has a strong tendency to render that person the fittest to whom it is
assigned. The extreme case of this state of society is that of a Highland
clan: and all other small societies of barbarous people are in the main
similar. The chief of a clan is despotic, so far as custom and opinion
and habit can render him so. He is not selected for any qualities of his,
for his office is in all cases hereditary. But he is bred to it, and practised
in it from his youth upwards; while every other member of the community is bred to, and practised in, something else, and has no opportunity of training himself to that. The position, moreover, of the society
itself, does not admit of the chief's being utterly destitute of the necessary qualifications for leading the clan in battle, and guiding them in
council. It is the condition of his existence and theirs, that he should
be capable of maintaining himself in circumstances of considerable
difficulty. As men generally contrive to acquire the faculties which they
cannot possibly do without, the head of a clan is scarcely ever absolutely
unfit for governing: the clansmen are fit for executing, and sometimes
for advising, but seldom for commanding. The leader, therefore, is still
the fittest, or at the least as fit as any one else: and the essential character
of a natural state of society is realized, for the people have confidence
in those who manage their affairs.

Between these two states of society, that in which capacity raises men
to power, and that in which power calls forth their capacity, there is
this important difference, that the former state does not contain in itself
the seeds of it own dissolution. A society which is directed by its most
capable members, wheresoever they are to be found, may doubtless
come to an end, as is shown by many instances, but at least its dissolution is never the direct consequence of its own organization, since
every new intellectual power which grows up, takes its natural place in
the existing social order, and is not obliged to break it in pieces in order
to make itself way. But when the possession of power is guaranteed to
particular persons independently of their capacity, those persons may
be the fittest to-day and the most incapable to-morrow: and these social
arrangements are exposed to certain destruction, from every cause
which raises up in the society itself, fitter persons for power than those
who possess it. For although mankind, in all ages except those of transition, are ever ready to obey and love those whom they recognize as
better able to govern them, than they are to govern themselves, it is not
in human nature to yield a willing obedience to men whom you think
no wiser than yourself, especially when you are told by those whom

you do think wiser, that they would govern you in a different manner. Unless therefore this state of society be so constituted as to prevent altogether the progress of civilization, that progress always ultimately overthrows it — the tendency of civilization being on the one hand, to render some of those who are excluded from power, fitter and fitter for it, and on the other hand (in a way hereafter to be explained) to render the monopolizers of power, actually less fit for it than they were originally.

Now, the proposition which I am about to prove is, that the above is a correct account of the process which has been going on for a considerable length of time in modern Europe: — that the qualification for power has been, and is, anything rather than fitness for it, either real or presumed: that nevertheless the holders of power, for a long time, possessed, from the necessary circumstances of society, greater fitness for it than was possessed by any other persons at that time; which fitness they have for some time been losing, while others through the advancement of civilization have been gaining it, until power, and fitness for power, have altogether ceased to correspond: and that this is one great cause, so far as political circumstances are concerned, of the general dissatisfaction with the present order of society, and the unsettled state of political opinion.

From the earliest periods of the nations of modern Europe, all worldly power has belonged to one particular class, the wealthy class. For many centuries the only wealth was land, and the only wealthy were the territorial aristocracy. At a later period, landed wealth ceased to be so greatly engrossed by a few noble families, and manufacturing and commercial wealth grew by little and little into large masses. Worldly power, under which expression I include all direct influence over the worldly affairs of the community, became proportionably diffused. It then belonged to two classes, but to them exclusively, the landed gentry, and the monied class; and in their hands it still remains.

For many ages these were felt by all to be the proper depositories of power, because they possessed, on the average, such qualifications for it as no other members of the community, in the then state of civilization, could rationally hope to acquire. It cannot, for example, be imagined that the villeins or serfs, or even the smaller freeholders, in those ages in which nothing was to be learnt from books, but all from practice and experience, could be so fit for commanding the nation in battle, or deliberating on its affairs in council, as those who had been taught to look to these as their appointed functions and occupations, who had been trained to fitness for them in every way which was suggested by the conceptions of those times, and who from constant practice, possessed at least the same kind of superiority in their business which an experienced workman possesses over one who has never handled a tool.

It is not pretended that the barons were in themselves very fit for power, or that they did not use it very ill; they did so, as history testifies, to a frightful extent: not that I agree in one-half of all that is said in their disparagement by many who, if cotemporary with them, would most probably have admired them, having no standard of approbation but the ideas of their own age. But those may be in themselves very unfit, than whom, nevertheless, an uncivilized age affords none fitter: and power, which is not accountable to those interested in its being properly employed, is likely to be abused, even though it be held by the most capable persons, not in a rude age only, but in the most highly civilized one. This is one of those principles which being true in all states and in all situations in which man has been found, or in which we can rationally expect to find him, must be allowed the paramount importance which is due to it, whatever be the state of society that we are considering. This may not always have been duly adverted to by the historical school of politicians (by whom, be it understood, I mean the really profound and philosophic inquirers into history in France and Germany, not the Plausibles, who in our own land of shallowness and charlatanerie, babble about induction without having ever considered what it is, relying on that rhetoric which is defined by Plato[1] as the art of appearing profoundly versed in a subject to those who know nothing at all about it). I say, those who have endeavoured to erect an inductive philosophy of history, may be charged with having taken insufficient account of the qualities in which mankind in all ages and nations are alike, their attention being unduly engrossed by the differences; but there is an error on the other side, to which those are peculiarly liable, who build their philosophy of politics upon what they term the universal principles of human nature. Such persons often form their judgments, in particular cases, as if, because there are universal principles of human nature, they imagined that all are such which they find to be true universally of the people of their own age and country. They should consider that if there are some tendencies of human nature, and some of the circumstances by which man is surrounded, which are the same in all ages and countries, these never form the whole of the tendencies, or of the circumstances, which exist in any particular age or country: each possesses, along with those invariable tendencies, others which are changeable, and peculiarly its own; and in no age, as civilization advances, are the prevailing tendencies exactly the same as in the preceding age, nor do those tendencies act under precisely the same combination of external circumstances.

We must not therefore (as some may be apt to do,) blame the people of the middle ages for not having sought securities against the irresponsible power of their rulers; persuading ourselves that in those or in any times, popular institutions might exist, if the many had sense to perceive their utility, and spirit to demand them. To find fault with our ancestors

1. Plato's *Gorgias* is almost certainly what Mill has in mind.

for not having annual parliaments, universal suffrage, and vote by ballot, would be like quarrelling with the Greeks and Romans for not using steam navigation, when we know it is so safe and expeditious; which would be, in short, simply finding fault with the third century before Christ for not being the eighteenth century after. It was necessary that many other things should be thought and done, before, according to the laws of human affairs, it was possible that steam navigation should be thought of. Human nature must proceed step by step, in politics as well as in physics. The people of the middle ages knew very well, whether they were oppressed or not; and the opinion of the many, added to the fear of vengeance from some injured individual, acted in a certain, though doubtless by no means a sufficient, extent, as a restraint upon oppression. For any more effectual restraint than this, society was not yet ripe. To have thrown off their masters, and taken others, would have been to buy a still worse government at the price of a convulsion: to contrive, establish, and work the machine of a responsible government, was an impossibility in the then state of the human mind. Though the idea had been conceived, it could not have been realized. Several antecedent stages in civilization had previously to be passed through. An insurrection of the peasants against their feudal lords, could, in the nature of things, have only been, what it actually was, a Jacquerie:[2] for any more rational effort there was needed a power of self-restraint for the purpose of union, and a confidence in each other, which they are not to be blamed for not having, since it could only be the slow result of a habit of acting in concert for other purposes, which, in an extensive country, can only co-exist with a high state of civilization. So soon as any portion of the people did acquire this habit of acting together, they did seek better political securities, and obtained them: witness the rise of the free cities, and corporations, all over Europe. The people therefore of the middle ages had as good a government as the circumstances of the middle ages admitted; their affairs were less badly managed, in that bad age, by their masters, than they could have managed them for themselves. The army of Godefroi de Bouillon in the first crusade, was not quite so efficient an instrument of warfare as that of the Duke of Wellington, in 1815: but it was considerably more so than that of Peter the Hermit,[3] which preceded it.

From these remarks it will be seen how greatly I differ, at once from those, who seeing the institutions of our ancestors to be bad for us, imagine that they were bad for those for whom they were made, and from those who ridiculously invoke the wisdom of our ancestors as

---

2. A peasant revolt; the French peasant was commonly called *Jacques*.
3. French monk (c. 1050–1115) who led a disorganized band of poor folk; they were massacred in 1096. Godfrey of Bouillon (c. 1060–1100), captured Jerusalem in 1099 as the culmination of the First Crusade. Arthur Wellesley, duke of Wellington (1769–1852), notable soldier, who defeated Napoleon at the Battle of Waterloo (1815) and thereafter played a central part in British conservative politics.

authority for institutions which in substance are now totally different, howsoever they may be the same in form. The institutions of our ancestors served passably well for our ancestors, and that from no wisdom of theirs; but from a cause to which, I am afraid, nearly all the good institutions which have ever existed, owed their origin, namely the force of circumstances: but the possessors of power in the present day are not the natural successors of the possessors of power in that day. They may show a valid title to inherit the property, perhaps, of the ancient Barons; but political power descends, as will be found in the long run, by a different law.

It is not necessary for me to point out that until a comparatively recent period, none but the wealthy, and even, I might say, the hereditarily wealthy, had it in their power to acquire the intelligence, the knowledge, and the habits, which are necessary to qualify a man, in any tolerable degree, for managing the affairs of his country. It is not necessary for me to show that this is no longer the case, nor what are the circumstances which have changed it: the improvement in the arts of life, giving ease and comfort to great numbers not possessed of the degree of wealth which confers political power: the increase of reading: the diffusion of elementary education: the increase of the town-population, which brings masses of men together, and accustoms them to examine and discuss important subjects with one another; and various other causes, which are known to every body. All this, however, is nothing more than the acquisition by other people in an inferior degree, of a few of the advantages which have always been within the reach of the higher classes, in a much greater degree: and if the higher classes had profited as they might have done by these advantages, and had kept their station in the vanguard of the march of improvement, they would not only at this moment have been sure to retain in their hands all the powers of government, subject perhaps to severer conditions of responsibility, but might possibly even have continued for a considerable time longer to retain them on the same footing as at present. For ample experience has proved that mankind (who, however prone they may be, in periods of transition, to even groundless suspicion and distrust, are as strongly addicted at all other times to the opposite extreme of blind and boundless confidence), will bear even great excesses of abused power, from those whom they recognize as fitter to hold the reins of government than themselves.

But the higher classes, instead of advancing, have retrograded in all the higher qualities of mind. In the humanizing effects of civilization they have indeed partaken, and, to some extent, in the diffusion of superficial knowledge, and are so far superior to their predecessors: but those predecessors were braced and nerved by the invigorating atmosphere of a barbarous age, and had all the virtues of a strong will and an energetic active mind, which their descendants are destitute of. For these qualities were not the fruits of an enlightened education skilfully pointed to that end, but of the peculiar position of the holders of power; and that position is no longer the same.

All is not absolutely unfounded in the notion we imbibe at school, from the modern writers on the decline of the ancient commonwealths, that luxury deadens and enervates the mind. It is true that these writers (whose opinion, truly, was the result of no process of thought in their own imitative souls, but a faint impression left by a ray of the stoic philosophy of Greece and Rome themselves, refracted or bent out of its direction by the muddy medium through which it had passed) were wrong in laying it down as a principle that pleasure enervates; as if pleasure, only to be earned by labour and won by heroic deeds, ever did or ever could enervate the mind of any one. What really enervates, is the secure and unquestioned possession, without any exertion, of all those things, to gain which, mankind in general are wont to exert themselves. This secure and lazy possession, the higher classes have now for some generations enjoyed; their predecessors in the same station and privileges did not enjoy it.

Who, for example, that looks over the catalogue of the Kings who have reigned in Europe for the last two centuries, would not conclude, from that and the nature of the case combined, that the station of a hereditary king was the very most unfavourable to be found in this sublunary world, for the acquisition of any talents for governing? Is not the incapacity of the monarch allowed for, as an inevitable inconvenience, even by the most strenuous supporters of monarchy; represented at best as an evil susceptible of palliation, and preventing other evils far more fatal? From the beginning of the eighteenth century it has passed into a philosophic truism, that kings are generally unfit to govern, and likely even to delegate their power not to statesmen, but to favourites, unless forced to choose those Ministers whom the public voice recommends to them. Yet this maxim is far from being borne out by history. A decided majority of all the kings of England previous to the Revolution, will be found to have been men who, in every endowment belonging to their age, might be compared to the best men in it. The same may be said of the Emperors of Germany, and even of the Kings of France, of Spain, the Dukes of Burgundy, and so on. Would you know why? Think of Edward the Second and Richard the Second.[4] In that turbulent age, no rank or station rendered the situation of a man without considerable personal endowments, a secure one. If the king possessed eminent talents, he might be nearly absolute: if he was a slave to ease and dissipation, not only his importance was absolutely null, but his throne and his life itself were constantly in danger. The Barons stood no less in need of mental energy and ability. Power, though not earned by capacity, might be greatly increased by it, and

---

4. Edward II (1284–1327) and Richard II (1377–1399) were deposed and murdered by their dissatisfied nobility.

could not be retained or enjoyed without it. The possessor of power
was not in the situation of one who is rewarded without exertion, but
of one who feels a great prize within his grasp, and is stimulated to
every effort necessary to make it securely his own.

But the virtues which insecurity calls forth, ceased with insecurity
itself. In a civilized age, though it may be difficult to *get*, it is very easy
to *keep*: if a man does not earn what he gets before he gets it, he has
little motive to earn it thereafter. The greater the power a man has
upon these terms, the less he is likely to deserve it. Accordingly, as Mr.
Hallam[5] has remarked, Great Britain has had since WILLIAM III. no
monarch of more than ordinary personal endowments; nor will she ever
more, unless the chapter of accidents should open at a page inscribed
with very singular characters. We may add, that the House of Peers has
produced, since the same epoch, hardly any remarkable men; though
some such have, from time to time, been aggregated to the order. As
soon as these facts became manifest, it was easy to see a termination to
hereditary monarchy and hereditary aristocracy: for we never shall again
return to the age of violence and insecurity, when men were forced,
whatever might be their taste for incapacity, to become men of talents
in spite of themselves: and mankind will not always consent to allow a
fat elderly gentleman[6] to fill the first place, without insisting upon his
doing something to deserve it. I do not undertake to say in what particular year hereditary distinctions will be abolished, nor do I say that
I would vote for their abolition, if it were proposed now, in the existing
state of society and opinion: but to the philosopher, who contemplates
the past and future fortunes of mankind as one series, and who counts
a generation or two for no more in marking the changes of the moral,
than an age or two in those of the physical world, the ultimate fate of
such distinctions is already decided.

There was an intermediate stage in the history of our own island, in
which it was yet a question whether the Crown should share in the
government of the country as the master of the aristocracy, or only as
the first and most powerful of its members. Though the progress of
civilization had given to the gentry of England, personal security independently of honourable exertion, it had not yet given them undisputed power. They were nothing, except through the Parliament, and
the Parliament as yet, was nothing, except through their energy and
talents. The great names by which the seventeenth century of English
history has been immortalized, belonged almost without an exception
to the same class which now possesses the governing power. What a
contrast! Think, good heavens! that Sir John Elliot, and John Hampden,
and Sir John Colepepper, and Sir Thomas Wentworth, were *country
gentlemen* — and think who are the parliamentary leaders of that class

5. Henry Hallam (1777–1859), a noted constitutional historian.
6. George IV (1762–1830) became king in 1820; after years of debauchery, he was exceedingly
   fat.

in our own day: a Knatchbull, a Bankes, a Gooch, a Lethbridge![7] Think even of the most respectable names among the English landholders of our time, such as Lord Wharncliffe, or Mr. Coke. The remainder of the great politicians of that age, the Bacons, the Cecils, the Walsinghams, the Seldens, the Iretons, the Pyms, the Cokes, were mostly lawyers.[8] But what lawyers, and how strikingly distinguished, as well by their origin as by the range of their faculties and acquirements, from our successful Barristers, our Sugdens and Copleys! They were almost to a man, the younger or even the elder sons of the first families among the English gentry who studied the law as being what it then in some degree was, a liberal profession, a pursuit fit for a gentleman, and not for a mere drudge; exercising at least the higher faculties, by the comprehension of principles, (though frequently absurd ones), not the mere memory, by the heaping together of unconnected details: and who studied it chiefly that it might serve them in fulfilling the exalted mission, to which they were called by an ambition justly to be called noble, since it required of them great sacrifices, and could be gratified only by the accomplishment of what was then nearest to their country's weal.

Applied to these men, the expression, natural leaders of the people, has some meaning: and then and then only it was that our institutions worked well, for they made this country the nurse of more that is exalted in sentiment, and expansive and profound in thought, than has been produced by all other countries in the modern world taken together, until a recent period. The whole of their effect is now the direct contrary — to degrade our morals, and to narrow and blunt our understandings: nor shall we ever be what we might be, nor even what we once were, until our institutions are adapted to the present state of civilization, and made compatible with the future progress of the human mind. But this will, I trust, more clearly appear, when, in the next paper, the historical survey which I have here taken of the conditions of worldly power, shall also have been taken of the conditions of moral influence.

IV

It has been stated, in the preceding paper, that the conditions which confer worldly power are still, amidst all changes of circumstances, the same as in the middle ages — namely, the possession of wealth, or the being employed and trusted by the wealthy. In the middle ages, this

7. Mill contrasts famous figures from both sides of the conflict between king and Parliament in seventeenth-century England and their nineteenth-century counterparts. John Hampden (1594–1643) led the fight against "ship money," one of Charles I's attempts to raise money without parliamentary approval. Thomas Wentworth (1595–1641) was, as earl of Strafford, Charles's chief adviser; he was executed to appease Parliament.
8. Again, Mill contrasts great figures of the Tudor and Stuart governments with modern nonentities. Henry Ireton (1611–1651) and John Pym (1584–1643) were leading parliamentarians. Edward Coke (1552–1634) was the greatest common lawyer of all time. The Cecil family is prominent in British politics to this day.

form of government might have been approved, even by a philosopher, if a philosopher had been possible in those ages: not, surely, for its intrinsic excellence; not because mankind enjoyed, or could have enjoyed, the blessings of good government under it: but there are states of society in which we must not seek for a good government, but for the least bad one. It is part of the inevitable lot of mankind, that when they themselves are in a backward state of civilization, they are unsusceptible of being well governed.

But, now, mankind are capable of being better governed than the wealthy classes have ever heretofore governed them: while those classes, instead of having improved, have actually retrograded in capacity for government. The abuses of their power have not diminished, though now showing themselves no otherwise than in forms compatible with the mildness of modern manners, and being of that kind which provokes contempt, mingled with resentment, rather than terror and hatred, as of yore.

Such of the above propositions as required illustration appearing to have sufficiently received it in the foregoing paper, I proceed to take a similar survey of the changes which mankind have undergone in respect to the conditions on which moral influence, or power over the minds of mankind, is dependent.

There are three distinguishable sources of moral influence: — eminent wisdom and virtue, real or supposed; the power of addressing mankind in the name of religion; and, finally, worldly power.

It is not necessary to illustrate the manner in which superiority of wisdom and virtue, or in which religion, preengages men's minds with the opinions and feelings in favour of which those authorities declare themselves. It is equally superfluous to insist upon the influence exercised over the minds of men by worldly power. The tendency of the human mind to the worship of power, is well understood. It is matter of common complaint, that even the Supreme Being is adored by an immense majority as the Almighty, not as the All-good; as he who can destroy, not as he who has blessed. It is a familiar fact, that the vulgar, in all parts of the world, have in general little or no rule of conduct or of opinion, but to do as their betters do, and to think as their betters think: and this very word *betters*, is speaking proof of the fact which we allege — meaning, as it does, not their *wisers*, or their *honesters*, but their *richers*, and those placed in authority over them.

All persons, from the most ignorant to the most instructed, from the most stupid to the most intelligent, have their minds more or less under the dominion of one or other, or all, of the influences which have just been mentioned. All bow down, with a submission more or less implicit, to the authority of superior minds, or of the interpreters of the divine will, or of their superiors in rank and station.

When an opinion is sanctioned by all these authorities, or by any one of them, the others not opposing, it becomes the received opinion.

At all periods of history in which there has existed a general agreement among these three authorities, there have existed *received doctrines*: a phrase the sense of which is now almost forgotten. The most marked character of such periods is a firm confidence in inherited opinions. Men cleave with a strong and fervent faith to the doctrine which they have imbibed from their infancy: though in conduct they be tempted to swerve from it, the belief remains in their hearts, fixed and immoveable, and has an irresistible hold upon the consciences of all good men. When, on the contrary, the three authorities are divided among themselves, or against each other, a violent conflict rages among opposing doctrines, until one or other prevails, or until mankind settle down into a state of general uncertainty and scepticism. At present, we are in a mixed state; some fight fiercely under their several banners, and these chiefly the least instructed; while the others (those few excepted who have strength to stand by themselves) are blown about by every breath, having no steady opinion — or at least no deep-rooted conviction that their opinion is true.

Society, therefore, has its natural state, and its transitional state, with respect to moral influence as well as to worldly power. Let us bestow a few words upon the natural state, and upon the nature of those varieties of the social order in which it has hitherto been realized.

It is in states of society in which the holders of power are chosen by the people (or by the most highly civilized portion of the people) for their supposed fitness, that we should most expect to find the three authorities acting together, and giving their sanction to the same doctrines. As men are raised to worldly power for their supposed wisdom and virtue, two of the three sources of moral influence are united in the same individuals. And although the rulers of such societies, being the creatures of the people's choice, have not, *qua* rulers, that ascendancy over the minds of the people, which power obtained and held independently of their will, commonly possesses; nevertheless, the station to which they are elevated gives them greater opportunities of rendering their wisdom and their virtue visible, while it also fixes the outward stamp of general recognition upon that merit, which would otherwise operate upon each mind only in proportion to its confidence in its own power of discriminating the most worthy.

Accordingly, in the best-constituted commonwealths of the ancient world, this unity of moral influence did to a very great degree exist. And in the great popular government of our own times, it exists with respect to the general doctrines of the constitution, and many maxims of national policy, and the list of received doctrines is increasing as rapidly as the differences of opinion among the persons possessing moral influence will allow.

I say, only the *best constituted* commonwealths of antiquity — and chiefly Athens, Sparta, and Rome — because, in the others, the form of the government, and the circumstances of society itself, being in a perpetual flux, the elements of moral influence never remained long enough in the same hands, to allow time for constitutional doctrines, or received maxims of policy, to grow up. But, in the three common-wealths which I have named, such constitutional doctrines, and such received maxims of policy, did exist, and the community was intensely attached to them.

The great authority for political doctrines in all these governments was the wisdom of ancestors: their old laws, their old maxims, the opin-ions of their ancient statesmen. This may sound strange to those who have imbibed the silly persuasion, that fickleness and love of innovation are the characteristics of popular governments. It is, however, matter of authentic history. It is not seen in reading Mitford, who always believed his prejudices above his eyes — but it is seen in reading Demosthenes, who shows in every page that he regards the authority of ancestors, not merely as an argument, but as one of the strongest of arguments; and steps out of his way to eulogise the wisdom of the ancient laws and lawgivers, with a frequency which proves it to have been the most popular of topics, and one on which his unequalled tact and sagacity taught him mainly to rely. All the other Athenian orators, down to the speeches in Thucydides; Cicero,[9] and all that we know of the Roman orators; Plato, and almost all the monuments which remain to us of the ideas of Athens, Sparta, and Rome, teem with evidence of the same fact. In all this there is nothing but what the known constitution of human nature would have enabled us to surmise: it is precisely what marks these commonwealths to have been in a natural state of society. When a government, whether it be a popular one or not, works well for the people among whom it exists, and satisfies their highest con-ceptions of a good social order, there is naturally a strong, and generally a very just, reverence for the memory of its founders. This would not have been thought strange three-quarters of a century ago. Robertson,[1] the historian, speaks with the utmost simplicity, of "that attachment to ancient forms, and aversion to innovation, which are the unfailing char-acteristics of popular assemblies." Europe had not then entered into the state of transition of which the first overt manifestation was the breaking out of the French revolution. Since that epoch, those near-sighted people who can see nothing, beyond their own age, have mis-taken that desire of novelty, and disregard of the authority of ancestors, which characterise an age of transition, for the properties of a popular government: just as if the same symptoms did not constantly attend every change, no matter of what nature, in the spirit of the age; as if

---

9. Thucydides' *History of the Pelopponesian War* is rich in speeches made by the leading figures of the day. Cicero's speeches, though intended to secure a conviction or acquittal, also made substantial political points.
1. William Robertson (1721–1793), Scots historian featured largely in Mill's childhood reading.

we might not be quite sure that there was as much scoffing at the
wisdom of ancestors in the Court of Augustus, as in the National Convention of France.[2]

The authority of ancestors, so deeply reverenced at Athens and
Rome, was the authority of the wisest and best men for many successive
generations. If, instead of upholding and applauding the ancient maxims, the ablest and most experienced contemporaries had affirmed
them to be the rude conceptions of barbarians, the many would have
lost their faith in them, and would have been as we are now. Nor had
authority more than its just weight: it did not supersede reason, but
guided it: for every relic which remains to us, of what was addressed to
the Athenian Demos, for example, by their orators and politicians, is
full of strong sense, cogent argument, and the most manly and forcible
appeals to the reason of the people. The speeches of the great orators,
and those in Thucydides,[3] are monuments of long-sighted policy, and
keen and sagacious observation of life and human nature, which will
be prized as long as the world shall endure or as wisdom shall be
understood and appreciated in it.

It is well known that respect and deference for old age formed a
conspicuous feature both in the public and private morality of the ancient commonwealths: and there is no surer mark of a natural state of
society in respect to moral influence. So deeply, however, have the
notions and feelings of an age of transition taken root among us, that
if there are some who wonder that this reverence should no longer
exist, there are probably many more who wonder that it should ever
have existed, and view it as a sort of superstition, or as one of the
numerous oddities of those peculiar people, the ancients: if, indeed,
they believe it at all; for it may be almost a misapplication of terms to
say that a man believes a fact, although he may never dream of doubting it; as religious writers know well, when they treat of what they call
practical infidelity. We can hardly be said to believe that, which we do
not conceive with any distinctness or vivacity. What we read of Greece
and Rome is so remote from what we have ever seen; we are helped
by so few familiar analogies to penetrate our minds with its spirit, and
make ourselves, as it were, at home in it, that some strength of imagination is requisite to conceive it with the intensity and life which is
essential to any thing deserving the name of belief. We do not believe
ancient history, we only fancy we believe it—our belief deserves no
higher name than simple acquiescence—it scarcely amounts to more
than that conventional assent, which we give to the mythology of the
same nations.

2. The National Convention—which met from September 20, 1792, to October 26, 1795—
   abolished the monarchy, governed France during the Reign of Terror, and succumbed to the
   need for stability in 1795.
3. Mill refers to the speeches that Thucydides puts into the mouths of the leading figures in his
   History of the Pelopponesian War and probably those of Demosthenes (384–322 B.C.).

Unquestionably, if the mental state of the old men of the present day were their natural state, there would be little reason for paying much deference to their modes of thinking. But narrowness of mind, and obstinate prejudice, are not the necessary, or the natural concomitants of old age. Old men have generally both their opinions and their feelings more deeply rooted than the young; but is it an evil to have strong convictions, and steady unfluctuating feelings? It is on the contrary, essential to all dignity or solidity of character, and to all fitness for guiding or governing mankind. It constitutes prejudice, only when society is at one of those turns or vicissitudes in its history, at which it becomes necessary that it should change its opinions and its feelings. There is but little wisdom in any one head, whatever quantity there may be in the society collectively, when the young are wiser than the old. We should not forget that, in the natural state of things, the old would, as a matter of course, be further advanced than the young, simply because they have been longer on the road. If this be not the case at present, it is because we have come to a bend in the road, and they not knowing it, continued to advance in the same line, got to the wrong side of the hedge, and allowed even the hindmost to pass them by. If the old know less than the young, it is because it is hard to unlearn; but society, fortunately, has not so frequent need to unlearn, as to learn.

All old men might have, and some old men really have, knowledge which it is altogether impossible that a young man, however great his capacity, should possess a very large measure of, namely, that which is derived from personal experience. There are some states of civilization in which this is every thing — rude states, it is true. In these, accordingly, the authority of age is almost unlimited. Nowhere is it so great as among the North American Indians: for there, the knowledge and judgment of every man must be nearly in proportion to the length of his individual experience, as the cunning of a fox may be not inaccurately measured by his years. Among the Greeks and Romans, though, in comparison, highly civilized nations, wisdom, notwithstanding, was less the fruit of speculative study, than of intercourse with the world, practice in business, and the long habit of deliberating on public affairs. It was there a recognized maxim, that old men were fittest to devise, and young men to execute.

In an age of literature, there is no longer, of necessity, the same wide interval between the knowledge of the old, and that which is attainable by the young. The experience of all former ages, recorded in books, is open to the young man as to the old; and this, doubtless, comprises much more than the individual experience of any one man; but it does not comprise all. There are things which books cannot teach. A young man *cannot*, unless his history has been a most extraordinary one, possess either that knowledge of life, which is necessary in the most difficult and important practical business, or that knowledge of the more recondite parts of human nature, which is equally necessary for the foundation of sound ethical and even political principles, but which is almost the exclusive privilege of him who, like Ulysses, has been πολυτλασ:[4] which he, whose mind has not passed through numerous states, both moral and intellectual, cannot find out by himself—though he may undoubtedly take upon trust from other minds, such faint, uncertain, and shadowy conceptions, as we have of a plant or an animal about which we have merely read. It is true that our old men, educated as they were, have little enough of all these advantages; but young men *cannot* have them. If they are not in the old men, they are nowhere.

That the habits of old men are fixed, their principles riveted, and that they swerve not easily from them, instead of a defect, should naturally be the highest recommendation. It would be so, if the habits which they acquired in their youth, were still suitable to the state of the human mind in their old age. When it is otherwise, indeed, the greater flexibility of the young, their greater accessibility to new ideas and new feelings, all which would otherwise be termed unsteadiness, renders them the sole hope of society. But this is nothing to be proud of, or to rejoice at; it is one of the great causes which combine to render this state of transition a most dangerous passage to society. The indispensable requisites for wise thinking and wise conduct in great affairs, are severed from each other: they are apart, and are not all found in the same men; nay, they are found in two sets of men, who are, for the most part, warring with each other. The young must prevail, though it were only by outliving their antagonists; but the most important of the qualifications for making a good use of success, are still to be acquired by them during the struggle. In turbulent times, knowledge of life and business are rapidly obtained; but a comprehensive knowledge of human nature is scarcely to be acquired, but by calm reflexion and observation, in times of political tranquillity; for when minds are excited, and one man is ranged against another, there are few who do not contract an invincible repugnance, not only to the errors of their opponents, but to the truths to which those errors are allied. Through this state, however, we must struggle; and happy will be the day when it will once more be true, that with length of years cometh wisdom, and when the necessary privations and annoyances of declining life shall again, as heretofore, be compensated by the honour and the gratitude due to increased powers of usefulness, fittingly employed.

V

In commencing this series of papers, I intended, and attempted, that the divisions of my discourse should correspond with those of my subject, and that each number should comprehend within its own limits

4. Affected by many things, experienced (Greek).

all which was necessary to the expansion and illustration of one single idea. The nature of the publication, which, as being read by more persons capable of understanding the drift of such speculations (and by fewer, in proportion, who are unfit for them) than any other single work, I considered myself fortunate in being enabled to adopt as a vehicle for my ideas, compels me to limit the length of each article more than is compatible with my original plan. I can no longer always hope that every paper should be complete within itself, and the present number, had it appeared in its proper place, would have formed the continuation of the last.

In endeavouring to give an intelligible notion of what I have termed the *natural* state of society, in respect of moral influence — namely, that state in which the opinions and feelings of the people are, with their voluntary acquiescence, formed *for* them, by the most cultivated minds which the intelligence and morality of the times call into existence; and in drawing attention to the striking differences between this *natural* state and our present *transitional* condition, in which there are no persons to whom the mass of the uninstructed habitually defer, and in whom they trust for finding the right, and for pointing it out; I have hitherto illustrated the former state only by the example of those commonwealths, in which the most qualified men are studiously picked out because of their qualifications, and invested with that worldly power, which, if it were in any other hands, would divide or eclipse their moral influence: but which, placed in theirs, and acting partly as a *certificate* of authority, and partly as a *cause*, tends naturally to render their power over the minds of their fellow-citizens paramount and irresistible.

But it is not solely in such societies that there is found a united body of moral authority, sufficient to extort acquiescence from the unin-quiring, or uninformed majority. It is found, likewise, in all societies where religion possesses a sufficient ascendency, to subdue the minds of the possessors of worldly power, and where the spirit of the prevailing religion is such as excludes the possibility of material conflict of opinion among its teachers.

These conditions exist among two great stationary communities — the Hindoos and the Turks;[5] and are doubtless the chief cause which keeps those communities stationary. The same union of circumstances has been hitherto found only in one *progressive* society — but that, the greatest which had ever existed: Christendom in the middle ages.

For many centuries, undivided moral influence over the nations of Europe, the unquestioned privilege of forming the opinions and feel-ings of the Christian world, was enjoyed, and most efficiently exercised by the Catholic clergy. Their word inspired in the rest of mankind the most fervent faith. It not only absolutely excluded doubt, but caused

5. Mill refers to the entire Ottoman Empire, already in decay, but still occupying a great area.

the doubter to be regarded with sentiments of profound abhorrence, which moralists had never succeeded in inspiring for the most revolting of crimes. It is certainly possible to feel perfectly sure of an opinion, without believing that whosoever doubts it will be damned, and should be burnt: and this last is by no means one of those peculiarities of a natural state of society which I am at all anxious to see restored. But the deep earnest feeling of firm and unwavering conviction, which, it pre-supposes, we may, without being unreasonable, lament that it was impossible, and could not *but* be impossible, in the intellectual anarchy of a general revolution in opinion, to transfer unimpaired to the truth.

The priesthood did not claim a right to dictate to mankind, either in belief or practice, beyond the province of religion and morals, but the political interests of mankind came not the less within their pale, because they seldom assumed the authority to regulate those concerns by specific precepts. They gave the sanction of their irresistible authority to one comprehensive rule, that which enjoined unlimited obedience to the temporal sovereign: an obligation from which they absolved the conscience of the believer, only when the sovereign disputed their authority within their peculiar province: and in that case they were invariably triumphant, like all those to whom it is given to call forth the moral sentiments of mankind in all their energy, against the inducements of mere physical hopes and fears.

The Catholic clergy, at the time when they possessed this undisputed authority in matters of conscience and belief, were, in point of fact, the fittest persons who *could* have possessed it—the then state of society, in respect of moral influence, answers to the description of a *natural* state.

Now, when we consider for how long a period the Catholic clergy were the only members of the European community who could even read; that they were the sole depositaries of all the treasures of thought, and reservoirs of intellectual delight, handed down to us from the ancients; that the sanctity of their persons permitted to them alone, among nations of semibarbarians, the tranquil pursuit of peaceful occupations and studies; that, howsoever defective the morality which they taught, they had at least a mission for curbing the unruly passions of mankind, and teaching them to set a value upon a distant end, paramount to immediate temptations, and to prize gratifications consisting of mental feelings above bodily sensation; that, situate in the position of the rivals to the temporal sovereign, drafted chiefly from the inferior classes of society, from men who otherwise would have been serfs, and the most lowly among them all having the road open before him, even to the papal chair, they had the strongest motives to avail themselves of the means afforded by Christianity, for inculcating the natural equality of mankind, the superiority of love and sacrifice above mere courage and bodily prowess, of menacing the great with the only terrors to which they were accessible, and speaking to their consciences in the name of the only superior whom they acknowledged, in behalf of the low. Reflecting on these things, I cannot persuade myself to doubt that the ascendancy of the Catholic clergy was to be desired, for that day, even by the philosopher; and that it has been a potent cause, if even it was not an indispensable condition, of the present civilization of Europe. Nor is this an apology for the vices of the Catholic religion: those vices were great and flagrant, and there was no natural connection between them; and the more civilizing and humanizing features in which all that there was of good in it resided. We may regret that the influence of the priesthood was not superseded by a better influence: but when in those days did any such influence exist?

I conclude, therefore, that, during a part of the middle ages, not only worldly power, as already shown, but moral influence also, was indisputedly exercised by the most competent persons; and that the conditions of a natural state of society were then fully realized.

But the age of transition arrived. A time came when that which had overmatched and borne down the strongest obstacles to improvement, became itself incompatible with improvement. Mankind outgrew their religion, and that, too, at a period when they had not yet outgrown their government, because the texture of the latter was more yielding, and could be stretched. We all know how lamentably effectual an instrument the influence of the Catholic priesthood then became, for restraining that expansion of the human intellect, which could not any longer consist with their ascendancy, or with the belief of the doctrines which they taught.

The more advanced communities of Europe succeeded, after a terrific struggle, in effecting their total or partial emancipation: in some, the Reformation achieved a victory—in others, a toleration; while, by a fate unhappily too common, the flame which had been kindled where the pile awaited the spark, spread into countries where the materials were not yet sufficiently prepared; and instead of burning down the hateful edifice, it consumed all that existed capable of nourishing itself, and was extinguished. The germs of civilization to come were scorched up and destroyed; the hierarchy reigned stronger than ever, amidst the intellectual solitude which it had made: and the countries which were thus denuded of the means of further advancement, fell back into barbarism irretrievable—except by foreign conquest. Such is the inevitable end, when, unhappily, changes to which the spirit of the age is favourable, can be successfully resisted. Civilization becomes the terror of the ruling powers, and that they may retain their seat, it must be their deliberate endeavour to barbarize mankind. There has been, since that day, one such attempt, and only one, which has had a momentary success: it was that of a man in whom all the evil influences of his age were concentered with an intensity and energy truly terrific, less tempered by any of its good influences than could appear possible in the times in which he lived—I need scarcely say that I refer to Napoleon.

May his abortive effort to uncivilize human nature, to uncultivate the mind of man, and turn it into a desolate waste, be the last!

It remains to trace the history of moral influence in the nations of Europe, subsequently to the Reformation.

In the countries which remained Catholic, but where the Catholic hierarchy did not retain sufficient moral ascendancy to succeed in stopping the progress of civilization, the church was compelled, by the decline of its separate influence, to link itself more and more closely with the temporal sovereignty. And thus did it retard its own downfall, until the spirit of the age became too strong for the two united, and both fell together to the ground.

I have said that the three sources of moral influence are, supposed wisdom and virtue, the sacerdotal office, and the possession of worldly power. But in Protestant countries, the authority of the ministers of religion, considered as an independent source of moral influence, must be blotted out from the catalogue. None of the churches which were the successors of the Catholic church in the nations in which the Reformation prevailed, succeeded, as churches, to any portion of the moral influence of their predecessor. The reason is, that no Protestant church ever claimed a special mission from the Deity to itself; or ever numbered among the obligations of religion, that of receiving its doctrines from teachers accredited by that particular church. The Catholics received the priest from God, and their religion from the priest. But in the Protestant sects, you resorted to the teacher, because you had already decided, or because it had been decided for you, that you would adopt his religion. In the popular religions you chose your own creed, and having so done, you naturally had recourse to its minister; — in the state religions, your creed was chosen for you by your worldly superiors, and you were instigated by conscience, or, it may be, urged by motives of a more worldly nature, to resort for religious instruction to the minister of their appointment.

Every head of a family, even of the lowest rank, in Scotland, is a theologian; he discusses points of doctrine with his neighbours, and expounds the scripture to his family. He defers, indeed, though with no slavish deference, to the opinion of his minister; but in what capacity? only as a man whom his understanding owns as being at least more versed in the particular subject — as being probably a wiser, and possibly, a better man than himself. This is not the influence of an interpreter of religion, as such; it is that of a purer heart, and a more cultivated intelligence. It is not the ascendancy of a priest: it is the combined authority of a professor of religion, and an esteemed private friend.

What I have said of the Scottish church, may be said of all Protestant churches, except state churches (which the Scottish church, notwithstanding its national endowment, is not). It may be said of all dissenters from our own establishment; except, indeed, those who inherit their religion, and adhere to it (not an uncommon case) as they would to any other family connexion. To the followers of the Church of England, a similar observation is wholly inapplicable: those excepted, who would abide by that communion for its doctrine, were it a dissenting sect. The people in general have not, nor ever had, any reason or motive for adhering to the established religion, except that it was the religion of their political superiors: and in the same ratio as their attachment to those superiors has declined, so has their adherence to the established church. From the time when the Church of England became firmly seated in its temporalities; from the period when its title to the fee-simple of our consciences acquired the sanctity of prescription, and when it was enabled to dispense with any support but what it derived from the stable foundations of the social fabric of which it formed a part; it sunk from its independent rank, into an integral part, or a kind of appendage, of the aristocracy. It merged into the higher classes: and what moral influence it possessed, was merely a portion of the general moral influence of temporal superiors.

From the termination, therefore, of that period of intellectual excitement and hardy speculation which succeeded the crisis of the Reformation, and which was prolonged in our own country to the end of the seventeenth century; — that moral influence, that power over the minds of mankind, which had been for so many ages the unquestioned heritage of the Catholic clergy, passed into the hands of the wealthy classes, and became united with worldly power. The ascendancy of the aristocracy was not so dictatorial and enthralling as that of the Catholic priesthood; because it was backed in a far inferior degree by the terrors of religion: and because unity of doctrine was not maintained, by the same powerful means, among the dominant class itself. Nevertheless, the higher classes set the fashion, as in dress, so in opinion. The opinions generally received among them, were the prevalent ones throughout the rest of the nation. A bookish man here and there might have his individual theories, but they made no converts. All who had no opinions of their own, assumed those of their superiors. Few men wrote and published doctrines which the higher classes did not approve; or if published, their books were successfully cried down, or at best, were little read or attended to. Such questions, and such only, as divided the aristocracy, were (modestly) debated by the people: whose various denominations or divisions were each headed by an aristocratic *coterie*. Even the Dissenters made amends for their preference of a vulgar religion, by evincing a full measure of pliability and acquiescence in all that concerned politics and social life; though the banner they in general followed, was that of a section of the aristocracy less wedded than the other section to the monopoly of the sect which possessed advowsons and archbishoprics.

The wealthy classes, then, from the revolution downwards, possessed all that existed both of moral authority and worldly power. Under their influence grew up the received doctrines of the British constitution; the opinions, respecting the proper limits of the powers of government, and the proper mode of constituting and administering it, which were long characteristic of Englishmen. Along with these arose a vast variety of current opinions respecting morality, education, and the structure of society. And feelings in unison with those opinions, spread far, and took a deep root in the English mind.

At no time, during this period, could the predominant class be said, with truth, to comprise among its members all the persons qualified to govern men's minds, or to direct their temporal interests, whom the state of society afforded. As a whole, however, that class contained, for a long time, a larger share of civilization and mental culture, than all other classes taken together. The difficulties, to men of merit and energy, of lifting themselves into that class, were not insuperable; and the leading and active spirits among the governing body, had capacity to comprehend intellectual superiority, and to value it. The conditions, therefore, of a natural state of society were for some time, upon the whole, tolerably well fulfilled.

But they have now ceased to be fulfilled. The government of the wealthy classes was, after all, the government of an irresponsible few; it therefore swarmed with abuses. Though the people, by the growth of their intelligence, became more and more sensible of whatever was vicious in their government, they might possibly have borne with it, had they themselves remained as they were formerly, unfit, and conscious of their unfitness, for the business of government. But the comparative freedom of the practical administration of our Constitution — the extensive latitude of action which it allowed to the energies of individuals — enabled the people to train themselves in every habit necessary for self-government; for the rational management of their own affairs. I believe it would be impossible to mention any portion whatever of the business of government (except some parts of the defence of the country against external enemies), of which the exact counterpart is not, in some instance or other, performed by a committee chosen by the people themselves: performed with less means, and under incomparably greater difficulties, but performed unexceptionably, and to the general satisfaction of the persons interested. It is notorious that much of the most important part of what in most other countries composes the business of government, is here performed wholly by voluntary associations: and other portions are done by the government in so clumsy and slovenly a manner, that it is found necessary to have recourse to voluntary associations as a subsidiary resource.

When the people were thus trained to self-government, and had learned by experience that they were fit for it, they could not continue to suppose that none but persons of rank and fortune were entitled to have a voice in the government, or were competent to criticise its pro-

ceedings. The superior capacity of the higher ranks for the exercise of
worldly power is now a broken spell.

It *was* in the power of those classes, possessed as they were of leisure
and boundless opportunities of mental culture, to have kept themselves
on the level of the most advanced intellects of the age; not to have
been overtopped by the growth around them of a mass of intelligence,
superior, on the average, to their own. They might also have preserved
the confidence of the people in the integrity of their purposes, by abat-
ing each abuse, in proportion as the public conscience rose against it.
They might thus have retained, in right of their virtue and intellect,
that moral ascendancy which an intelligent people never long continues to yield to mere power. But they have flung away their advantages.

I have already adverted to the decline of the higher classes in active
talent, as they became enervated by lazy enjoyment. In the same ratio
in which they have advanced in humanity and refinement, they have
fallen off in energy of intellect and strength of will. Many of them were
formerly versed in business: and into the hands of such, the remainder
committed the management of the nation's affairs. Now, the men of
hereditary wealth are mostly inexperienced in business, and unfit for it.
Many of them formerly knew life and the world: but their knowledge
of life is now little more than the knowledge of two or three hundred
families, with whom they are accustomed to associate; and it may be
safely asserted, that not even a fellow of a college is more ignorant
of the world, or more grossly mistakes the signs of the times, than
an English nobleman. Their very opinions, — which, before they had
passed into aphorisms, were the result of choice, and something like
an act of the intelligence, — are now merely hereditary. Their minds
were once active — they are now passive: they once generated impressions — they now merely take them. What are now their political
maxims? Traditional texts, relating, directly or indirectly, to the privileges of their order, and to the exclusive fitness of men of their own
sort for governing. What is their public virtue? Attachment to these
texts, and to the prosperity and grandeur of England, on condition that
she shall never swerve from them; idolatry of certain abstractions, called
church constitution, agriculture, trade, and others: by dint of which
they have gradually contrived, in a manner, to exclude from their minds
the very idea of their living and breathing fellow-citizens, as the subjects
of moral obligation in their capacity of rulers. They love their country
as Bonaparte[6] loved his army — for whose glory he felt the most ardent
zeal, at a time when all the men who composed it, one with another,
were killed off every two or three years. They do not love England as
one loves human beings, but as a man loves his house or his acres.

Being such persons as has now been described, and being at last

6. Napoleon Bonaparte (1769–1821), emperor of France.

completely found out by the more intelligent, they no longer retain sufficient moral influence to give, as heretofore, vogue and currency to their opinions. But they retain—and the possessors of worldly power must always retain—enough of that influence, to prevent any opinions, which they do not acknowledge, from passing into received doctrines. They must, therefore, be divested of the monopoly of worldly power, ere the most virtuous and best-instructed of the nation will acquire that ascendancy over the opinions and feelings of the rest, by which alone England can emerge from this crisis of transition, and enter once again into a natural state of society.

A few months before the first of these papers was written, it would have seemed a paradox to assert that the present area is one of moral and social transition. The same proposition now seems almost the tritest of truisms. The revolution which had already taken place in the human mind, is rapidly shaping external things to its own form and proportions.

That we are in a state of transition, is a point which needs no further illustration. That the passage we are in the midst of, will conduct us to a healthier state, has perhaps been rendered probable in the preceding papers, to some few who might otherwise have questioned it.

But it greatly imports us to obtain a far deeper insight into the futurity which awaits us, and into the means by which the blessings of that futurity may be best improved, and its dangers avoided.

How shall we attain this insight? By a careful survey of the properties which are characteristic of the English national mind, in the present age—for on these the future fate of our country must depend.

But "fit audience," even "though few," cannot be found for such discussions, at a moment when the interests of the day and of the hour naturally and properly engross every mind. The sequel of these papers must therefore be postponed until the interval of repose, after the present bustle and tumult. I shall resume my subject as early as possible after the passing of the Reform Bill.[7]

7. Not in fact passed until June 1832.

On Liberty

"The grand, leading principle, towards which every argument unfolded in these pages directly converges, is the absolute and essential
importance of human development in its richest diversity."
Wilhelm von Humboldt, *Sphere and Duties of Government.*
[Trans. Joseph Coulthard (London: Chapman, 1854), p. 65.]

To the beloved and deplored memory of her who was the inspirer,
and in part the author, of all that is best in my writings — the friend
and wife whose exalted sense of truth and right was my strongest
incitement, and whose approbation was my chief reward — I dedicate this volume. Like all that I have written for many years, it
belongs as much to her as to me; but the work as it stands has
had, in a very insufficient degree, the inestimable advantage of her
revision: some of the most important portions having been reserved
for a more careful re-examination, which they are now never destined to receive. Were I but capable of interpreting to the world
one half the great thoughts and noble feelings which are buried
in her grave, I should be the medium of a greater benefit to it,
than is ever likely to arise from anything that I can write, un-
prompted and unassisted by her all but unrivalled wisdom.

Chapter I

INTRODUCTORY

The subject of this Essay is not the so-called Liberty of the Will so
unfortunately opposed to the misnamed doctrine of Philosophical Necessity; but Civil, or Social Liberty: the nature and limits of the power
which can be legitimately exercised by society over the individual. A
question seldom stated, and hardly ever discussed, in general terms, but
which profoundly influences the practical controversies of the age by
its latent presence, and is likely soon to make itself recognized as the
vital question of the future. It is so far from being new, that, in a certain
sense, it has divided mankind, almost from the remotest ages; but in
the stage of progress into which the more civilised portions of the species have now entered, it presents itself under new conditions, and
requires a different and more fundamental treatment.

The struggle between Liberty and Authority is the most conspicuous
feature in the portions of history with which we are earliest familiar,
particularly in that of Greece, Rome, and England. But in old times
this contest was between subjects, or some classes of subjects, and the
Government. By liberty, was meant protection against the tyranny of
the political rulers. The rulers were conceived (except in some of the

popular governments of Greece) as in a necessarily antagonistic position to the people whom they ruled. They consisted of a governing One, or a governing tribe or caste, who derived their authority from inheritance or conquest, who, at all events, did not hold it at the pleasure of the governed, and whose supremacy men did not venture, perhaps did not desire, to contest, whatever precautions might be taken against its oppressive exercise. Their power was regarded as necessary, but also as highly dangerous; as a weapon which they would attempt to use against their subjects, no less than against external enemies. To prevent the weaker members of the community from being preyed upon by innumerable vultures, it was needful that there should be an animal of prey stronger than the rest, commissioned to keep them down. But as the king of the vultures would be no less bent upon preying on the flock than any of the minor harpies, it was indispensable to be in a perpetual attitude of defence against his beak and claws. The aim, therefore, of patriots was to set limits to the power which the ruler should be suffered to exercise over the community; and this limitation was what they meant by liberty. It was attempted in two ways. First, by obtaining a recognition of certain immunities, called political liberties or rights, which it was to be regarded as a breach of duty in the ruler to infringe, and which if he did infringe, specific resistance, or general rebellion, was held to be justifiable. A second, and generally a later expedient, was the establishment of constitutional checks, by which the consent of the community, or of a body of some sort, supposed to represent its interests, was made a necessary condition to some of the more important acts of the governing power. To the first of these modes of limitation, the ruling power, in most European countries, was compelled, more or less, to submit. It was not so with the second; and, to attain this, or when already in some degree possessed, to attain it more completely, became everywhere the principal object of the lovers of liberty. And so long as mankind were content to combat one enemy by another, and to be ruled by a master, on condition of being guaranteed more or less efficaciously against his tyranny, they did not carry their aspirations beyond this point.

A time, however, came, in the progress of human affairs, when men ceased to think it a necessity of nature that their governors should be an independent power, opposed in interest to themselves. It appeared to them much better that the various magistrates of the State should be their tenants or delegates, revocable at their pleasure. In that way alone, it seemed, could they have complete security that the powers of government would never be abused to their disadvantage. By degrees this new demand for elective and temporary rulers became the prominent object of the exertions of the popular party, wherever any such party existed; and superseded, to a considerable extent, the previous efforts to limit the power of rulers. As the struggle proceeded for making the ruling power emanate from the periodical choice of the ruled, some persons began to think that too much importance had been attached to the limitation of the power itself. *That* (it might seem) was a resource against rulers whose interests were habitually opposed to those of the people. What was now wanted was, that the rulers should be identified with the people; that their interest and will should be the interest and will of the nation. The nation did not need to be protected against its own will. There was no fear of its tyrannising over itself. Let the rulers be effectually responsible to it, promptly removable by it, and it could afford to trust them with power of which it could itself dictate the use to be made. Their power was but the nation's own power, concentrated, and in a form convenient for exercise. This mode of thought, or rather perhaps of feeling, was common among the last generation of European liberalism, in the Continental section of which it still apparently predominates. Those who admit any limit to what a government may do, except in the case of such governments as they think ought not to exist, stand out as brilliant exceptions among the political thinkers of the Continent. A similar tone of sentiment might by this time have been prevalent in our own country, if the circumstances which for a time encouraged it, had continued unaltered.

But, in political and philosophical theories, as well as in persons, success discloses faults and infirmities which failure might have concealed from observation. The notion, that the people have no need to limit their power over themselves, might seem axiomatic, when popular government was a thing only dreamed about, or read of as having existed at some distant period of the past. Neither was that notion necessarily disturbed by such temporary aberrations as those of the French Revolution, the worst of which were the work of a usurping few, and which, in any case, belonged, not to the permanent working of popular institutions, but to a sudden and convulsive outbreak against monarchical and aristocratic depotism. In time, however, a democratic republic came to occupy a large portion of the earth's surface, and made itself felt as one of the most powerful members of the community of nations; and elective and responsible government became subject to the observations and criticisms which wait upon a great existing fact. It was now perceived that such phrases as "self-government," and "the power of the people over themselves," do not express the true state of the case. The "people" who exercise the power are not always the same people with those over whom it is exercised; and the "self-government" spoken of is not the government of each by himself, but of each by all the rest. The will of the people, moreover, practically means the will of the most numerous or the most active *part* of the people; the majority, or those who succeed in making themselves accepted as the majority; the people, consequently, *may* desire to oppress a part of their number; and precautions are as much needed against this as against any other abuse of power. The limitation, therefore, of the power of government over individuals loses none of its importance when the holders of power are regularly accountable to the community, that is, to the strongest party therein. This view of things, recommending itself equally to the intelligence of thinkers and to the inclination of those important classes in European society to whose real or supposed interests democracy is adverse, has had no difficulty in establishing itself; and in political speculations "the tyranny of the majority" is now generally included among the evils against which society requires to be on its guard.

Like other tyrannies, the tyranny of the majority was at first, and is still vulgarly, held in dread, chiefly as operating through the acts of the public authorities. But reflecting persons perceived that when society is itself the tyrant — society collectively over the separate individuals who compose it — its means of tyrannising are not restricted to the acts which it may do by the hands of its political functionaries. Society can and does execute its own mandates; and if it issues wrong mandates instead of right, or any mandates at all in things with which it ought not to meddle, it practises a social tyranny more formidable than many kinds of political oppression, since, though not usually upheld by such extreme penalties, it leaves fewer means of escape, penetrating much more deeply into the details of life, and enslaving the soul itself.[1] Protection, therefore, against the tyranny of the magistrate is not enough: there needs protection also against the tyranny of the prevailing opinion and feeling; against the tendency of society to impose, by other means than civil penalties, its own ideas and practices as rules of conduct on those who dissent from them; to fetter the development, and, if possible, prevent the formation, of any individuality not in harmony with its ways, and compels all characters to fashion themselves upon the model of its own. There is a limit to the legitimate interference of collective opinion with individual independence: and to find that limit, and maintain it against encroachment, is as indispensable to a good condition of human affairs, as protection against political despotism.

But though this proposition is not likely to be contested in general terms, the practical question, where to place the limit — how to make the fitting adjustment between individual independence and social control — is a subject on which nearly everything remains to be done. All that makes existence valuable to any one, depends on the enforcement of restraints upon the actions of other people. Some rules of conduct, therefore, must be imposed, by law in the first place, and by opinion on many things which are not fit subjects for the operation of law. What these rules should be is the principal question in human affairs; but if we except a few of the most obvious cases, it is one of those which least progress has been made in resolving. No two ages,

1. James Madison (1751–1836) seems to have originated the expression and the idea. Alexis de Tocqueville (1805–1859), extended its scope as suggested here (*Democracy in America*, vol. 1, chap. 15). Madison's fears in *The Federalist* no. 10 were confined to what the majority might do to the property of the well-off.

and scarcely any two countries, have decided it alike; and the decision of one age or country is a wonder to another. Yet the people of any given age and country no more suspect any difficulty in it, than if it were a subject on which mankind had always been agreed. The rules which obtain among themselves appear to them self-evident and self-justifying. This all but universal illusion is one of the examples of the magical influence of custom, which is not only, as the proverb says, a second nature, but is continually mistaken for the first. The effect of custom, in preventing any misgiving respecting the rules of conduct which mankind impose on one another, is all the more complete because the subject is one on which it is not generally considered necessary that reasons should be given, either by one person to others or by each to himself. People are accustomed to believe, and have been encouraged in the belief by some who aspire to the character of philosophers, that their feelings, on subjects of this nature, are better than reasons, and render reasons unnecessary. The practical principle which guides them to their opinions on the regulation of human conduct, is the feeling in each person's mind that everybody should be required to act as he, and those with whom he sympathises, would like them to act. No one, indeed, acknowledges to himself that his standard of judgment is his own liking; but an opinion on a point of conduct, not supported by reasons, can only count as one person's preference; and if the reasons, when given, are a mere appeal to a similar preference felt by other people, it is still only many people's liking instead of one. To an ordinary man, however, his own preference, thus supported, is not only a perfectly satisfactory reason, but the only one he generally has for any of his notions of morality, taste, or propriety, which are not expressly written in his religious creed; and his chief guide in the interpretation even of that. Men's opinions, accordingly, on what is laudable or blamable, are affected by all the multifarious causes which influence their wishes in regard to the conduct of others, and which are as numerous as those which determine their wishes on any other subject. Sometimes their reason — at other times their prejudices or superstitions: often their social affections, not seldom their antisocial ones, their envy or jealousy, their arrogance or contemptuousness: but most commonly their desires or fears for themselves — their legitimate or illegitimate self-interest. Wherever there is an ascendant class, a large portion of the morality of the country emanates from its class interests, and its feelings of class superiority. The morality between Spartans and Helots, between planters and negroes, between princes and subjects, between nobles and roturiers,[2] between men and women, has been for the most part the creation of these class interests and feelings: and the sentiments thus generated react in turn upon the moral feelings of the

---

2. Plebeian or commoner (French). The Helots were serfs or slaves owned by Spartan landowners.

members of the ascendant class, in their relations among themselves. Where, on the other hand, a class, formerly ascendant, has lost its ascendancy, or where its ascendancy is unpopular, the prevailing moral sentiments frequently bear the impress of an impatient dislike of superiority. Another grand determining principle of the rules of conduct, both in act and forbearance, which have been enforced by law or opinion, has been the servility of mankind towards the supposed preferences or aversions of their temporal masters or of their gods. This servility, though essentially selfish, is not hypocrisy; it gives rise to perfectly genuine sentiments of abhorrence; it made men burn magicians and heretics. Among so many baser influences, the general and obvious interests of society have of course had a share, and a large one, in the direction of the moral sentiments: less, however, as a matter of reason, and on their own account, than as a consequence of the sympathies and antipathies which grew out of them: and sympathies and antipathies which had little or nothing to do with the interests of society, have made themselves felt in the establishment of moralities with quite as great force.

The likings and dislikings of society, or of some powerful portion of it, are thus the main thing which has practically determined the rules laid down for general observance, under the penalties of law or opinion. And in general, those who have been in advance of society in thought and feeling, have left this condition of things unassailed in principle, however they may have come into conflict with it in some of its details. They have occupied themselves rather in inquiring what things society ought to like or dislike, than in questioning whether its likings or dislikings should be a law to individuals. They preferred endeavouring to alter the feelings of mankind on the particular points on which they were themselves heretical, rather than make common cause in defence of freedom, with heretics generally. The only case in which the higher ground has been taken on principle and maintained with consistency, by any but an individual here and there, is that of religious belief: a case instructive in many ways, and not least so as forming a most striking instance of the fallibility of what is called the moral sense: for the *odium theologicum*,[3] in a sincere bigot, is one of the most unequivocal cases of moral feeling. Those who first broke the yoke of what called itself the Universal Church,[4] were in general as little willing to permit differences of religious opinion as that church itself. But when the heat of the conflict was over, without giving a complete victory to any party, and each church or sect was reduced to limit its hopes to retaining possession of the ground it already occupied; minorities, seeing that they had no chance of becoming majorities, were under the necessity of pleading to those whom they could not convert, for permission to

3. Religious hatred (Latin).
4. The Roman Catholic Church.

differ. It is accordingly on this battlefield, almost solely, that the rights of the individual against society have been asserted on broad grounds of principle, and the claim of society to exercise authority over dissentients openly controverted. The great writers to whom the world owes what religious liberty it possesses, have mostly asserted freedom of conscience as an indefeasible right, and denied absolutely that a human being is accountable to others for his religious belief. Yet so natural to mankind is intolerance in whatever they really care about, that religious freedom has hardly anywhere been practically realised, except where religious indifference, which dislikes to have its peace disturbed by theological quarrels, has added its weight to the scale. In the minds of almost all religious persons, even in the most tolerant countries, the duty of toleration is admitted with tacit reserves. One person will bear with dissent in matters of church government, but not of dogma; another can tolerate anybody, short of a Papist or a Unitarian; another every one who believes in revealed religion; a few extend their charity a little further, but stop at the belief in a God and in a future state. Wherever the sentiment of the majority is still genuine and intense, it is found to have abated little of its claim to be obeyed.

In England, from the peculiar circumstances of our political history, though the yoke of opinion is perhaps heavier, that of law is lighter, than in most other countries of Europe; and there is considerable jealousy of direct interference, by the legislative or the executive power, with private conduct; not so much from any just regard for the independence of the individual, as from the still subsisting habit of looking on the government as representing an opposite interest to the public. The majority have not yet learnt to feel the power of the government their power, or its opinions their opinions. When they do so, individual liberty will probably be as much exposed to invasion from the government, as it already is from public opinion. But, as yet, there is a considerable amount of feeling ready to be called forth against any attempt of the law to control individuals in things in which they have not hitherto been accustomed to be controlled by it; and this with very little discrimination as to whether the matter is, or is not, within the legitimate sphere of legal control; insomuch that the feeling, highly salutary on the whole, is perhaps quite as often misplaced as well grounded in the particular instances of its application. There is, in fact, no recognised principle by which the propriety or impropriety of government interference is customarily tested. People decide according to their personal preferences. Some, whenever they see any good to be done, or evil to be remedied, would willingly instigate the government to undertake the business; while others prefer to bear almost any amount of social evil, rather than add one to the departments of human interest amenable to governmental control. And men range themselves on one or the other side in any particular case, according to this general direction of their sentiments; or according to the degree of interest which they feel in the particular thing which it is proposed that the government should do, or according to the belief they entertain that the government would, or would not, do it in the manner they prefer; but very rarely on account of any opinion to which they consistently adhere, as to what things are fit to be done by a government. And it seems to me that in consequence of this absence of rule or principle, one side is at present as often wrong as the other; the interference of government is, with about equal frequency, improperly invoked and improperly condemned.

The object of this Essay is to assert one very simple principle, as entitled to govern absolutely the dealings of society with the individual in the way of compulsion and control, whether the means used be physical force in the form of legal penalties, or the moral coercion of public opinion. That principle is, that the sole end for which mankind are warranted, individually or collectively, in interfering with the liberty of action of any of their number, is self-protection. That the only purpose for which power can be rightfully exercised over any member of a civilised community, against his will, is to prevent harm to others. His own good, either physical or moral, is not a sufficient warrant. He cannot rightfully be compelled to do or forbear because it will be better for him to do so, because it will make him happier, because, in the opinions of others, to do so would be wise, or even right. These are good reasons for remonstrating with him, or reasoning with him, or persuading him, or entreating him, but not for compelling him, or visiting him with any evil in case he do otherwise. To justify that, the conduct from which it is desired to deter him must be calculated to produce evil to some one else. The only part of the conduct of any one, for which he is amenable to society, is that which concerns others. In the part which merely concerns himself, his independence is, of right, absolute. Over himself, over his own body and mind, the individual is sovereign.

It is, perhaps hardly necessary to say that this doctrine is meant to apply only to human beings in the maturity of their faculties. We are not speaking of children, or of young persons below the age which the law may fix as that of manhood or womanhood. Those who are still in a state to require being taken care of by others, must be protected against their own actions as well as against external injury. For the same reason, we may leave out of consideration those backward states of society in which the race itself may be considered as in its nonage. The early difficulties in the way of spontaneous progress are so great, that there is seldom any choice of means for overcoming them; and a ruler full of the spirit of improvement is warranted in the use of any expedients that will attain an end, perhaps otherwise unattainable. Despotism is a legitimate mode of government in dealing with barbarians, provided the end be their improvement, and the means justified by actually effecting that end. Liberty, as a principle, has no application to any state of things anterior to the time when mankind have become capable of being improved by free and equal discussion. Until then, there is nothing for them but implicit obedience to an Akbar or a Charlemagne,[5] if they are so fortunate as to find one. But as soon as mankind have attained the capacity of being guided to their own improvement by conviction or persuasion (a period long since reached in all nations with whom we need here concern ourselves), compulsion, either in the direct form or in that of pains and penalties for non-compliance, is no longer admissible as a means to their own good, and justifiable only for the security of others.

It is proper to state that I forego any advantage which could be derived to my argument from the idea of abstract right, as a thing independent of utility. I regard utility as the ultimate appeal on all ethical questions; but it must be utility in the largest sense, grounded on the permanent interests of man as a progressive being. Those interests, I contend, authorise the subjection of individual spontaneity to external control, only in respect to those actions of each, which concern the interest of other people. If any one does an act hurtful to others, there is a *prima facie*[6] case for punishing him, by law, or, where legal penalties are not safely applicable, by general disapprobation. There are also many positive acts for the benefit of others, which he may rightfully be compelled to perform; such as to give evidence in a court of justice; to bear his fair share in the common defence, or in any other joint work necessary to the interest of the society of which he enjoys the protection; and to perform certain acts of individual beneficence, such as saving a fellow-creature's life, or interposing to protect the defenceless against ill-usage, things which whenever it is obviously a man's duty to do, he may rightfully be made responsible to society for not doing. A person may cause evil to others not only by his actions but by his inaction, and in either case he is justly accountable to them for the injury. The latter case, it is true, requires a much more cautious exercise of compulsion than the former. To make any one answerable for doing evil to others is the rule; to make him answerable for not preventing evil is, comparatively speaking, the exception. Yet there are many cases clear enough and grave enough to justify that exception. In all things which regard the external relations of the individual, he is *de jure*[7] amenable to those whose interests are concerned, and, if need be, to society as their protector. There are often good reasons for not holding him to the responsibility; but these reasons must arise from the special expediencies of the case: either because it is a kind of case in

5. United much of western Europe in the Holy Roman Empire and was a renowned patron of art and learning (742–814). Akbar (1542–1605), a renowned Mogul emperor of India.
6. On the face of it (Latin).
7. Of right (Latin).

which he is on the whole likely to act better, when left to his own discretion, than when controlled in any way in which society have it in their power to control him; or because the attempt to exercise control would produce other evils, greater than those which it would prevent. When such reasons as these preclude the enforcement of responsibility, the conscience of the agent himself should step into the vacant judgment seat, and protect those interests of others which have no external protection; judging himself all the more rigidly, because the case does not admit of his being made accountable to the judgment of his fellow-creatures.

But there is a sphere of action in which society, as distinguished from the individual, has, if any, only an indirect interest; comprehending all that portion of a person's life and conduct which affects only himself, or if it also affects others, only with their free, voluntary, and undeceived consent and participation. When I say only himself, I mean directly, and in the first instance; for whatever affects himself, may affect others *through* himself; and the objection which may be grounded on this contingency, will receive consideration in the sequel. This, then, is the appropriate region of human liberty. It comprises, first, the inward domain of consciousness; demanding liberty of conscience in the most comprehensive sense; liberty of thought and feeling; absolute freedom of opinion and sentiment on all subjects, practical or speculative, scientific, moral, or theological. The liberty of expressing and publishing opinions may seem to fall under a different principle, since it belongs to that part of the conduct of an individual which concerns other people; but, being almost of as much importance as the liberty of thought itself, and resting in great part on the same reasons, is practically inseparable from it. Secondly, the principle requires liberty of tastes and pursuits; of framing the plan of our life to suit our own character; of doing as we like, subject to such consequences as may follow: without impediment from our fellow-creatures, so long as what we do does not harm them, even though they should think our conduct foolish, perverse, or wrong. Thirdly, from this liberty of each individual, follows the liberty, within the same limits, of combination among individuals; freedom to unite, for any purpose not involving harm to others: the persons combining being supposed to be of full age, and not forced or deceived.

No society in which these liberties are not, on the whole, respected, is free, whatever may be its form of government; and none is completely free in which they do not exist absolute and unqualified. The only freedom which deserves the name, is that of pursuing our own good in our own way, so long as we do not attempt to deprive others of theirs, or impede their efforts to obtain it. Each is the proper guardian of his own health, whether bodily, or mental and spiritual. Mankind are greater gainers by suffering each other to live as seems good to themselves, than by compelling each to live as seems good to the rest.

Though this doctrine is anything but new, and, to some persons, may have the air of a truism, there is no doctrine which stands more directly opposed to the general tendency of existing opinion and practice. Society has expended fully as much effort in the attempt (according to its lights) to compel people to conform to its notions of personal as of social excellence. The ancient commonwealths thought themselves entitled to practise, and the ancient philosophers countenanced, the regulation of every part of private conduct by public authority, on the ground that the State had a deep interest in the whole bodily and mental discipline of every one of its citizens; a mode of thinking which may have been admissible in small republics surrounded by powerful enemies, in constant peril of being subverted by foreign attack or internal commotion, and to which even a short interval of relaxed energy and self-command might so easily be fatal that they could not afford to wait for the salutary permanent effects of freedom. In the modern world, the greater size of political communities, and, above all, the separation between spiritual and temporal authority (which placed the direction of men's consciences in other hands than those which controlled their worldly affairs), prevented so great an interference by law in the details of private life; but the engines of moral repression have been wielded more strenuously against divergence from the reigning opinion in self-regarding, than even in social matters; religion, the most powerful of the elements which have entered into the formation of moral feeling, having almost always been governed either by the ambition of a hierarchy, seeking control over every department of human conduct, or by the spirit of Puritanism.[8] And some of those modern reformers who have placed themselves in strongest opposition to the religions of the past, have been noway behind either churches or sects in their assertion of the right of spiritual domination: M. Comte,[9] in particular, whose social system, as unfolded in his *Système de Politique Positive*, aims at establishing (though by moral more than by legal appliances) a despotism of society over the individual, surpassing anything contemplated in the political ideal of the most rigid disciplinarian among the ancient philosophers.

Apart from the peculiar tenets of individual thinkers, there is also in the world at large an increasing inclination to stretch unduly the powers of society over the individual, both by the force of opinion and even by that of legislation; and as the tendency of all the changes taking place in the world is to strengthen society, and diminish the power of the individual, this encroachment is not one of the evils which tend

8. Mill probably did not mean the views of seventeenth-century Church of England reformers so much as straitlaced opinion generally.
9. Auguste Comte (1798–1857), French sociologist—he coined the term—and inventor of Positivism, a supposedly scientific religious and political creed.

spontaneously to disappear, but, on the contrary, to grow more and more formidable. The disposition of mankind, whether as rulers or as fellow-citizens, to impose their own opinions and inclinations as a rule of conduct on others, is so energetically supported by some of the best and by some of the worst feelings incident to human nature, that it is hardly ever kept under restraint by anything but want of power; and as the power is not declining, but growing, unless a strong barrier of moral conviction can be raised against the mischief, we must expect, in the present circumstances of the world, to see it increase.

It will be convenient for the argument, if, instead of at once entering upon the general thesis, we confine ourselves in the first instance to a single branch of it, on which the principle here stated is, if not fully, yet to a certain point, recognised by the current opinions. This one branch is the Liberty of Thought: from which it is impossible to separate the cognate liberty of speaking and of writing. Although these liberties, to some considerable amount, form part of the political morality of all countries which profess religious toleration and free institutions, the grounds, both philosophical and practical, on which they rest, are perhaps not so familiar to the general mind, nor so thoroughly appreciated by many even of the leaders of opinion, as might have been expected. Those grounds, when rightly understood, are of much wider application than to only one division of the subject, and a thorough consideration of this part of the question will be found the best introduction to the remainder. Those to whom nothing which I am about to say will be new, may therefore, I hope, excuse me, if on a subject which for now three centuries has been so often discussed, I venture on one discussion more.

Chapter II

OF THE LIBERTY OF THOUGHT AND DISCUSSION

The time, it is to be hoped, is gone by, when any defence would be necessary of the "liberty of the press" as one of the securities against corrupt or tyrannical government. No argument, we may suppose, can now be needed, against permitting a legislature or an executive, not identified in interest with the people, to prescribe opinions to them, and determine what doctrines or what arguments they shall be allowed to hear. This aspect of the question, besides, has been so often and so triumphantly enforced by preceding writers, that it needs not be specially insisted on in this place. Though the law of England, on the subject of the press, is as servile to this day as it was in the time of the Tudors,[1] there is little danger of its being actually put in force against

---

1. The ruling royal family in England from 1485 (Henry VII) to 1603 (Elizabeth I).

political discussion, except during some temporary panic, when fear of insurrection drives ministers and judges from their propriety;[2] and, speaking generally, it is not, in constitutional countries, to be apprehended, that the government, whether completely responsible to the people or not, will often attempt to control the expression of opinion, except when in doing so it makes itself the organ of the general intolerance of the public. Let us suppose, therefore, that the government is entirely at one with the people, and never thinks of exerting any power of coercion unless in agreement with what it conceives to be their voice. But I deny the right of the people to exercise such coercion, either by themselves or by their government. The power itself is illegitimate. The best government has no more title to it than the worst. It is as noxious, or more noxious, when exerted in accordance with public opinion, than when in opposition to it. If all mankind minus one were of one opinion, and only one person were of the contrary opinion, mankind would be no more justified in silencing that one person, than he, if he had the power, would be justified in silencing mankind. Were an opinion a personal possession of no value except to the owner; if to be obstructed in the enjoyment of it were simply a private injury, it would make some difference whether the injury was inflicted only on a few persons or on many. But the peculiar evil of silencing the expression of an opinion is, that it is robbing the human race; posterity as well as the existing generation; those who dissent from the opinion, still more than those who hold it. If the opinion is right, they are deprived of the opportunity of exchanging error for truth: if wrong, they lose, what is almost as great a benefit, the clearer perception and livelier impression of truth, produced by its collision with error.

It is necessary to consider separately these two hypotheses, each of

2. These words had scarcely been written, when, as if to give them an emphatic contradiction, occurred the Government Press Prosecutions of 1858. That ill-judged interference with the liberty of public discussion has not, however, induced me to alter a single word in the text, nor has it at all weakened my conviction that, moments of panic excepted, the era of pains and penalties for political discussion has, in our own country, passed away. For, in the first place, the prosecutions were not persisted in; and, in the second, they were never, properly speaking, political prosecutions. The offence charged was not that of criticising institutions, or the acts or persons of rulers, but of circulating what was deemed an immoral doctrine, the lawfulness of Tyrannicide.

If the arguments of the present chapter are of any validity, there ought to exist the fullest liberty of professing and discussing, as a matter of ethical conviction, any doctrine, however immoral it may be considered. It would, therefore, be irrelevant and out of place to examine here, whether the doctrine of Tyrannicide deserves that title. I shall content myself with saying that the subject has been at all times one of the open questions of morals; that the act of a private citizen in striking down a criminal, who, by raising himself above the law, has placed himself beyond the reach of legal punishment or control, has been accounted by whole nations, and by some of the best and wisest of men, not a crime, but an act of exalted virtue; and that, right or wrong, it is not of the nature of assassination, but of civil war. As such, I hold that the instigation to it, in a specific case, may be a proper subject of punishment, but only if an overt act has followed, and at least a probable connection can be established between the act and the instigation. Even then, it is not a foreign government, but the very government assailed, which alone, in the exercise of self-defence, can legitimately punish attacks directed against its own existence [Mill's note].

which has a distinct branch of the argument corresponding to it. We can never be sure that the opinion we are endeavouring to stifle is a false opinion; and if we were sure, stifling it would be an evil still.

First: the opinion which it is attempted to suppress by authority may possibly be true. Those who desire to suppress it, of course deny its truth; but they are not infallible. They have no authority to decide the question for all mankind, and exclude every other person from the means of judging. To refuse a hearing to an opinion, because they are sure that it is false, is to assume that *their* certainty is the same thing as *absolute* certainty. All silencing of discussion is an assumption of infallibility. Its condemnation may be allowed to rest on this common argument, not the worse for being common.

Unfortunately for the good sense of mankind, the fact of their fallibility is far from carrying the weight in their practical judgment which is always allowed to it in theory; for while every one well knows himself to be fallible, few think it necessary to take any precautions against their own fallibility, or admit the supposition that any opinion, of which they feel very certain, may be one of the examples of the error to which they acknowledge themselves to be liable. Absolute princes, or others who are accustomed to unlimited deference, usually feel this complete confidence in their own opinions on nearly all subjects. People more happily situated, who sometimes hear their opinions disputed, and are not wholly unused to be set right when they are wrong, place the same unbounded reliance only on such of their opinions as are shared by all who surround them, or to whom they habitually defer; for in proportion to a man's want of confidence in his own solitary judgment, does he usually repose, with implicit trust, on the infallibility of "the world" in general. And the world, to each individual, means the part of it with which he comes in contact; his party, his sect, his church, his class of society; the man may be called, by comparison, almost liberal and large-minded to whom it means anything so comprehensive as his own country or his own age. Nor is his faith in this collective authority at all shaken by his being aware that other ages, countries, sects, churches, classes, and parties have thought, and even now think, the exact reverse. He devolves upon his own world the responsibility of being in the right against the dissentient worlds of other people; and it never troubles him that mere accident has decided which of these numerous worlds is the object of his reliance, and that the same causes which make him a Churchman in London, would have made him a Buddhist or a Confucian in Pekin.[3] Yet it is as evident in itself, as any amount of argument can make it, that ages are no more infallible than individuals; every age having held many opinions which subsequent ages have deemed not only false but absurd; and it is as certain that many opinions now gen-

3. Peking, now Beijing. "Churchman": member of the Church of England.

eral will be rejected by future ages, as it is that many, once general, are rejected by the present.

The objection likely to be made to this argument would probably take some such form as the following. There is no greater assumption of infallibility in forbidding the propagation of error, than in any other thing which is done by public authority on its own judgment and responsibility. Judgment is given to men that they may use it. Because it may be used erroneously, are men to be told that they ought not to use it at all? To prohibit what they think pernicious, is not claiming exemption from error, but fulfilling the duty incumbent on them, although fallible, of acting on their conscientious conviction. If we were never to act on our opinions, because those opinions may be wrong, we should leave all our interests uncared for, and all our duties unperformed. An objection which applies to all conduct can be no valid objection to any conduct in particular. It is the duty of governments, and of individuals, to form the truest opinions they can; to form carefully, and never impose them upon others unless they are quite sure of being right. But when they are sure (such reasoners may say), it is not conscientiousness but cowardice to shrink from acting on their opinions, and allow doctrines which they honestly think dangerous to the welfare of mankind, either in this life or in another, to be scattered abroad without restraint, because other people, in less enlightened times, have persecuted opinions now believed to be true. Let us take care, it may be said, not to make the same mistake: but governments and nations have made mistakes in other things, which are not denied to be fit subjects for the exercise of authority: they have laid on bad taxes, made unjust wars. Ought we therefore to lay on no taxes, and, under whatever provocation, make no wars? Men and governments, must act to the best of their ability. There is no such thing as absolute certainty, but there is assurance sufficient for the purposes of human life. We may, and must, assume our opinion to be true for the guidance of our own conduct: and it is assuming no more when we forbid bad men to pervert society by the propagation of opinions which we regard as false and pernicious.

I answer, that it is assuming very much more. There is the greatest difference between presuming an opinion to be true, because, with every opportunity for contesting it, it has not been refuted, and assuming its truth for the purpose of not permitting its refutation. Complete liberty of contradicting and disproving our opinion is the very condition which justifies us in assuming its truth for purposes of action; and on no other terms can a being with human faculties have any rational assurance of being right.

When we consider either the history of opinion, or the ordinary conduct of human life, to what is it to be ascribed that the one and the other are no worse than they are? Not certainly to the inherent force of the human understanding; for, on any matter not self-evident, there are ninety-nine persons totally incapable of judging of it for one who is capable; and the capacity of the hundredth person is only comparative; for the majority of the eminent men of every past generation held many opinions now known to be erroneous, and did or approved numerous things which no one will now justify. Why is it, then, that there is on the whole a preponderance among mankind of rational opinions and rational conduct? If there really is this preponderance — which there must be unless human affairs are, and have always been, in an almost desperate state — it is owing to a quality of the human mind, the source of everything respectable in man either as an intellectual or as a moral being, namely, that his errors are corrigible. He is capable of rectifying his mistakes, by discussion and experience. Not by experience alone. There must be discussion, to show how experience is to be interpreted. Wrong opinions and practices gradually yield to fact and argument; but facts and arguments, to produce any effect on the mind, must be brought before it. Very few facts are able to tell their own story, without comments to bring out their meaning. The whole strength and value, then, of human judgment, depending on the one property, that it can be set right when it is wrong, reliance can be placed on it only when the means of setting it right are kept constantly at hand. In the case of any person whose judgment is really deserving of confidence, how has it become so? Because he has kept his mind open to criticism on his opinions and conduct. Because it has been his practice to listen to all that could be said against him; to profit by as much of it as was just, and expound to himself, and upon occasion to others, the fallacy of what was fallacious. Because he has felt, that the only way in which a human being can make some approach to knowing the whole of a subject, is by hearing what can be said about it by persons of every variety of opinion, and studying all modes in which it can be looked at by every character of mind. No wise man ever acquired his wisdom in any mode but this; nor is it in the nature of human intellect to become wise in any other manner. The steady habit of correcting and completing his own opinion by collating it with those of others, so far from causing doubt and hesitation in carrying it into practice, is the only stable foundation for a just reliance on it: for, being cognisant of all that can, at least obviously, be said against him, and having taken up his position against all gainsayers — knowing that he has sought for objections and difficulties, instead of avoiding them, and has shut out no light which can be thrown upon the subject from any quarter — he has a right to think his judgment better than that of any person, or any multitude, who have not gone through a similar process.

It is not too much to require that what the wisest of mankind, those who are best entitled to trust their own judgment, find necessary to warrant their relying on it, should be submitted to by that miscellaneous collection of a few wise and many foolish individuals, called the public.

The most intolerant of churches, the Roman Catholic Church, even at the canonisation of a saint, admits, and listens patiently to, a "devil's advocate."[4] The holiest of men, it appears, cannot be admitted to post-humous honours, until all that the devil could say against him is known and weighed. If even the Newtonian philosophy[5] were not permitted to be questioned, mankind could not feel as complete assurance of its truth as they now do. The beliefs which we have most warrant for have no safeguard to rest on, but a standing invitation to the whole world to prove them unfounded. If the challenge is not accepted, or is accepted and the attempt fails, we are far enough from certainty still; but we have done the best that the existing state of human reason admits of; we have neglected nothing that could give the truth a chance of reaching us: if the lists are kept open, we may hope that if there be a better truth, it will be found when the human mind is capable of receiving it; and in the meantime we may rely on having attained such approach to truth as is possible in our own day. This is the amount of certainty attainable by a fallible being, and this the sole way of attaining it.

Strange it is, that men should admit the validity of the arguments for free discussion, but object to their being "pushed to an extreme"; not seeing that unless the reasons are good for an extreme case, they are not good for any case. Strange that they should imagine that they are not assuming infallibility, when they acknowledge that there should be free discussion on all subjects which can possibly be *doubtful*, but think that some particular principle or doctrine should be forbidden to be questioned because it is so *certain*, that is, because *they are certain* that it is certain. To call any proposition certain, while there is any one who would deny its certainty if permitted, but who is not permitted, is to assume that we ourselves, and those who agree with us, are the judges of certainty, and judges without hearing the other side.

In the present age — which has been described as "destitute of faith, but terrified at scepticism"[6] — in which people feel sure, not so much that their opinions are true, as that they should not know what to do without them — the claims of an opinion to be protected from public attack are rested not so much on its truth, as on its importance to society. There are, it is alleged, certain beliefs so useful, not to say indispensable, to well-being that it is as much the duty of governments to uphold those beliefs, as to protect any other of the interests of society. In a case of such necessity, and so directly in the line of their duty, something less than infallibility may, it is maintained, warrant, and even bind, governments to act on their own opinion, confirmed by the general opinion of mankind. It is also often argued, and still oftener

---

4. The *advocatus diaboli* (Latin); the term is used in any context where someone is called on to speak against the official view.
5. The system of physics created by Sir Isaac Newton (1642–1727).
6. Thomas Carlyle, "Memoirs of the Life of Scott," in *Critical and Miscellaneous Essays* (1880), 520.

thought, that none but bad men would desire to weaken these salutary
beliefs; and there can be nothing wrong, it is thought, in restraining
bad men, and prohibiting what only such men would wish to practise.
This mode of thinking makes the justification of restraints on discussion
not a question of the truth of doctrines, but of their usefulness; and
flatters itself by that means to escape the responsibility of claiming to
be an infallible judge of opinions. But those who thus satisfy themselves, do not perceive that the assumption of infallibility is merely
shifted from one point to another. The usefulness of an opinion is itself
matter of opinion: as disputable, as open to discussion, and requiring
discussion as much as the opinion itself. There is the same need of an
infallible judge of opinions to decide an opinion to be noxious, as to
decide it to be false, unless the opinion condemned has full opportunity
of defending itself. And it will not do to say that the heretic may be
allowed to maintain the utility or harmlessness of his opinion, though
forbidden to maintain its truth. The truth of an opinion is part of its
utility. If we would know whether or not it is desirable that a proposition
should be believed, is it possible to exclude the consideration of
whether or not it is true? In the opinion, not of bad men, but of the
best men, no belief which is contrary to truth can be really useful: and
can you prevent such men from urging that plea, when they are
charged with culpability for denying some doctrine which they are told
is useful, but which they believe to be false? Those who are on the side
of received opinions never fail to take all possible advantage of this
plea: you do not find *them* handling the question of utility as if it could
be completely abstracted from that of truth: on the contrary, it is, above
all, because their doctrine is "the truth," that the knowledge or the
belief of it is held to be so indispensable. There can be no fair discussion of the question of usefulness when an argument so vital may be
employed on one side, but not on the other. And in point of fact, when
law or public feeling do not permit the truth of an opinion to be disputed, they are just as little tolerant of a denial of its usefulness. The
utmost they allow is an extenuation of its absolute necessity, or of the
positive guilt of rejecting it.

In order more fully to illustrate the mischief of denying a hearing to
opinions because we, in our own judgment, have condemned them, it
will be desirable to fix down the discussion to a concrete case; and I
choose, by preference, the cases which are least favourable to me — in
which the argument against freedom of opinion, both on the score of
truth and on that of utility, is considered the strongest. Let the opinions
impugned be the belief in a God and in a future state, or any of the
commonly received doctrines of morality. To fight the battle on such
ground gives a great advantage to an unfair antagonist; since he will be
sure to say (and many who have no desire to be unfair will say it
internally), Are these the doctrines which you do not deem sufficiently
certain to be taken under the protection of law? Is the belief in a God

one of the opinions to feel sure of which you hold to be assuming infallibility? But I must be permitted to observe, that it is not the feeling sure of a doctrine (be it what it may) which I call an assumption of infallibility. It is the undertaking to decide that question *for others*, without allowing them to hear what can be said on the contrary side. And I denounce and reprobate this pretension not the less, if put forth on the side of my most solemn convictions. However positive any one's persuasion may be, not only of the falsity but of the pernicious consequences — not only of the pernicious consequences, but (to adopt expressions which I altogether condemn) the immorality and impiety of an opinion; yet if, in pursuance of that private judgment, though backed by the public judgment of his country or his cotemporaries, he prevents the opinion from being heard in its defence, he assumes infallibility. And so far from the assumption being less objectionable or less dangerous because the opinion is called immoral or impious, this is the case of all others in which it is most fatal. These are exactly the occasions on which the men of one generation commit those dreadful mistakes which excite the astonishment and horror of posterity. It is among such that we find the instances memorable in history, when the arm of the law has been employed to root out the best men and the noblest doctrines; with deplorable success as to the men, though some of the doctrines have survived to be (as if in mockery) invoked in defence of similar conduct towards those who dissent from *them*, or from their received interpretation.

Mankind can hardly be too often reminded, that there was once a man named Socrates,[7] between whom and the legal authorities and public opinion of his time there took place a memorable collision. Born in an age and country abounding in individual greatness, this man has been handed down to us by those who best knew both him and the age, as the most virtuous man in it; while *we* know him as the head and prototype of all subsequent teachers of virtue, the source equally of the lofty inspiration of Plato and the judicious utilitarianism of Aristotle, "*i maëstri di color che sanno*,"[8] the two headsprings of ethical as of all other philosophy. This acknowledged master of all the eminent thinkers who have since lived — whose fame, still growing after more than two thousand years, all but outweighs the whole remainder of the names which make his native city illustrious — was put to death by his countrymen, after a judicial conviction, for impiety and immorality. Impiety, in denying the gods recognised by the State; indeed his accuser asserted (see the "Apologia"[9]) that he believed in no gods at all. Im-

---

7. Plato's teacher (c. 469–399 B.C.), executed by the Athenian democracy for questioning moral and religious tradition.
8. The masters of them that know (Latin); a play on Dante's phrase about Aristotle in the *Divine Comedy, Inferno* 4.131. Plato (427–347 B.C.), pupil of Socrates, famous as a critic of democracy, and author of *The Republic*. Aristotle (384–322 B.C.), a pupil of Plato, was a more moderate critic of democracy and an advocate of a complex constitutional polity.
9. *The Apology*, Plato's dialogue about Socrates' trial.

morality, in being, by his doctrines and instructions, a "corruptor of youth." Of these charges the tribunal, there is every ground for believing, honestly found him guilty, and condemned the man who probably of all then born had deserved best of mankind to be put to death as a criminal.

To pass from this to the only other instance of judicial iniquity, the mention of which, after the condemnation of Socrates, would not be an anti-climax: the event which took place on Calvary rather more than eighteen hundred years ago. The man who left on the memory of those who witnessed his life and conversation such an impression of his moral grandeur that eighteen subsequent centuries have done homage to him as the Almighty in person, was ignominiously put to death, as what? As a blasphemer. Men did not merely mistake their benefactor; they mistook him for the exact contrary of what he was, and treated him as that prodigy of impiety which they themselves are now held to be for their treatment of him. The feelings with which mankind now regard these lamentable transactions, especially the later of the two, render them extremely unjust in their judgment of the unhappy actors. These were, to all appearance, not bad men — not worse than men commonly are, but rather the contrary; men who possessed in a full, or somewhat more than a full measure, the religious, moral and patriotic feelings of their time and people: the very kind of men who, in all times, our own included, have every chance of passing through life blameless and respected. The high-priest[1] who rent his garments when the words were pronounced, which, according to all the ideas of his country, constituted the blackest guilt, was in all probability quite as sincere in his horror and indignation as the generality of respectable and pious men now are in the religious and moral sentiments they profess; and most of those who now shudder at his conduct, if they had lived in his time, and been born Jews, would have acted precisely as he did. Orthodox Christians who are tempted to think that those who stoned to death the first martyrs must have been worse men than they themselves are, ought to remember that one of those persecutors was Saint Paul.[2]

Let us add one more example, the most striking of all, if the impressiveness of an error is measured by the wisdom and virtue of him who falls into it. If ever any one, possessed of power, had grounds for thinking himself the best and most enlightened among his contemporaries, it was the Emperor Marcus Aurelius.[3] Absolute monarch of the whole civilised world, he preserved through life not only the most unblemished justice, but what was less to be expected from his Stoical breeding, the tenderest heart. The few failings which are attributed to

---

1. Caiaphas; the account is in Matthew 26.65.
2. Born Saul (d. c. A.D. 67), he had earlier persecuted the Jewish followers of Jesus.
3. Roman emperor and Stoic philosopher (121–180). The Stoics were followers of Zeno of Citium (c. 336–264 B.C.); they advocated complete mastery of the emotions as essential to virtue.

him were all on the side of indulgence: while his writings, the highest ethical product of the ancient mind, differ scarcely perceptibly, if they differ at all, from the most characteristic teachings of Christ. This man, a better Christian in all but the dogmatic sense of the word than almost any of the ostensibly Christian sovereigns who have since reigned, persecuted Christianity. Placed at the summit of all the previous attainments of humanity, with an open, unfettered intellect, and a character which led him of himself to embody in his moral writings the Christian ideal, he yet failed to see that Christianity was to be a good and not an evil to the world, with his duties to which he was so deeply penetrated. Existing society he knew to be in a deplorable state. But such as it was, he saw, or thought he saw, that it was held together, and prevented from being worse, by belief and reverence of the received divinities. As a ruler of mankind, he deemed it his duty not to suffer society to fall in pieces; and saw not how, if its existing ties were removed, any others could be formed which could again knit it together. The new religion openly aimed at dissolving these ties: unless, therefore, it was his duty to adopt that religion, it seemed to be his duty to put it down. Inasmuch then as the theology of Christianity did not appear to him true or of divine origin; inasmuch as this strange history of a crucified God was not credible to him, and a system which purported to rest entirely upon a foundation to him so wholly unbelievable, could not be foreseen by him to be that renovating agency which, after all abatements, it has in fact proved to be; the gentlest and most amiable of philosophers and rulers, under a solemn sense of duty, authorised the persecution of Christianity. To my mind this is one of the most tragical facts in all history. It is a bitter thought, how different a thing the Christianity of the world might have been, if the Christian faith had been adopted as the religion of the empire under the auspices of Marcus Aurelius instead of those of Constantine.[4] But it would be equally unjust to him and false to truth to deny, that no one plea which can be urged for punishing anti-Christian teaching was wanting to Marcus Aurelius for punishing, as he did, the propagation of Christianity. No Christian more firmly believes that Atheism is false, and tends to the dissolution of society, than Marcus Aurelius believed the same things of Christianity; he who, of all men then living, might have been thought the most capable of appreciating it. Unless any one who approves of punishment for the promulgation of opinions, flatters himself that he is a wiser and better man than Marcus Aurelius — more deeply versed in the wisdom of his time, more elevated in his intellect above it — more earnest in his search for truth, or more single-minded in his devotion to it when found; let him abstain from that assumption of the joint infallibility of himself and the multitude, which the great Antoninus made with so unfortunate a result.

4. Constantine the Great (c. 288–337) made Christianity lawful in 313 and persecuted dissenters.

Aware of the impossibility of defending the use of punishment for restraining irreligious opinions by any argument which will not justify Marcus Antoninus, the enemies of religious freedom, when hard pressed, occasionally accept this consequence, and say, with Dr. Johnson,[5] that the persecutors of Christianity were in the right; that persecution is an ordeal through which truth ought to pass, and always passes successfully, legal penalties being, in the end, powerless against truth, though sometimes beneficially effective against mischievous errors. This is a form of the argument for religious intolerance sufficiently remarkable not to be passed without notice.

A theory which maintains that truth may justifiably be persecuted because persecution cannot possibly do it any harm, cannot be charged with being intentionally hostile to the reception of new truths; but we cannot commend the generosity of its dealing with the persons to whom mankind are indebted for them. To discover to the world something which deeply concerns it, and of which it was previously ignorant; to prove to it that it had been mistaken on some vital point of temporal or spiritual interest, is as important a service as a human being can render to his fellow-creatures, and in certain cases, as in those of the early Christians and of the Reformers, those who think with Dr. Johnson believe it to have been the most precious gift which could be bestowed on mankind. That the authors of such splendid benefits should be requited by martyrdom; that their reward should be to be dealt with as the vilest of criminals, is not, upon this theory, a deplorable error and misfortune, for which humanity should mourn in sackcloth and ashes, but the normal and justifiable state of things. The propounder of a new truth, according to this doctrine, should stand, as stood, in the legislation of the Locrians,[6] the proposer of a new law, with a halter round his neck, to be instantly tightened if the public assembly did not, on hearing his reasons, then and there adopt his proposition. People who defend this mode of treating benefactors cannot be supposed to set much value on the benefit; and I believe this view of the subject is mostly confined to the sort of persons who think that new truths may have been desirable once, but that we have had enough of them now.

But, indeed, the dictum that truth always triumphs over persecution is one of those pleasant falsehoods which men repeat after one another till they pass into commonplaces, but which all experience refutes. History teems with instances of truth put down by persecution. If not suppressed for ever, it may be thrown back for centuries. To speak only of religious opinions: the Reformation broke out at least twenty times before Luther, and was put down, Arnold of Brescia was put down. Fra

5. Lexicographer, critic, and poet (1709–1784).
6. The inhabitants of Locri, a Greek colony in southern Italy. They had the first written legal code in Europe and were reluctant to amend it.

Dolcino was put down. Savonarola was put down. The Albigeois were put down. The Vaudois were put down. The Lollards were put down. The Hussites[7] were put down. Even after the era of Luther, wherever persecution was persisted in, it was successful. In Spain, Italy, Flanders, the Austrian empire, Protestantism was rooted out; and, most likely, would have been so in England, had Queen Mary lived, or Queen Elizabeth[8] died. Persecution has always succeeded, save where the heretics were too strong a party to be effectually persecuted. No reasonable person can doubt that Christianity might have been extirpated in the Roman Empire. It spread, and became predominant, because the persecutions were only occasional, lasting but a short time, and separated by long intervals of almost undisturbed propagandism. It is a piece of idle sentimentality that truth, merely as truth, has any inherent power denied to error of prevailing against the dungeon and the stake. Men are not more zealous for truth than they often are for error, and a sufficient application of legal or even of social penalties will generally succeed in stopping the propagation of either. The real advantage which truth has consists in this, that when an opinion is true, it may be extinguished once, twice, or many times, but in the course of ages there will generally be found persons to rediscover it, until some one of its reappearances falls on a time when from favourable circumstances it escapes persecution until it has made such head as to withstand all subsequent attempts to suppress it.

It will be said, that we do not now put to death the introducers of new opinions: we are not like our fathers who slew the prophets, we even build sepulchres to them. It is true we no longer put heretics to death; and the amount of penal infliction which modern feeling would probably tolerate, even against the most obnoxious opinions, is not sufficient to extirpate them. But let us not flatter ourselves that we are yet free from the stain even of legal persecution. Penalties for opinion, or at least for its expression, still exist by law; and their enforcement is not, even in these times, so unexampled as to make it all incredible that they may some day be revived in full force. In the year 1857, at the summer assizes of the county of Cornwall, an unfortunate man, said to be of unexceptionable conduct in all relations of life, was sentenced

---

7. Followers of John Huss (1369–1415), a disciple of Wyclif. Martin Luther (1483–1546), German priest and theologian who led the Protestant Reformation. Arnold of Brescia (1090?–1155), leader of resistance to the papacy's secular power; he was eventually executed as a rebel. Dolcino of Novario (d. 1307), tortured to death as a heretic. Savonarola (1452–1498), critic of Church corruption, briefly the leader of the Florentine Republic, and executed for heresy. The Albigeois, better known as the Albigensians, were a heretical sect that flourished in the Languedoc in the late twelfth century. The vaudois were followers of Pierre Waldo, a twelfth-century ascetic. The Lollards were roving preachers and followers of John Wyclif (1324–1384), an English reformer.

8. Elizabeth I (1533–1603), queen of England from 1558 to 1603, secured the survival of the Church of England. Mary Tudor (1516–1558), queen of England from 1553 to 1558, tried to restore Catholicism in England.

to twenty-one months' imprisonment, for uttering, and writing on a
gate, some offensive words concerning Christianity.[9] Within a month
of the same time, at the Old Bailey, two persons, on two separate occasions, were rejected as jurymen, and one of them grossly insulted by
the judge and by one of the counsel, because they honestly declared
that they had no theological belief;[1] and a third, a foreigner, for the
same reason, was denied justice against a thief.[2] This refusal of redress
took place in virtue of the legal doctrine, that no person can be allowed
to give evidence in a court of justice who does not profess belief in a
God (any god is sufficient) and in a future state; which is equivalent
to declaring such persons to be outlaws, excluded from the protection
of the tribunals; who may not only be robbed or assaulted with impunity, if no one but themselves, or persons of similar opinions, be present, but any one else may be robbed or assaulted with impunity, if the
proof of the fact depends on their evidence. The assumption on which
this is grounded is that the oath is worthless of a person who does not
believe in a future state; a proposition which betokens much ignorance
of history in those who assent to it (since it is historically true that a
large proportion of infidels in all ages have been persons of distinguished integrity and honour); and would be maintained by no one
who had the smallest conception how many of the persons in greatest
repute with the world, both for virtues and attainments, are well known,
at least to their intimates, to be unbelievers. The rule, besides, is sui-
cidal, and cuts away its own foundation. Under pretence that atheists
must be liars, it admits the testimony of all atheists who are willing to
lie, and rejects only those who brave the obloquy of publicly confessing
a detested creed rather than affirm a falsehood. A rule thus self-
convicted of absurdity so far as regards its professed purpose, can be
kept in force only as a badge of hatred, a relic of persecution; a persecution, too, having the peculiarity that the qualification for under-
going it is the being clearly proved not to deserve it. The rule, and the
theory it implies, are hardly less insulting to believers than to infidels.
For if he who does not believe in a future state necessarily lies, it follows
that they who do believe are only prevented from lying, if prevented
they are, by the fear of hell. We will not do the authors and abettors
of the rule the injury of supposing that the conception which they have
formed of Christian virtue is drawn from their own consciousness.

    These, indeed, are but rags and remnants of persecution, and may
be thought to be not so much an indication of the wish to persecute,
as an example of that very frequent infirmity of English minds, which
makes them take a preposterous pleasure in the assertion of a bad principle, when they are no longer bad enough to desire to carry it really

---

9. Thomas Pooley, Bodmin Assiges, July 31, 1857. In December following, he received a free
   pardon from the Crown [Mill's note].
1. George Jacob Holyoake, August 17, 1857; Edward Trielove, July 1857 [Mill's note].
2. Baron de Gleichen, Marlborough Street Police Court, August 4, 1857 [Mill's note].

into practice. But unhappily there is no security in the state of the public mind that the suspension of worse forms of legal persecution, which has lasted for about the space of a generation, will continue. In this age the quiet surface of routine is as often ruffled by attempts to resuscitate past evils, as to introduce new benefits. What is boasted of at the present time as the revival of religion, is always, in narrow and uncultivated minds, at least as much the revival of bigotry; and where there is the strong permanent leaven of intolerance in the feelings of a people, which at all times abides in the middle classes of this country, it needs but little to provoke them into actively persecuting those whom they have never ceased to think proper objects of persecution.[3] For it is this — it is the opinions men entertain, and the feelings they cherish, respecting those who disown the beliefs they deem important, which makes this country not a place of mental freedom. For a long time past, the chief mischief of the legal penalties is that they strengthen the social stigma. It is that stigma which is really effective, and so effective is it, that the profession of opinions which are under the ban of society is much less common in England than is, in many other countries, the avowal of those which incur risk of judicial punishment. In respect to all persons but those whose pecuniary circumstances make them independent of the good will of other people, opinion, on this subject, is as efficacious as law; men might as well be imprisoned, as excluded from the means of earning their bread. Those whose bread is already secured, and who desire no favours from men in power, or from bodies of men, or from the public, have nothing to fear from the open avowal of any opinions, but to be ill-thought of and ill-spoken of, and this it ought not to require a very heroic mould to enable them to bear. There is no room for any appeal *ad misericordiam*[4] in behalf of such persons. But though we do not now inflict so much evil on those who think differently from us as it was formerly our custom to do, it may be that

3. Ample warning may be drawn from the large infusion of the passions of a persecutor, which mingled with the general display of the worst parts of our national character on the occasion of the Sepoy insurrection. The ravings of fanatics or charlatans from the pulpit may be unworthy of notice; but the heads of the Evangelical party have announced as their principle for the government of Hindoos and Mahomedans, that no schools be supported by public money in which the Bible is not taught, and by necessary consequence that no public employment be given to any but real or pretended Christians. An Under-Secretary of State in a speech delivered to his constituents on the 12th of November, 1857, is reported to have said: "Toleration of their faith" (the faith of a hundred millions of British subjects), "the superstition which they called religion, by the British Government, had had the effect of retarding the ascendancy of the British name, and preventing the salutary growth of Christianity. . . . Toleration was the great corner-stone of the religious liberties of this country; but do not let them abuse that precious word toleration. As he understood it, it meant the complete liberty to all, freedom of worship, *among Christians, who worshipped upon the same foundation.* It meant toleration of all sects and denominations of *Christians who believed in the one mediation.*" I desire to call attention to the fact, that a man who has been deemed fit to fill a high office in the government of this country under a liberal ministry, maintains the doctrine that all who do not believe in the divinity of Christ are beyond the pale of toleration. Who, after this imbecile display, can indulge the illusion that religious persecution has passed away, never to return? [Mill's note].
4. For mercy (Latin).

we do ourselves as much evil as ever by our treatment of them. Socrates
was put to death, but the Socratic philosophy rose like the sun in
heaven, and spread its illumination over the whole intellectual firma-
ment. Christians were cast to the lions, but the Christian church grew
up a stately and spreading tree, overtopping the older and less vigorous
growths, and stifling them by its shade. Our merely social intolerance
kills no one, roots out no opinions, but induces men to disguise them,
or to abstain from any active effort for their diffusion. With us, heretical
opinions do not perceptibly gain, or even lose, ground in each decade
or generation; they never blaze out far and wide, but continue to smoulder in the narrow circles of thinking and studious persons among whom
they originate, without ever lighting up the general affairs of mankind
with either a true or a deceptive light. And thus is kept up a state of
things very satisfactory to some minds, because, without the unpleasant
process of fining or imprisoning anybody, it maintains all prevailing
opinions outwardly undisturbed, while it does not absolutely interdict
the exercise of reason by dissentients afflicted with the malady of
thought. A convenient plan for having peace in the intellectual world,
and keeping all things going on therein very much as they do already.
But the price paid for this sort of intellectual pacification is the sacrifice
of the entire moral courage of the human mind. A state of things in
which a large portion of the most active and inquiring intellects find
it advisable to keep the general principles and grounds of their convictions within their own breasts, and attempt, in what they address to the
public, to fit as much as they can of their own conclusions to premises
which they have internally renounced, cannot send forth the open,
fearless characters, and logical, consistent intellects who once adorned
the thinking world. The sort of men who can be looked for under it,
are either mere conformers to commonplace, or time-servers for truth,
whose arguments on all great subjects are meant for their hearers, and
are not those which have convinced themselves. Those who avoid this
alternative, do so by narrowing their thoughts and interest to things
which can be spoken of without venturing within the region of principles, that is, to small practical matters, which would come right of
themselves, if but the minds of mankind were strengthened and enlarged, and which will never be made effectually right until then: while
that which would strengthen and enlarge men's minds, free and daring
speculation on the highest subjects, is abandoned.

Those in whose eyes this reticence on the part of heretics is no evil
should consider, in the first place, that in consequence of it there is
never any fair and thorough discussion of heretical opinions; and that
such of them as could not stand such a discussion, though they may
be prevented from spreading, do not disappear. But it is not the minds
of heretics that are deteriorated most by the ban placed on all inquiry
which does not end in the orthodox conclusions. The greatest harm
done is to those who are not heretics, and whose whole mental devel-

opment is cramped, and their reason cowed, by the fear of heresy. Who can compute what the world loses in the multitude of promising intellects combined with timid characters, who dare not follow out any bold, vigorous, independent train of thought, lest it should land them in something which would admit of being considered irreligious or immoral? Among them we may occasionally see some man of deep conscientiousness, and subtle and refined understanding, who spends a life in sophisticating with an intellect which he cannot silence, and exhausts the resources of ingenuity in attempting to reconcile the promptings of his conscience and reason with orthodoxy, which yet he does not, perhaps, to the end succeed in doing. No one can be a great thinker who does not recognise, that as a thinker it is his first duty to follow his intellect to whatever conclusions it may lead. Truth gains more even by the errors of one who, with due study and preparation, thinks for himself, than by the true opinions of those who only hold them because they do not suffer themselves to think. Not that it is solely, or chiefly, to form great thinkers, that freedom of thinking is required. On the contrary, it is as much and even more indispensable to enable average human beings to attain the mental stature which they are capable of. There have been, and may again be, great individual thinkers in a general atmosphere of mental slavery. But there never has been, nor ever will be, in that atmosphere an intellectually active people. Where any people has made a temporary approach to such a character, it has been because the dread of heterodox speculation was for a time suspended. Where there is a tacit convention that principles are not to be disputed; where the discussion of the greatest questions which can occupy humanity is considered to be closed, we cannot hope to find that generally high scale of mental activity which has made some periods of history so remarkable. Never when controversy avoided the subjects which are large and important enough to kindle enthusiasm, was the mind of a people stirred up from its foundations, and the impulse given which raised even persons of the most ordinary intellect to something of the dignity of thinking beings. Of such we have had an example in the condition of Europe during the times immediately following the Reformation; another, though limited to the Continent and to a more cultivated class, in the speculative movement of the latter half of the eighteenth century; and a third, of still briefer duration, in the intellectual fermentation of Germany during the Goethian and Fichtean[5] period. These periods differed widely in the particular opinions which they developed; but were alike in this, that during all three the yoke of authority was broken. In each, an old mental despotism had been thrown off, and no new one had yet taken its place. The impulse given at these three periods has made Europe what it now is.

---

5. Johann Gottlieb Fichte (1762–1814), German philosopher and theorist of nationalism. Johann Wolfgang Goethe (1749–1832), German poet, dramatist, novelist, and statesman.

Every single improvement which has taken place either in the human mind or in institutions, may be traced distinctly to one or other of them. Appearances have for some time indicated that all three impulses are well nigh spent; and we can expect no fresh start until we again assert our mental freedom.

Let us now pass to the second division of the argument, and dismissing the supposition that any of the received opinions may be false, let us assume them to be true, and examine into the worth of the manner in which they are likely to be held, when their truth is not freely and openly canvassed. However unwillingly a person who has a strong opinion may admit the possibility that his opinion may be false, he ought to be moved by the consideration that, however true it may be, if it is not fully, frequently, and fearlessly discussed, it will be held as a dead dogma, not a living truth.

There is a class of persons (happily not quite so numerous as formerly) who think it enough if a person assents undoubtingly to what they think true, though he has no knowledge whatever of the grounds of the opinion, and could not make a tenable defence of it against the most superficial objections. Such persons, if they can once get their creed taught from authority, naturally think that no good, and some harm, comes of its being allowed to be questioned. Where their influence prevails, they make it nearly impossible for the received opinion to be rejected wisely and considerately, though it may still be rejected rashly and ignorantly; for to shut out discussion entirely is seldom possible, and when it once gets in, beliefs not grounded on conviction are apt to give way before the slightest semblance of an argument. Waiving, however, this possibility — assuming that the true opinion abides in the mind, but abides as a prejudice, a belief independent of, and proof against, argument — this is not the way in which truth ought to be held by a rational being. This is not knowing the truth. Truth, thus held, is but one superstition the more, accidentally clinging to the words which enunciate a truth.

If the intellect and judgment of mankind ought to be cultivated, a thing which Protestants at least do not deny, on what can these faculties be more appropriately exercised by any one, than on the things which concern him so much that it is considered necessary for him to hold opinions on them? If the cultivation of the understanding consists in one thing more than in another, it is surely in learning the grounds of one's own opinions. Whatever people believe, on subjects on which it is of the first importance to believe rightly, they ought to be able to defend against at least the common objections. But, some one may say, "Let them be *taught* the grounds of their opinions. It does not follow that opinions must be merely parroted because they are never heard controverted. Persons who learn geometry do not simply commit the theorems to memory, but understand and learn likewise the demonstrations; and it would be absurd to say that they remain ignorant of the grounds of geometrical truths, because they never hear any one deny, and attempt to disprove them." Undoubtedly: and such teaching suffices on a subject like mathematics, where there is nothing at all to be said on the wrong side of the question. The peculiarity of the evidence of mathematical truths is that all the argument is on one side. There are no objections, and no answers to objections. But on every subject on which difference of opinion is possible, the truth depends on a balance to be struck between two sets of conflicting reasons. Even in natural philosophy, there is always some other explanation possible of the same facts; some geocentric theory instead of heliocentric, some phlogiston instead of oxygen; and it has to be shown why that other theory cannot be the true one: and until this is shown, and until we know how it is shown, we do not understand the grounds of our opinion. But when we turn to subjects infinitely more complicated, to morals, religion, politics, social relations, and the business of life, three-fourths of the arguments for every disputed opinion consist in dispelling the appearances which favour some opinion different from it. The greatest orator, save one, of antiquity, has left it on record that he always studied his adversary's case with as great, if not still greater, intensity than even his own. What Cicero practised as the means of forensic success requires to be imitated by all who study any subject in order to arrive at the truth. He who knows only his own side of the case, knows little of that. His reasons may be good, and no one may have been able to refute them. But if he is equally unable to refute the reasons on the opposite side; if he does not so much as know what they are, he has no ground for preferring either opinion. The rational position for him would be suspension of judgment, and unless he contents himself with that, he is either led by authority, or adopts, like the generality of the world, the side to which he feels most inclination. Nor is it enough that he should hear the arguments of adversaries from his own teachers, presented as they state them, and accompanied by what they offer as refutations. That is not the way to do justice to the arguments, or bring them into real contact with his own mind. He must be able to hear them from persons who actually believe them; who defend them in earnest, and do their very utmost for them. He must know them in their most plausible and persuasive form; he must feel the whole force of the difficulty which the true view of the subject has to encounter and dispose of; else he will never really possess himself of the portion of truth which meets and removes that difficulty. Ninety-nine in a hundred of what are called educated men are in this condition; even of those who can argue fluently for their opinions. Their conclusion may be true, but it might be false for anything they know: they have never thrown themselves into the mental position of those who think differently from them, and considered what such persons may have to say; and consequently they do not, in any proper sense of the word, know the doctrine which they themselves profess. They do not know those parts of it which explain and justify the remainder; the considerations which show that a fact which seemingly conflicts with another is reconcilable with it, or that, of two apparently strong reasons, one and not the other ought to be preferred. All that part of the truth which turns the scale, and decides the judgment of a completely informed mind, they are strangers to; nor is it ever really known, but to those who have attended equally and impartially to both sides, and endeavoured to see the reasons of both in the strongest light. So essential is this discipline to a real understanding of moral and human subjects, that if opponents of all important truths do not exist, it is indispensable to imagine them, and supply them with the strongest arguments which the most skilful devil's advocate can conjure up.

To abate the force of these considerations, an enemy of free discussion may be supposed to say, that there is no necessity for mankind in general to know and understand all that can be said against or for their opinions by philosophers and theologians. That it is not needful for common men to be able to expose all the misstatements or fallacies of an ingenious opponent. That it is enough if there is always somebody capable of answering them, so that nothing likely to mislead uninstructed persons remains unrefuted. That simple minds, having been taught the obvious grounds of the truths inculcated on them, may trust to authority for the rest, and being aware that they have neither knowledge nor talent to resolve every difficulty which can be raised, may repose in the assurance that all those which have been raised have been or can be answered, by those who are specially trained to the task.

Conceding to this view of the subject the utmost that can be claimed for it by those most easily satisfied with the amount of understanding of truth which ought to accompany the belief of it; even so, the argument for free discussion is no way weakened. For even this doctrine acknowledges that mankind ought to have a rational assurance that all objections have been satisfactorily answered; and how are they to be answered if that which requires to be answered is not spoken? or how can the answers be known to be satisfactory, if the objectors have no opportunity of showing that it is unsatisfactory? If not the public, at least the philosophers and theologians who are to resolve the difficulties, must make themselves familiar with those difficulties in their most puzzling form; and this cannot be accomplished unless they are freely stated, and placed in the most advantageous light which they admit of. The Catholic Church has its own way of dealing with this embarrassing problem. It makes a broad separation between those who can be permitted to receive its doctrines on conviction, and those who must accept them on trust. Neither, indeed, are allowed any choice as to what they will accept; but the clergy, such at least as can be fully confided in, may admissibly and meritoriously make themselves acquainted with the arguments of opponents, in order to answer them, and may, therefore, read heretical books; the laity, not unless by special permission, hard to be obtained. This discipline recognises a knowledge of the enemy's case as beneficial to the teachers, but finds means, consistent with this, of denying it to the rest of the world: thus giving to the *élite* more mental culture, though not more mental freedom, than it allows to the mass. By this device it succeeds in obtaining the kind of mental superiority which its purposes require; for though culture without freedom never made a large and liberal mind, it can make a clever *nisi prius*[6] advocate of a cause. But in countries professing Protestantism, this resource is denied; since Protestants hold, at least in theory, that the responsibility for the choice of a religion must be borne by each for himself, and cannot be thrown off upon teachers. Besides, in the present state of the world, it is practically impossible that writings which are read by the instructed can be kept from the uninstructed. If the teachers of mankind are to be cognisant of all that they ought to know, everything must be free to be written and published without restraint.

If, however, the mischievous operation of the absence of free discussion, when the received opinions are true, were confined to leaving men ignorant of the grounds of those opinions, it might be thought that this, if an intellectual, is no moral evil, and does not affect the worth of the opinions, regarded in their influence on the character. The fact, however, is, that not only the grounds of the opinion are forgotten in the absence of discussion, but too often the meaning of the opinion itself. The words which convey it cease to suggest ideas, or suggest only a small portion of those they were originally employed to communicate. Instead of a vivid conception and a living belief there remain only a few phrases retained by rote; or, if any part, the shell and husk only of the meaning is retained, the finer essence being lost. The great chapter in human history which this fact occupies and fills, cannot be too earnestly studied and meditated on.

It is illustrated in the experience of almost all ethical doctrines and religious creeds. They are all full of meaning and vitality to those who originate them, and to the direct disciples of the originators. Their meaning continues to be felt in undiminished strength, and is perhaps brought out into even fuller consciousness, so long as the struggle lasts to give the doctrine or creed an ascendancy over other creeds. At last it either prevails, and becomes the general opinion, or its progress stops; it keeps possession of the ground it has gained, but ceases to spread further. When either of these results has become apparent, controversy on the subject flags, and gradually dies away. The doctrine has taken its place, if not as a received opinion, as one of the admitted sects or divisions of opinion: those who hold it have generally inherited, not adopted it; and conversion from one of these doctrines to another, being now an exceptional fact, occupies little place in the thoughts their pro-

6. A legal tag meaning a law is to be accounted valid unless shown to be otherwise (Latin); here meaning an advocate who takes the validity of his own cause for granted.

fessors. Instead of being, as at first, constantly on the alert either to defend themselves against the world, or to bring the world over to them, they have subsided into acquiescence, and neither listen, when they can help it, to arguments against their creed, nor trouble dissentients (if there be such) with arguments in its favour. From this time may usually be dated the decline in the living power of the doctrine. We often hear the teachers of all creeds lamenting the difficulty of keeping up in the minds of believers a lively apprehension of the truth which they nominally recognise, so that it may penetrate the feelings, and acquire a real mastery over the conduct. No such difficulty is complained of while the creed is still fighting for its existence: even the weaker combatants then know and feel what they are fighting for, and the difference between it and other doctrines; and in that period of every creed's existence, not a few persons may be found, who have realised its fundamental principles in all the forms of thought, have weighed and considered them in all their important bearings, and have experienced the full effect on the character which belief in that creed ought to produce in a mind thoroughly imbued with it. But when it has come to be an hereditary creed, and to be received passively, not actively — when the mind is no longer compelled, in the same degree as at first, to exercise its vital powers on the questions which its belief presents to it, there is a progressive tendency to forget all of the belief except the formularies, or to give it a dull and torpid assent, as if accepting it on trust dispensed with the necessity of realising it in consciousness, or testing it by personal experience, until it almost ceases to connect itself at all with the inner life of the human being. Then are seen the cases, so frequent in this age of the world as almost to form the majority, in which the creed remains as it were outside the mind, incrusting and petrifying it against all other influences addressed to the higher parts of our nature; manifesting its power by not suffering any fresh and living conviction to get in, but itself doing nothing for the mind or heart, except standing sentinel over them to keep them vacant.

To what an extent doctrines intrinsically fitted to make the deepest impression upon the mind may remain in it as dead beliefs, without being ever realised in the imagination, the feelings, or the understanding, is exemplified by the manner in which the majority of believers hold the doctrines of Christianity. By Christianity I here mean what is accounted such by all churches and sects — the maxims and precepts contained in the New Testament. These are considered sacred, and accepted as laws, by all professing Christians. Yet it is scarcely too much to say that not one Christian in a thousand guides or tests his individual conduct by reference to those laws. The standard to which he does refer it, is the custom of his nation, his class, or his religious profession. He has thus, on the one hand, a collection of ethical maxims, which he believes to have been vouchsafed to him by infallible wisdom as rules for his government; and on the other a set of every-day judgments and practices, which go a certain length with some of those maxims, not so great a length with others, stand in direct opposition to some, and are, on the whole, a compromise between the Christian creed and the interests and suggestions of worldly life. To the first of these standards he gives his homage; to the other his real allegiance. All Christians believe that the blessed are the poor and humble, and those who are ill-used by the world; that it is easier for a camel to pass through the eye of a needle than for a rich man to enter the kingdom of heaven; that they should judge not, lest they be judged; that they should swear not at all; that they should love their neighbour as themselves; that if one take their cloak, they should give him their coat also; that they should take no thought for the morrow; that if they would be perfect they should sell all that they have and give it to the poor. They are not insincere when they say that they believe these things. They do believe them, as people believe what they have always heard lauded and never discussed. But in the sense of that living belief which regulates conduct, they believe these doctrines just up to the point to which it is usual to act upon them. The doctrines in their integrity are serviceable to pelt adversaries with; and it is understood that they are to be put forward (when possible) as the reasons for whatever people do that they think laudable. But any one who reminded them that the maxims require an infinity of things which they never even think of doing, would gain nothing but to be classed among those very unpopular characters who affect to be better than other people. The doctrines have no hold on ordinary believers — are not a power in their minds. They have an habitual respect for the sound of them, but no feeling which spreads from the words to the things signified, and forces the mind to take *them* in, and make them conform to the formula. Whenever conduct is concerned, they look round for Mr. A and B to direct them how far to go in obeying Christ.

Now we may be well assured that the case was not thus, but far otherwise, with the early Christians. Had it been thus, Christianity never would have expanded from an obscure sect of the despised Hebrews into the religion of the Roman empire. When their enemies said, "See how these Christians love one another"[7] (a remark not likely to be made by anybody now), they assuredly had a much livelier feeling of the meaning of their creed than they have ever had since. And to this cause, probably, it is chiefly owing that Christianity now makes so little progress in extending its domain, and after eighteen centuries is still nearly confined to Europeans and the descendants of Europeans. Even with the strictly religious, who are much in earnest about their doctrines, and attach a greater amount of meaning to many of them than people in general, it commonly happens that the part which is

---

7. From Tertullian's (late second century) *Apologeticus* 39.7.

thus comparatively active in their minds is that which was made by Calvin, or Knox,[8] or some such person much nearer in character to themselves. The sayings of Christ coexist passively in their minds, producing hardly any effect beyond what is caused by mere listening to words so amiable and bland. There are many reasons, doubtless, why doctrines which are the badge of a sect retain more of their vitality than those common to all recognised sects, and why more pains are taken by teachers to keep their meaning alive; but one reason certainly is, that the peculiar doctrines are more questioned, and have to be oftener defended against open gainsayers. Both teachers and learners go to sleep at their post, as soon as there is no enemy in the field.

The same thing holds true, generally speaking, of all traditional doctrines — those of prudence and knowledge of life, as well as of morals or religion. All languages and literatures are full of general observations on life, both as to what it is, and how to conduct oneself in it; observations which everybody knows, which everybody repeats, or hears with acquiescence, which are received as truisms, yet of which most people first truly learn the meaning when experience, generally of a painful kind, has made it a reality to them. How often, when smarting under some unforeseen misfortune or disappointment, does a person call to mind some proverb or common saying, familiar to him all his life, the meaning of which, if he had ever before felt it as he does now, would have saved him from the calamity. There are indeed reasons for this, other than the absence of discussion; there are many truths of which the full meaning *cannot* be realised until personal experience has brought it home. But much more of the meaning even of these would have been understood, and what was understood would have been far more deeply impressed on the mind, if the man had been accustomed to hear it argued *pro* and *con* by people who did understand it. The fatal tendency of mankind to leave off thinking about a thing when it is no longer doubtful, is the cause of half their errors. A contemporary author has well spoken of "the deep slumber of a decided opinion."[9]

But what! (it may be asked) Is the absence of unanimity an indispensable condition of true knowledge? Is it necessary that some part of mankind should persist in error to enable any to realise the truth? Does a belief cease to be real and vital as soon as it is generally received — and is a proposition never thoroughly understood and felt unless some doubt of it remains? As soon as mankind have unanimously accepted a truth, does the truth perish within them? The highest aim and best result of improved intelligence, it has hitherto been thought, is to unite mankind more and more in the acknowledgement of all important

8. John Knox (1505–72), Scots Protestant theologian, founder of the Presbyterian Church. Jean Calvin (1509–1564), French Protestant theologian, ruler of Geneva, and author of *Institutes of the Christian Religion*.
9. Not identified.

truths; and does the intelligence only last as long as it has not achieved its object? Do the fruits of conquest perish by the very completeness of the victory?

I affirm no such thing. As mankind improve, the number of doctrines which are no longer disputed or doubted will be constantly on the increase: and the well-being of mankind may almost be measured by the number and gravity of the truths which have reached the point of being uncontested. The cessation, on one question after another, of serious controversy, is one of the necessary incidents of the consolidation of opinion; a consolidation of salutary in the case of true opinions, as it is dangerous and noxious when the opinions are erroneous. But though this gradual narrowing of the bounds of diversity of opinion is necessary in both senses of the term, being at once inevitable and indispensable, we are not therefore obliged to conclude that all its consequences must be beneficial. The loss of so important an aid to the intelligent and living apprehension of a truth, as is afforded by the necessity of explaining it to, or defending it against, opponents, though not sufficient to outweigh, is no trifling drawback from, the benefit of its universal recognition. Where this advantage can no longer be had, I confess I should like to see the teachers of mankind endeavouring to provide a substitute for it; some contrivance for making the difficulties of the question as present to the learner's consciousness, as if they were pressed upon him by a dissentient champion, eager for his conversion.

But instead of seeking contrivances for this purpose, they have lost those they formerly had. The Socratic dialectics, so magnificently exemplified in the dialogues of Plato, were a contrivance of this description. They were essentially a negative discussion of the great question of philosophy and life, directed with consummate skill to the purpose of convincing any one who had merely adopted the commonplaces of received opinion that he did not understand the subject—that he as yet attached no definite meaning to the doctrines he professed; in order that, becoming aware of his ignorance, he might be put in the way to obtain a stable belief, resting on a clear apprehension both of the meaning of doctrines and of their evidence. The school disputations of the Middle Ages had a somewhat similar object. They were intended to make sure that the pupil understood his own opinion, and (by necessary correlation) the opinion opposed to it, and could enforce the grounds of the one and confute those of the other. These last-mentioned contests had indeed the incurable defect, that the premises appealed to were taken from authority, not from reason; and, as a discipline to the mind, they were in every respect inferior to the powerful dialectics which formed the intellects of the "Socratici viri";[1] but the modern mind owes far more to both than it is generally willing to admit, and the present modes of education contain nothing which in the smallest degree sup-

1. Socrates' students, i.e., thinkers ready to argue their views against opponents.

plies the place either of the one or of the other. A person who derives all his instruction from teachers or books, even if he escape the beset-ting temptation of contenting himself with cram, is under no com-pulsion to hear both sides; accordingly it is far from a frequent accomplishment, even among thinkers, to know both sides; and the weakest part of what everybody says in defence of his opinion is what he intends as a reply to antagonists. It is the fashion of the present time to disparage negative logic — that which points out weaknesses in theory or errors in practice, without establishing positive truths. Such negative criticism would indeed be poor enough as an ultimate result; but as a means to attaining any positive knowledge or conviction worthy the name, it cannot be valued too highly; and until people are again sys-tematically trained to it, there will be few great thinkers, and a low general average of intellect, in any but the mathematical and physical departments of speculation. On any other subject no one's opinions deserve the name of knowledge, except so far as he has either had forced upon him by others, or gone through of himself, the same men-tal process which would have been required of him in carrying on an active controversy with opponents. That, therefore, which when absent, it is so indispensable, but so difficult, to create, how worse than absurd it is to forego, when spontaneously offering itself! If there are any per-sons who contest a received opinion, or who will do so if law or opinion will let them, let us thank them for it, open our minds to listen to them, and rejoice that there is some one to do for us what we otherwise ought, if we have any regard for either the certainty or the vitality of our convictions, to do with much greater labour for ourselves.

It still remains to speak of one of the principal causes which make diversity of opinion advantageous, and will continue to do so until man-kind shall have entered a stage of intellectual advancement which at present seems at an incalculable distance. We have hitherto considered only two possibilities: that the received opinion may be false, and some other opinion, consequently, true; or that, the received opinion being true, a conflict with the opposite error is essential to a clear apprehen-sion and deep feeling of its truth. But there is a commoner case than either of these; when the conflicting doctrines, instead of being one true and the other false, share the truth between them; and the non-conforming opinion is needed to supply the remainder of the truth, of which the received doctrine embodies only a part. Popular opinions, on subjects not palpable to sense, are often true, but seldom or never the whole truth. They are a part of the truth; sometimes a greater, sometimes a smaller part, but exaggerated, distorted, and disjointed from the truths by which they ought to be accompanied and limited. Heretical opinions, on the other hand, are generally some of these suppressed and neglected truths, bursting the bonds which kept them down, and either seeking reconciliation with the truth contained in the common opinion, or fronting it as enemies, and setting themselves up, with similar exclusiveness, as the whole truth. The latter case is hitherto the most frequent, as, in the human mind, one-sidedness has always been the rule, and many-sidedness the exception. Hence, even in revolutions of opinion, one part of the truth usually sets while another rises. Even progress, which ought to superadd, for the most part only substitutes, one partial and incomplete truth for another; improvement consisting chiefly in this, that the new fragment of truth is more wanted, more adapted to the needs of the time, than that which it displaces. Such being the partial character of prevailing opinions, even when resting on a true foundation, every opinion which embodies somewhat of the portion of truth which the common opinion omits, ought to be considered precious, with whatever amount of error and confusion that truth may be blended. No sober judge of human affairs will feel bound to be indignant because those who force on our notice truths which we should otherwise have overlooked, overlook some of those which we see. Rather, he will think that so long as popular truth is one-sided, it is more desirable than otherwise that unpopular truth should have one-sided assertors too; such being usually the most energetic, and the most likely to compel reluctant attention to the fragment of wisdom which they proclaim as if it were the whole.

Thus, in the eighteenth century, when nearly all the instructed, and all those of the uninstructed who were led by them, were lost in admiration of what is called civilisation, and of the marvels of modern science, literature, and philosophy, and while greatly over-rating the amount of unlikeness between the men of modern and those of ancient times, indulged the belief that the whole of the difference was in their own favour; with what a salutary shock did the paradoxes of Rousseau[2] explode like bombshells in the midst, dislocating the compact mass of one-sided opinion, and forcing its elements to recombine in a better form and with additional ingredients. Not that the current opinions were on the whole farther from the truth than Rousseau's were; on the contrary, they were nearer to it; they contained more of positive truth, and very much less of error. Nevertheless there lay in Rousseau's doctrine, and has floated down the stream of opinion along with it, a considerable amount of exactly those truths which the popular opinion wanted; and these are the deposit which was left behind when the flood subsided. The superior worth of simplicity of life, the enervating and demoralising effect of the trammels and hypocrisies of artificial society, are ideas which have never been entirely absent from cultivated minds since Rousseau wrote; and they will in time produce their due effect,

2. Jean-Jacques Rousseau (1712–1778), Genevan political and moral thinker, composer, and novelist; author of *The Social Contract* (1762).

though at present needing to be asserted as much as ever, and to be asserted by deeds, for words, on this subject, have nearly exhausted their power.

In politics, again, it is almost a commonplace, that a party of order or stability, and a party of progress or reform, are both necessary elements of a healthy state of political life; until the one or the other shall have so enlarged its mental grasp as to be a party equally of order and of progress, knowing and distinguishing what is fit to be preserved from what ought to be swept away. Each of these modes of thinking derives its utility from the deficiencies of the other; but it is in a great measure the opposition of the other that keeps each within the limits of reason and sanity. Unless opinions favourable to democracy and to aristocracy, to property and to equality, to co-operation and to competition, to luxury and to abstinence, to sociality and individuality, to liberty and discipline, and all the other standing antagonisms of practical life, are expressed with equal freedom, and enforced and defended with equal talent and energy, there is no chance of both elements obtaining their due; one scale is sure to go up, and the other down. Truth, in the great practical concerns of life, is so much a question of the reconciling and combining of opposites, that very few have minds sufficiently capacious and impartial to make the adjustment with an approach to correctness, and it has to be made by the rough process of a struggle between combatants fighting under hostile banners. On any of the great open questions just enumerated, if either of the two opinions has a better claim than the other, not merely to be tolerated, but to be encouraged and countenanced, it is the one which happens at the particular time and place to be in a minority. That is the opinion which, for the time being, represents the neglected interests, the side of human well-being which is in danger of obtaining less than its share. I am aware that there is not, in this country, any intolerance of differences of opinion on most of these topics. They are adduced to show, by admitted and multiplied examples, the universality of the fact, that only through diversity of opinion is there, in the existing state of human intellect, a chance of fair play to all sides of the truth. When there are persons to be found who form an exception to the apparent unanimity of the world on any subject, even if the world is in the right, it is always probable that dissentients have something worth hearing to say for themselves, and that truth would lose something by their silence.

It may be objected, "But *some* received principles, especially on the highest and most vital subjects, are more than half-truths. The Christian morality, for instance, is the whole truth on that subject, and if any one teaches a morality which varies from it, he is wholly in error." As this is of all cases the most important in practice, none can be fitter to test the general maxim. But before pronouncing what Christian morality is or is not, it would be desirable to decide what is meant by Christian morality. If it means the morality of the New Testament, I wonder that any one who derives his knowledge of this from the book itself, can suppose that it was announced, or intended, as a complete doctrine of morals. The Gospel always refers to a pre-existing morality, and confines its precepts to the particulars in which that morality was to be corrected, or superseded by a wider and higher; expressing itself, moreover, in terms most general, often impossible to be interpreted literally, and possessing rather the impressiveness of poetry or eloquence than the precision of legislation. To extract from it a body of ethical doctrine, has never been possible without eking it out from the Old Testament, that is, from a system elaborate indeed, but in many respects barbarous, and intended only for a barbarous people. St. Paul, a declared enemy to this Judaical mode of interpreting the doctrine and filling up the scheme of his Master, equally assumes a pre-existing morality, namely that of the Greeks and Romans; and his advice to Christians is in a great measure a system of accommodation to that; even to the extent of giving an apparent sanction to slavery. What is called Christian, but should rather be termed theological morality, was not the work of Christ or the Apostles, but is of much later origin, having been gradually built up by the Catholic church of the first five centuries, and though not implicitly adopted by moderns and Protestants, has been much less modified by them than might have been expected. For the most part, indeed, they have contented themselves with cutting off the additions which had been made to it in the Middle Ages, each sect supplying the place by fresh additions, adapted to its own character and tendencies. That mankind owe a great debt to this morality, and to its early teachers, I should be the last person to deny; but I do not scruple to say of it that it is, in many important points, incomplete and one-sided, and that unless ideas and feelings, not sanctioned by it, had contributed to the formation of European life and character, human affairs would have been in a worse condition than they now are. Christian morality (so called) has all the characters of a reaction; it is, in great part, a protest against Paganism. Its ideal is negative rather than positive; passive rather than active; Innocence rather than Nobleness; Abstinence from Evil, rather than energetic Pursuit of Good; in its precepts (as has been well said) "thou shall not" predominates unduly over "thou shalt." In its horror of sensuality, it made an idol of asceticism, which has been gradually compromised away into one of legality. It holds out the hope of heaven and the threat of hell, as the appointed and appropriate motives to a virtuous life: in this falling far below the best of the ancients, and doing what lies in it to give to human morality an essentially selfish character, by disconnecting each man's feelings of duty from the interests of his fellow-creatures, except so far as a self-interested inducement is offered to him for consulting them. It is essentially a doctrine of passive obedience; it inculcates submission to all authorities found established; who indeed are not to be actively obeyed when they command what religion forbids, but who are not to be resisted, far less rebelled against, for any amount of wrong to ourselves. And while, in the morality of the best Pagan nations, duty to the State holds even a disproportionate place, infringing on the just liberty of the individual; in purely Christian ethics, that grand department of duty is scarcely noticed or acknowledged. It is in the Koran, not the New Testament, that we read the maxim — "A ruler who appoints any man to an office, when there is in his dominions another man better qualified for it, sins against God and against the State."[3] What little recognition the idea of obligation to the public obtains in modern morality is derived from Greek and Roman sources, not from Christian; as, even in the morality of private life, whatever exists of magnanimity, highmindedness, personal dignity, even the sense of honour, is derived from the purely human, not the religious part of our education, and never could have grown out of a standard of ethics in which the only worth, professedly recognised, is that of obedience.

I am as far as any one from pretending that these defects are necessarily inherent in the Christian ethics in every manner in which it can be conceived, or that the many requisites of a complete moral doctrine which it does not contain do not admit of being reconciled with it. Far less would I insinuate this of the doctrines and precepts of Christ himself. I believe that the sayings of Christ are all that I can see any evidence of their having been intended to be; that they are irreconcilable with nothing which a comprehensive morality requires; that everything which is excellent in ethics may be brought within them, with no greater violence to their language than has been done to it by all who have attempted to deduce from them any practical system of conduct whatever. But it is quite consistent with this to believe that they contain, and were meant to contain, only a part of the truth; that many essential elements of the highest morality are among the things which are not provided for, nor intended to be provided for, in the recorded deliverances of the Founder of Christianity, and which have been entirely thrown aside in the system of ethics erected on the basis of those deliverances by the Christian Church. And this being so, I think it a great error to persist in attempting to find in the Christian doctrine that complete rule for our guidance which its author intended it to sanction and enforce, but only partially to provide. I believe, too, that this narrow theory is becoming a grave practical evil, detracting greatly from the moral training and instruction which so many well-meaning persons are now at length exerting themselves to promote. I much fear that by attempting to form the mind and feelings on an exclusively religious type, and discarding those secular standards (as for want of a better name they may be called) which heretofore co-existed with and supplemented the Christian ethics, receiving some of its spirit,

3. Mill is in error; the quotation is not in the Koran.

and infusing into it some of theirs, there will result, and is even now resulting, a low, abject, servile type of character, which, submit itself as it may to what it deems the Supreme Will, is incapable of rising to or sympathising in the conception of Supreme Goodness. I believe that other ethics than any which can be evolved from exclusively Christian sources, must exist side by side with Christian ethics to produce the moral regeneration of mankind; and that the Christian system is no exception to the rule, that in an imperfect state of the human mind the interests of truth require a diversity of opinions. It is not necessary that in ceasing to ignore the moral truths not contained in Christianity men should ignore any of those which it does contain. Such prejudice, or oversight, when it occurs, is altogether an evil; but it is one from which we cannot hope to be always exempt, and must be regarded as the price paid for an inestimable good. The exclusive pretension made by a part of the truth to be the whole, must and ought to be protested against; and if a reactionary impulse should make the protestors unjust in their turn, this one-sidedness, like the other, may be lamented, but must be tolerated. If Christians would teach infidels to be just to Christianity, they should themselves be just to infidelity. It can do truth no service to blink the fact, known to all who have the most ordinary acquaintance with literary history, that a large portion of the noblest and most valuable moral teaching has been the work, not only of men who did not know, but of men who knew and rejected, the Christian faith.

I do not pretend that the most unlimited use of the freedom of enunciating all possible opinions would put an end to the evils of religious or philosophical sectarianism. Every truth which men of narrow capacity are in earnest about, is sure to be asserted, inculcated, and in many ways even acted on, as if no other truth existed in the world, or at all events none that could limit or qualify the first. I acknowledge that the tendency of all opinions to become sectarian is not cured by the freest discussion, but is often heightened and exacerbated thereby; the truth which ought to have been, but was not, seen, being rejected all the more violently because proclaimed by persons regarded as opponents. But it is not on the impassioned partisan, it is on the calmer and more disinterested bystander, that this collision of opinions works its salutary effect. Not the violent conflict between parts of the truth, but the quiet suppression of half of it, is the formidable evil; there is always hope when people are forced to listen to both sides; it is when they attend only to one that errors harden into prejudices, and truth itself ceases to have the effect of truth, by being exaggerated into falsehood. And since there are few mental attributes more rare than that judicial faculty which can sit in intelligent judgment between two sides of a question, of which only one is represented by an advocate before it, truth has no chance but in proportion as every side of it, every opinion which embodies any fraction of the truth, not only finds advocates, but is so advocated as to be listened to.

We have now recognised the necessity to the mental well-being of mankind (on which all their other well-being depends) of freedom of opinion, and freedom of the expression of opinion, on four distinct grounds; which we will now briefly recapitulate.

First, if any opinion is compelled to silence, that opinion may, for aught we can certainly know, be true. To deny this is to assume our own infallibility.

Secondly, though the silenced opinion be an error, it may, and very commonly does, contain a portion of truth; and since the general or prevailing opinion on any subject is rarely or never the whole truth, it is only by the collision of adverse opinions that the remainder of the truth has any chance of being supplied.

Thirdly, even if the received opinion be not only true, but the whole truth; unless it is suffered to be, and actually is, vigorously and earnestly contested, it will, by most of those who receive it, be held in the manner of a prejudice, with little comprehension or feeling of its rational grounds. And not only this, but, fourthly, the meaning of the doctrine itself will be in danger of being lost, or enfeebled, and deprived of its vital effect on the character and conduct; the dogma becoming a mere formal profession, inefficacious for good, but cumbering the ground, and preventing the growth of any real and heartfelt conviction, from reason or personal experience.

Before quitting the subject of freedom of opinion, it is fit to take some notice of those who say that the free expression of all opinions should be permitted, on condition that the manner be temperate, and do not pass the bounds of fair discussion. Much might be said on the impossibility of fixing where these supposed bounds are to be placed; for if the test be offence to those whose opinions are attacked, I think experience testifies that this offence is given whenever the attack is telling and powerful, and that every opponent who pushes them hard, and whom they find it difficult to answer, appears to them, if he shows any strong feeling on the subject, an intemperate opponent. But this, though an important consideration in a practical point of view, merges in a more fundamental objection. Undoubtedly the manner of asserting an opinion, even though it be a true one, may be very objectionable, and may justly incur severe censure. But the principal offences of the kind are such as it is mostly impossible, unless by accidental self-betrayal, to bring home to conviction. The gravest of them is, to argue sophistically, to suppress facts or arguments, to misstate the elements of the case, or misrepresent the opposite opinion. But all this, even to the most aggravated degree, is so continually done in perfect good faith, by persons who are not considered, and in many other respects may not deserve to be considered, ignorant or incompetent, that it is rarely possible, on adequate grounds, conscientiously to stamp the misrepresentation as morally culpable; and still less could law presume to interfere with this kind of controversial misconduct. With regard to what is commonly meant by intemperate discussion, namely invective, sarcasm, personality, and the like, the denunciation of these weapons would deserve more sympathy if it were ever proposed to interdict them equally to both sides; but it is only desired to restrain the employment of them against the prevailing opinion: against the unprevailing they may not only be used without general disapproval, but will be likely to obtain for him who uses them the praise of honest zeal and righteous indignation. Yet whatever mischief arises from their use is greatest when they are employed against the comparatively defenceless; and whatever unfair advantage can be derived by any opinion from this mode of asserting it, accrues almost exclusively to received opinions. The worst offence of this kind which can be committed by a polemic is to stigmatise those who hold the contrary opinion as bad and immoral men. To calumny of this sort, those who hold any unpopular opinion are peculiarly exposed, because they are in general few and uninfluential, and nobody but themselves feels much interested in seeing justice done them; but this weapon is, from the nature of the case, denied to those who attack a prevailing opinion: they can neither use it with safety to themselves, nor, if they could, would it do anything but recoil on their own cause. In general, opinions contrary to those commonly received can only obtain a hearing by studied moderation of language, and the most cautious avoidance of unnecessary offence, from which they hardly ever deviate even in a slight degree without losing ground: while unmeasured vituperation employed on the side of the prevailing opinion really does deter people from professing contrary opinions, and from listening to those who profess them. For the interest, therefore, of truth and justice, it is far more important to restrain this employment of vituperative language than the other; and, for example, if it were necessary to choose, there would be much more need to discourage offensive attacks on infidelity than on religion. It is, however, obvious that law and authority have no business with restraining either, while opinion ought, in every instance, to determine its verdict by the circumstances of the individual case; condemning every one, on whichever side of the argument he places himself, in whose mode of advocacy either want of candour, or malignity, bigotry, or intolerance of feeling manifest themselves; but not inferring these vices from the side which a person takes, though it be the contrary side of the question to our own; and giving merited honour to every one, whatever opinion he may hold, who has calmness to see and honesty to state what his opponents and their opinions really are, exaggerating nothing to their discredit, keeping nothing back which tells, or can be supposed to tell, in their favour. This is the real morality of public discussion: and if often violated, I am happy to think that there are many controversialists

who to a great extent observe it, and a still greater number who conscientiously strive towards it.

Chapter III

OF INDIVIDUALITY, AS ONE OF THE ELEMENTS OF WELL-BEING

Such being the reasons which make it imperative that human beings
should be free to form opinions, and to express their opinions without
reserve; and such the baneful consequences to the intellectual, and
through that to the moral nature of man, unless this liberty is either
conceded, or asserted in spite of prohibition; let us next examine
whether the same reasons do not require that men should be free to
act upon their opinions — to carry these out in their lives, without hindrance, either physical or moral, from their fellow-men, so long as it is
at their own risk and peril. This last proviso is of course indispensable.
No one pretends that actions should be as free as opinions. On the
contrary, even opinions lose their immunity when the circumstances
in which they are expressed are such as to constitute their expression a
positive instigation to some mischievous act. An opinion that corn-
dealers are starvers of the poor, or that private property is robbery, ought
to be unmolested when simply circulated through the press, but may
justly incur punishment when delivered orally to an excited mob assembled before the house of a corn-dealer, or when handed about
among the same mob in the form of a placard. Acts, of whatever kind,
which, without justifiable cause, do harm to others, may be, and in the
more important cases absolutely require to be, controlled by the unfavourable sentiments, and, when needful, by the active interference of
mankind. The liberty of the individual must be thus far limited; he
must not make himself a nuisance to other people. But if he refrains
from molesting others in what concerns them, and merely acts according to his own inclination and judgment in things which concern himself, the same reasons which show that opinion should be free, prove
also that he should be allowed, without molestation, to carry his opinions into practice at his own cost. That mankind are not infallible; that
their truths, for the most part, are only half-truths; that unity of opinion,
unless resulting from the fullest and freest comparison of opposite opinions, is not desirable, and diversity not an evil, but a good, until mankind are much more capable than at present of recognising all sides of
the truth, are principles applicable to men's modes of action, not less
than to their opinions. As it is useful that while mankind are imperfect
there should be different opinions, so it is that there should be different
experiments of living; that free scope should be given to varieties of
character, short of injury to others; and that the worth of different
modes of life should be proved practically, when any one thinks fit to
try them. It is desirable, in short, that in things which do not primarily

concern others, individuality should assert itself. Where, not the person's own character, but the traditions or customs of other people are the rule of conduct, there is wanting one of the principal ingredients of human happiness, and quite the chief ingredient of individual and social progress.

In maintaining this principle, the greatest difficulty to be encountered does not lie in the appreciation of means towards an acknowledged end, but in the indifference of persons in general to the end itself. If it were felt that the free development of individuality is one of the leading essentials of well-being; that it is not only a coordinate element with all that is designated by the terms civilisation, instruction, education, culture, but is itself a necessary part and condition of all those things; there would be no danger that liberty should be undervalued, and the adjustment of the boundaries between it and social control would present no extraordinary difficulty. But the evil is, that individual spontaneity is hardly recognised by the common modes of thinking as having any intrinsic worth, or deserving any regard on its own account. The majority, being satisfied with the ways of mankind as they now are (for it is they who make them what they are), cannot comprehend why those ways should not be good enough for everybody; and what is more, spontaneity forms no part of the ideal of the majority of moral and social reformers, but is rather looked on with jealousy, as a troublesome and perhaps rebellious obstruction to the general acceptance of what these reformers, in their own judgment, think would be best for mankind. Few persons, out of Germany, even comprehend the meaning of the doctrine which Wilhelm von Humboldt, so eminent both as a *savant*[4] and as a politician, made the text of a treatise — that "the end of man, or that which is prescribed by the eternal or immutable dictates of reason, and not suggested by vague and transient desires, is the highest and most harmonious development of his powers to a complete and consistent whole"; that, therefore, the object "towards which every human being must ceaselessly direct his efforts, and on which especially those who design to influence their fellow-men must ever keep their eyes, is the individuality of power and development;" that for this there are two requisites, "freedom, and variety of situations;" and that from the union of these arise "individual vigour and manifold diversity," which combine themselves in "originality."[5]

Little, however, as people are accustomed to a doctrine like that of Von Humboldt, and surprising as it may be to them to find so high a value attached to individuality, the question, one must nevertheless think, can only be one of degree. No one's idea of excellence in conduct is that people should do absolutely nothing but copy one another. No one would assert that people ought not to put into their mode of

4. Man of learning (French).
5. *The Sphere of Duties of Government*, from the German of Baron Wilhelm von Humboldt, pp. 11–13 [Mill's note].

life, and into the conduct of their concerns, any impress whatever of their own judgment, or of their own individual character. On the other hand, it would be absurd to pretend that people ought to live as if nothing whatever had been known in the world before they came into it; as if experience had as yet done nothing towards showing that one mode of existence, or of conduct, is preferable to another. Nobody denies that people should be so taught and trained in youth as to know and benefit by the ascertained results of human experience. But it is the privilege and proper condition of a human being, arrived at the maturity of his faculties, to use and interpret experience in his own way. It is for him to find out what part of recorded experience is properly applicable to his own circumstances and character. The traditions and customs of other people are, to a certain extent, evidence of what their experience has taught *them*; presumptive evidence, and as such, have a claim to his deference: but, in the first place, their experience may be too narrow; or they may not have interpreted it rightly. Secondly, their interpretation of experience may be correct, but unsuitable to him. Customs are made for customary circumstances and customary characters; and his circumstances or his character may be uncustomary. Thirdly, though the customs be both good as customs, and suitable to him, yet to conform to custom, merely *as* custom, does not educate or develop in him any of the qualities which are the distinctive endowment of a human being. The human faculties of perception, judgment, discriminative feeling, mental activity, and even moral preference, are exercised only in making a choice. He who does anything because it is the custom makes no choice. He gains no practice either in discerning or in desiring what is best. The mental and moral, like the muscular powers, are improved only by being used. The faculties are called into no exercise by doing a thing merely because others do it, no more than by believing a thing only because others believe it. If the grounds of an opinion are not conclusive to the person's own reason, his reason cannot be strengthened, but is likely to be weakened, by his adopting it: and if the inducements to an act are not such as are consentaneous to his own feelings and character (where affection, or the rights of others, are not concerned) it is so much done towards rendering his feelings and character inert and torpid, instead of active and energetic.

He who lets the world, or his own portion of it, choose his plan of life for him, has no need of any other faculty than the ape-like one of imitation. He who chooses his plan for himself, employs all his faculties. He must use observation to see, reasoning and judgment to foresee, activity to gather materials for decision, discrimination to decide, and when he has decided, firmness and self-control to hold to his deliberate decision. And these qualities he requires and exercises exactly in proportion as the part of his conduct which he determines according to his own judgment and feelings is a large one. It is possible that he might be guided in some good path, and kept out of harm's way, without any of these things. But what will be his comparative worth as a human being? It really is of importance, not only what men do, but also what manner of men they are that do it. Among the works of man, which human life is rightly employed in perfecting and beautifying, the first in importance surely is man himself. Supposing it were possible to get houses built, corn grown, battles fought, causes tried, and even churches erected and prayers said, by machinery—by automatons in human form—it would be a considerable loss to exchange for these automatons even the men and women who at present inhabit the more civilised parts of the world, and who assuredly are but starved specimens of what nature can and will produce. Human nature is not a machine to be built after a model, and set to do exactly the work prescribed for it, but a tree, which requires to grow and develop itself on all sides, according to the tendency of the inward forces which make it a living thing.

It will probably be conceded that it is desirable people should exercise their understandings, and that an intelligent following of custom, or even occasionally an intelligent deviation from custom, is better than a blind and simply mechanical adhesion to it. To a certain extent it is admitted that our understanding should be our own: but there is not the same willingness to admit that our desires and impulses should be our own likewise; or that to possess impulses of our own, and of any strength, is anything but a peril and a snare. Yet desires and impulses are as much a part of a perfect human being as beliefs and restraints: and strong impulses are only perilous when not properly balanced; when one set of aims and inclinations is developed into strength, while others, which ought to co-exist with them, remain weak and inactive. It is not because men's desires are strong that they act ill; it is because their consciences are weak. There is no natural connection between strong impulses and a weak conscience. The natural connection is the other way. To say that one person's desires and feelings are stronger and more various than those of another, is merely to say that he has more of the raw material of human nature, and is therefore capable, perhaps of more evil, but certainly of more good. Strong impulses are but another name for energy. Energy may be turned to bad uses; but more good may always be made of an energetic nature, than of an indolent and impassive one. Those who have most natural feeling, are always those whose cultivated feelings may be made the strongest. The same strong susceptibilities which make the personal impulses vivid and powerful, are also the source from whence are generated the most passionate love of virtue, and the sternest self-control. It is through the cultivation of these that society both does its duty and protects its interest: not by rejecting the stuff of which heroes are made, because it knows not how to make them. A person whose desires and impulses are his own—are the expression of his own nature, as it has been developed and modified by his own culture—is said to have a character.

One whose desires and impulses are not his own, has no character, no more than a steam-engine has a character. If, in addition to being his own, his impulses are strong, and are under the government of a strong will, he has an energetic character. Whoever thinks that individuality of desires and impulses should not be encouraged to unfold itself, must maintain that society has no need of strong natures — is not the better for containing many persons who have much character — and that a high general average of energy is not desirable.

In some early states of society, these forces might be, and were, too much ahead of the power which society then possessed of disciplining and controlling them. There has been a time when the element of spontaneity and individuality was in excess, and the social principle had a hard struggle with it. The difficulty then was to induce men of strong bodies or minds to pay obedience to any rules which required them to control their impulses. To overcome this difficulty, law and discipline, like the Popes struggling against the Emperors, asserted a power over the whole man, claiming to control all his life in order to control his character — which society had not found any other sufficient means of binding. But society has now fairly got the better of individuality; and the danger which threatens human nature is not the excess, but the deficiency, of personal impulses and preferences. Things are vastly changed since the passions of those who were strong by station or by personal endowment were in a state of habitual rebellion against laws and ordinances, and required to be rigorously chained up to enable the persons within their reach to enjoy any particle of security. In our times, from the highest class of society down to the lowest, every one lives as under the eye of a hostile and dreaded censorship. Not only in what concerns others, but in what concerns only themselves, the individual or the family do not ask themselves — what do I prefer? or, what would suit my character and disposition? or, what would allow the best and highest in me to have fair play, and enable it to grow and thrive? They ask themselves, what is suitable to my position? what is usually done by persons of my station and pecuniary circumstances? or (worse still) what is usually done by persons of a station and circumstances superior to mine? I do not mean that they choose what is customary in preference to what suits their own inclination. It does not occur to them to have any inclination, except for what is customary. Thus the mind itself is bowed to the yoke: even in what people do for pleasure, conformity is the first thing thought of; they like in crowds; they exercise choice only among things commonly done: peculiarity of taste, eccentricity of conduct, are shunned equally with crimes: until by dint of not following their own nature they have no nature to follow: their human capacities are withered and starved: they become incapable of any strong wishes or native pleasures, and are generally without either opinions or feelings of home growth, or properly their own. Now is this, or is it not, the desirable condition of human nature?

It is so, on the Calvinistic theory. According to that, the one great offence of man is self-will. All the good of which humanity is capable is comprised in obedience. You have no choice; thus you must do, and no otherwise: "whatever is not a duty, is a sin." Human nature being radically corrupt, there is no redemption for any one until human nature is killed within him. To one holding this theory of life, crushing out any of the human faculties, capacities, and susceptibilities, is no evil: man needs no capacity, but that of surrendering himself to the will of God: and if he uses any of his faculties for any other purpose but to do that supposed will more effectually, he is better without them. This is the theory of Calvinism; and it is held, in a mitigated form, by many who do not consider themselves Calvinists; the mitigation consisting in giving a less ascetic interpretation to the alleged will of God; asserting it to be his will that mankind should gratify some of their inclinations; of course not in the manner they themselves prefer, but in the way of obedience, that is, in a way prescribed to them by authority; and, therefore, by the necessary condition of the case, the same for all.

In some such insidious form there is at present a strong tendency to this narrow theory of life, and to the pinched and hidebound type of human character which it patronises. Many persons, no doubt, sincerely think that human beings thus cramped and dwarfed are as their Maker designed them to be; just as many have thought that trees are a much finer thing when clipped into pollards, or cut out into figures of animals, than as nature made them. But if it be any part of religion to believe that man was made by a good Being, it is more consistent with that faith to believe that this Being gave all human faculties that they might be cultivated and unfolded, not rooted out and consumed, and that he takes delight in every nearer approach made by his creatures to the ideal conception embodied in them, every increase in any of their capabilities of comprehension, of action, or of enjoyment. There is a different type of human excellence from the Calvinistic: a conception of humanity as having its nature bestowed on it for other purposes than merely to be abnegated. "Pagan self-assertion" is one of the elements of human worth, as well as "Christian self-denial."[6] There is a Greek ideal of self-development, which the Platonic and Christian ideal of self-government blends with, but does not supersede. It may be better to be a John Knox than an Alicibiades,[7] but it is better to be a Pericles than either; nor would a Pericles, if we had one in these days, be without anything good which belonged to John Knox.

It is not by wearing down into uniformity all that is individual in themselves, but by cultivating it, and calling it forth, within the limits imposed by the rights and interests of others, that human beings be-

6. Sterling's *Essays* [Mill's note].
7. An Athenian general and politician of great charm and little self-restraint (450–404 B.C.).

come a noble and beautiful object of contemplation; and as the works partake the character of those who do them, by the same process human life also becomes rich, diversified, and animating, furnishing more abundant aliment to high thoughts and elevating feelings, and strengthening the tie which binds every individual to the race, by making the race infinitely better worth belonging to. In proportion to the development of his individuality, each person becomes more valuable to himself, and is therefore capable of being more valuable to others. There is a greater fulness of life about his own existence, and when there is more life in the units there is more in the mass which is composed of them. As much compression as is necessary to prevent the stronger specimens of human nature from encroaching on the rights of others, cannot be dispensed with; but for this there is ample compensation even in the point of view of human development. The means of development which the individual loses by being prevented from gratifying his inclinations to the injury of others, are chiefly obtained at the expense of the development of other people. And even to himself there is a full equivalent in the better development of the social part of his nature, rendered possible by the restraint put upon the selfish part. To be held to rigid rules of justice for the sake of others, develops the feelings and capacities which have the good of others for their object. But to be restrained in things not affecting their good, by their mere displeasure, develops nothing valuable, except such force of character as may unfold itself in resisting the restraint. If acquiesced in, it dulls and blunts the whole nature. To give any fair play to the nature of each, it is essential that different persons should be allowed to lead different lives. In proportion as this latitude has been exercised in any age, has that age been noteworthy to posterity. Even despotism does not produce its worst effects, so long as individuality exists under it; and whatever crushes individuality is despotism, by whatever name it may be called, and whether it professes to be enforcing the will of God or the injunctions of men.

Having said that the individuality is the same thing with development, and that it is only the cultivation of individuality which produces, or can produce, well-developed human beings, I might here close the argument: for what more or better can be said of any condition of human affairs than that it brings human beings themselves nearer to the best things they can be? or what worse can be said of any obstruction to good than that it prevents this? Doubtless, however, these considerations will not suffice to convince those who most need convincing; and it is necessary further to show, that these developed human beings are of some use to the undeveloped — to point out to those who do not desire liberty, and would not avail themselves of it, that they may be in some intelligible manner rewarded for allowing other people to make use of it without hindrance.

In the first place, then, I would suggest that they might possibly learn something from them. It will not be denied by anybody, that originality is a valuable element in human affairs. There is always need of persons not only to discover new truths, and point out when what were once truths are true no longer, but also to commence new practices, and set the example of more enlightened conduct, and better taste and sense in human life. This cannot well be gainsaid by anybody who does not believe that the world has already attained perfection in all its ways and practices. It is true that this benefit is not capable of being rendered by everybody alike: there are but few persons, in comparison with the whole of mankind, whose experiments, if adopted by others, would be likely to be any improvement on established practice. But these few are the salt of the earth; without them, human life would become a stagnant pool. Not only is it they who introduce good things which did not before exist; it is they who keep the life in those which already exist. If there were nothing new to be done, would human intellect cease to be necessary? Would it be a reason why those who do the old things should forget why they are done, and do them like cattle, not like human beings? There is only too great a tendency in the best beliefs and practices to degenerate into the mechanical; and unless there were a succession of persons whose ever-recurring originality prevents the grounds of those beliefs and practices from becoming merely traditional, such dead matter would not resist the smaller shock from anything really alive, and there would be no reason why civilisation should not die out, as in the Byzantine Empire. Persons of genius, it is true, are, and are always likely to be, a small minority; but in order to have them, it is necessary to preserve the soil in which they grow. Genius can only breathe freely in an *atmosphere* of freedom. Persons of genius are, *ex vi termini*,[8] more individual than any other people — less capable, consequently, of fitting themselves, without hurtful compression, into any of the small number of moulds which society provides in order to save its members the trouble of forming their own character. If from timidity they consent to be forced into one of these moulds, and to let all that part of themselves which cannot expand under the pressure remain unexpanded, society will be little the better for their genius. If they are of a strong character, and break their fetters, they become a mark for the society which has not succeeded in reducing them to commonplace, to point out with solemn warning as "wild," "erratic," and the like; much as if one should complain of the Niagara river for not flowing smoothly between its banks like a Dutch canal.

I insist thus emphatically on the importance of genius, and the necessity of allowing it to unfold itself freely both in thought and in practice, being well aware that no one will deny the position in theory, but knowing also that almost every one, in reality, is totally indifferent to it. People think genius a fine thing if it enables a man to write an

---

8. By definition (Latin).

exciting poem, or paint a picture. But in its true sense, that of originality in thought and action, though no one says that it is not a thing to be admired, nearly all, at heart, think that they can do very well without it. Unhappily this is too natural to be wondered at. Originality is the one thing which unoriginal minds cannot feel the use of. They cannot see what it is to do for them: how should they? If they could see what it would do for them, it would not be originality. The first service which originality has to render them, is that of opening their eyes: which being once fully done, they would have a chance of being themselves original. Meanwhile, recollecting that nothing was ever yet done which some one was not the first to do, and that all good things which exist are the fruits of originality, let them be modest enough to believe that there is something still left for it to accomplish, and assure themselves that they are more in need of originality, the less they are conscious of the want.

In sober truth, whatever homage may be professed, or even paid, to real or supposed mental superiority, the general tendency of things throughout the world is to render mediocrity the ascendant power among mankind. In ancient history, in the Middle Ages, and in a diminishing degree through the long transition from feudality to the present time, the individual was a power in himself; and if he had either great talents or a high social position, he was a considerable power. At present individuals are lost in the crowd. In politics it is almost a triviality to say that public opinion now rules the world. The only power deserving the name is that of masses, and of governments while they make themselves the organ of the tendencies and instincts of masses. This is as true in the moral and social relations of private life as in public transactions. Those whose opinions go by the name of public opinion are not always the same sort of public: in America they are the whole white population; in England, chiefly the middle class. But they are always a mass, that is to say, collective mediocrity. And what is a still greater novelty, the mass do not now take their opinions from dignitaries in Church or State, from ostensible leaders, or from books. Their thinking is done for them by men much like themselves, addressing them or speaking in their name, on the spur of the moment, through the newspapers. I am not complaining of all this. I do not assert that anything better is compatible, as a general rule, with the present low state of the human mind. But that does not hinder the government of mediocrity from being mediocre government. No government by a democracy or a numerous aristocracy, either in its political acts or in the opinions, qualities, and tone of mind which it fosters, ever did or could rise above mediocrity, except in so far as the sovereign Many have let themselves be guided (which in their best times they always have done) by the counsels and influence of a more highly gifted and instructed One or Few. The initiation of all wise or noble things comes and must come from individuals; generally at first from some one individual. The honour and glory of the average man is that he is capable of following that initiative; that he can respond internally to wise and noble things, and be led to them with his eyes open. I am not countenancing the sort of "hero-worship" which applauds the strong man of genius for forcibly seizing on the government of the world and making it do his bidding in spite of itself. All he can claim is, freedom to point out the way. The power of compelling others into it is not only inconsistent with the freedom and development of all the rest, but corrupting to the strong man himself. It does seem, however, that when the opinions of masses of merely average men are everywhere become or becoming the dominant power, the counterpoise and corrective to that tendency would be the more and more pronounced individuality of those who stand on the higher eminences of thought. It is in these circumstances most especially, that exceptional individuals, instead of being deterred, should be encouraged in acting differently from the mass. In other times there was no advantage in their doing so, unless they acted not only differently but better. In this age, the mere example of non-conformity, the mere refusal to bend the knee to custom, is itself a service. Precisely because the tyranny of opinion is such as to make eccentricity a reproach, it is desirable, in order to break through that tyranny, that people should be eccentric. Eccentricity has always abounded when and where strength of character has abounded; and the amount of eccentricity in a society has generally been proportional to the amount of genius, mental vigour, and moral courage it contained. That so few now dare to be eccentric marks the chief danger of the time.

I have said that it is important to give the freest scope possible to uncustomary things, in order that it may in time appear which of these are fit to be converted into customs. But independence of action, and disregard of custom, are not solely deserving of encouragement for the chance they afford that better modes of action, and customs more worthy of general adoption, may be struck out; nor is it only persons of decided mental superiority who have a just claim to carry on their lives in their own way. There is no reason that all human existence should be constructed on some one or some small number of patterns. If a person possesses any tolerable amount of common sense and experience, his own mode of laying out his existence is the best, not because it is the best in itself, but because it is his own mode. Human beings are not like sheep; and even sheep are not undistinguishably alike. A man cannot get a coat or a pair of boots to fit him unless they are either made to his measure, or he has a whole warehouseful to choose from: and is it easier to fit him with a life than with a coat, or are human beings more like one another in their whole physical and spiritual conformation than in the shape of their feet? If it were only that people have diversities of taste, that is reason enough for not attempting to shape them all after one model. But different persons also require different conditions for their spiritual development; and can no more exist healthily in the same moral, than all the variety of plants can in the same physical, atmosphere and climate. The same things which are helps to one person towards the cultivation of higher nature are hindrances to another. The same mode of life is a healthy excitement to one, keeping all his faculties of action and enjoyment in their best order, while to another it is a distracting burthen, which suspends or crushes all internal life. Such are the differences among human beings in their sources of pleasure, their susceptibilities of pain, and the operation on them of different physical and moral agencies, that unless there is a corresponding diversity in their modes of life, they neither obtain their fair share of happiness, nor grow up to the mental, moral, and aesthetic stature of which their nature is capable. Why then should tolerance, as far as the public sentiment is concerned, extend only to tastes and modes of life which extort acquiescence by the multitude of their adherents? Nowhere (except in some monastic institutions) is diversity of taste entirely unrecognised; a person may, without blame, either like or dislike rowing, or smoking, or music, or athletic exercises, or chess, or cards, or study, because both those who like each of these things, and those who dislike them, are too numerous to be put down. But the man, and still more the woman, who can be accused either of doing "what nobody does," or of not doing "what everybody does," is the subject of as much depreciatory remark as if he or she had committed some grave moral delinquency. Persons require to possess a title, or some other badge of rank, or of the consideration of people of rank, to be able to indulge somewhat in the luxury of doing as they like without detriment to their estimation. To indulge somewhat, I repeat: for whoever allow themselves much of that indulgence, incur the risk of something worse than disparaging speeches — they are in peril of a commission *de lunatico*,[9] and of having their property taken from them and given to their relations.[1]

There is one characteristic of the present direction of public opinion

9. A commission to ascertain the presence of insanity (Latin).
1. There is something both contemptible and frightful in the sort of evidence on which, of late years, any person can be judicially declared unfit for the management of his affairs; and after his death, his disposal of his property can be set aside, if there is enough of it to pay the expenses of litigation — which are charged on the property itself. All the minute details of his daily life are pried into, and whatever is found which, seen through the medium of the perceiving and describing faculties of the lowest of the low, bears an appearance unlike absolute commonplace, is laid before the jury as evidence of insanity, and often with success; the jurors being little, if at all, less vulgar and ignorant than the witnesses; while the judges, with that extraordinary want of knowledge of human nature and life which continually astonishes us in English lawyers, often help to mislead them. These trials speak volumes as to the state of feeling and opinion among the vulgar with regard to human liberty. So far from setting any value on individuality — so far from respecting the right of each individual to act, in things indifferent, as seems good to his own judgment and inclinations, judges and juries cannot even conceive that a person in a state of sanity can desire such freedom. In former days, when it was proposed to burn atheists, charitable people used to suggest putting them in a madhouse instead: it would be nothing surprising now-a-days were we to see this done, and the doers applauding themselves, because, instead of persecuting for religion, they had adopted so humane and Christian a mode of treating these unfortunates, not without a silent satisfaction at their having thereby obtained their deserts [Mill's note].

peculiarly calculated to make it intolerant of any marked demonstration of individuality. The general average of mankind are not only moderate in intellect, but also moderate in inclinations: they have no tastes or wishes strong enough to incline them to do anything unusual, and they consequently do not understand those who have, and class all such with the wild and intemperate whom they are accustomed to look down upon. Now, in addition to this fact which is general, we have only to suppose that a strong movement has set in towards the improvement of morals, and it is evident what we have to expect. In these days such a movement has set in; much has actually been effected in the way of increased regularity of conduct and discouragement of excesses; and there is a philanthropic spirit abroad, for the exercise of which there is no more inviting field than the moral and prudential improvement of our fellow-creatures. These tendencies of the times cause the public to be more disposed than at most former periods to prescribe general rules of conduct, and endeavour to make every one conform to the approved standard. And that standard, express or tacit, is to desire nothing strongly. Its ideal of character is to be without any marked character; to maim by compression, like a Chinese lady's foot, every part of human nature which stands out prominently, and tends to make the person markedly dissimilar in outline to commonplace humanity.

As is usually the case with ideals which exclude one-half of what is desirable, the present standard of approbation produces only an inferior imitation of the other half. Instead of great energies guided by vigorous reason, and strong feelings strongly controlled by a conscientious will, its result is weak feelings and weak energies, which therefore can be kept in outward conformity to rule without any strength either of will or of reason. Already energetic characters on any large scale are becoming merely traditional. There is now scarcely any outlet for energy in this country except business. The energy expended in this may still be regarded as considerable. What little is left from that employment is expended on some hobby; which may be a useful, even a philanthropic hobby, but is always some one thing, and generally a thing of small dimensions. The greatness of England is now all collective; individually small, we only appear capable of anything great by our habit of combining; and with this our moral and religious philanthropists are perfectly contented. But it was men of another stamp than this that made England what is has been; and men of another stamp will be needed to prevent its decline.

The despotism of custom is everywhere the standing hindrance to human advancement, being in unceasing antagonism to that disposition to aim at something better than customary, which is called, according to circumstances, the spirit of liberty, or that of progress or improvement. The spirit of improvement is not always a spirit of liberty, for it may aim at forcing improvements on an unwilling people; and the spirit of liberty, in so far as it resists such attempts, may ally itself locally and temporarily with the opponents of improvement; but the only unfailing and permanent source of improvement is liberty, since by it there are as many possible independent centres of improvement as there are individuals. The progressive principle, however, in either shape, whether as the love of liberty or of improvement, is antagonistic to the sway of Custom, involving at least emancipation from that yoke; and the contest between the two constitutes the chief interest of the history of mankind. The greater part of the world has, properly speaking, no history, because the despotism of Custom is complete. This is the case over the whole East. Custom is there, in all things, the final appeal; justice and right mean conformity to custom; the argument of custom no one, unless some tyrant intoxicated with power, thinks of resisting. And we see the result. Those nations must once have had originality; they did not start out of the ground populous, lettered, and versed in many of the arts of life; they made themselves all this, and were then the greatest and most powerful nations of the world. What are they now? The subjects or dependents of tribes whose forefathers wandered in the forests when theirs had magnificent palaces and gorgeous temples, but over whom custom exercised only a divided rule with liberty and progress. A people, it appears, may be progressive for a certain length of time, and then stop: when does it stop? When it ceases to possess individuality. If a similar change should befall the nations of Europe, it will not be in exactly the same shape: the despotism of custom with which these nations are threatened is not precisely stationariness. It proscribes singularity, but it does not preclude change, provided all change together. We have discarded the fixed costumes of our forefathers; every one must still dress like other people, but the fashion may change once or twice a year. We thus take care that when there is a change, it shall be for change's sake, and not from any idea of beauty or convenience; for the same idea of beauty or convenience would not strike all the world at the same moment, and be simultaneously thrown aside by all at another moment. But we are progressive as well as changeable: we continually make new inventions in mechanical things, and keep them until they are again superseded by better; we are eager for improvement in politics, in education, even in morals, though in this last our idea of improvement chiefly consists in persuading or forcing other people to be as good as ourselves. It is not progress that we object to; on the contrary, we flatter ourselves that we are the most progressive people who ever lived. It is individuality that we war against: we should think we had done wonders if we had made ourselves all alike; forgetting that the unlikeness of one person to another is generally the first thing which draws the attention of either to the imperfection of his own type, and the superiority of another, or the possibility, by combining the advantages of both, of producing something better than either. We have a warning example in China—a nation of much talent, and, in some respects, even wisdom, owing to the rare good fortune of having been provided at an early period with a particularly good set of customs, the work, in some measure, of men to whom even the most enlightened European must accord, under certain limitations, the title of sages and philosophers. They are remarkable, too, in the excellence of their apparatus for impressing, as far as possible, the best wisdom they possess upon every mind in the community, and securing that those who have appropriated most of it shall occupy the posts of honour and power. Surely the people who did this have discovered the secret of human progressiveness, and must have kept themselves steadily at the head of the movement of the world. On the contrary, they have become stationary — have remained so for thousands of years; and if they are ever to be farther improved, it must be by foreigners. They have succeeded beyond all hope in what English philanthropists are so industriously working at — in making a people all alike, all governing their thoughts and conduct by the same maxims and rules; and these are the fruits. The modern *régime* of public opinion is, in an unorganised form, what the Chinese educational and political systems are in an organised; and unless individuality shall be able successfully to assert itself against this yoke, Europe, notwithstanding its noble antecedents and its professed Christianity, will tend to become another China.

What is it that has hitherto preserved Europe from this lot? What has made the European family of nations an improving, instead of a stationary portion of mankind? Not any superior excellence in them, which, when it exists, exists as the effect, not as the cause; but their remarkable diversity of character and culture. Individuals, classes, nations, have been extremely unlike one another: they have struck out a great variety of paths, each leading to something valuable; and although at every period those who travelled in different paths have been intolerant of one another, and each would have thought it an excellent thing if all the rest could have been compelled to travel his road, their attempts to thwart each other's development have rarely had any permanent success, and each has in time endured to receive the good which the others have offered. Europe is, in my judgment, wholly indebted to this plurality of paths for its progressive and many-sided development. But it already begins to possess this benefit in a considerably less degree. It is decidedly advancing towards the Chinese ideal of making all people alike. M. de Tocqueville, in his last important work,[2] remarks how much more that Frenchmen of the present day resemble one another than did those even of the last generation. The same remark might be made of Englishmen in a far greater degree. In a passage already quoted from Wilhelm von Humboldt, he points out two things as necessary conditions of human development, because necessary to render people unlike one another; namely, freedom, and variety of situations. The second of these two conditions is in this country every day

2. Alexis de Tocqueville's *L'ancien régime et la révolution* (1856).

diminishing. The circumstances which surround different classes and individuals, and shape their characters, are daily becoming more assimilated. Formerly, different ranks, different neighbourhoods, different trades and professions, lived in what might be called different worlds; at present to a great degree in the same. Comparatively speaking, they now read the same things, listen to the same things, see the same things, go to the same places, have their hopes and fears directed to the same objects, have the same rights and liberties, and the same means of asserting them. Great as are the differences of position which remain, they are nothing to those which have ceased. And the assimilation is still proceeding. All the political changes of the age promote it, since they all tend to raise the low and to lower the high. Every extension of education promotes it, because education brings people under common influences, and gives them access to the general stock of facts and sentiments. Improvement in the means of communication promotes it, by bringing the inhabitants of distant places into personal contact, and keeping up a rapid flow of changes of residence between one place and another. The increase of commerce and manufactures promotes it, by diffusing more widely the advantages of easy circumstances, and opening all objects of ambition, even the highest, to general competition, whereby the desire of rising becomes no longer the character of a particular class, but of all classes. A more powerful agency than even all these, in bringing about a general similarity among mankind, is the complete establishment, in this and other free countries, of the ascendancy of public opinion in the State. As the various social eminences which enabled persons entrenched on them to disregard the opinion of the multitude gradually become levelled; as the very idea of resisting the will of the public, when it is positively known that they have a will, disappears more and more from the minds of practical politicians; there ceases to be any social support for nonconformity — any substantive power in society which, itself opposed to the ascendancy of numbers, is interested in taking under its protection opinions and tendencies at variance with those of the public.

The combination of all these causes forms so great a mass of influences hostile to Individuality, that it is not easy to see how it can stand its ground. It will do so with increasing difficulty, unless the intelligent part of the public can be made to feel its value — to see that it is good there should be differences, even though not for the better, even though, as it may appear to them, some should be for the worse. If the claims of individuality are ever to be asserted, the time is now, while much is still wanting to complete the enforced assimilation. It is only in the earlier stages that any stand can be successfully made against the encroachment. The demand that all other people shall resemble ourselves grows by what it feeds on. If resistance waits till life is reduced *nearly* to one uniform type, all deviations from that type will come to be considered impious, immoral, even monstrous and contrary to na-

ture. Mankind speedily become unable to conceive diversity, when they
have been for some time unaccustomed to see it.

Chapter IV

OF THE LIMITS TO THE AUTHORITY OF SOCIETY
OVER THE INDIVIDUAL

What, then, is the rightful limit to the sovereignty of the individual
over himself? Where does the authority of society begin? How much
of human life should be assigned to individuality, and how much to
society?

Each will receive its proper share, if each has that which more particularly concerns it. To individuality should belong the part of life in
which it is chiefly the individual that is interested; to society, the part
which chiefly interests society.

Though society is not founded on a contract, and though no good
purpose is answered by inventing a contract in order to deduce social
obligations from it, every one who receives the protection of society
owes a return for the benefit, and the fact of living in society renders
it indispensable that each should be bound to observe a certain line of
conduct towards the rest. This conduct consists, first, in not injuring
the interests of one another; or rather certain interests, which, either
by express legal provision, or by tacit understanding, ought to be considered as rights; and secondly, in each person's bearing his share (to
be fixed on some equitable principle) of the labours and sacrifices in-
curred for defending the society or its members from injury and molestation. These conditions society is justified in enforcing, at all costs
to those who endeavour to withhold fulfilment. Nor is this all that
society may do. The acts of an individual may be hurtful to others, or
wanting in due consideration for their welfare, without going to the
length of violating any of their constituted rights. The offender may
then be justly punished by opinion, though not by law. As soon as any
part of a person's conduct affects prejudicially the interests of others,
society has jurisdiction over it, and the question whether the general
welfare will or will not be promoted by interfering with it, becomes
open to discussion. But there is no room for entertaining any such
question when a person's conduct affects the interests of no persons
besides himself, or needs not affect them unless they like (all the persons concerned being of full age, and the ordinary amount of understanding). In all such cases, there should be perfect freedom, legal and
social, to do the action and stand the consequences.

It would be a great misunderstanding of this doctrine to suppose that
it is one of selfish indifference, which pretends that human beings have
no business with each other's conduct in life, and that they should not
concern themselves about the well-doing or well-being of one another,

unless their own interest is involved. Instead of any diminution, there is need of a great increase of disinterested exertion to promote the good of others. But disinterested benevolence can find other instruments to persuade people to their good than whips and scourges, either of the literal or the metaphorical sort. I am the last person to undervalue the self-regarding virtues; they are only second in importance, if even second, to the social. It is equally the business of education to cultivate both. But even education works by conviction and persuasion as well as by compulsion, and it is by the former only that, when the period of education is passed, the self-regarding virtues should be inculcated. Human beings owe to each other help to distinguish the better from the worse, and encouragement to choose the former and avoid the latter. They should be forever stimulating each other to increased exercise of their higher faculties, and increased direction of their feelings and aims towards wise instead of foolish, elevating instead of degrading, objects and contemplations. But neither one person, nor any number of persons, is warranted in saying to another human creature of ripe years, that he shall not do with his life for his own benefit what he chooses to do with it. He is the person most interested in his own well-being: the interest which any other person, except in cases of strong personal attachment, can have in it, is trifling, compared with that which he himself has; the interest which society has in him individually (except as to his conduct to others) is fractional, and altogether indirect; while with respect to his own feelings and circumstances, the most ordinary man or woman has means of knowledge immeasurably surpassing those that can be possessed by any one else. The interference of society to overrule his judgment and purposes in what only regards himself must be grounded on general presumptions; which may be altogether wrong, and even if right, are as likely as not to be misapplied to individual cases, by persons no better acquainted with the circumstances of such cases than those are who look at them merely from without. In this department, therefore, of human affairs, Individuality has its proper field of action. In the conduct of human beings towards one another it is necessary that general rules should for the most part be observed, in order that people may know what they have to expect: but in each person's own concerns his individual spontaneity is entitled to free exercise. Considerations to aid his judgment, exhortations to strengthen his will, may be offered to him, even obtruded on him, by others: but he himself is the final judge. All errors which he is likely to commit against advice and warning are far outweighed by the evil of allowing others to constrain him to what they deem his good.

I do not mean that the feelings with which a person is regarded by others ought not to be in any way affected by his self-regarding qualities or deficiencies. This is neither possible nor desirable. If he is eminent in any of the qualities which conduce to his own good, he is, so far, a proper object of admiration. He is so much the nearer to the ideal perfection of human nature. If he is grossly deficient in those qualities, a sentiment the opposite of admiration will follow. There is a degree of folly, and a degree of what may be called (though the phrase is not unobjectionable) lowness or depravation of taste, which, though it cannot justify doing harm to the person who manifests it renders him necessarily and properly a subject of distaste, or, in extreme cases, even of contempt: a person could not have the opposite qualities in due strength without entertaining these feelings. Though doing no wrong to any one, a person may so act as to compel us to judge him, and feel to him, as a fool, or as a being of an inferior order: and since this judgment and feeling are a fact which he would prefer to avoid, it is doing him a service to warn him of it beforehand, as of any other disagreeable consequence to which he exposes himself. It would be well, indeed, if this good office were much more freely rendered than the common notions of politeness at present permit, and if one person could honestly point out to another that he thinks him in fault, without being considered unmannerly or presuming. We have a right, also, in various ways, to act upon our unfavourable opinion of any one, not to the oppression of his individuality, but in the exercise of ours. We are not bound, for example, to seek his society; we have a right to avoid it (though not to parade the avoidance), for we have a right to choose the society most acceptable to us. We have a right, and it may be our duty, to caution others against him, if we think his example or conversation likely to have a pernicious effect on those with whom he associates. We may give others a preference over him in optional good offices, except those which tend to his improvement. In these various modes a person may suffer very severe penalties at the hands of others for faults which directly concern only himself; but he suffers these penalties only in so far as they are the natural, and, as it were, the spontaneous consequences of the faults themselves, not because they are purposely inflicted on him for the sake of punishment. A person who shows rashness, obstinacy, self-conceit — who cannot live within moderate means — who cannot restrain himself from hurtful indulgences — who pursues animal pleasures at the expense of those of feeling and intellect — must expect to be lowered in the opinion of others, and to have a less share of their favourable sentiments; but of this he has no right to complain, unless he has merited their favour by special excellence in his social relations, and has thus established a title to their good offices, which is not affected by his demerits towards himself.

What I contend for is, that the inconveniences which are strictly inseparable from the unfavourable judgment of others, are the only ones to which a person should ever be subjected for that portion of his conduct and character which concerns his own good, but which does not affect the interest of others in their relations with him. Acts injurious to others require a totally different treatment. Encroachment on their rights; infliction on them of any loss or damage not justified by his own rights; falsehood or duplicity in dealing with them; unfair or ungenerous use of advantages over them; even selfish abstinence from defending them against injury — these are fit objects of moral reprobation, and, in grave cases, of moral retribution and punishment. And not only these acts, but the dispositions which lead to them, are properly immoral, and fit subjects of disapprobation which may rise to abhorrence. Cruelty of disposition; malice and ill-nature; that most anti-social and odious of all passions, envy; dissimulation and insincerity, irascibility on insufficient cause, and resentment disproportioned to the provocation; the love of domineering over others; the desire to engross more than one's share of advantages (the πλεονεξια[3] of the Greeks), the pride which derives gratification from the abasement of others; the egotism which thinks self and its concerns more important than everything else, and decides all doubtful questions in its own favour; — these are moral vices, and constitute a bad and odious moral character: unlike the self-regarding faults previously mentioned, which are not properly immoralities, and to whatever pitch they may be carried, do not constitute wickedness. They may be proofs of any amount of folly, or want of personal dignity and self-respect; but they are only a subject of moral reprobation when they involve a breach of duty to others, for whose sake the individual is bound to have care for himself. What are called duties to ourselves are not socially obligatory, unless circumstances render them at the same time duties to others. The term duty to oneself, when it means anything more than prudence, means self-respect or self-development, and for none of these is any one accountable to his fellow creatures, because for none of them is it for the good of mankind that he be held accountable to them.

The distinction between the loss of consideration which a person may rightly incur by defect of prudence or of personal dignity, and the reprobation which is due to him for an offence against the rights of others, is not a merely nominal distinction. It makes a vast difference both in our feelings and in our conduct towards him whether he displeases us in things in which we think we have a right to control him, or in things in which we know that we have not. If he displeases us, we may express our distaste, and we may stand aloof from a person as well as from a thing that displeases us; but we shall not therefore feel called on to make his life uncomfortable. We shall reflect that he already bears, or will bear, the whole penalty of his error; if he spoils his life by mismanagement, we shall not, for that reason, desire to spoil it still further: instead of wishing to punish him, we shall rather endeavour to alleviate his punishment, by showing him how he may avoid or cure the evils his conduct tends to bring upon him. He may be to us an object of pity, perhaps of dislike, but not of anger or resentment; we shall not treat him like an enemy of society: the worst we shall think

3. *Pleonexia*, greed.

ourselves justified in doing is leaving him to himself, if we do not interfere benevolently by showing interest or concern for him. It is far otherwise if he has infringed the rules necessary for the protection of his fellow-creatures, individually or collectively. The evil consequences of his acts do not then fall on himself, but on others; and society, as the protector of all its members, must retaliate on him; must inflict pain on him for the express purpose of punishment, and must take care that it be sufficiently severe. In the one case, he is an offender at our bar, and we are called on not only to sit in judgment on him, but, in one shape or another, to execute our own sentence: in the other case, it is not our part to inflict any suffering on him, except what may incidentally follow from our using the same liberty in the regulation of our own affairs, which we allow to him in his.

The distinction here pointed out between the part of a person's life which concerns only himself, and that which concerns others, many persons will refuse to admit. How (it may be asked) can any part of the conduct of a member of society be a matter of indifference to the other members? No person is an entirely isolated being; it is impossible for a person to do anything seriously or permanently hurtful to himself, without mischief reaching at least to his near connections, and often far beyond them. If he injures his property, he does harm to those who directly or indirectly derived support from it, and usually diminishes, by a greater or less amount, the general resources of the community. If he deteriorates his bodily or mental faculties, he not only brings evil upon all who depended on him for any portion of their happiness, but disqualifies himself for rendering the services which he owes to his fellow-creatures generally; perhaps becomes a burthen on their affection or benevolence; and if such conduct were very frequent, hardly any offence that is committed would detract more from the general sum of good. Finally, if by his vices or follies a person does no direct harm to others, he is nevertheless (it may be said) injurious by his example; and ought to be compelled to control himself, for the sake of those whom the sight or knowledge of his conduct might corrupt or mislead.

And even (it will be added) if the consequences of misconduct could be confined to the vicious or thoughtless individual, ought society to abandon to their own guidance those who are manifestly unfit for it? If protection against themselves is confessedly due to children and persons under age, is not society equally bound to afford it to persons of mature years who are equally incapable of self-government? If gambling, or drunkenness, or incontinence, or idleness, or uncleanliness, are as injurious to happiness, and as great a hindrance to improvement, as many or most of the acts prohibited by law, why (it may be asked) should not law, so far as is consistent with practicability and social convenience, endeavour to repress these also? And as a supplement to the unavoidable imperfections of law, ought not opinion at least to organise a powerful police against these vices, and visit rigidly with social penalties those who are known to practise them? There is no question here (it may be said) about restricting individuality, or impeding the trial of new and original experiments in living. The only things it is sought to prevent are things which have been tried and condemned from the beginning of the world until now; things which experience has shown not to be useful or suitable to any person's individuality. There must be some length of time and amount of experience after which a moral or prudential truth may be regarded as established: and it is merely desired to prevent generation after generation from falling over the same precipice which has been fatal to their predecessors.

I fully admit that the mischief which a person does to himself may seriously affect, both through their sympathies and their interests, those nearly connected with him and, in a minor degree, society at large. When, by conduct of this sort, a person is led to violate a distinct and assignable obligation to any other person or persons, the case is taken out of the self-regarding class, and becomes amenable to moral disapprobation in the proper sense of the term. If, for example, a man, through intemperance or extravagance, becomes unable to pay his debts, or, having undertaken the moral responsibility of a family, becomes from the same cause incapable of supporting or educating them, he is deservedly reprobated, and might be justly punished; but it is for the breach of duty to his family or creditors, not for the extravagance. If the resources which ought to have been devoted to them, had been diverted from them for the most prudent investment, the moral culpability would have been the same. George Barnwell[4] murdered his uncle to get money for his mistress, but if he had done it to set himself up in business, he would equally have been hanged. Again, in the frequent case of a man who causes grief to his family by addiction to bad habits, he deserves reproach for his unkindness or ingratitude; but so he may for cultivating habits not in themselves vicious, if they are painful to those with whom he passes his life, or who from personal ties are dependent on him for their comfort. Whoever fails in the consideration generally due to the interests and feelings of others, not being compelled by some more imperative duty, or justified by allowable self-preference, is a subject of moral disapprobation for that failure, but not for the cause of it, nor for the errors, merely personal to himself, which may have remotely led to it. In like manner, when a person disables himself, by conduct purely self-regarding, from the performance of some definite duty incumbent on him to the public, he is guilty of a social offence. No person ought to be punished simply for being drunk; but a soldier or a policeman should be punished for being drunk on duty. Whenever, in short, there is a definite damage, or a definite risk

4. The protagonist of a popular ballad of the early eighteenth century.

of damage, either to an individual or to the public, the case is taken out of the province of liberty, and placed in that of morality or law.

But with regard to the merely contingent, or, as it may be called, constructive injury which a person causes to society, by conduct which neither violates any specific duty to the public, nor occasions perceptible hurt to any assignable individual except himself; the inconvenience is one which society can afford to bear, for the sake of the greater good of human freedom. If grown persons are to be punished for not taking proper care of themselves, I would rather it were for their own sake, than under pretence of preventing them from imparing their capacity of rendering to society benefits which society does not pretend it has a right to exact. But I cannot consent to argue the point as if society had no means of bringing its weaker members up to its ordinary standard of rational conduct, except waiting till they do something irrational, and then punishing them, legally or morally, for it. Society has had absolute power over them during all the early portion of their existence: it has had the whole period of childhood and nonage in which to try whether it could make them capable of rational conduct in life. The existing generation is master both of the training and the entire circumstances of the generation to come; it cannot indeed make them perfectly wise and good, because it is itself so lamentably deficient in goodness and wisdom; and its best efforts are not always, in individual cases, its most successful ones; but it is perfectly well able to make the rising generation, as a whole, as good as, and a little better than, itself. If society lets any considerable number of its members grow up mere children, incapable of being acted on by rational consideration of distant motives, society has itself to blame for the consequences. Armed not only with all the powers of education, but with the ascendancy which the authority of a received opinion always exercises over the minds who are least fitted to judge for themselves; and aided by the *natural* penalties which cannot be prevented from falling on those who incur the distaste or the contempt of those who know them; let not society pretend that it needs, besides all this, the power to issue commands and enforce obedience in the personal concerns of individuals, in which, on all principles of justice and policy, the decision ought to rest with those who are to abide the consequences. Nor is there anything which tends more to discredit and frustrate the better means of influencing conduct than a resort to the worse. If there be among those whom it is attempted to coerce into prudence or temperance any of the material of which vigorous and independent characters are made, they will infallibly rebel against the yoke. No such person will ever feel that others have a right to control him in his concerns, such as they have to prevent him from injuring them in theirs; and it easily comes to be considered a mark of spirit and courage to fly in the face of such usurped authority, and do with ostentation the exact opposite of what it enjoins; as in the fashion of grossness which succeeded, in the time of Charles II.,[5] to the fanatical moral intolerance of the Puritans. With respect to what is said of the necessity of protecting society from the bad example set to others by the vicious or the self-indulgent; it is true that bad example may have a pernicious effect, especially the example of doing wrong to others with impunity to the wrong-doer. But we are now speaking of conduct which, while it does no wrong to others, is supposed to do great harm to the agent himself: and I do not see how those who believe this can think otherwise than that the example, on the whole, must be more salutary than hurtful, since, if it displays the misconduct, it displays also the painful or degrading consequences which, if the conduct is justly censured, must be supposed to be in all or most cases attendant on it.

But the strongest of all the arguments against the interference of the public with purely personal conduct is that, when it does interfere, the odds are that it interferes wrongly, and in the wrong place. On questions of social morality, of duty to others, the opinion of the public, that is, of an overruling majority, though often wrong, is likely to be still oftener right; because on such questions they are only required to judge of their own interests; of the manner in which some mode of conduct, if allowed to be practised, would affect themselves. But the opinion of a similar majority, imposed as a law on the minority, on questions of self-regarding conduct, is quite as likely to be wrong as right; for in these cases public opinion means, at the best, some people's opinion of what is good or bad for other people; while very often it does not even mean that; the public, with the most perfect indifference, passing over the pleasure or convenience of those whose conduct they censure, and considering only their own preference. There are many who consider as an injury to themselves any conduct which they have a distaste for, and resent it as an outrage to their feelings; as a religious bigot, when charged with disregarding the religious feelings of others, has been known to retort that they disregard his feelings, by persisting in their abominable worship or creed. But there is no parity between the feeling of a person for his own opinion, and the feeling of another who is offended at his holding it; no more than between the desire of a thief to take a purse, and the desire of the right owner to keep it. And a person's taste is as much his own peculiar concern as his opinion or his purse. It is easy for any one to imagine an ideal public which leaves the freedom and choice of individuals in all uncertain matters undisturbed, and only requires them to abstain from modes of conduct which universal experience has condemned. But where has there been seen a public which set any such limit to its censorship? or when does the public trouble itself about universal experience? In its interferences with

5. King of England (1660–85), famous for his mistresses.

personal conduct it is seldom thinking of anything but the enormity of acting or feeling differently from itself; and this standard of judgment, thinly disguised, is held up to mankind as the dictate of religion and philosophy, by nine-tenths of all moralists and speculative writers. These teach that things are right because they are right; because we feel them to be so. They tell us to search in our own minds and hearts for laws of conduct binding on ourselves and on all others. What can the poor public do but apply these instructions, and make their own personal feelings of good and evil, if they are tolerably unanimous in them, obligatory on all the world?

The evil here pointed out is not one which exists only in theory; and it may perhaps be expected that I should specify the instances in which the public of this age and country improperly invests its own prefer-ences with the character of moral laws. I am not writing an essay on the aberrations of existing moral feeling. That is too weighty a subject to be discussed parenthetically, and by way of illustration. Yet examples are necessary to show that the principle I maintain is of serious and practical moment, and that I am not endeavouring to erect a barrier against imaginary evils. And it is not difficult to show, by abundant instances, that to extend the bounds of what may be called moral police, until it encroaches on the most unquestionably legitimate liberty of the individual, is one of the most universal of all human propensities.

As a first instance, consider the antipathies which men cherish on no better grounds than that persons whose religious opinions are dif-ferent from theirs do not practise their religious observances, especially their religious abstinences. To cite a rather trivial example, nothing in the creed or practice of Christians does more to envenom the hatred of Mahomedans against them than the fact of their eating pork. There are few acts which Christians and Europeans regard with more unaf-fected disgust than Mussulmans[6] regard this particular mode of satis-fying hunger. It is, in the first place, an offence against their religion; but this circumstance by no means explains either the degree or the kind of their repugnance; for wine also is forbidden by their religion, and to partake of it is by all Mussulmans accounted wrong, but not disgusting. Their aversion to the flesh of the "unclean beast" is, on the contrary, of that peculiar character, resembling an instinctive antipathy, which the idea of uncleanness, when once it thoroughly sinks into the feelings, seems always to excite even in those whose personal habits are anything but scrupulously cleanly, and of which the sentiment of reli-gious impurity, so intense in the Hindoos, is a remarkable example. Suppose now that in a people, of whom the majority were Mussulmans, that majority should insist upon not permitting pork to be eaten within the limits of the country. This would be nothing new in Mahomedan

6. Muslims.

countries.[7] Would it be a legitimate exercise of the moral authority of
public opinion? and if not, why not? The practice is really revolting to
such a public. They also sincerely think that it is forbidden and ab-
horred by the Deity. Neither could the prohibition be censured as religious persecution. It might be religious in its origin, but it would not
be persecution for religion, since nobody's religion makes it a duty to
eat pork. The only tenable ground of condemnation would be that with
the personal tastes and self-regarding concerns of individuals the public
has no business to interfere.

To come somewhat nearer home: the majority of Spaniards consider
it a gross impiety, offensive in the highest degree to the Supreme Being,
to worship him in any other manner than the Roman Catholic; and
no other public worship is lawful on Spanish soil. The people of all
Southern Europe look upon a married clergy as not only irreligious,
but unchaste, indecent, gross, disgusting. What do Protestants think of
these perfectly sincere feelings, and of the attempt to enforce them
against non-Catholics? Yet, if mankind are justified in interfering with
each other's liberty in things which do not concern the interests of
others, on what principle is it possible consistently to exclude these
cases? or who can blame people for desiring to suppress what they
regard as a scandal in the sight of God and man? No stronger case can
be shown for prohibiting anything which is regarded as a personal immorality, than is made out for suppressing these practices in the eyes
of those who regard them as impieties; and unless we are willing to
adopt the logic of persecutors, and to say that we may persecute others
because we are right, and that they must not persecute us because they
are wrong, we must beware of admitting a principle of which we should
resent as a gross injustice the application to ourselves.

The preceding instances may be objected to, although unreasonably,
as drawn from contingencies impossible among us: opinion, in this
country, not being likely to enforce abstinence from meats, or to interfere with people for worshipping, and for either marrying or not marrying, according to their creed or inclination. The next example,
however, shall be taken from an interference with liberty which we
have by no means passed all danger of. Wherever the Puritans have
been sufficiently powerful, as in New England, and in Great Britain at
the time of the Commonwealth, they have endeavoured, with considerable success, to put down all public, and nearly all private, amuse-

---

7. The case of the Bombay Parsees is a curious instance in point. When this industrious and
enterprising tribe, the descendants of the Persian fire-worshippers, flying from their native
country before the Caliphs, arrived in Western India, they were admitted to toleration by the
Hindoo sovereigns, on condition of not eating beef. When those regions afterwards fell under
the dominion of Mahomedan conquerors, the Parsees obtained from them a continuance of
indulgence, on condition of refraining from pork. What was at first obedience to authority
became a second nature, and the Parsees to this day abstain both from beef and pork. Though
not required by their religion, the double abstinence has had time to grow into a custom of
their tribe; and custom, in the East, is a religion [Mill's note].

ments: especially music, dancing, public games, or other assemblages
for purposes of diversion, and the theatre. There are still in this country
large bodies of persons by whose notions of morality and religion these
recreations are condemned; and those persons belonging chiefly to the
middle class, who are the ascendant power in the present social and
political condition of the kingdom, it is by no means impossible that
persons of these sentiments may at some time or other command a
majority in Parliament. How will the remaining portion of the community like to have the amusements that shall be permitted to them
regulated by the religious and moral sentiments of the stricter Calvinists
and Methodists?[8] Would they not, with considerable peremptoriness,
desire these intrusively pious members of society to mind their own
business? This is precisely what should be said to every government
and every public, who have the pretension that no person shall enjoy
any pleasure which they think wrong. But if the principle of the pretension be admitted, no one can reasonably object to its being acted
on in the sense of the majority, or other preponderating power in the
country; and all persons must be ready to conform to the idea of a
Christian commonwealth, as understood by the early settlers in New
England, if a religious profession similar to theirs should ever succeed
in regaining its lost ground, as religions supposed to be declining have
so often been known to do.

To imagine another contingency, perhaps more likely to be realised
than the one last mentioned. There is confessedly a strong tendency in
the modern world towards a democratic constitution of society, accompanied or not by popular political institutions. It is affirmed that in the
country where this tendency is most completely realised — where both
society and the government are most democratic — the United States —
the feeling of the majority, to whom any appearance of a more showy
or costly style of living than they can hope to rival is disagreeable,
operates as a tolerably effectual sumptuary law, and that in many parts
of the Union it is really difficult for a person possessing a very large
income to find any mode of spending it which will not incur popular
disapprobation. Though such statements as these are doubtless much
exaggerated as a representation of existing facts, the state of things they
describe is not only a conceivable and possible, but a probable result
of democratic feeling, combined with the notion that the public has a
right to a veto on the manner in which individuals shall spend their
incomes. We have only further to suppose a considerable diffusion of
Socialist opinions, and it may become infamous in the eyes of the
majority to possess more property than some very small amount, or any
income not earned by manual labour. Opinions similar in principle to
these already prevail widely among the artisan class, and weigh oppres-

---

8. Followers of John Wesley (1703–1791), an Anglican preacher who eventually broke with the
   Church of England.

sively on those who are amenable to the opinion chiefly of that class, namely, its own members. It is known that the bad workmen who form the majority of the operatives in many branches of industry, are decidedly of opinion that bad workmen ought to receive the same wages as good, and that no one ought to be allowed, through piecework or otherwise, to earn by superior skill or industry more than others can without it. And they employ a moral police, which occasionally becomes a physical one, to deter skillful workmen from receiving, and employers from giving, a larger remuneration for a more useful service. If the public have any jurisdiction over private concerns, I cannot see that these people are in fault, or that any individuals's particular public can be blamed for asserting the same authority over his individual conduct which the general public asserts over people in general.

But, without dwelling upon supposititious cases, there are, in our own day, gross usurpations upon the liberty of private life actually practised, and still greater ones threatened with some expectation of success, and opinions propounded which assert an unlimited right in the public not only to prohibit by law everything which it thinks wrong, but, in order to get at what it thinks wrong, to prohibit a number of things which it admits to be innocent.

Under the name of preventing intemperance, the people of one English colony, and of nearly half the United States, have been interdicted by law from making any use whatever of fermented drinks, except for medical purposes: for prohibition of their sale is in fact, as it is intended to be, prohibition of their use. And though the impracticability of executing the law has caused its repeal in several of the States which had adopted it, including the one from which it derives its name,[9] an attempt has notwithstanding been commenced, and is prosecuted with considerable zeal by many of the professed philanthropists, to agitate for a similar law in this country. The association, or "Alliance"[1] as it terms itself, which has been formed for this purpose, has acquired some notoriety through the publicity given to a correspondence between its secretary and one of the very few English public men who hold that a politician's opinions ought to be founded on principles. Lord Stanley's[2] share in this correspondence is calculated to strengthen the hopes already built on him, by those who know how rare such qualities as are manifested in some of his public appearances unhappily are among those who figure in political life. The organ of the Alliance, who would "deeply deplore the recognition of any principle which could be wrested to justify bigotry and persecution," undertakes to point out the "broad and impassable barrier" which divides such principles from those of the association. "All matters relating to thought, opinion, con-

9. I.e., the Maine Law, passed in 1815, which imposed Prohibition.
1. The United Kingdom Alliance for the Legislative Suppression of the Sale of Intoxicating Liquors was founded in 1853.
2. Edward Henry Stanley (1826–1893), British statesman.

science, appear to me," he says, "to be without the sphere of legislation; all pertaining to social act, habit, relation, subject only to a discretionary power vested in the State itself, and not in the individual, to be within it." No mention is made of a third class, different from either of these, viz., acts and habits which are not social, but individual; although it is to this class, surely, that the act of drinking fermented liquors belongs. Selling fermented liquors, however, is trading, and trading is a social act. But the infringement complained of is not on the liberty of the seller, but on that of the buyer and consumer; since the State might just as well forbid him to drink wine as purposely make it impossible for him to obtain it. The secretary, however, says, "I claim, as a citizen, a right to legislate whenever my social rights are invaded by the social act of another." And now for the definition of these "social rights." "If anything invades my social rights, certainly the traffic in strong drink does. It destroys my primary right of security, by constantly creating and stimulating social disorder. It invades my right of equality, by deriving a profit from the creation of a misery I am taxed to support. It impedes my right to free moral and intellectual development, by surrounding my path with dangers, and by weakening and demoralising society, from which I have a right to claim mutual aid and intercourse." A theory of "social rights" the like of which probably never before found its way into distinct language: being nothing short of this—that it is the absolute social right of every individual, that every other individual shall act in every respect exactly as he ought; that whosoever fails thereof in the smallest particular violates my social right, and entitles me to demand from the legislature the removal of the grievance. So monstrous a principle is far more dangerous than any single interference with liberty; there is no violation of liberty which it would not justify; it acknowledges no right to any freedom whatever, except perhaps to that of holding opinions in secret, without ever disclosing them: for, the moment an opinion which I consider noxious passes any one's lips, it invades all the "social rights" attributed to me by the Alliance. The doctrine ascribes to all mankind a vested interest in each other's moral, intellectual, and even physical perfection, to be defined by each claimant according to his own standard.

Another important example of illegitimate interference with the rightful liberty of the individual, not simply threatened, but long since carried into triumphant effect, is Sabbatarian legislation. Without doubt, abstinence on one day in the week, so far as the exigencies of life permit, from the usual daily occupation, though in no respect religiously binding on any except Jews, is a highly beneficial custom. And inasmuch as this custom cannot be observed without a general consent to that effect among the industrious classes, therefore, in so far as some persons by working may impose the same necessity on others, it may be allowable and right that the law should guarantee to each the observance by others of the custom, by suspending the greater operations

of industry on a particular day. But this justification, grounded on the
direct interest which others have in each individual's observance of the
practice, does not apply to the self-chosen occupations in which a person may think fit to employ his leisure; nor does it hold good, in the
smallest degree, for legal restrictions on amusements. It is true that the
amusement of some is the day's work of others; but the pleasure, not
to say the useful recreation, of many, is worth the labour of a few,
provided the occupation is freely chosen, and can be freely resigned.
The operatives are perfectly right in thinking that if all worked on Sunday, seven days' work would have to be given for six days' wages; but
so long as the great mass of employments are suspended, the small
number who for the enjoyment of others must still work, obtain a proportional increase of earnings; and they are not obliged to follow those
occupations if they prefer leisure to emolument. If a further remedy is
sought, it might be found in the establishment by custom of a holiday
on some other day of the week for those particular classes of persons.
The only ground, therefore, on which restrictions on Sunday amusements can be defended, must be that they are religiously wrong; a
motive of legislation which can never be too earnestly protested against.
"Deorum injuriæ Diis curiæ."[3] It remains to be proved that society or
any of its officers holds a commission from on high to avenge any
supposed offence to Omnipotence, which is not also a wrong to our
fellow-creatures. The notion that it is one man's duty that another
should be religious, was the foundation of all the religious persecutions
ever perpetrated, and, if admitted, would fully justify them. Though the
feeling which breaks out in the repeated attempts to stop railway travelling on Sunday, in the resistance to the opening of Museums, and
the like, has not the cruelty of the old persecutors, the state of mind
indicated by it is fundamentally the same. It is a determination not to
tolerate others in doing what is permitted by their religion, because it
is not permitted by the persecutor's religion. It is a belief that God not
only abominates the act of the misbeliever, but will not hold us guiltless
if we leave him unmolested.

I cannot refrain from adding to these examples of the little account
commonly made of human liberty, the language of downright persecution which breaks out from the press of this country whenever it feels
called on to notice the remarkable phenomenon of Mormonism.[4]
Much might be said on the unexpected and instructive fact that an
alleged new revelation, and a religion founded on it, the product of
palpable imposture, not even supported by the *prestige* of extraordinary
qualities in its founder, is believed by hundreds of thousands, and has
been made the foundation of a society, in the age of newspapers, rail-

3. Insults to the Gods are the Gods' business (Latin).
4. The creed of the Church of Latter-Day Saints, founded by Joseph Smith (1805–1844). The
   Mormons, led by Brigham Young (1801–1877), fled to the American West to escape persecution, settling in what is now Utah.

ways, and the electric telegraph. What here concerns us is, that this religion, like other and better religions, has its martyrs: that its prophet and founder was, for his teaching, put to death by a mob; that others of its adherents lost their lives by the same lawless violence; that they were forcibly expelled, in a body, from the country in which they first grew up; while, now that they have been chased into a solitary recess in the midst of a desert, many in this country openly declare that it would be right (only that it is not convenient) to send an expedition against them, and compel them by force to conform to the opinions of other people. The article of the Mormonite doctrine which is the chief provocative to the antipathy which thus breaks through the ordinary restraints of religious tolerance, is its sanction of polygamy; which, though permitted to Mahomedans, and Hindoos, and Chinese, seems to excite unquenchable animosity when practised by persons who speak English and profess to be a kind of Christians. No one has a deeper disapprobation than I have of this Mormon institution; both for other reasons, and because, far from being in any way countenanced by the principle of liberty, it is a direct infraction of that principle, being a mere riveting of the chains of one half of the community, and an emancipation of the other from reciprocity of obligation towards them. Still, it must be remembered that this relation is as much voluntary on the part of the women concerned in it, and who may be deemed the sufferers by it, as is the case with any other form of the marriage institution; and however surprising this fact may appear, it has its explanation in the common ideas and customs of the world, which teaching women to think marriage the one thing needful, make it intelligible that many a woman should prefer being one of several wives, to not being a wife at all. Other countries are not asked to recognise such unions, or release any portion of their inhabitants from their own laws on the score of Mormonite opinions. But when the dissentients have conceded to the hostile sentiments of others far more than could justly be demanded; when they have left the countries to which their doctrines were unacceptable, and established themselves in a remote corner of the earth, which they have been the first to render habitable to human beings; it is difficult to see on what principles but those of tyranny they can be prevented from living there under what laws they please, provided they commit no aggression on other nations, and allow perfect freedom of departure to those who are dissatisfied with their ways. A recent writer, in some respects of considerable merit, proposes (to use his own words) not a crusade, but a *civilisade*, against this polygamous community, to put an end to what seems to him a retrograde step in civilisation. It also appears so to me, but I am not aware that any community has a right to force another to be civilised. So long as the sufferers by the bad law do not invoke assistance from other communities, I cannot admit that persons entirely unconnected with them ought to step in and require that a condition of things with which all

who are directly interested appear to be satisfied, should be put an end
to because it is a scandal to persons some thousands of miles distant,
who have no part or concern in it. Let them send missionaries, if they
please, to preach against it; and let them, by any fair means (of which
silencing the teachers is not one), oppose the progress of similar doctrines among their own people. If civilisation has got the better of barbarism when barbarism had the world to itself, it is too much to profess
to be afraid lest barbarism, after having been fairly got under, should
revive and conquer civilisation. A civilisation that can thus succumb to
its vanquished enemy, must first have become so degenerate, that neither its appointed priests and teachers, nor anybody else, has the capacity, or will take the trouble, to stand up for it. If this be so, the
sooner such a civilisation receives notice to quit the better. It can only
go on from bad to worse, until destroyed and regenerated (like the
Western Empire) by energetic barbarians.

Chapter V

APPLICATIONS

The principles asserted in these pages must be more generally admitted as the basis for discussion of details, before a consistent application of them to all the various departments of government and morals
can be attempted with any prospect of advantage. The few observations
I propose to make on questions of detail are designed to illustrate the
principles, rather than to follow them out to their consequences. I offer,
not so much applications, as specimens of application; which may serve
to bring into greater clearness the meaning and limits of the two maxims which together form the entire doctrine of this Essay, and to assist
the judgment in holding the balance between them, in the cases where
it appears doubtful which of them is applicable to the case.

The maxims are, first, that the individual is not accountable to society
for his actions, in so far as these concern the interests of no person but
himself. Advice, instruction, persuasion, and avoidance by other people
if thought necessary by them for their own good, are the only measures
by which society can justifiably express its dislike or disapprobation of
his conduct. Secondly, that for such actions as are prejudicial to the
interests of others, the individual is accountable, and may be subjected
either to social or to legal punishment, if society is of opinion that the
one or the other is requisite for its protection.

In the first place, it must by no means be supposed, because damage,
or probability of damage, to the interests of others, can alone justify the
interference of society, that therefore it always does justify such interference. In many cases, an individual, in pursuing a legitimate object,
necessarily and therefore legitimately causes pain or loss to others, or
intercepts a good which they had a reasonable hope of obtaining. Such

oppositions of interest between individuals often arise from bad social institutions, but are unavoidable while those institutions last; and some would be unavoidable under any institutions. Whoever succeeds in an overcrowded profession, or in a competitive examination; whoever is preferred to another in any contest for an object which both desire, reaps benefit from the loss of others, from their wasted exertion and their disappointment. But it is, by common admission, better for the general interest of mankind, that persons should pursue their objects undeterred by this sort of consequences. In other words, society admits no right, either legal or moral, in the disappointed competitors to immunity from this kind of suffering; and feels called on to interfere, only when means of success have been employed which it is contrary to the general interest to permit — namely, fraud or treachery, and force.

Again, trade is a social act. Whoever undertakes to sell any description of goods to the public, does what affects the interest of other persons, and of society in general; and thus his conduct, in principle, comes within the jurisdiction of society: accordingly, it was once held to be the duty of governments, in all cases which were considered of importance, to fix prices, and regulate the processes of manufacture. But it is now recognised, though not till after a long struggle, that both the cheapness and the good quality of commodities are most effectually provided for by leaving the producers and sellers perfectly free, under the sole check of equal freedom to the buyers for supplying themselves elsewhere. This is the so-called doctrine of Free Trade, which rests on grounds different from, though equally solid with, the principle of individual liberty asserted in this Essay. Restrictions on trade, or on production for purposes of trade, are indeed restraints; and all restraint, *quâ* restraint, is an evil: but the restraints in question affect only that part of conduct which society is competent to restrain, and are wrong solely because they do not really produce the results which it is desired to produce by them. As the principle of individual liberty is not involved in the doctrine of Free Trade, so neither is it in most of the questions which arise respecting the limits of that doctrine; as, for example, what amount of public control is admissible for the prevention of fraud by adulteration; how far sanitary precautions, or arrangements to protect workpeople employed in dangerous occupations, should be enforced on employers. Such questions involve considerations of liberty, only in so far as leaving people to themselves is always better, *cæteris paribus*,[5] than controlling them: but that they may be legitimately controlled for these ends is in principle undeniable. On the other hand, there are questions relating to interference with trade which are essentially questions of liberty; such as the Maine Law, already touched upon; the prohibition of the importation of opium into China; the restriction of the sale of poisons; all cases, in short, where the object of the interfer-

5. Other things equal (Latin).

ence is to make it impossible or difficult to obtain a particular commodity. These interferences are objectionable, not as infringements on
the liberty of the producer or seller, but on that of the buyer.

One of these examples, that of the sale of poisons, opens a new
question; the proper limits of what may be called the functions of police; how far liberty may legitimately be invaded for the prevention of
crime, or of accident. It is one of the undisputed functions of government to take precautions against crime before it has been committed,
as well as to detect and punish it afterwards. The preventive function
of government, however, is far more liable to be abused, to the prejudice of liberty, than the punitory function; for there is hardly any part
of the legitimate freedom of action of a human being which would not
admit of being represented, and fairly too, as increasing the facilities
for some form or other of delinquency. Nevertheless, if a public authority, or even a private person, sees any one evidently preparing to
commit a crime, they are not bound to look on inactive until the crime
is committed, but may interfere to prevent it. If poisons were never
bought or used for any purpose except the commission of murder, it
would be right to prohibit their manufacture and sale. They may, however, be wanted not only for innocent but for useful purposes, and
restrictions cannot be imposed in the one case without operating in the
other. Again, it is a proper office of public authority to guard against
accidents. If either a public officer or any one else saw a person attempting to cross a bridge which had been ascertained to be unsafe,
and there were no time to warn him of his danger, they might seize
him and turn him back, without any real infringement of his liberty;
for liberty consists in doing what one desires, and he does not desire
to fall into the river. Nevertheless, when there is not a certainty, but
only a danger of mischief, no one but the person himself can judge of
the sufficiency of the motive which may prompt him to incur the risk:
in this case, therefore (unless he is a child, or delirious, or in some
state of excitement or absorption incompatible with the full use of the
reflecting faculty), he ought, I conceive, to be only warned of the danger; not forcibly prevented from exposing himself to it. Similar considerations, applied to such a question as the sale of poisons, may enable
us to decide which among the possible modes of regulation are or are
not contrary to principle. Such a precaution, for example, as that of
labelling the drug with some word expressive of its dangerous character,
may be enforced without violation of liberty: the buyer cannot wish not
to know that the thing he possesses has poisonous qualities. But to
require in all cases the certificate of a medical practitioner would make
it sometimes impossible, always expensive, to obtain the article for legitimate uses. The only mode apparent to me, in which difficulties may
be thrown in the way of crime committed through this means, without
any infringement worth taking into account upon the liberty of those
who desire the poisonous substance for other purposes, consists in pro-

viding what, in the apt language of Bentham, is called "pre-appointed evidence." This provision is familiar to every one in the case of contracts. It is usual and right that the law, when a contract is entered into, should require as the condition of its enforcing performance, that certain formalities should be observed, such as signatures, attestation of witnesses, and the like, in order that in case of subsequent dispute there may be evidence to prove that the contract was really entered into, and that there was nothing in the circumstances to render it legally invalid: the effect being to throw great obstacles in the way of fictitious contracts, or contracts made in circumstances which, if known, would destroy their validity. Precautions of a similar nature might be enforced in the sale of articles adapted to be instruments of crime. The seller, for example, might be required to enter in a register the exact time of the transaction, the name and address of the buyer, the precise quality and quantity sold; to ask the purpose for which it was wanted, and record the answer he received. When there was no medical prescription, the presence of some third person might be required to bring home the fact to the purchaser, in case there should afterwards be reason to believe that the article had been applied to criminal purposes. Such regulations would in general be no material impediment to obtaining the article, but a very considerable one to making an improper use of it without detection.

The right inherent in society, to ward off crimes against itself by antecedent precautions, suggests the obvious limitations to the maxim, that purely self-regarding misconduct cannot properly be meddled with in the way of prevention or punishment. Drunkenness, for example, in ordinary cases, is not a fit subject for legislative interference; but I should deem it perfectly legitimate that a person, who had once been convicted of any act of violence to others under the influence of drink, should be placed under a special legal restriction, personal to himself; that if he were afterwards found drunk, he should be liable to a penalty, and that if when in that state he committed another offence, the punishment to which he would be liable for that other offence should be increased in severity. The making himself drunk, in a person whom drunkenness excites to do harm to others, is a crime against others. So, again, idleness, except in a person receiving support from the public, or except when it constitutes a breach of contract, cannot without tyranny be made a subject of legal punishment; but if, either from idleness or from any other avoidable cause, a man fails to perform his legal duties to others, as for instance to support his children, it is no tyranny to force him to fulfil that obligation, by compulsory labour, if no other means are available.

Again, there are many acts which, being directly injurious only to the agents themselves, ought not to be legally interdicted, but which, if done publicly, are a violation of good manners, and coming thus within the category of offences against others, may rightly be prohibited.

Of this kind are offences against decency; on which it is unnecessary to dwell, the rather as they are only connected indirectly with our subject, the objection to publicity being equally strong in the case of many actions not in themselves condemnable, nor supposed to be so.

There is another question to which an answer must be found, consistent with the principles which have been laid down. In cases of personal conduct supposed to be blameable, but which respect for liberty precludes society from preventing or punishing, because the evil directly resulting falls wholly on the agent; what the agent is free to do, ought other persons to be equally free to counsel or instigate? This question is not free from difficulty. The case of a person who solicits another to do an act is not strictly a case of self-regarding conduct. To give advice or offer inducements to any one is a social act, and may, therefore, like actions in general which affect others, be supposed amenable to social control. But a little reflection corrects the first impression, by showing that if the case is not strictly within the definition of individual liberty, yet the reasons on which the principle of individual liberty is grounded are applicable to it. If people must be allowed, in whatever concerns only themselves, to act as seems best to themselves, at their own peril, they must equally be free to consult with one another about what is fit to be so done; to exchange opinions, and give and receive suggestions. Whatever it is permitted to do, it must be permitted to advise to do. The question is doubtful only when the instigator derives a personal benefit from his advice; when he makes it his occupation, for subsistence or pecuniary gain, to promote what society and the State consider to be an evil. Then, indeed, a new element of complication is introduced; namely, the existence of classes of persons with an interest opposed to what is considered as the public weal, and whose mode of living is grounded on the counteraction of it. Ought this to be interfered with, or not? Fornication, for example, must be tolerated, and so must gambling; but should a person be free to be a pimp, or to keep a gambling-house? The case is one of those which lie on the exact boundary line between two principles, and it is not at once apparent to which of the two it properly belongs. There are arguments on both sides. On the side of toleration it may be said that the fact of following anything as an occupation, and living or profiting by the practice of it, cannot make that criminal which would otherwise be admissible; that the act should either be consistently permitted or consistently prohibited; that if the principles which we have hitherto defended are true, society has no business, *as* society, to decide anything to be wrong which concerns only the individual; that it cannot go beyond dissuasion, and that one person should be as free to persuade as another to dissuade. In opposition to this it may be contended, that although the public, or the State, are not warranted in authoritatively deciding, for purposes of repression or punishment, that such or such conduct affecting only the interests of the individual is good or bad, they are fully justified in assuming, if they regard it as bad, that its being so or not is at least a disputable question: That, this being supposed, they cannot be acting wrongly in endeavouring to exclude the influence of solicitations which are not disinterested, of instigators who cannot possibly be impartial—who have a direct personal interest on one side, and that side the one which the State believes to be wrong, and who confessedly promote it for personal objects only. There can surely, it may be urged, be nothing lost, no sacrifice of good, by so ordering matters that persons shall make their election, either wisely or foolishly, on their own prompting, as free as possible from the arts of persons who stimulate their inclinations for interested purposes of their own. Thus (it may be said) though the statutes respecting unlawful games are utterly indefensible—though all persons should be free to gamble in their own or each other's houses, or in any place of meeting established by their own subscriptions, and open only to the members and their visitors—yet public gambling-houses should not be permitted. It is true that the prohibition is never effectual, and that whatever amount of tyrannical power may be given to the police, gambling-houses can always be maintained under other pretences; but they may be compelled to conduct their operations with a certain degree of secrecy and mystery, so that nobody knows anything about them but those who seek them; and more than this society ought not to aim at. There is considerable force in these arguments. I will not venture to decide whether they are sufficient to justify the moral anomaly of punishing the accessary, when the principal is (and must be) allowed to go free; of fining or imprisoning the procurer, but not the fornicator—the gambling-house keeper, but not the gambler. Still less ought the common operations of buying and selling to be interfered with on analogous grounds. Almost every article which is bought and sold may be used in excess, and the sellers have a pecuniary interest in encouraging that excess; but no argument can be founded on this, in favour, for instance, of the Maine Law; because the class of dealers in strong drinks, though interested in their abuse, are indispensably required for the sake of their legitimate use. The interest, however, of these dealers in promoting intemperance is a real evil, and justifies the State in imposing restrictions and requiring guarantees which, but for that justification, would be infringements of legitimate liberty.

A further question is, whether the State, while it permits, should nevertheless indirectly discourage conduct which it deems contrary to the best interests of the agent; whether, for example, it should take measures to render the means of drunkenness more costly, or add to the difficulty of procuring them by limiting the number of the places of sale. On this as on most other practical questions, many distinctions require to be made. To tax stimulants for the sole purpose of making them more difficult to be obtained, is a measure differing only in degree from their entire prohibition; and would be justifiable only if that were justifiable. Every increase of cost is a prohibition, to those whose means do not come up to the augmented price; and to those who do, it is a penalty laid on them for gratifying a particular taste. Their choice of pleasures, and their mode of expending their income, after satisfying their legal and moral obligations to the State and to individuals, are their own concern, and must rest with their own judgment. These considerations may seem at first sight to condemn the selection of stimulants as special subjects of taxation for the purposes of revenue. But it must be remembered that taxation for fiscal purposes is absolutely inevitable; that in most countries it is necessary that a considerable part of that taxation should be indirect; that the State, therefore, cannot help imposing penalties, which to some persons may be prohibitory, on the use of some articles of consumption. It is hence the duty of the State to consider, in the imposition of taxes, what commodities the consumers can best spare; and *à fortiori*,[6] to select in preference those of which it deems the use, beyond a very moderate quantity, to be positively injurious. Taxation, therefore, of stimulants, up to the point which produces the largest amount of revenue (supposing that the State needs all the revenue which it yields) is not only admissible, but to be approved of.

The question of making the sale of these commodities a more or less exclusive privilege, must be answered differently, according to the purposes to which the restriction is intended to be subservient. All places of public resort require the restraint of a police, and places of this kind peculiarly, because offences against society are especially apt to originate there. It is, therefore, fit to confine the power of selling these commodities (at least for consumption on the spot) to persons of known or vouched-for respectability of conduct; to make such regulations respecting hours of opening and closing as may be requisite for public surveillance, and to withdraw the licence if breaches of the peace repeatedly take place through the connivance or incapacity of the keeper of the house, or if it becomes a rendezvous for concocting and preparing offences against the law. Any further restriction I do not conceive to be, in principle, justifiable. The limitation in number, for instance, of beer and spirit houses, for the express purpose of rendering them more difficult of access, and diminishing the occasions of temptation, not only exposes all to an inconvenience because there are some by whom the facility would be abused, but is suited only to a state of society in which the labouring classes are avowedly treated as children or savages, and placed under an education of restraint, to fit them for future admission to the privileges of freedom. This is not the principle on which the labouring classes are professedly governed in any free country; and no person who sets due value on freedom will give his adhesion to their being so governed, unless after all efforts have been

6. With even stronger reason (Latin).

exhausted to educate them for freedom and govern them as freemen, and it has been definitively proved that they can only be governed as children. The bare statement of the alternative shows the absurdity of supposing that such efforts have been made in any case which needs be considered here. It is only because the institutions of this country are a mass of inconsistencies, that things find admittance into our practice which belong to the system of despotic, or what is called paternal, government, while the general freedom of our institutions precludes the exercise of the amount of control necessary to render the restraint of any real efficacy as a moral education.

It was pointed out in an early part of this Essay, that the liberty of the individual, in things wherein the individual is alone concerned, implies a corresponding liberty in any number of individuals to regulate by mutual agreement such things as regard them jointly, and regard no persons but themselves. This question presents no difficulty, so long as the will of all the persons implicated remains unaltered; but since that will may change, it is often necessary, even in things in which they alone are concerned, that they should enter into engagements with one another; and when they do, it is fit, as a general rule, that those engagements should be kept. Yet, in the laws, probably, of every country, this general rule has some exceptions. Not only persons are not held to engagements which violate the rights of third parties, but it is sometimes considered a sufficient reason for releasing them from an engagement, that it is injurious to themselves. In this and most other civilised countries, for example, an engagement by which a person should sell himself, or allow himself to be sold, as a slave, would be null and void; neither enforced by law nor by opinion. The ground for thus limiting his power of voluntarily disposing of his own lot in life, is apparent, and is very clearly seen in this extreme case. The reason for not interfering, unless for the sake of others, with a person's voluntary acts, is consideration for his liberty. His voluntary choice is evidence that what he so chooses is desirable, or at least endurable, to him, and his good is on the whole best provided for by allowing him to take his own means of pursuing it. But by selling himself for a slave, he abdicates his liberty; he foregoes any future use of it beyond that single act. He therefore defeats, in his own case, the very purpose which is the justification of allowing him to dispose of himself. He is no longer free; but is thenceforth in a position which has no longer the presumption in its favour, that would be afforded by his voluntarily remaining in it. The principle of freedom cannot require that he should be free not to be free. It is not freedom to be allowed to alienate his freedom. These reasons, the force of which is so conspicuous in this peculiar case, are evidently of far wider application; yet a limit is everywhere set to them by the necessities of life, which continually require, not indeed that we should resign our freedom, but that we should consent to this and the other limitation of it. The principle, however, which demands uncontrolled freedom of action in all that concerns only the agents themselves, requires that those who have become bound to one another, in things which concern no third party, should be able to release one another from the engagement: and even without such voluntary release there are perhaps no contracts or engagements, except those that relate to money or money's worth, of which one can venture to say that there ought to be no liberty whatever of retractation. Baron Wilhelm von Humboldt, in the excellent essay from which I have already quoted, states it as his conviction, that engagements which involve personal relations or services should never be legally binding beyond a limited duration of time; and that the most important of these engagements, marriage, having the peculiarity that its objects are frustrated unless the feelings of both the parties are in harmony with it, should require nothing more than the declared will of either party to dissolve it. This subject is too important, and too complicated, to be discussed in a parenthesis, and I touch on it only so far as is necessary for purposes of illustration. If the conciseness and generality of Baron Humboldt's dissertation had not obliged him in this instance to content himself with enunciating his conclusion without discussing the premises, he would doubtless have recognised that the question cannot be decided on grounds so simple as those to which he confines himself. When a person, either by express promise or by conduct, has encouraged another to rely upon his continuing to act in a certain way—to build expectations and calculations, and stake any part of his plan of life upon that supposition—a new series of moral obligations arises on his part towards that person, which may possibly be overruled, but cannot be ignored. And again, if the relation between two contracting parties has been followed by consequences to others; if it has placed third parties in any peculiar position, or, as in the case of marriage, has even called third parties into existence, obligations arise on the part of both the contracting parties towards those third persons, the fulfilment of which, or at all events the mode of fulfilment, must be greatly affected by the continuance or disruption of the relation between the original parties to the contract. It does not follow, nor can I admit, that these obligations extend to requiring the fulfilment of the contract at all costs to the happiness of the reluctant party; but they are a necessary element in the question; and even if, as Von Humboldt maintains, they ought to make no difference in the *legal* freedom of the parties to release themselves from the engagement (and I also hold that they ought not to make *much* difference), they necessarily make a great difference in the *moral* freedom. A person is bound to take all these circumstances into account before resolving on a step which may affect such important interests of others; and if he does not allow proper weight to those interests, he is morally responsible for the wrong. I have made these obvious remarks for the better illustration of the general principle of liberty, and not because they are at all needed on the particular question, which, on the contrary, is usually discussed as if the interest of children was everything, and that of grown persons nothing.

I have already observed that, owing to the absence of any recognised general principles, liberty is often granted where it should be withheld, as well as withheld where it should be granted; and one of the cases in which, in the modern European world, the sentiment of liberty is the strongest, is a case where in my view, it is altogether misplaced. A person should be free to do as he likes in his own concerns; but he ought not to be free to do as he likes in acting for another, under the pretext that the affairs of the other are his own affairs. The State, while it respects the liberty of each in what specially regards himself, is bound to maintain a vigilant control over his exercise of any power which it allows him to possess over others. This obligation is almost entirely disregarded in the case of the family relations, a case, in its direct influence on human happiness, more important than all others taken together. The almost despotic power of husbands over wives needs not be enlarged upon here, because nothing more is needed for the complete removal of the evil than that wives should have the same rights, and should receive the protection of law in the same manner, as all other persons; and because, on this subject, the defenders of established injustice do not avail themselves of the plea of liberty, but stand forth openly as the champions of power. It is in the case of children that misapplied notions of liberty are a real obstacle to the fulfilment by the State of its duties. One would almost think that a man's children were supposed to be literally, and not metaphorically, a part of himself, so jealous is opinion of the smallest interference of law with his absolute and exclusive control over them; more jealous than of almost any interference with his own freedom of action: so much less do the generality of mankind value liberty than power. Consider, for example, the case of education. Is it not almost a self-evident axiom, that the State should require and compel the education, up to a certain standard, of every human being who is born its citizen? Yet who is there that is not afraid to recognise and assert this truth? Hardly any one indeed will deny that it is one of the most sacred duties of the parents (or, as law and usage now stand, the father), after summoning a human being into the world, to give to that being an education fitting him to perform his part well in life towards others and towards himself. But while this is unanimously declared to be the father's duty, scarcely anybody, in this country, will bear to hear of obliging him to perform it. Instead of his being required to make any exertion or sacrifice for securing education to his child, it is left to his choice to accept it or not when it is provided gratis! It still remains unrecognised, that to bring a child into existence without a fair prospect of being able, not only to provide food for its body, but instruction and training for its mind, is a moral crime, both against the unfortunate offspring and against society; and that if the parent does not fulfil this obligation, the State ought to see it fulfilled, at the charge, as far as possible, of the parent.

Were the duty of enforcing universal education once admitted there would be an end to the difficulties about what the State should teach, and how it should teach, which now convert the subject into a mere battlefield for sects and parties, causing the time and labour which should have been spent in educating, to be wasted in quarrelling about education. If the government would make up its mind to require for every child a good education, it might save itself the trouble of providing one. It might leave to parents to obtain the education where and how they pleased, and content itself with helping to pay the school fees of the poorer classes of children, and defraying the entire school expenses of those who have no one else to pay for them. The objections which are urged with reason against State education do not apply to the enforcement of education by the State, but to the State's taking upon itself to direct that education; which is a totally different thing. That the whole or any large part of the education of the people should be in State hands, I go as far as any one in deprecating. All that has been said of the importance of individuality of character, and diversity in opinions and modes of conduct, involves, as of the same unspeakable importance, diversity of education. A general State education is a mere contrivance for moulding people to be exactly like one another: and as the mould in which it casts them is that which pleases the predominant power in the government, whether this be a monarch, a priesthood, an aristocracy, or the majority of the existing generation; in proportion as it is efficient and successful, it establishes a despotism over the mind, leading by natural tendency to one over the body. An education established and controlled by the State should only exist, if it exist at all, as one among many competing experiments, carried on for the purpose of example and stimulus, to keep the others up to a certain standard of excellence. Unless, indeed, when society in general is in so backward a state that it could not or would not provide for itself any proper institutions of education unless the government undertook the task: then, indeed, the government may, as the less of two great evils, take upon itself the business of schools and universities, as it may that of joint stock companies, when private enterprise, in a shape fitted for undertaking great works of industry, does not exist in the country. But in general, if the country contains a sufficient number of persons qualified to provide education under government auspices, the same persons would be able and willing to give an equally good education on the voluntary principle, under the assurance of remuneration afforded by a law rendering education compulsory, combined with State aid to those unable to defray the expense.

The instrument for enforcing the law could be no other than public examinations, extending to all children, and beginning at an early age.

An age might be fixed at which every child must be examined, to ascertain if he (or she) is able to read. If a child proves unable, the father, unless he has some sufficient ground of excuse, might be subjected to a moderate fine, to be worked out, if necessary, by his labour, and the child might be put to school at his expense. Once in every year the examination should be renewed, with a gradually extending range of subjects, so as to make the universal acquisition, and what is more, retention, of a certain minimum of general knowledge virtually compulsory. Beyond that minimum there should be voluntary examinations on all subjects, at which all who come up to a certain standard of proficiency might claim a certificate. To prevent the State from exercising, through these arrangements, an improper influence over opinion, the knowledge required for passing an examination (beyond the merely instrumental parts of knowledge, such as languages and their use) should, even in the higher classes of examinations, be confined to facts and positive science exclusively. The examinations on religion, politics, or other disputed topics, should not turn on the truth or falsehood of opinions, but on the matter of fact that such and such an opinion is held, on such grounds, by such authors, or schools, or churches. Under this system, the rising generation would be no worse off in regard to all disputed truths than they are at present; they would be brought up either churchmen or dissenters as they now are, the State merely taking care that they should be instructed churchmen, or instructed dissenters. There would be nothing to hinder them from being taught religion, if their parents chose, at the same schools where they were taught other things. All attempts by the State to bias the conclusions of its citizens on disputed subjects are evil; but it may very properly offer to ascertain and certify that a person possesses the knowledge requisite to make his conclusions, on any given subject, worth attending to. A student of philosophy would be the better for being able to stand an examination both in Locke and in Kant, whichever of the two he takes up with, or even if with neither: and there is no reasonable objection to examining an atheist in the evidences of Christianity, provided he is not required to profess a belief in them. The examinations, however, in the higher branches of knowledge should, I conceive, be entirely voluntary. It would be giving too dangerous a power to governments were they allowed to exclude any one from professions, even from the profession of teacher, for alleged deficiency of qualifications: and I think, with Wilhelm von Humboldt, that degrees, or other public certificates of scientific or professional acquirements, should be given to all who present themselves for examination, and stand the test; but that such certificates should confer no advantage over competitors other than the weight which may be attached to their testimony by public opinion.

It is not in the matter of education only that misplaced notions of liberty prevent moral obligations on the part of parents from being

recognised, and legal obligations from being imposed, where there are
the strongest grounds for the former always, and in many cases for the
latter also. The fact itself, of causing the existence of a human being,
is one of the most responsible actions in the range of human life. To
undertake this responsibility — to bestow a life which may be either a
curse or a blessing — unless the being on whom it is to be bestowed
will have at least the ordinary chances of a desirable existence, is a
crime against that being. And in a country either over-peopled, or
threatened with being so, to produce children, beyond a very small
number, with the effect of reducing the reward of labour by their competition, is a serious offence against all who live by the remuneration
of their labour. The laws which, in many countries on the Continent,
forbid marriage unless the parties can show that they have the means
of supporting a family, do not exceed the legitimate powers of the State:
and whether such laws be expedient or not (a question mainly dependent on local circumstances and feelings), they are not objectionable as violations of liberty. Such laws are interferences of the State
to prohibit a mischievous act — an act injurious to others, which ought
to be a subject of reprobation, and social stigma, even when it is not
deemed expedient to superadd legal punishment. Yet the current ideas
of liberty, which bend so easily to real infringements of the freedom of
the individual in things which concern only himself, would repel the
attempt to put any restraint upon his inclinations when the consequence of their indulgence is a life or lives of wretchedness and depravity to the offspring, with manifold evils to those sufficiently within
reach to be in any way affected by their actions. When we compare
the strange respect of mankind for liberty, with their strange want of
respect for it, we might imagine that a man had an indispensable right
to do harm to others, and no right at all to please himself without giving
pain to any one.

I have reserved for the last place a large class of questions respecting
the limits of government interference, which, though closely connected
with the subject of this Essay, do not, in strictness, belong to it. These
are cases in which the reasons against interference do not turn upon
the principle of liberty: the question is not about restraining the actions
of individuals, but about helping them; it is asked whether the government should do, or cause to be done, something for their benefit, instead of leaving it to be done by themselves, individually or in voluntary
combination.

The objection to government interference, when it is not such as to
involve infringement of liberty, may be of three kinds.

The first is, when the thing to be done is likely to be better done by
individuals than by the government. Speaking generally, there is no
one so fit to conduct any business, or to determine how or by whom
it shall be conducted, as those who are personally interested in it. This
principle condemns the interferences, once so common, of the legis-

lature, or the officers of government, with the ordinary processes of industry. But this part of the subject has been sufficiently enlarged upon by political economists, and is not particularly related to the principles of this Essay.

The second objection is more nearly allied to our subject. In many cases, though individuals may not do the particular thing so well, on the average, as the officers of government, it is nevertheless desirable that it should be done by them, rather than by the government, as a means to their own mental education—a mode of strengthening their active faculties, exercising their judgment, and giving them a familiar knowledge of the subjects with which they are thus left to deal. This is a principal, though not the sole, recommendation of jury trial (in cases not political); of free and popular local and municipal institutions; of the conduct of industrial and philanthropic enterprises by voluntary associations. These are not questions of liberty, and are connected with that subject only by remote tendencies; but they are questions of development. It belongs to a different occasion from the present to dwell on these things as parts of national education; as being, in truth, the peculiar training of a citizen, the practical part of the political education of a free people, taking them out of the narrow circle of personal and family selfishness, and accustoming them to the comprehension of joint interests, the management of joint concerns—habituating them to act from public or semi-public motives, and guide their conduct by aims which unite instead of isolating them from one another. Without these habits and powers, a free constitution can neither be worked nor preserved; as is exemplified by the too-often transitory nature of political freedom in countries where it does not rest upon a sufficient basis of local liberties. The management of purely local business by the localities, and of the great enterprises of industry by the union of those who voluntarily supply the pecuniary means, is further recommended by all the advantages which have been set forth in this Essay as belonging to individuality of development, and diversity of modes of action. Government operations tend to be everywhere alike. With individuals and voluntary associations, on the contrary, there are varied experiments, and endless diversity of experience. What the State can usefully do is to make itself a central depository, and active circulator and diffuser, of the experience resulting from many trials. Its business is to enable each experimentalist to benefit by the experiments of others; instead of tolerating no experiments but its own.

The third and most cogent reason for restricting the interference of government is the great evil of adding unnecessarily to its power. Every function superadded to those already exercised by the government causes its influence over hopes and fears to be more widely diffused, and converts, more and more, the active and ambitious part of the public into hangers-on of the government, or of some party which aims at becoming the government. If the roads, the railways, the banks, the insurance offices, the great joint-stock companies, the universities, and the public charities, were all of them branches of the government; if, in addition, the municipal corporations and local boards, with all that now devolves on them, became departments of the central administration; if the employés of all these different enterprises were appointed and paid by the government, and looked to the government for every rise in life; not all the freeom of the press and popular constitution of the legislature would make this or any other country free otherwise than in name. And the evil would be greater, the more efficiently and scientifically the administrative machinery was constructed — the more skilful the arrangements for obtaining the best qualified hands and heads with which to work it. In England it has of late been proposed that all the members of the civil service of government should be selected by competitive examination, to obtain for these employments the most intelligent and instructed persons procurable; and much has been said and written for and against this proposal. One of the arguments most insisted on by its opponents is that the occupation of a permanent official servant of the State does not hold out sufficient prospects of emolument and importance to attract the highest talents, which will always be able to find a more inviting career in the professions, or in the service of companies and other public bodies. One would not have been surprised if this argument had been used by the friends of the proposition, as an answer to its principal difficulty. Coming from the opponents it is strange enough. What is urged as an objection is the safety-valve of the proposed system. If indeed all the high talent of the country *could* be drawn into the service of the government, a proposal tending to bring about that result might well inspire uneasiness. If every part of the business of society which required organised concert, or large and comprehensive views, were in the hands of the government, and if government offices were universally filled by the ablest men, all the enlarged culture and practised intelligence in the country, except the purely speculative, would be concentrated in a numerous bureaucracy, to whom alone the rest of the community would look for all things: the multitude for direction and dictation in all they had to do; the able and aspiring for personal advancement. To be admitted into the ranks of this bureaucracy, and when admitted, to rise therein, would be the sole objects of ambition. Under this régime, not only is the outside public ill-qualified, for want of practical experience, to criticise or check the mode of operation of the bureaucracy, but even if the accidents of despotic or the natural working of popular institutions occasionally raise to the summit a ruler or rulers of reforming inclinations, no reform can be effected which is contrary to the interest of the bureaucracy. Such is the melancholy condition of the Russian empire, as shown in the accounts of those who have had sufficient opportunity of observation. The Czar himself is powerless against the bureaucratic body; he can send any one of them to Siberia, but he cannot govern without them, or against their will. On every decree of his they have a tacit veto, by merely refraining from carrying it into effect. In countries of more advanced civilisation and of a more insurrectionary spirit, the public, accustomed to expect everything to be done for them by the State, or at least to do nothing for themselves without asking from the State not only leave to do it, but even how it is to be done, naturally hold the State responsible for all evil which befalls them, and when the evil exceeds their amount of patience, they rise against the government, and make what is called a revolution; whereupon somebody else, with or without legitimate authority from the nation, vaults into the seat, issues his orders to the bureaucracy, and everything goes on much as it did before; the bureaucracy being unchanged, and nobody else being capable of taking their place.

A very different spectacle is exhibited among a people accustomed to transact their own business. In France, a large part of the people, having been engaged in military service, many of whom have held at least the rank of non-commissioned officers, there are in every popular insurrection several persons competent to take the lead, and improvise some tolerable plan of action. What the French are in military affairs, the Americans are in every kind of civil business; let them be left without a government, every body of Americans is able to improvise one, and to carry on that or any other public business with a sufficient amount of intelligence, order, and decision. This is what every free people ought to be: and a people capable of this is certain to be free; it will never let itself be enslaved by any man or body of men because these are able to seize and pull the reins of the central administration. No bureaucracy can hope to make such a people as this do or undergo anything that they do not like. But where everything is done through the bureaucracy, nothing to which the bureaucracy is really adverse can be done at all. The constitution of such countries is an organisation of the experience and practical ability of the nation into a disciplined body for the purpose of governing the rest; and the more perfect that organisation is in itself, the more successful in drawing to itself and educating for itself the persons of greatest capacity from all ranks of the community, the more complete is the bondage of all, the members of the bureaucracy included. For the governors are as much the slaves of their organisation and discipline as the governed are of the governors. A Chinese mandarin is as much the tool and creature of a despotism as the humblest cultivator. An individual Jesuit is to the utmost degree of abasement the slave of his order, though the order itself exists for the collective power and importance of its members.

It is not, also, to be forgotten, that the absorption of all the principal ability of the country into the governing body is fatal, sooner or later, to the mental activity and progressiveness of the body itself. Banded together as they are — working a system which, like all systems, necessarily proceeds in a great measure by fixed rules — the official body are under the constant temptation of sinking into indolent routine, or, if they now and then desert that mill-horse round, of rushing into some half-examined crudity which has struck the fancy of some leading member of the corps; and the sole check to these closely allied, though seemingly opposite, tendencies, the only stimulus which can keep the ability of the body itself up to a high standard, is liability to the watchful criticism of equal ability outside the body. It is indispensable, therefore, that the means should exist, independently of the government, of forming such ability, and furnishing it with the opportunities and experience necessary for a correct judgment of great practical affairs. If we would possess permanently a skilful and efficient body of functionaries — above all, a body able to originate and willing to adopt improvements; if we would not have our bureaucracy degenerate into a pedantocracy, this body must not engross all the occupations which form and cultivate the faculties required for the government of mankind.

To determine the point at which evils, so formidable to human freedom and advancement, begin, or rather at which they begin to predominate over the benefits attending the collective application of the force of society, under its recognised chiefs, for the removal of the obstacles which stand in the way of its well-being; to secure as much of the advantages of centralised power and intelligence as can be had without turning into governmental channels too great a proportion of the general activity — is one of the most difficult and complicated questions in the art of government. It is, in a great measure, a question of detail, in which many and various considerations must be kept in view, and no absolute rule can be laid down. But I believe that the practical principle in which safety resides, the ideal to be kept in view, the standard by which to test all arrangements intended for overcoming the difficulty, may be conveyed in these words: the greatest dissemination of power consistent with efficiency; but the greatest possible centralisation of information, and diffusion of it from the centre. Thus, in municipal administration, there would be, as in the New England States, a very minute division among separate officers, chosen by the localities, of all business which is not better left to the persons directly interested; but besides this, there would be, in each department of local affairs, a central superintendence, forming a branch of the general government. The organ of this superintendence would concentrate, as in a focus, the variety of information and experience derived from the conduct of that branch of public business in all the localities, from everything analogous which is done in foreign countries, and from the general principles of political science. This central organ should have a right to know all that is done, and its special duty should be that of making the knowledge acquired in one place available for others. Emancipated from the petty prejudices and narrow views of a locality by its elevated position and comprehensive sphere of observation, its advice would naturally carry much authority; but its actual power, as a permanent

institution, should, I conceive, be limited to compelling the local officers to obey the laws laid down for their guidance. In all things not
provided for by general rules, those officers should be left to their own
judgment, under responsibility to their constituents. For the violation
of rules, they should be responsible to law, and the rules themselves
should be laid down by the legislature; the central administrative authority only watching over their execution, and if they were not properly
carried into effect, appealing, according to the nature of the case, to
the tribunals to enforce the law, or to the constituencies to dismiss the
functionaries who had not executed it according to its spirit. Such, in
its general conception, is the central superintendence which the Poor
Law Board[7] is intended to exercise over the administrators of the Poor
Rate throughout the country. Whatever powers the Board exercises beyond this limit, were right and necessary in that peculiar case, for the
cure of rooted habits of maladministration in matters deeply affecting
not the localities merely, but the whole community; since no locality
has a moral right to make itself by mismanagement a nest of pauperism,
necessarily overflowing into other localities, and impairing the moral
and physical condition of the whole labouring community. The powers
of administrative coercion and subordinate legislation possessed by the
Poor Law Board (but which, owing to the state of opinion on the subject, are very scantily exercised by them), though perfectly justifiable in
a case of first-rate national interest, would be wholly out of place in the
superintendence of interests purely local. But a central organ of information and instruction for all the localities, would be equally valuable
in all departments of administration. A government cannot have too
much of the kind of activity which does not impede, but aids and
stimulates, individual exertion and development. The mischief begins
when, instead of calling forth the activity and powers of individuals and
bodies, it substitutes its own activity for theirs; when, instead of inform-
ing, advising, and, upon occasion, denouncing, it makes them work in
fetters, or bids them stand aside and does their work instead of them.
The worth of a State, in the long run, is the worth of the individuals
composing it; and a State which postpones the interests of *their* mental
expansion and elevation, to a little more of administrative skill, or of
that semblance of it which practice gives, in the details of business; a
State which dwarfs its men, in order that they may be more docile
instruments in its hands even for beneficial purposes — will find that
with small men no great thing can really be accomplished; and that
the perfection of machinery to which it has sacrificed everything, will
in the end avail it nothing, for want of the vital power which, in order
that the machine might work more smoothly, it has preferred to banish.

---

7. The board was the agency that supervised the administration of the Poor Law of 1834.

The Subjection of Women

1

The object of this Essay is to explain as clearly as I am able, the grounds of an opinion which I have held from the very earliest period when I had formed any opinions at all on social or political matters, and which, instead of being weakened or modified, has been constantly growing stronger by the progress of reflection and the experience of life: That the principle which regulates the existing social relations between the two sexes — the legal subordination of one sex to the other — is wrong in itself, and now one of the chief hindrances to human improvement; and that it ought to be replaced by a principle of perfect equality, admitting no power or privilege on the one side, nor disability on the other.

The very words necessary to express the task I have undertaken, show how arduous it is. But it would be a mistake to suppose that the difficulty of the case must lie in the insufficiency or obscurity of the grounds of reason on which my conviction rests. The difficulty is that which exists in all cases in which there is a mass of feeling to be contended against. So long as an opinion is strongly rooted in the feelings, it gains rather than loses in stability by having a preponderating weight of argument against it. For if it were accepted as a result of argument, the refutation of the argument might shake the solidity of the conviction; but when it rests solely on feeling, the worse it fares in argumentative contest, the more persuaded its adherents are that their feeling must have some deeper ground, which the arguments do not reach; and while the feeling remains, it is always throwing up fresh intrenchments of argument to repair any breach made in the old. And there are so many causes tending to make the feelings connected with this subject the most intense and most deeply-rooted of all those which gather round and protect old institutions and customs, that we need not wonder to find them as yet less undermined and loosened than any of the rest by the progress of the great modern spiritual and social transition; nor suppose that the barbarisms to which men cling longest must be less barbarisms than those which they earlier shake off.

In every respect the burthen is hard on those who attack an almost universal opinion. They must be very fortunate as well as unusually capable if they obtain a hearing at all. They have more difficulty in obtaining a trial, than any other litigants have in getting a verdict. If they do extort a hearing, they are subjected to a set of logical requirements totally different from those exacted from other people. In all other cases, the burthen of proof is supposed to lie with the affirmative.

If a person is charged with a murder, it rests with those who accuse him to give proof of his guilt, not with himself to prove his innocence. If there is a difference of opinion about the reality of any alleged historical event, in which the feelings of men in general are not much interested, as the Siege of Troy for example, those who maintain that the event took place are expected to produce their proofs, before those who take the other side can be required to say anything; and at no time are these required to do more than show that the evidence produced by the others is of no value. Again, in practical matters, the burthen of proof is supposed to be with those who are against liberty; who contend for any restriction or prohibition; either any limitation of the general freedom of human action, or any disqualification or disparity of privilege affecting one person or kind of persons, as compared with others. The *a priori* presumption is in favor of freedom and impartiality. It is held that there should be no restraint not required by the general good, and that the law should be no respecter of persons, but should treat all alike, save where dissimilarity of treatment is required by positive reasons, either of justice or of policy. But of none of these rules of evidence will the benefit be allowed to those who maintain the opinion I profess. It is useless for me to say that those who maintain the doctrine that men have a right to command and women are under an obligation to obey, or that men are fit for government and women unfit, are on the affirmative side of the question, and that they are bound to show positive evidence for the assertions, or submit to their rejection. It is equally unavailing for me to say that those who deny to women any freedom or privilege rightly allowed to men, having the double presumption against them that they are opposing freedom and recommending partiality, must be held to the strictest proof of their case, and unless their success be such as to exclude all doubt, the judgment ought to go against them. These would be thought good pleas in any common case; but they will not be thought so in this instance. Before I could hope to make any impression, I should be expected not only to answer all that has ever been said by those who take the other side of the question, but to imagine all that could be said by them — to find them in reasons, as well as answer all I find: and besides refuting all arguments for the affirmative, I shall be called upon for invincible positive arguments to prove a negative. And even if I could do all this, and leave the opposite party with a host of unanswered arguments against them, and not a single unrefuted one on their side, I should be thought to have done little; for a cause supported on the one hand by universal usage, and on the other by so great a preponderance of popular sentiment, is supposed to have a presumption in its favor, superior to any conviction which an appeal to reason has power to produce in any intellects but those of a high class.

I do not mention these difficulties to complain of them; first, because it would be useless; they are inseparable from having to contend

through people's understandings against the hostility of their feelings
and practical tendencies: and truly the understandings of the majority
of mankind would need to be much better cultivated than has ever yet
been the case, before they can be asked to place such reliance in their
own power of estimating arguments, as to give up practical principles
in which they have been born and bred and which are the basis of
much of the existing order of the world, at the first argumentative attack
which they are not capable of logically resisting. I do not therefore
quarrel with them for having too little faith in argument, but for having
too much faith in custom and the general feeling. It is one of the
characteristic prejudices of the reaction of the nineteenth century
against the eighteenth, to accord to the unreasoning elements in human
nature the infallibility which the eighteenth century is supposed to have
ascribed to the reasoning elements. For the apotheosis of Reason we
have substituted that of Instinct; and we call everything instinct which
we find in ourselves and for which we cannot trace any rational foundation. This idolatry, infinitely more degrading than the other, and the
most pernicious of the false worships of the present day, of all of which
it is now the main support, will probably hold its ground until it gives
way before a sound psychology, laying bare the real root of much that
is bowed down to as the intention of Nature and the ordinance of God.
As regards the present question, I am willing to accept the unfavorable
conditions which the prejudice assigns to me. I consent that established
custom, and the general feeling, should be deemed conclusive against
me, unless that custom and feeling from age to age can be shown to
have owed their existence to other causes than their soundness, and to
have derived their power from the worse rather than the better parts of
human nature. I am willing that judgment should go against me, unless
I can show that my judge has been tampered with. The concession is
not so great as it might appear; for to prove this, is by far the easiest
portion of my task.

The generality of a practice is in some cases a strong presumption
that it is, or at all events once was, conducive to laudable ends. This
is the case, when the practice was first adopted, or afterwards kept up,
as a means to such ends, and was grounded on experience of the mode
in which they could be most effectually attained. If the authority of
men over women, when first established, had been the result of a
conscientious comparison between different modes of constituting the
government of society; if, after trying various other modes of social
organization — the government of women over men, equality between
the two, and such mixed and divided modes of government as might
be invented — it had been decided, on the testimony of experience, that
the mode in which women are wholly under the rule of men, having
no share at all in public concerns, and each in private being under the
legal obligation of obedience to the man with whom she has associated
her destiny, was the arrangement most conducive to the happiness and

well being of both; its general adoption might then be fairly thought to be some evidence that, at the time when it was adopted, it was the best: though even then the considerations which recommended it may, like so many other primeval social facts of the greatest importance, have subsequently, in the course of ages, ceased to exist. But the state of the case is in every respect the reverse of this. In the first place, the opinion in favor of the present system, which entirely subordinates the weaker sex to the stronger, rests upon theory only; for there never has been trial made of any other: so that experience, in the sense in which it is vulgarly opposed to theory, cannot be pretended to have pronounced any verdict. And in the second place, the adoption of this system of inequality never was the result of deliberation, or forethought, or any social ideas, or any notion whatever of what conduced to the benefit of humanity or the good order of society. It arose simply from the fact that from the very earliest twilight of human society, every woman (owing to the value attached to her by men, combined with her inferiority in muscular strength) was found in a state of bondage to some man. Laws and systems of polity always begin by recognizing the relations they find already existing between individuals. They convert what was a mere physical fact into a legal right, give it the sanction of society, and principally aim at the substitution of public and organized means of asserting and protecting these rights, instead of the irregular and lawless conflict of physical strength. Those who had already been compelled to obedience became in this manner legally bound to it. Slavery, from being a mere affair of force between the master and the slave, became regularized and a matter of compact among the masters, who, binding themselves to one another for common protection, guaranteed by their collective strength the private possessions of each, including his slaves. In early times, the great majority of the male sex were slaves, as well as the whole of the female. And many ages elapsed, some of them ages of high cultivation, before any thinker was bold enough to question the rightfulness, and the absolute social necessity, either of the one slavery or of the other. By degrees such thinkers did arise: and (the general progress of society assisting) the slavery of the male sex has, in all the countries of Christian Europe at least (though, in one of them,[1] only within the last few years) been at length abolished, and that of the female sex has been gradually changed into a milder form of dependence. But this dependence, as it exists at present, is not an original institution, taking a fresh start from considerations of justice and social expediency — it is the primitive state of slavery lasting on, through successive mitigations and modifications occasioned by the same causes which have softened the general manners, and brought all human relations more under the control of justice and the influence of humanity. It has not lost the taint of its brutal origin. No presumption in its favor,

1. Russian serfdom was abolished in 1861 by Emperor Alexander II.

therefore, can be drawn from the fact of its existence. The only such presumption which it could be supposed to have, must be grounded on its having lasted till now, when so many other things which came down from the same odious source have been done away with. And this, indeed, is what makes it strange to ordinary ears, to hear it asserted that the inequality of rights between men and women has no other source than the law of the strongest.

That this statement should have the effect of a paradox, is in some respects creditable to the progress of civilization, and the improvement of the moral sentiments of mankind. We now live—that is to say, one or two of the most advanced nations of the world now live—in a state in which the law of the strongest seems to be entirely abandoned as the regulating principle of the world's affairs: nobody professes it, and, as regards most of the relations between human beings, nobody is permitted to practice it. When any one succeeds in doing so, it is under cover of some pretext which gives him the semblance of having some general social interest on his side. This being the ostensible state of things, people flatter themselves that the rule of mere force is ended; that the law of the strongest cannot be the reason of existence of anything which has remained in full operation down to the present time. However any of our present institutions may have begun, it can only, they think, have been preserved to this period of advanced civilization by a well-grounded feeling of its adaptation to human nature, and conduciveness to the general good. They do not understand the great vitality and durability of institutions which place right on the side of might; how intensely they are clung to; how the good as well as the bad propensities and sentiments of those who have power in their hands, become identified with retaining it; how slowly these bad institutions give way, one at a time, the weakest first, beginning with those which are least interwoven with the daily habits of life; and how very rarely those who have obtained legal power because they first had physical, have ever lost their hold of it until the physical power had passed over to the other side. Such shifting of the physical force not having taken place in the case of women; this fact, combined with all the peculiar and characteristic features of the particular case, made it certain from the first that this branch of the system of right founded on might, though softened in its most atrocious features at an earlier period than several of the others, would be the very last to disappear. It was inevitable that this one case of a social relation grounded on force, would survive through generations of institutions grounded on equal justice, an almost solitary exception to the general character of their laws and customs; but which, so long as it does not proclaim its own origin, and as discussion has not brought out its true character, is not felt to jar with modern civilization, any more than domestic slavery among the Greeks jarred with their notion of themselves as a free people.

The truth is, that people of the present and the last two or three generations have lost all practical sense of the primitive condition of humanity; and only the few who have studied history accurately, or have much frequented the parts of the world occupied by the living representatives of ages long past, are able to form any mental picture of what society then was. People are not aware how entirely, in former ages, the law of superior strength was the rule of life; how publicly and openly it was avowed, I do not say cynically or shamelessly — for these words imply a feeling that there was something in it to be ashamed of, and no such notion could find a place in the faculties of any person in those ages, except a philosopher or a saint. History gives a cruel experience of human nature, in shewing how exactly the regard due to the life, possessions, and entire earthly happiness of any class of persons, was measured by what they had the power of enforcing; how all who made any resistance to authorities that had arms in their hands, however dreadful might be the provocation, had not only the law of force but all other laws, and all the notions of social obligation against them; and in the eyes of those whom they resisted, were not only guilty of crime, but of the worst of all crimes, deserving the most cruel chastisement which human beings could inflict. The first small vestige of a feeling of obligation in a superior to acknowledge any right in inferiors, began when he had been induced, for convenience, to make some promise to them. Though these promises, even when sanctioned by the most solemn oaths, were for many ages revoked or violated on the most trifling provocation or temptation, it is probable that this, except by persons of still worse than the average morality, was seldom done without some twinges of conscience. The ancient republics, being mostly grounded from the first upon some kind of mutual compact, or at any rate formed by an union of persons not very unequal in strength, afforded, in consequence, the first instance of a portion of human relations fenced round, and placed under the dominion of another law than that of force. And though the original law of force remained in full operation between them and their slaves, and also (except so far as limited by express compact) between a commonwealth and its subjects, or other independent commonwealths; the banishment of that primitive law even from so narrow a field, commenced the regeneration of human nature, by giving birth to sentiments of which experience soon demonstrated the immense value even for material interests, and which thenceforward only required to be enlarged, not created. Though slaves were no part of the commonwealth, it was in the free states that slaves were first felt to have rights as human beings. The Stoics[2] were, I believe, the first (except so far as the Jewish law constitutes an exception)

---

2. The most influential movement in classical philosophy, from about 300 B.C. to A.D. 200. They were famous for emphasizing the need for self-control and a complete command of the emotions.

who taught as a part of morality that men were bound by moral obligations to their slaves. No one, after Christianity became ascendant, could ever again have been a stranger to this belief, in theory; nor, after the rise of the Catholic Church, was it ever without persons to stand up for it. Yet to enforce it was the most arduous task which Christianity ever had to perform. For more than a thousand years the Church kept up the contest, with hardly any perceptible success. It was not for want of power over men's minds. Its power was prodigious. It could make kings and nobles resign their most valued possessions to enrich the Church. It could make thousands, in the prime of life and the height of worldly advantages, shut themselves up in convents to work out their salvation by poverty, fasting, and prayer. It could send hundreds of thousands across land and sea, Europe and Asia, to give their lives for the deliverance of the Holy Sepulcher. It could make kings relinquish wives who were the object of their passionate attachment, because the Church declared that they were within the seventh (by our calculation the fourteenth) degree of relationship. All this it did; but it could not make men fight less with one another, nor tyrannize less cruelly over the serfs, and when they were able, over burgesses. It could not make them renounce either of the applications of force; force militant, or force triumphant. This they could never be induced to do until they were themselves in their turn compelled by superior force. Only by the growing power of kings was an end put to fighting except between kings or competitors for kingship; only by the growth of a wealthy and warlike bourgeoisie in the fortified towns, and of a plebeian infantry which proved more powerful in the field than the undisciplined chivalry, was the insolent tyranny of the nobles over the bourgeoisie and peasantry brought within some bounds. It was persisted in not only until, but long after, the oppressed had obtained a power enabling them often to take conspicuous vengeance; and on the Continent much of it continued to the time of the French Revolution, though in England the earlier and better organization of the democratic classes put an end to it sooner, by establishing equal laws and free national institutions.

If people are mostly so little aware how completely, during the greater part of the duration of our species, the law of force was the avowed rule of general conduct, any other being only a special and exceptional consequence of peculiar ties — and from how very recent a date it is that the affairs of society in general have been even pretended to be regulated according to any moral law; as little do people remember or consider, how institutions and customs which never had any ground but the law of force, last on into ages and states of general opinion which never would have permitted their first establishment. Less than forty years ago, Englishmen might still by law hold human beings in bondage as saleable property: within the present century they might kidnap them and carry them off, and work them literally to death.[3] This absolutely extreme case of the law of force, condemned by those who can tolerate almost every other form of arbitrary power, and which, of all others, presents features the most revolting to the feelings of all who look at it from an impartial position, was the law of civilized and Christian England within the memory of persons now living: and in one half of Anglo-Saxon America three or four years ago, not only did slavery exist, but the slave trade, and the breeding of slaves expressly for it, was a general practice between slave states. Yet not only was there a greater strength of sentiment against it, but, in England at least, a less amount either of feeling or of interest in favor of it, than of any other of the customary abuses of force: for its motive was the love of gain, unmixed and undisguised; and those who profited by it were a very small numerical fraction of the country, while the natural feeling of all who were not personally interested in it, was unmitigated abhorrence. So extreme an instance makes it almost superfluous to refer to any other: but consider the long duration of absolute monarchy. In England at present it is the almost universal conviction that military despotism is a case of the law of force, having no other origin or justification. Yet in all the great nations of Europe except England it either still exists, or has only just ceased to exist, and has even now a strong party favorable to it in all ranks of the people, especially among persons of station and consequence. Such is the power of an established system, even when far from universal; when not only in almost every period of history there have been great and well-known examples of the contrary system, but these have almost invariably been afforded by the most illustrious and most prosperous communities. In this case, too, the possessor of the undue power, the person directly interested in it, is only one person, while those who are subject to it and suffer from it are literally all the rest. The yoke is naturally and necessarily humiliating to all persons, except the one who is on the throne, together with, at most, the one who expects to succeed to it. How different are these cases from that of the power of men over women! I am not now prejudging the question of its justifiableness. I am showing how vastly more permanent it could not but be, even if not justifiable, than these other dominations which have nevertheless lasted down to our own time. Whatever gratification of pride there is in the possession of power, and whatever personal interest in its exercise, is in this case not confined to a limited class, but common to the whole male sex. Instead of being, to most of its supporters, a thing desirable chiefly in the abstract, or, like the political ends usually contended for by factious, of little private importance to any but the leaders; it comes home to the person and hearth of every male head of a family, and of every one who looks forward to

---

3. Slavery in the British West Indies was abolished in 1833; the slave trade was abolished in 1807.

being so. The clodhopper exercises, or is to exercise, his share of the power equally with the highest nobleman. And the case is that in which the desire of power is the strongest: for every one who desires power, desires it most over those who are nearest to him, with whom his life is passed, with whom he has most concerns in common, and in whom any independence of his authority is oftenest likely to interfere with his individual preferences. If, in the other cases specified, power manifestly grounded only on force, and having so much less to support them, are so slowly and with so much difficulty got rid of, much more must it be so with this, even if it rests on no better foundation than those. We must consider, too, that the possessors of the power have facilities in this case, greater than in any other, to prevent any uprising against it. Every one of the subjects lives under the very eye, and almost, it may be said, in the hands, of one of the masters—in closer intimacy with him than with any of her fellow-subjects; with no means of combining against him, no power of even locally overmastering him, and, on the other hand, with the strongest motives for seeking his favor and avoiding to give him offence. In struggles for political emancipation, everybody knows how often its champions are bought off by bribes, or daunted by terrors. In the case of women, each individual of the subject-class is in a chronic state of bribery and intimidation combined. In setting up the standard of resistance, a large number of the leaders, and still more of the followers, must make an almost complete sacrifice of the pleasures or the alleviations of their own individual lot. If ever any system of privilege and enforced subjection had its yoke tightly riveted on the necks of those who are kept down by it, this has. I have not yet shown that it is a wrong system: but every one who is capable of thinking on the subject must see that even if it is, it was certain to outlast all other forms of unjust authority. And when some of the grossest of the other forms still exist in many civilized countries, and have only recently been got rid of in others, it would be strange if that which is so much the deepest-rooted had yet been perceptibly shaken anywhere. There is more reason to wonder that the protests and testimonies against it should have been so numerous and so weighty as they are.

Some will object, that a comparison cannot fairly be made between the government of the male sex and the forms of unjust power which I have adduced in illustration of it, since these are arbitrary, and the effect of mere usurpation, while it on the contrary is natural. But was there ever any domination which did not appear natural to those who possessed it? There was a time when the division of mankind into two classes, a small one of masters and a numerous one of slaves, appeared, even to the most cultivated minds, to be a natural, and the only natural, condition of the human race. No less an intellect, and one which contributed no less to the progress of human thought, than Aristotle,[4] held

4. *Politics* 1.4–7.

this opinion without doubt or misgiving; and rested it on the same premises on which the same assertion in regard to the dominion of men over women is usually based, namely that there are different natures among mankind, free natures, and slave natures; that the Greeks were of a free nature, the barbarian races of Thracians and Asiatics of a slave nature. But why need I go back to Aristotle? Did not the slave-owners of the Southern United States maintain the same doctrine, with all the fanaticism with which men cling to the theories that justify their passions and legitimate their personal interests? Did they not call heaven and earth to witness that the dominion of the white man over the black is natural, that the black race is by nature incapable of freedom, and marked out for slavery? some even going so far as to say that the freedom of manual laborers is an unnatural order of things anywhere. Again, the theorists of absolute monarchy have always affirmed it to be the only natural form of government; issuing from the patriarchal, which was the primitive and spontaneous form of society, framed on the model of the paternal, which is anterior to society itself, and, as they contend, the most natural authority of all. Nay, for that matter, the law of force itself, to those who could not plead any other, has always seemed the most natural of all grounds for the exercise of authority. Conquering races hold it to be Nature's own dictate that the conquered should obey the conquerors, or, as they euphoniously paraphrase it, that the feebler and more unwarlike races should submit to the braver and manlier. The smallest acquaintance with human life in the middle ages, shows how supremely natural the dominion of the feudal nobility over men of low condition appeared to the nobility themselves, and how unnatural the conception seemed, of a person of the inferior class claiming equality with them, or exercising authority over them. It hardly seemed less so to the class held in subjection. The emancipated serfs and burgesses, even in their most vigorous struggles, never made any pretension to a share of authority; they only demanded more or less of limitation to the power of tyrannizing over them. So true is it that unnatural generally means only uncustomary, and that everything which is usual appears natural. The subjection of women to men being a universal custom, any departure from it quite naturally appears unnatural. But how entirely, even in this case, the feeling is dependent on custom, appears by ample experience. Nothing so much astonishes the people of distant parts of the world, when they first learn anything about England, as to be told that it is under a queen: the thing seems to them so unnatural as to be almost incredible. To Englishmen this does not seem in the least degree unnatural, because they are used to it; but they do feel it unnatural that women should be soldiers or members of parliament. In the feudal ages, on the contrary, war and politics were not thought unnatural to women, because not unusual; it seemed natural that women of the privileged classes should be of manly character, inferior in nothing but bodily strength to their husbands and fathers. The independence of women seemed rather less unnatural to the Greeks than to other ancients, on account of the fabulous Amazons (whom they believed to be historical), and the partial example afforded by the Spartan women; who, though no less subordinate by law than in other Greek states, were more free in fact, and being trained to bodily exercises in the same manner with men, gave ample proof that they were not naturally disqualified for them. There can be little doubt that Spartan experience suggested to Plato,[5] among many other of his doctrines, that of the social and political equality of the two sexes.

But, it will be said, the rule of men over women differs from all these others in not being a rule of force: it is accepted voluntarily; women make no complaint, and are consenting parties to it. In the first place, a great number of women do not accept it. Ever since there have been women able to make their sentiments known by their writings (the only mode of publicity which society permits to them), an increasing number of them have recorded protests against their present social condition: and recently many thousands of them, headed by the most eminent women known to the public, have petitioned Parliament for their admission to the Parliamentary Suffrage. The claim of women to be educated as solidly, and in the same branches of knowledge, as men, is urged with growing intensity, and with a great prospect of success; while the demand for their admission into professions and occupations hitherto closed against them, becomes every year more urgent. Though there are not in this country, as there are in the United States, periodical Conventions and an organized party to agitate for the Rights of Women, there is a numerous and active Society[6] organized and managed by women, for the more limited object of obtaining the political franchise. Nor is it only in our own country and in America that women are beginning to protest, more or less collectively, against the disabilities under which they labour. France, and Italy, and Switzerland, and Russia now afford examples of the same thing. How many more women there are who silently cherish similar aspirations, no one can possibly know; but there are abundant tokens how many *would* cherish them, were they not so strenuously taught to repress them as contrary to the proprieties of their sex. It must be remembered, also, that no enslaved class ever asked for complete liberty at once. When Simon de Montfort[7] called the deputies of the commons to sit for the first time in Parliament, did any of them dream of demanding that an assembly, elected by their constituents, should make and destroy ministries, and dictate to the king in affairs of state? No such thought entered into the imagination of the most ambitious of them. The nobility had already these

5. *The Republic* 5.449–57.
6. The National Society for Women's Suffrage, founded in 1867.
7. Englishman (c. 1208–1265), who led baronial resistance to King Henry III and called the first English Parliament in 1265.

pretensions; the commons pretended to nothing but to be exempt from arbitrary taxation, and from the gross individual oppression of the king's officers. It is a political law of nature that those who are under any power of ancient origin, never begin by complaining of the power itself, but only of its oppressive exercise. There is never any want of women who complain of ill usage by their husbands. There would be infinitely more, if complaint were not the greatest of all provocatives to a repetition and increase of the ill usage. It is this which frustrates all attempts to maintain the power but protect the woman against its abuses. In no other case (except that of a child) is the person who has been proved judicially to have suffered an injury, replaced under the physical power of the culprit who inflicted it. Accordingly wives, even in the most extreme and protracted cases of bodily ill usage, hardly ever dare avail themselves of the laws made for their protection: and if, in a moment of irrepressible indignation, or by the interference of neighbors, they are induced to do so, their whole effort afterwards is to disclose as little as they can, and to beg off their tyrant from his merited chastisement.

All causes, social and natural, combine to make it unlikely that women should be collectively rebellious to the power of men. They are so far in a position different from all other subject classes, that their masters require something more from them than actual service. Men do not want solely the obedience of women, they want their sentiments. All men, except the most brutish, desire to have, in the woman most nearly connected with them, not a forced slave but a willing one, not a slave merely, but a favorite. They have therefore put everything in practice to enslave their minds. The masters of all other slaves rely, for maintaining obedience, on fear; either fear of themselves, or religious fears. The masters of women wanted more than simple obedience, and they turned the whole force of education to effect their purpose. All women are brought up from the very earliest years in the belief that their ideal of character is the very opposite to that of men; not self-will, and government by self-control, but submission, and yielding to the control of others. All the moralities tell them that it is the duty of women, and all the current sentimentalities that it is their nature, to live for others; to make complete abnegation of themselves, and to have no life but in their affections. And by their affections are meant the only ones they are allowed to have — those to the men with whom they are connected, or to the children who constitute an additional and indefeasible tie between them and a man. When we put together three things — first, the natural attraction between opposite sexes; secondly, the wife's entire dependence on the husband, every privilege or pleasure she has being either his gift, or depending entirely on his will; and lastly, that the principal object of human pursuit, consideration, and all objects of social ambition, can in general be sought or obtained by her only through him, it would be a miracle if the object of being attractive to men had not become the polar star of feminine education and formation of character. And, this great means of influence over the minds of women having been acquired, an instinct of selfishness made men avail themselves of it to the utmost as a means of holding women in subjection, by representing to them meekness, submissiveness, and resignation of all individual will into the hands of a man, as an essential part of sexual attractiveness. Can it be doubted that any of the other yokes which mankind have succeeded in breaking, would have subsisted till now if the same means had existed, and had been as sedulously used, to bow down their minds to it? If it had been made the object of the life of every young plebeian to find personal favour in the eyes of some patrician, of every young serf with some seigneur;[8] if domestication with him, and a share of his personal affections, had been held out as the prize which they all should look out for, the most gifted and aspiring being able to reckon on the most desirable prizes; and if, when this prize had been obtained, they had been shut out by a wall of brass from all interests not centering in him, all feelings and desires but those which he shared or inculcated; would not serfs and seigneurs, plebeians and patricians, have been as broadly distinguished at this day as men and women are? and would not all but a thinker here and there, have believed the distinction to be a fundamental and unalterable fact in human nature?

The preceding considerations are amply sufficient to show that custom, however universal it may be, affords in this case no presumption, and ought not to create any prejudice, in favour of the arrangements which place women in social and political subjection to men. But I may go farther, and maintain that the course of history, and the tendencies of progressive human society, afford not only no presumption in favor of this system of inequality of rights, but a strong one against it; and that, so far as the whole course of human improvement up to this time, the whole stream of modern tendencies, warrants any inference on the subject, it is, that this relic of the past is discordant with the future, and must necessarily disappear.

For, what is the peculiar character of the modern world — the difference which chiefly distinguishes modern institutions, modern social ideas, modern life itself, from those of times long past? It is, that human beings are no longer born to their place in life, and chained down by an inexorable bond to the place they are born to, but are free to employ their faculties, and such favorable chances as offer, to achieve the lot which may appear to them most desirable. Human society of old was constituted on a very different principle. All were born to a fixed social position, and were mostly kept in it by law, or interdicted from any means by which they could emerge from it. As some men are born white and others black, so some were born slaves and others freemen and citizens; some were born patricians, other plebeians; some were

8. Lord.

born feudal nobles, others commoners and *roturiers*.[9] A slave or serf could never make himself free, nor, except by the will of his master, become so. In most European countries it was not till towards the close of the middle ages, and as a consequence of the growth of regal power, that commoners could be ennobled. Even among nobles, the eldest son was born the exclusive heir to the paternal possessions, and a long time elapsed before it was fully established that the father could disinherit him. Among the industrious classes, only those who were born members of a guild, or were admitted into it by its members, could lawfully practice their calling within its local limits; and nobody could practice any calling deemed important, in any but the legal manner — by processes authoritatively prescribed. Manufacturers have stood in the pillory for presuming to carry on their business by new and improved methods. In modern Europe, and most in those parts of it which have participated most largely in all other modern improvements, diametrically opposite doctrines now prevail. Law and government do not undertake to prescribe by whom any social or industrial operation shall or shall not be conducted, or what modes of conducting them shall be lawful. These things are left to the unfettered choice of individuals. Even the laws which required that workmen should serve an apprenticeship, have in this country been repealed: there being ample assurance that in all cases in which an apprenticeship is necessary, its necessity will suffice to enforce it. The old theory was, that the least possible should be left to the choice of the individual agent; that all he had to do should, as far as practicable, be laid down for him by superior wisdom. Left to himself he was sure to go wrong. The modern conviction, the fruit of a thousand years of experience, is, that things in which the individual is the person directly interested, never go right but as they are left to his own discretion; and that any regulation of them by authority, except to protect the rights of others, is sure to be mischievous. This conclusion, slowly arrived at, and not adopted until almost every possible application of the contrary theory had been made with disastrous result, now (in the industrial department) prevails universally in the most advanced countries, almost universally in all that have pretensions to any sort of advancement. It is not that all processes are supposed to be equally good, or all persons to be equally qualified for everything; but that freedom of individual choice is now known to be the only thing which procures the adoption of the best processes, and throws each operation into the hands of those who are best qualified for it. Nobody thinks it necessary to make a law that only a strong-armed man shall be a blacksmith. Freedom and competition suffice to make blacksmiths strong-armed men, because the weak-armed can earn more by engaging in occupations for which they are more fit. In consonance with this doctrine, it is felt to be an overstepping of the proper

9. Plebeians or nonnobles (French).

bounds of authority to fix beforehand, on some general presumption, that certain persons are not fit to do certain things. It is now thoroughly known and admitted that if some such presumptions exist, no such presumption is infallible. Even if it be well grounded in a majority of cases, which it is very likely not to be, there will be a minority of exceptional cases in which it does not hold: and in those it is both an injustice to the individuals, and a detriment to society, to place barriers in the way of their using their faculties for their own benefit and for that of others. In the cases, on the other hand, in which the unfitness is real, the ordinary motives of human conduct will on the whole suffice to prevent the incompetent person from making, or from persisting in, the attempt.

If this general principle of social and economical science is not true; if individuals, with such help as they can derive from the opinion of those who know them, are not better judges than the law and the government, of their own capacities and vocation; the world cannot too soon abandon this principle, and return to the old system of regulations and disabilities. But if the principle is true, we ought to act as if we believed it, and not to ordain that to be born a girl instead of a boy, any more than to be born black instead of white, or a commoner instead of a nobleman, shall decide the person's position through all life — shall interdict people from all the more elevated social positions, and from all, except a few, respectable occupations. Even were we to admit the utmost that is ever pretended as to the superior fitness of men for all the functions now reserved to them, the same argument applies which forbids a legal qualification for members of Parliament. If only once in a dozen years the conditions of eligibility exclude a fit person, there is a real loss, while the exclusion of thousands of unfit persons is no gain; for if the constitution of the electoral body disposes them to choose unfit persons, there are always plenty of such persons to choose from. In all things of any difficulty and importance, those who can do them well are fewer than the need, even with the most unrestricted latitude of choice: and any limitation of the field of selection deprives society of some chances of being served by the competent, without ever saving it from the incompetent.

At present, in the more improved countries, the disabilities of women are the only case, save one, in which laws and institutions take persons at their birth, and ordain that they shall never in all their lives be allowed to compete for certain things. The one exception is that of royalty. Persons still are born to the throne; no one, not of the reigning family, can ever occupy it, and no one even of that family can, by any means but the course of hereditary succession, attain it. All other dignities and social advantages are open to the whole male sex: many indeed are only attainable by wealth, but wealth may be striven for by any one, and is actually obtained by many men of the very humblest origin. The difficulties, to the majority, are indeed insuperable without the aid of fortunate accidents; but no male human being is under any legal ban: neither law nor opinion superadd artificial obstacles to the natural ones. Royalty, as I have said, is excepted: but in this case every one feels it to be an exception — an anomaly in the modern world, in marked opposition to its customs and principles, and to be justified only by extraordinary special expediencies, which, though individuals and nations differ in estimating their weight, unquestionably do in fact exist. But in this exceptional case, in which a high social function is, for important reasons, bestowed on birth instead of being put up to competition, all free nations contrive to adhere in substance to the principle from which they nominally derogate; for they circumscribe this high function by conditions avowedly intended to prevent the person to whom it ostensibly belongs from really performing it; while the person by whom it is performed, the responsible minister, does obtain the post by a competition from which no full-grown citizen of the male sex is legally excluded. The disabilities, therefore, to which women are subject from the mere fact of their birth, are the solitary examples of the kind in modern legislation. In no instance except this, which comprehends half the human race, are the higher social functions closed against any one by a fatality of birth which no exertions, and no change of circumstances, can overcome; for even religious disabilities (besides that in England and in Europe they have practically almost ceased to exist) do not close any career to the disqualified person in case of conversion.

The social subordination of women thus stands out an isolated fact in modern social institutions; a solitary breach of what has become their fundamental law; a single relic of an old world of thought and practice exploded in everything else, but retained in the one thing of most universal interest; as if a gigantic dolmen, or a vast temple of Jupiter Olympius,[1] occupied the site of St. Paul's and received daily worship, while the surrounding Christian churches were only resorted to on fasts and festivals. This entire discrepancy between one social fact and all those which accompany it, and the radical opposition between its nature and the progressive movement which is the boast of the modern world, and which has successively swept away everything else of an analogous character, surely affords, to a conscientious observer of human tendencies, serious matter for reflection. It raises a prima facie presumption on the unfavorable side, far outweighing any which custom and usage could in such circumstances create on the favourable; and should at least suffice to make this, like the choice between republicanism and royalty, a balanced question.

The least that can be demanded is, that the question should not be considered as prejudged by existing fact and existing opinion, but open

---

1. The supreme god in the Roman pantheon. "Dolmen": a sacred megalith, supposed to play a part in Druidic ritual.

to discussion on its merits, as a question of justice and expediency: the decision on this, as on any of the other social arrangements of mankind, depending on what an enlightened estimate of tendencies and consequences may show to be most advantageous to humanity in general, without distinction of sex. And the discussion must be a real discussion, descending to foundations, and not resting satisfied with vague and general assertions. It will not do, for instance, to assert in general terms, that the experience of mankind has pronounced in favor of the existing system. Experience cannot possibly have decided between two courses, so long as there has only been experience of one. If it be said that the doctrine of the equality of the sexes rests only on theory, it must be remembered that the contrary doctrine also has only theory to rest upon. All that is proved in its favor by direct experience, is that mankind have been able to exist under it, and to attain the degree of improvement and prosperity which we now see; but whether that prosperity has been attained sooner, or is now greater, than it would have been under the other system, experience does not say. On the other hand, experience does say, that every step in improvement has been so invariably accompanied by a step made in raising the social position of women, that historians and philosophers have been led to adopt their elevation or debasement as on the whole the surest test and most correct measure of the civilization of a people or an age. Through all the progressive period of human history, the condition of women has been approaching nearer to equality with men. This does not of itself prove that the assimilation must go on to complete equality; but it assuredly affords some presumption that such is the case.

Neither does it avail anything to say that the *nature* of the two sexes adapts them to their present functions and position, and renders these appropriate to them. Standing on the ground of common sense and the constitution of the human mind, I deny that any one knows, or can know, the nature of the two sexes, as long as they have only been seen in their present relation to one another. If men had ever been found in society without women, or women without men, or if there had been a society of men and women in which the women were not under the control of the men, something might have been positively known about the mental and moral differences which may be inherent in the nature of each. What is now called the nature of women is an eminently artificial thing — the result of forced repression in some directions, unnatural stimulation in others. It may be asserted without scruple, that no other class of dependents have had their character so entirely distorted from its natural proportions by their relation with their masters; for, if conquered and slave races have been, in some respects, more forcibly repressed, whatever in them has not been crushed down by an iron heel has generally been let alone, and if left with any liberty of development, it has developed itself according to its own laws; but in the case of women, a hot-house and stove cultivation has always been carried on of some of the capabilities of their nature, for the benefit and pleasure of their masters. Then, because certain products of the general vital force sprout luxuriantly and reach a great development in this heated atmosphere and under this active nurture and watering, while other shoots from the same root, which are left outside in the wintry air, with ice purposely heaped all round them, have a stunted growth, and some are burnt off with fire and disappear; men, with that inability to recognize their own work which distinguishes the unanalytic mind, indolently believe that the tree grows of itself in the way they have made it grow, and that it would die if one half of it were not kept in a vapor bath and the other half in the snow.

Of all difficulties which impede the progress of thought, and the formation of well-grounded opinions on life and social arrangements, the greatest is now the unspeakable ignorance and inattention of mankind in respect to the influences which form human character. Whatever any portion of the human species now are, or seem to be, such, it is supposed, they have a natural tendency to be: even when the most elementary knowledge of the circumstances in which they have been placed, clearly points out the causes that made them what they are. Because a cottier[2] deeply in arrears to his landlord is not industrious, there are people who think that the Irish are naturally idle. Because constitutions can be overthrown when the authorities appointed to execute them turn their arms against them, there are people who think the French incapable of free government. Because the Greeks cheated the Turks, and the Turks only plundered the Greeks, there are persons who think that the Turks are naturally more sincere: and because women, as is often said, care nothing about politics except their personalities, it is supposed that the general good is naturally less interesting to women than to men. History, which is now so much better understood than formerly, teaches another lesson: if only by showing the extraordinary susceptibility of human nature to external influences, and the extreme variableness of those of its manifestations which are supposed to be most universal and uniform. But in history, as in travelling, men usually see only what they already had in their own minds; and few learn much from history, who do not bring much with them to its study.

Hence, in regard to that most difficult question, what are the natural differences between the two sexes — a subject on which it is impossible in the present state of society to obtain complete and correct knowledge — while almost everybody dogmatizes upon it, almost all neglect and make light of the only means by which any partial insight can be obtained into it. This is, an analytic study of the most important department of psychology, the laws of the influence of circumstances on

2. One who practices a form of tenure closely related to sharecropping; discussed by Mill in *Principles of Political Economy* (2.9).

THE SUBJECTION OF WOMEN

character. For, however great and apparently ineradicable the moral and intellectual differences between men and women might be, the evidence of their being natural differences could only be negative. Those only could be inferred to be natural which could not possibly be artificial — the residuum, after deducting every characteristic of either sex which can admit of being explained from education or external circumstances. The profoundest knowledge of the laws of the formation of character is indispensable to entitle any one to affirm even that there is any difference, much more what the difference is, between the two sexes considered as moral and rational beings; and since no one, as yet, has that knowledge, (for there is hardly any subject which, in proportion to its importance, has been so little studied), no one is thus far entitled to any positive opinion on the subject. Conjectures are all that can at present be made; conjectures more or less probable, according as more or less authorized by such knowledge as we yet have of the laws of psychology, as applied to the formation of character.

Even the preliminary knowledge, what the differences between the sexes now are, apart from all questions as to how they are made what they are, is still in the crudest and most incomplete state. Medical practitioners and physiologists have ascertained, to some extent, the differences in bodily constitution; and this is an important element to the psychologist: but hardly any medical practitioner is a psychologist. Respecting the mental characteristics of women; their observations are of no more worth than those of common men. It is a subject on which nothing final can be known, so long as those who alone can really know it, women themselves, have given but little testimony, and that little, mostly suborned. It is easy to know stupid women. Stupidity is much the same all the world over. A stupid person's notions and feelings may confidently be inferred from those which prevail in the circle by which the person is surrounded. Not so with those whose opinions and feelings are an emanation from their own nature and faculties. It is only a man here and there who has any tolerable knowledge of the character even of the women of his own family. I do not mean, of their capabilities; these nobody knows, not even themselves, because most of them have never been called out. I mean their actually existing thoughts and feelings. Many a man thinks he perfectly understands women, because he has had amatory relations with several, perhaps with many of them. If he is a good observer, and his experience extends to quality as well as quantity, he may have learnt something of one narrow department of their nature — an important department, no doubt. But of all the rest of it, few persons are generally more ignorant, because there are few from whom it is so carefully hidden. The most favorable case which a man can generally have for studying the character of a woman, is that of his own wife: for the opportunities are greater, and the cases of complete sympathy not so unspeakably rare. And in fact, this is the source from which any knowledge worth having on the subject has, I believe, generally come. But most men have not had the opportunity of studying in this way more than a single case: accordingly one can, to an almost laughable degree, infer what a man's wife is like, from his opinions about women in general. To make even this one case yield any result, the woman must be worth knowing, and the man not only a competent judge, but of a character so sympathetic in itself, and so well adapted to hers, that he can either read her mind by sympathetic intuition, or has nothing in himself which makes her shy of disclosing it. Hardly anything, I believe, can be more rare than this conjunction. It often happens that there is the most complete unity of feeling and community of interests as to all external things, yet the one has as little admission into the internal life of the other as if they were common acquaintance. Even with true affection, authority on the one side and subordination on the other prevent perfect confidence. Though nothing may be intentionally withheld, much is not shown. In the analogous relation of parent and child, the corresponding phenomenon must have been in the observation of every one. As between father and son, how many are the cases in which the father, in spite of real affection on both sides, obviously to all the world does not know, nor suspect, parts of the son's character familiar to his companions and equals. The truth is, that the position of looking up to another is extremely unpropitious to complete sincerity and openness with him. The fear of losing ground in his opinion or in his feelings is so strong, that even in an upright character, there is an unconscious tendency to show only the best side, or the side which, though not the best, is that which he most likes to see: and it may be confidently said that thorough knowledge of one another hardly ever exists, but between persons who, besides being intimates, are equals. How much more true, then, must all this be, when the one is not only under the authority of the other, but has it inculcated on her as a duty to reckon everything else subordinate to his comfort and pleasure, and to let him neither see nor feel anything coming from her, except what is agreeable to him. All these difficulties stand in the way of a man's obtaining any thorough knowledge even of the one woman whom alone, in general, he has sufficient opportunity of studying. When we further consider that to understand one woman is not necessarily to understand any other woman; that even if he could study many women of one rank, or of one country, he would not thereby understand women of other ranks or countries; and even if he did, they are still only the women of a single period of history; we may safely assert that the knowledge which men can acquire of women, even as they have been and are, without reference to what they might be, is wretchedly imperfect and superficial, and always will be so, until women themselves have told all that they have to tell.

And this time has not come; nor will it come otherwise than gradually. It is but of yesterday that women have either been qualified by literary accomplishments, or permitted by society, to tell anything to the general public. As yet very few of them dare tell anything, which men, on whom their literary success depends, are unwilling to hear. Let us remember in what manner, up to a very recent time, the expression, even by a male author, of uncustomary opinions, or what are deemed eccentric feelings, usually was, and in some degree still is, received; and we may form some faint conception under what impediments a woman, who is brought up to think custom and opinion her sovereign rule, attempts to express in books anything drawn from the depths of her own nature. The greatest woman who has left writings behind her sufficient to give her an eminent rank in the literature of her country, thought it necessary to prefix as a motto to her boldest work, "Un homme peut braver l'opinion; une femme doit s'y soumettre."[3] The greater part of what women write about women is mere sycophancy to men. In the case of unmarried women, much of it seems only intended to increase their chance of a husband. Many, both married and unmarried, overstep the mark, and inculcate a servility beyond what is desired or relished by any man, except the very vulgarest. But this is not so often the case as, even at a quite late period, it still was. Literary women are becoming more freespoken, and more willing to express their real sentiments. Unfortunately, in this country especially, they are themselves such artificial products, that their sentiments are compounded of a small element of individual observation and consciousness, and a very large one of acquired associations. This will be less and less the case, but it will remain true to a great extent, as long as social institutions do not admit the same free development of originality in women which is possible to men. When that time comes, and not before, we shall see, and not merely hear, as much as it is necessary to know of the nature of women, and the adaptation of other things to it.

I have dwelt so much on the difficulties which at present obstruct any real knowledge by men of the true nature of women, because in this as in so many other things "opinio copiæ inter maximas causas inopiæ est";[4] and there is little chance of reasonable thinking on the matter, while people flatter themselves that they perfectly understand a subject of which most men know absolutely nothing, and of which it is at present impossible that any man, or all men taken together, should have knowledge which can qualify them to lay down the law to women as to what is, or is not, their vocation. Happily, no such knowledge is necessary for any practical purpose connected with the position of women in relation to society and life. For, according to all the principles involved in modern society, the question rests with women themselves — to be decided by their own experience, and by the use of

3. "Title page of Mme. de Stael's 'Delphine' " [Mill's note]. The French translates as "A man may defy public opinion, but a woman must submit to it."
4. Believing oneself rich is one of the main causes of poverty (Latin).

their own faculties. There are no means of finding what either one person or many can do, but by trying—and no means by which any one else can discover for them what it is for their happiness to do or leave undone.

One thing we may be certain of—that what is contrary to women's nature to do, they never will be made to do by simply giving their nature free play. The anxiety of mankind to interfere in behalf of nature, for fear lest nature should not succeed in effecting its purpose, is an altogether unnecessary solicitude. What women by nature cannot do, it is quite superfluous to forbid them from doing. What they can do, but not so well as the men who are their competitors, competition suffices to exclude them from; since nobody asks for protective duties and bounties in favor of women; it is only asked that the present bounties and protective duties in favor of men should be recalled. If women have a greater natural inclination for some things than for others, there is no need of laws or social inculcation to make the majority of them do the former in preference to the latter. Whatever women's services are most wanted for, the free play of competition will hold out the strongest inducements to them to undertake. And, as the words imply, they are most wanted for the things for which they are most fit; by the apportionment of which to them, the collective faculties of the two sexes can be applied on the whole with the greatest sum of valuable result.

The general opinion of men is supposed to be, that the natural vocation of a woman is that of a wife and mother. I say, is supposed to be, because, judging from acts—from the whole of the present constitution of society—one might infer that their opinion was the direct contrary. They might be supposed to think that the alleged natural vocation of women was of all things the most repugnant to their nature; insomuch that if they are free to do anything else—if any other means of living, or occupation of their time and faculties, is open, which has any chance of appearing desirable to them—there will not be enough of them who will be willing to accept the condition said to be natural to them. If this is the real opinion of men in general, it would be well that it should be spoken out. I should like to hear somebody openly enunciating the doctrine (it is already implied in much that is written on the subject)—"It is necessary to society that women should marry and produce children. They will not do so unless they are compelled. Therefore it is necessary to compel them." The merits of the case would then be clearly defined. It would be exactly that of the slaveholders of South Carolina and Louisiana. "It is necessary that cotton and sugar should be grown. White men cannot produce them. Negroes will not, for any wages which we choose to give. *Ergo* they must be compelled." An illustration still closer to the point is that of impressment. Sailors must absolutely be had to defend the country. It often happens that they will not voluntarily enlist. Therefore there must be the power of forcing them. How often has this logic been used! and, but for one flaw in it, without doubt it would have been successful up to this day. But it is open to the retort—First pay the sailors the honest value of their labor. When you have made it as well worth their while to serve you, as to work for other employers, you will have no more difficulty than others have in obtaining their services. To this there is no logical answer except "I will not": and as people are now not only ashamed, but are not desirous, to rob the laborer of his hire, impressment is no longer advocated. Those who attempt to force women into marriage by closing all other doors against them, lay themselves open to a similar retort. If they mean what they say, their opinion must evidently be, that men do not render the married condition so desirable to women, as to induce them to accept it for its own recommendations. It is not a sign of one's thinking the boon one offers very attractive, when one allows only Hobson's choice, "that or none."[5] And here, I believe, is the clue to the feelings of those men, who have a real antipathy to the equal freedom of women. I believe they are afraid, not lest women should be unwilling to marry, for I do not think that any one in reality has that apprehension; but lest they should insist that marriage should be on equal conditions; lest all women of spirit and capacity should prefer doing almost anything else, not in their own eyes degrading, rather than marry, when marrying is giving themselves a master, and a master too of all their earthly possessions. And truly, if this consequence were necessarily incident to marriage, I think that the apprehension would be very well founded. I agree in thinking it probable that few women, capable of anything else, would, unless under an irresistible *entrainement*, rendering them for the time insensible to anything but itself, choose such a lot, when any other means were open to them of filling a conventionally honorable place in life: and if men are determined that the law of marriage shall be a law of despotism, they are quite right, in point of mere policy, in leaving to women only Hobson's choice. But, in that case, all that has been done in the modern world to relax the chain on the minds of women, has been a mistake. They never should have been allowed to receive a literary education. Women who read, much more women who write, are, in the existing constitution of things, a contradiction and a disturbing element: and it was wrong to bring women up with any acquirements but those of an odalisque, or of a domestic servant.

2

It will be well to commence the detailed discussion of the subject by the particular branch of it to which the course of our observations has led us: the conditions which the laws of this and all other countries

5. I.e., take it or leave it. Hobson was a Cambridge ostler, perhaps only fictional, who insisted that his clients take the horse nearest the door or go without.

annex to the marriage contract. Marriage being the destination appointed by society for women, the prospect they are brought up to, and the object which it is intended should be sought by all of them, except those who are too little attractive to be chosen by any man as his companion; one might have supposed that everything would have been done to make this condition as eligible to them as possible, that they might have no cause to regret being denied the option of any other. Society, however, both in this, and, at first, in all other cases, has preferred to attain its object by foul rather than fair means: but this is the only case in which it has substantially persisted in them even to the present day. Originally women were taken by force, or regularly sold by their father to the husband. Until a late period in European history, the father had the power to dispose of his daughter in marriage at his own will and pleasure, without any regard to hers. The Church, indeed, was so far faithful to a better morality as to require a formal "yes" from the woman at the marriage ceremony; but there was nothing to shew that the consent was other than compulsory; and it was practically impossible for the girl to refuse compliance if the father persevered, except perhaps when she might obtain the protection of religion by a determined resolution to take monastic vows. After marriage, the man had anciently (but this was anterior to Christianity) the power of life and death over his wife. She could invoke no law against him; he was her sole tribunal and law. For a long time he could repudiate her, but she had no corresponding power in regard to him. By the old laws of England, the husband was called the *lord* of the wife; he was literally regarded as her sovereign, inasmuch that the murder of a man by his wife was called treason (*petty* as distinguished from *high* treason), and was more cruelly avenged than was usually the case with high treason, for the penalty was burning to death. Because the various enormities have fallen into disuse (for most of them were never formally abolished, or not until they had long ceased to be practiced) men suppose that all is now as it should be in regard to the marriage contract; and we are continually told that civilization and Christianity have restored to the woman her just rights. Meanwhile the wife is the actual bondservant of her husband: no less so, as far as legal obligation goes, than slaves commonly so called. She vows a lifelong obedience to him at the altar, and is held to it all through her life by law. Casuists may say that the obligation of obedience stops short of participation in crime, but it certainly extends to everything else. She can do no act whatever but by his permission, at least tacit. She can acquire no property but for him; the instant it becomes hers, even if by inheritance, it becomes *ipso facto* his. In this respect the wife's position under the common law of England is worse than that of slaves in the laws of many countries:[6]

6. The Married Woman's Property Act of 1882 provided some redress, as had earlier acts in 1857 and 1870.

by the Roman law, for example, a slave might have his peculium, which to a certain extent the law guaranteed to him for his exclusive use. The higher classes in this country have given an analogous advantage to their women, through special contracts setting aside the law, by conditions of pin-money, etc.: since parental feeling being stronger with fathers than the class feeling of their own sex, a father generally prefers his own daughter to a son-in-law who is a stranger to him. By means of settlements, the rich usually contrive to withdraw the whole or part of the inherited property of the wife from the absolute control of the husband: but they do not succeed in keeping it under her own control; the utmost they can do only prevents the husband from squandering it, at the same time debarring the rightful owner from its use. The property itself is out of the reach of both; and as to the income derived from it, the form of settlement most favorable to the wife (that called "to her separate use") only precludes the husband from receiving it instead of her: it must pass through her hands, but if he takes it from her by personal violence as soon as she receives it, he can neither be punished, nor compelled to restitution. This is the amount of the protection which, under the laws of this country, the most powerful nobleman can give to his own daughter as respects her husband. In the immense majority of cases there is no settlement: and the absorption of all rights, all property, as well as all freedom of action, is complete. The two are called "one person in law," for the purpose of inferring that whatever is hers is his, but the parallel inference is never drawn that whatever is his is hers; the maxim is not applied against the man, except to make him responsible to third parties for her acts, as a master is for the acts of his slaves or of his cattle. I am far from pretending that wives are in general no better treated than slaves; but no slave is a slave to the same lengths, and in so full a sense of the word, as a wife is. Hardly any slave, except one immediately attached to the master's person, is a slave at all hours and all minutes; in general he has, like a soldier, his fixed task, and when it is done, or when he is off duty, he disposes, within certain limits, of his own time, and has a family life into which the master rarely intrudes. "Uncle Tom" under his first master had his own life in his "cabin," almost as much as any man whose work takes him away from home, is able to have in his own family. But it cannot be so with the wife. Above all, a female slave has (in Christian countries) an admitted right, and is considered under a moral obligation, to refuse to her master the last familiarity. Not so the wife: however brutal a tyrant she may unfortunately be chained to — though she may know that he hates her, though it may be his daily pleasure to torture her, and though she may feel it impossible not to loathe him — he can claim from her and enforce the lowest degradation of a human being, that of being made the instrument of an animal function contrary to her inclinations. While she is held in this worst description of slavery as to her own person, what is her position in regard to the children in whom she and her master have a joint interest? They are by law *his* children. He alone has any legal rights over them. Not one act can she do towards or in relation to them, except by delegation from him. Even after he is dead she is not their legal guardian, unless he by will has made her so. He could even send them away from her, and deprive her of the means of seeing or corresponding with them, until this power was in some degree restricted by Serjeant Talfourd's Act.[7] This is her legal state. And from this state she has no means of withdrawing herself. If she leaves her husband, she can take nothing with her, neither her children nor anything which is rightfully her own. If he chooses, he can compel her to return, by law, or by physical force; or he may content himself with seizing for his own use anything which she may earn, or which may be given to her by her relations. It is only legal separation by a decree of a court of justice, which entitles her to live apart, without being forced back into the custody of an exasperated jailer — or which empowers her to apply any earnings to her own use, without fear that a man whom perhaps she has not seen for twenty years will pounce upon her some day and carry all off. This legal separation, until lately, the courts of justice would only give at an expense which made it inaccessible to any one out of the higher ranks. Even now it is only given in cases of desertion, or of the extreme of cruelty; and yet complaints are made every day that it is granted too easily. Surely, if a woman is denied any lot in life but that of being the personal bodyservant of a despot, and is dependent for everything upon the chance of finding one who may be disposed to make a favorite of her instead of merely a drudge, it is a very cruel aggravation of her fate that she should be allowed to try this chance only once. The natural sequel and corollary from this state of things would be, that since her all in life depends upon obtaining a good master, she should be allowed to change again and again until she finds one. I am not saying that she ought to be allowed this privilege. That is a totally different consideration. The question of divorce, in the sense involving liberty of remarriage, is one into which it is foreign to my purpose to enter. All I now say is, that to those to whom nothing but servitude is allowed, the free choice of servitude is the only, though a most insufficient, alleviation. Its refusal completes the assimilation of the wife to the slave — and the slave under not the mildest form of slavery: for in some slave codes the slave could, under certain circumstances of ill usage, legally compel the master to sell him. But no amount of ill usage, without adultery superadded, will in England free a wife from her tormentor.

I have no desire to exaggerate, nor does the case stand in any need of exaggeration. I have described the wife's legal position, not her actual treatment. The laws of most countries are far worse than the people who execute them, and many of them are only able to remain laws by

7. Amended the law relating to the custody of infants (1839).

being seldom or never carried into effect. If married life were all that it might be expected to be, looking to the laws alone, society would be a hell upon earth. Happily there are both feelings and interests which in many men exclude, and in most, greatly temper, the impulses and propensities which lead to tyranny: and of those feelings, the tie which connects a man with his wife affords, in a normal state of things, incomparably the strongest example. The only tie which at all approaches to it, that between him and his children, tends, in all save exceptional cases, to strengthen, instead of conflicting with, the first. Because this is true; because men in general do not inflict, nor women suffer, all the misery which could be inflicted and suffered if the full power of tyranny with which the man is legally invested were acted on; the defenders of the existing form of the institution think that all its iniquity is justified, and that any complaint is merely quarreling with the evil which is the price paid for every great good. But the mitigations in practice, which are compatible with maintaining in full legal force this or any other kind of tyranny, instead of being any apology for despotism, only serve to prove what power human nature possesses of reacting against the vilest institutions, and with what vitality the seeds of good as well as those of evil in human character diffuse and propagate themselves. Not a word can be said for despotism in the family which cannot be said for political despotism. Every absolute king does not sit at his window to enjoy the groans of his tortured subjects, nor strips them of their last rag and turns them out to shiver in the road. The despotism of Louis XVI was not the despotism of Philippe le Bel, or of Nadir Shah, or of Caligula;[8] but it was bad enough to justify the French Revolution, and to palliate even its horrors. If an appeal be made to the intense attachments which exist between wives and their husbands, exactly as much may be said of domestic slavery. It was quite an ordinary fact in Greece and Rome for slaves to submit to death by torture rather than betray their masters. In the proscriptions of the Roman civil wars it was remarked that wives and slaves were heroically faithful, sons very commonly treacherous. Yet we know how cruelly many Romans treated their slaves. But in truth these intense individual feelings nowhere rise to such a luxuriant height as under the most atrocious institutions. It is part of the irony of life, that the strongest feelings of devoted gratitude of which human nature seems to be susceptible, are called forth in human beings towards those who, having the power entirely to crush their earthly existence, voluntarily refrain from using that power. How great a place in most men this sentiment fills, even

8. Widely reputed to be mad, he was certainly cruel (A.D. 12–41); he was Roman emperor from 37 to 41 and was murdered by the soldiers who had elevated him. His nickname, meaning "little boots," was given to him by his father's soldiers. Louis XVI (1754–1793), king of France, was deposed and eventually executed by the revolutionaries of 1789. Philippe le Bel, or Philip the Fair (1268–1314), a tough and astute king of France, who was famously unscrupulous. Nadir Shah (1688–1747), an Iranian adventurer, who was famous for his invasions of India and notorious for his cruelty.

in religious devotion, it would be cruel to inquire. We daily see how much their gratitude to Heaven appears to be stimulated by the contemplation of fellow-creatures to whom God has not been so merciful as he has to themselves.

Whether the institution to be defended is slavery, political absolution, or the absolutism of the head of a family, we are always expected to judge of it from its best instances; and we are presented with pictures of loving exercise of authority on one side, loving submission to it on the other — superior wisdom ordering all things for the greatest good of the dependents, and surrounded by their smiles and benedictions. All this would be very much to the purpose if any one pretended that there are no such things as good men. Who doubts that there may be great goodness, and great happiness, and great affection, under the absolute government of a good man? Meanwhile, laws and institutions require to be adapted, not to good men, but to bad. Marriage is not an institution designed for a select few. Men are not required, as a preliminary to the marriage ceremony, to prove by testimonials that they are fit to be trusted with the exercise of absolute power. The tie of affection and obligation to a wife and children is very strong with those whose general social feelings are strong, and with many who are little sensible to any other social ties; but there are all degrees of sensibility and insensibility to it, as there are all grades of goodness and wickedness in men, down to those whom no ties will bind, and on whom society has no action but through its *ultima ratio*, the penalties of the law. In every grade of this descending scale are men to whom are committed all the legal powers of a husband. The vilest malefactor has some wretched woman tied to him, against whom he can commit any atrocity except killing her, and, if tolerably cautious, can do that without much danger of the legal penalty. And how many thousands are there among the lowest classes in every country, who, without being in a legal sense malefactors in any other respect, because in every other quarter their aggressions meet with resistance, indulge the utmost habitual excesses of bodily violence towards the unhappy wife, who alone, at least of grown persons, can neither repel nor escape from their brutality; and towards whom the excess of dependence inspires their mean and savage natures, not with a generous forbearance, and a point of honour to behave well to one whose lot in life is trusted entirely to their kindness, but on the contrary with a notion that the law has delivered her to them as their thing, to be used at their pleasure, and that they are not expected to practice the consideration towards her which is required from them towards everybody else. The law, which till lately left even these atrocious extremes of domestic oppression practically unpunished, has within these few years made some feeble attempts to repress them. But its attempts have done little, and cannot be expected to do much, because it is contrary to reason and experience to suppose that there can be any real check to brutality, consistent with leaving the victim still in the power of the executioner. Until a conviction for personal violence, or at all events a repetition of it after a first conviction, entitles the woman *ipso facto* to a divorce, or at least to a judicial separation, the attempt to repress these "aggravated assaults" by legal penalties will break down for want of a prosecutor, or for want of a witness.

When we consider how vast is the number of men, in any great country, who are little higher than brutes, and that this never prevents them from being able, through the law of marriage, to obtain a victim, the breadth and depth of human misery caused in this shape alone by the abuse of the institution swells to something appalling. Yet these are only the extreme cases. They are the lowest abysses, but there is a sad succession of depth after depth before reaching them. In domestic as in political tyranny the case of absolute monsters chiefly illustrates the institution by showing that there is scarcely any horror which may not occur under it if the despot pleases, and thus setting in a strong light what must be the terrible frequency of things only a little less atrocious. Absolute fiends are as rare as angels, perhaps rarer: ferocious savages, with occasional touches of humanity, are however very frequent: and in the wide interval which separates these from any worthy representatives of the human species, how many are the forms and gradations of animalism and selfishness, often under an outward varnish of civilization and even cultivation, living at peace with the law, maintaining a creditable appearance to all who are not under their power, yet sufficient often to make the lives of all who are so, a torment and a burthen to them! It would be tiresome to repeat the commonplaces about the unfitness of men in general for power, which, after the political discussions of centuries, every one knows by heart, were it not that hardly any one thinks of applying these maxims to the case in which above all others they are applicable, that of power, not placed in the hands of a man here and there, but offered to every adult male, down to the basest and most ferocious. It is not because a man is not known to have broken any of the Ten Commandments, or because he maintains a respectable character in his dealings with those whom he cannot compel to have intercourse with him, or because he does not fly out into violent bursts of ill-temper against those who are not obliged to bear with him, that it is possible to surmise of what sort his conduct will be in the unrestraint of home. Even the commonest men reserve the violent, the sulky, the undisguisedly selfish side of their character for those who have no power to withstand it. The relation of superiors to dependents is the nursery of these vices of character, which, wherever else they exist, are an overflowing from that source. A man who is morose or violent to his equals, is sure to be one who has lived among inferiors, whom he could frighten or worry into submission. If the family in its best forms is, as it is often said to be, a school of sympathy, tenderness, and loving forgetfulness of self, it is still oftener, as respects its chief, a school of wilfulness, overbearingness, unbounded self-indulgence, and a double-dyed and idealized selfishness, of which sacrifice itself is only a particular form: the care for the wife and children being only care for them as parts of the man's own interests and belongings, and their individual happiness being immolated in every shape to his smallest preferences. What better is to be looked for under the existing form of the institution? We know that the bad propensities of human nature are only kept within bounds when they are allowed no scope for their indulgence. We know that from impulse and habit, when not from deliberate purpose, almost every one to whom others yield, goes on encroaching upon them, until a point is reached at which they are compelled to resist. Such being the common tendency of human nature; the almost unlimited power which present social institutions give to the man over at least one human being—the one with whom he resides, and whom he has always present—this power seeks out and evokes the latent germs of selfishness in the remotest corners of his nature—fans its faintest sparks and smoldering embers—offers to him a license for the indulgence of those points of his original character which in all other relations he would have found it necessary to repress and conceal, and the repression of which would in time have become a second nature. I know that there is another side to the question. I grant that the wife, if she cannot effectually resist, can at least retaliate; she, too, can make the man's life extremely uncomfortable, and by that power is able to carry many points which she ought, and many which she ought not, to prevail in. But this instrument of self-protection—which may be called the power of the scold, or the shrewish sanction—has the fatal defect, that it avails most against the least tyrannical superiors, and in favour of the least deserving dependents. It is the weapon of irritable and self-willed women; of those who would make the worst use of power if they themselves had it, and who generally turn this power to a bad use. The amiable cannot use such an instrument, the highminded disdain it. And on the other hand, the husbands against whom it is used most effectively are the gentler and more inoffensive; those who cannot be induced, even by provocation, to resort to any very harsh exercise of authority. The wife's power of being disagreeable generally only establishes a counter-tyranny, and makes victims in their turn chiefly of those husbands who are least inclined to be tyrants.

What is it, then, which really tempers the corrupting effects of the power, and makes it compatible with such amount of good as we actually see? Mere feminine blandishments, though of great effect in individual instances, have very little effect in modifying the general tendencies of the situation; for their power only lasts while the woman is young and attractive, often only while her charm is new, and not dimmed by familiarity; and on many men they have not much influence at any time. The real mitigating causes are, the personal affection which is the growth of time, in so far as the man's nature is susceptible of it, and the woman's character sufficiently congenial with his to excite it; their common interests as regards the children, and their general community of interest as concerns third persons (to which however there are very great limitations); the real importance of the wife to his daily comforts and enjoyments, and the value he consequently attaches to her on his personal account, which, in a man capable of feeling for others, lays the foundation of caring for her on her own; and lastly, the influence naturally acquired over almost all human beings by those near to their persons (if not actually disagreeable to them): who, both by their direct entreaties, and by the insensible contagion of their feelings and dispositions, are often able, unless counteracted by some equally strong personal influence, to obtain a degree of command over the conduct of the superior, altogether excessive and unreasonable. Through these various means, the wife frequently exercises even too much power over the man; she is able to affect his conduct in things in which she may not be qualified to influence it for good — in which her influence may be not only unenlightened, but employed on the morally wrong side; and in which he would act better if left to his own prompting. But neither in the affairs of families nor in those of states is power a compensation for the loss of freedom. Her power often gives her what she has no right to, but does not enable her to assert her own rights. A Sultan's favorite slave has slaves under her, over whom she tyrannizes; but the desirable thing would be that she should neither have slaves nor be a slave. By entirely sinking her own existence in her husband; by having no will (or persuading him that she has no will) but his, in anything which regards their joint relation, and by making it the business of her life to work upon his sentiments, a wife may gratify herself by influencing, and very probably perverting, his conduct, in those of his external relations which she has never qualified herself to judge of, or in which she is herself wholly influenced by some personal or other partiality or prejudice. Accordingly, as things now are, those who act most kindly to their wives, are quite as often made worse, as better, by the wife's influence, in respect to all interests extending beyond the family. She is taught that she has no business with things out of that sphere; and accordingly she seldom has any honest and conscientious opinion on them; and therefore hardly ever meddles with them for any legitimate purpose, but generally for an interested one. She neither knows nor cares which is the right side in politics, but she knows what will bring in money or invitations, give her husband a title, her son a place, or her daughter a good marriage.

But how, it will be asked, can any society exist without government? In a family, as in a state, some one person must be the ultimate ruler. Who shall decide when married people differ in opinion? Both cannot have their way, yet a decision one way or the other must be come to.

It is not true that in all voluntary association between two people, one of them must be absolute master: still less that the law must determine which of them it shall be. The most frequent case of voluntary association, next to marriage, is partnership in business: and it is not found or thought necessary to enact that in every partnership, one partner shall have entire control over the concern, and the others shall be bound to obey his orders. No one would enter into partnership on terms which would subject him to the responsibilities of a principal, with only the powers and privileges of a clerk or agent. If the law dealt with other contracts as it does with marriage, it would ordain that one partner should administer the common business as if it was his private concern; that the others should have only delegated powers; and that this one should be designated by some general presumption of law, for example as being the eldest. The law never does this: nor does experience show it to be necessary that any theoretical inequality of power should exist between the partners, or that the partnership should have any other conditions than what they may themselves appoint by their articles of agreement. Yet it might seem that the exclusive power might be conceded with less danger to the rights and interests of the inferior, in the case of partnership than in that of marriage, since he is free to cancel the power by withdrawing from the connexion. The wife has no such power, and even if she had, it is almost always desirable that she should try all measures before resorting to it.

It is quite true that things which have to be decided every day, and cannot adjust themselves gradually, or wait for a compromise, ought to depend on one will: one person must have their sole control. But it does not follow that this should always be the same person. The natural arrangement is a division of powers between the two; each being absolute in the executive branch of their own department, and any change of system and principle requiring the consent of both. The division neither can nor should be pre-established by the law, since it must depend on individual capacities and suitabilities. If the two persons chose, they might pre-appoint it by the marriage contract, as pecuniary arrangements are now often pre-appointed. There would seldom be any difficulty in deciding such things by mutual consent, unless the marriage was one of those unhappy ones in which all other things as well as this, become subjects of bickering and dispute. The division of rights would naturally follow the division of duties and functions; and that is already made by consent, or at all events not by law, but by general custom, modified and modifiable at the pleasure of the persons concerned.

The real practical decision of affairs, to whichever may be given the legal authority, will greatly depend, as it even now does, upon comparative qualifications. The mere fact that he is usually the eldest, will in most cases give the preponderance to the man; at least until they both attain a time of life at which the difference in their years is of no importance. There will naturally also be a more potential voice on the side, whichever it is, that brings the means of support. Inequality from this source does not depend on the law of marriage, but on the general conditions of human society, as now constituted. The influence of mental superiority, either general or special, and of superior decision of character, will necessarily tell for much. It always does so at present. And this fact shows how little foundation there is for the apprehension that the powers and responsibilities of partners in life (as of partners in business), cannot be satisfactorily apportioned by agreement between themselves. They always are so apportioned, except in cases in which the marriage institution is a failure. Things never come to an issue of downright power on one side, and obedience on the other, except where the connection altogether has been a mistake, and it would be a blessing to both parties to be relieved from it. Some may say that the very thing by which an amicable settlement of differences becomes possible, is the power of legal compulsion known to be in reserve; as people submit to an arbitration because there is a court of law in the background, which they know that they can be forced to obey. But to make the cases parallel, we must suppose that the rule of the court of law was, not to try the cause, but to give judgment always for the same side, suppose the defendant. If so, the amenability to it would be a motive with the plaintiff to agree to almost any arbitration, but it would be just the reverse with the defendant. The despotic power which the law gives to the husband may be a reason to make the wife assent to any compromise by which power is practically shared between the two, but it cannot be the reason why the husband does. That there is always among decently conducted people a practical compromise, though one of them at least is under no physical or moral necessity of making it, shows that the natural motives which lead to a voluntary adjustment of the united life of two persons in a manner acceptable to both, do on the whole, except in unfavorable cases, prevail. The matter is certainly not improved by laying down as an ordinance of law, that the superstructure of free government shall be raised upon a legal basis of despotism on one side and subjection on the other, and that every concession which the despot makes may, at his mere pleasure, and without any warning, be recalled. Besides that no freedom is worth much when held on so precarious a tenure, its conditions are not likely to be the most equitable when the law throws so prodigious a weight into one scale; when the adjustment rests between two persons one of whom is declared to be entitled to everything, the other not only entitled to nothing except during the good pleasure of the first, but under the strongest moral and religious obligation not to rebel under any excess of oppression.

A pertinacious adversary, pushed to extremities, may say, that husbands indeed are willing to be reasonable, and to make fair concessions to their partners without being compelled to it, but that wives are not: that if allowed any rights of their own, they will acknowledge no rights at all in any one else, and never will yield in anything, unless they can be compelled, by the man's mere authority, to yield in everything. This would have been said by many persons some generations ago, when satires on women were in vogue, and men thought it a clever thing to insult women for being what men made them. But it will be said by no one now who is worth replying to. It is not the doctrine of the present day that women are less susceptible of good feeling, and consideration for those with whom they are united by the strongest ties, than men are. On the contrary, we are perpetually told that women are better than men, by those who are totally opposed to treating them as if they were as good; so that the saying has passed into a piece of tiresome cant, intended to put a complimentary face upon an injury, and resembling those celebrations of royal clemency which, according to Gulliver,[9] the king of Lilliput always prefixed to his most sanguinary decrees. If women are better than men in anything, it surely is in individual self-sacrifice for those of their own family. But I lay little stress on this, so long as they are universally taught that they are born and created for self-sacrifice. I believe that equality of rights would abate the exaggerated self-abnegation which is the present artificial ideal of feminine character, and that a good woman would not be more self-sacrificing than the best man: but on the other hand, men would be much more unselfish and self-sacrificing than at present, because they would no longer be taught to worship their own will as such a grand thing that it is actually the law for another rational being. There is nothing which men so easily learn as this self-worship: all privileged persons, and all privileged classes, have had it. The more we descend in the scale of humanity, the intenser it is; and most of all in those who are not, and can never expect to be, raised above any one except an unfortunate wife and children. The honorable exceptions are proportionally fewer than in the case of almost any other human infirmity. Philosophy and religion, instead of keeping it in check, are generally suborned to defend it; and nothing controls it but that practical feeling of the equality of human beings, which is the theory of Christianity, but which Christianity will never practically teach, while it sanctions institutions grounded on an arbitrary preference of one human being over another.

There are, no doubt, women, as there are men, whom equality of consideration will not satisfy; with whom there is no peace while any will or wish is regarded but their own. Such persons are a proper subject for the law of divorce. They are only fit to live alone, and no human beings ought to be compelled to associate their lives with them. But the legal subordination tends to make such characters among women more, rather than less, frequent. If the man exerts his whole power, the woman is of course crushed: but if she is treated with indulgence, and permitted to assume power, there is no rule to set limits to her en-

9. In Jonathan Swift's *Gulliver's Travels* (1726).

croachments. The law, not determining her rights, but theoretically allowing her none at all, practically declares that the measure of what she has a right to, is what she can contrive to get.

The equality of married persons before the law, is not only the sole mode in which that particular relation can be made consistent with justice to both sides, and conducive to the happiness of both, but it is the only means of rendering the daily life of mankind, in any high sense, a school of moral cultivation. Though the truth may not be felt or generally acknowledged for generations to come, the only school of genuine moral sentiment is society between equals. The moral education of mankind has hitherto emanated chiefly from the law of force, and is adapted almost solely to the relations which force creates. In the less advanced states of society, people hardly recognize any relation with their equals. To be an equal is to be an enemy. Society, from its highest place to its lowest, is one long chain, or rather ladder, where every individual is either above or below his nearest neighbour, and wherever he does not command he must obey. Existing moralities accordingly, are mainly fitted to a relation of command and obedience. Yet command and obedience are but unfortunate necessities of human life: society in equality is its normal state. Already in modern life, and more and more as it progressively improves, command and obedience become exceptional facts in life, equal association its general rule. The morality of the first ages rested on the obligation to submit to power; that of the ages next following, on the right of the weak to the forbearance and protection of the strong. How much longer is one form of society and life to content itself with the morality made for another? We have had the morality of submission, and the morality of chivalry and generosity; the time is now come for the morality of justice. Whenever, in former ages, any approach has been made to society in equality, Justice has asserted its claims as the foundation of virtue. It was thus in the free republics of antiquity. But even in the best of these, the equals were limited to the free male citizens; slaves, women, and the unenfranchised residents were under the law of force. The joint influence of Roman civilization and of Christianity obliterated these distinctions, and in theory (if only partially in practice) declared the claims of the human being, as such, to be paramount to those of sex, class, or social position. The barriers which had begun to be levelled were raised again by the northern conquests; and the whole of modern history consists of the slow process by which they have since been wearing away. We are entering into an order of things in which justice will again be the primary virtue; grounded as before on equal, but now also on sympathetic association; having its root no longer in the instinct of equals for self-protection, but in a cultivated sympathy between them; and no one being now left out, but an equal measure being extended to all. It is no novelty that mankind do not distinctly foresee their own changes, and that their sentiments are adapted to past, not to coming ages. To see the futurity of the species has always been the privilege of the intellectual élite, or of those who have learnt from them; to have the feelings of that futurity has been the distinction, and usually the martyrdom, of a still rarer élite. Institutions, books, education, society, all go on training human beings for the old, long after the new has come; much more when it is only coming. But the true virtue of human beings is fitness to live together as equals; claiming nothing for themselves but what they as freely concede to every one else; regarding command of any kind as an exceptional necessity, and in all cases a temporary one; and preferring, whenever possible, the society of those with whom leading and following can be alternate and reciprocal. To these virtues, nothing in life as at present constituted gives cultivation by exercise. The family is a school of despotism, in which the virtues of despotism, but also its vices, are largely nourished. Citizenship, in free countries, is partly a school of society in equality; but citizenship fills only a small place in modern life, and does not come near the daily habits or inmost sentiments. The family, justly constituted, would be the real school of the virtues of freedom. It is sure to be a sufficient one of everything else. It will always be a school of obedience for the children, of command for the parents. What is needed is, that it should be a school of sympathy in equality, of living together in love, without power on one side or obedience on the other. This it ought to be between the parents. It would then be an exercise of those virtues which each requires to fit them for all other association, and a model to the children of the feelings and conduct which their temporary training by means of obedience is designed to render habitual, and therefore natural, to them. The moral training of mankind will never be adapted to the conditions of the life for which all other human progress is a preparation, until they practice in the family the same moral rule which is adapted to the normal constitution of human society. Any sentiment of freedom which can exist in a man whose nearest and dearest intimacies are with those of whom he is absolute master, is not the genuine or Christian love of freedom, but, what the love of freedom generally was in the ancients and in the middle ages — an intense feeling of the dignity and importance of his own personality; making him disdain a yoke for himself, of which he has no abhorrence whatever in the abstract, but which he is abundantly ready to impose on others for his own interest or glorification.

I readily admit (and it is the very foundation of my hopes) that numbers of married people even under the present law, (in the higher classes of England probably a great majority), live in the spirit of a just law of equality. Laws never would be improved, if there were not numerous persons whose moral sentiments are better than the existing laws. Such persons ought to support the principles here advocated; of which the only object is to make all other married couples similar to what these are now. But persons even of considerable moral worth, unless they are also thinkers, are very ready to believe that laws or practices, the evils of which they have not personally experienced, do not produce any evils, but (if seeming to be generally approved of) probably do good, and that it is wrong to object to them. It would, however, be a great mistake in such married people to suppose, because the legal conditions of the tie which unites them do not occur to their thoughts once in a twelvemonth, and because they live and feel in all respects as if they were legally equals, that the same is the case with all other married couples, wherever the husband is not a notorious ruffian. To suppose this, would be to show equal ignorance of human nature and of fact. The less fit a man is for the possession of power — the less likely to be allowed to exercise it over any person with that person's voluntary consent — the more does he hug himself in the consciousness of the power the law gives him, exact its legal rights to the utmost point which custom (the custom of men like himself) will tolerate, and take pleasure in using the power, merely to enliven the agreeable sense of possessing it. What is more; in the most naturally brutal and morally uneducated part of the lower classes, the legal slavery of the woman, and something in the merely physical subjection to their will as an instrument, causes them to feel a sort of disrespect and contempt towards their own wife which they do not feel towards any other woman, or any other human being, with whom they come in contact; and which makes her seem to them an appropriate subject for any kind of indignity. Let an acute observer of the signs of feeling, who has the requisite opportunities, judge for himself whether this is not the case: and if he finds that it is, let him not wonder at any amount of disgust and indignation that can be felt against institutions which lead naturally to this depraved state of the human mind.

We shall be told, perhaps, that religion imposes the duty of obedience; as every established fact which is too bad to admit of any other defence, is always presented to us as an injunction of religion. The Church, it is very true, enjoins it in her formularies, but it would be difficult to derive any such injunction from Christianity. We are told that St. Paul said, "Wives, obey your husbands:" but he also said, "Slaves, obey your masters."[1] It was not St. Paul's business, nor was it consistent with his object, the propagation of Christianity, to incite any one to rebellion against existing laws. The apostle's acceptance of all social institutions as he found them, is no more to be construed as a disapproval of attempts to improve them at the proper time, than his declaration, "The powers that be are ordained of God," gives his sanction to military despotism, and to that alone, as the Christian form of political government, or commands passive obedience to it. To pretend that Christianity was intended to stereotype existing forms of govern-

---

1. See Colossians 3.18: "Wives, submit yourselves unto your husbands, as it is fit in the Lord."
   See also Colossians 3.22: "Servants, obey your masters according to the flesh."

ment and society, and protect them against change, is to reduce it to the level of Islamism or of Brahminism. It is precisely because Christianity has not done this, that it has been the religion of the progressive portion of mankind, and Islamism, Brahminism, etc., have been those of the stationary portions; or rather (for there is no such thing as a really stationary society) of the declining portions. There have been abundance of people, in all ages of Christianity, who tried to make it something of the same kind; to convert us into a sort of Christian Mussulmans, with the Bible for a Koran, prohibiting all improvement: and great has been their power, and many have had to sacrifice their lives in resisting them. But they have been resisted, and the resistance has made us what we are, and will yet make us what we are to be.

After what has been said respecting the obligation of obedience, it is almost superfluous to say anything concerning the more special point included in the general one — a woman's right to her own property; for I need not hope that this treatise can make any impression upon those who need anything to convince them that a woman's inheritance or gains ought to be as much her own after marriage as before. The rule is simple: whatever would be the husband's or wife's if they were not married, should be under their exclusive control during marriage; which need not interfere with the power to tie up property by settlement, in order to preserve it for children. Some people are sentimentally shocked at the idea of a separate interest in money matters, as inconsistent with the ideal fusion of two lives into one. For my own part, I am one of the strongest supporters of community of goods, when resulting from an entire unity of feeling in the owners, which makes all things common between them. But I have no relish for a community of goods resting on the doctrine, that what is mine is yours but what is yours is not mine; and I should prefer to decline entering into such a compact with any one, though I were myself the person to profit by it.

This particular injustice and oppression to women, which is, to common apprehensions, more obvious than all the rest, admits of remedy without interfering with any other mischiefs: and there can be little doubt that it will be one of the earliest remedied. Already, in many of the new and several of the old States of the American Confederation,[2] provisions have been inserted even in the written Constitutions, securing to women equality of rights in this respect: and thereby improving materially the position, in the marriage relation, of those women at least who have property, by leaving them one instrument of power which they have not signed away; and preventing also the scandalous abuse of the marriage institution, which is perpetrated when a man entraps a girl into marrying him without a settlement, for the sole purpose of getting possession of her money. When the support of the family

_____

2. Mill did not mean the South; Texas and California made such provisions in 1845 and 1849, for instance.

depends, not on property, but on earnings, the common arrangement, by which the man earns the income and the wife superintends the domestic expenditure, seems to me in general the most suitable division of labour between the two persons. If, in addition to the physical suffering of bearing children, and the whole responsibility of their care and education in early years, the wife undertakes the careful and economical application of the husband's earnings to the general comfort of the family; she takes not only her fair share, but usually the larger share, of the bodily and mental exertion required by their joint existence. If she undertakes any additional portion, it seldom relieves her from this, but only prevents her from performing it properly. The care which she is herself disabled from taking of the children and the household, nobody else takes; those of the children who do not die, grow up as they best can, and the management of the household is likely to be so bad, as even in point of economy to be a great drawback from the value of the wife's earnings. In an otherwise just state of things, it is not, therefore, I think, a desirable custom, that the wife should contribute by her labor to the income of the family. In an unjust state of things, her doing so may be useful to her, by making her of more value in the eyes of the man who is legally her master; but, on the other hand, it enables him still farther to abuse his power, by forcing her to work, and leaving the support of the family to her exertions, while he spends most of his time in drinking and idleness. The *power* of earning is essential to the dignity of a woman, if she has not independent property. But if marriage were an equal contract, not implying the obligation of obedience; if the connection were no longer enforced to the oppression of those to whom it is purely a mischief, but a separation, on just terms (I do not now speak of a divorce), could be obtained by any woman who was morally entitled to it; and if she would then find all honorable employments as freely open to her as to men; it would not be necessary for her protection, that during marriage she should make this particular use of her faculties. Like a man when he chooses a profession, so, when a woman marries, it may in general be understood that she makes choice of the management of a household, and the bringing up of a family, as the first call upon her exertions, during as many years of her life as may be required for the purpose; and that she renounces, not all other objects and occupations, but all which are not consistent with the requirements of this. The actual exercise, in a habitual or systematic manner, of outdoor occupations, or such as cannot be carried on at home, would by this principle be practically interdicted to the greater number of married women. But the utmost latitude ought to exist for the adaptation of general rules to individual suitabilities; and there ought to be nothing to prevent faculties exceptionally adapted to any other pursuit, from obeying their vocation notwithstanding marriage: due provision being made for supplying otherwise any falling-short which might become inevitable, in her full performance of the ordinary functions of mistress of a family. These things, if once opinion were rightly directed on the subject, might with perfect safety be left to be regulated by opinion, without any interference of law.

3

On the other point which is involved in the just equality of women, their admissibility to all the functions and occupations hitherto retained as the monopoly of the stronger sex, I should anticipate no difficulty in convincing any one who has gone with me on the subject of the equality of women in the family. I believe that their disabilities elsewhere are only clung to in order to maintain their subordination in domestic life; because the generality of the male sex cannot yet tolerate the idea of living with an equal. Were it not for that, I think that almost every one, in the existing state of opinion in politics and political economy, would admit the injustice of excluding half the human race from the greater number of lucrative occupations, and from almost all high social functions; ordaining from their birth either that they are not, and cannot by any possibility become, fit for employments which are legally open to the stupidest and basest of the other sex, or else that however fit they may be, those employments shall be interdicted to them, in order to be preserved for the exclusive benefit of males. In the last two centuries, when (which was seldom the case) any reason beyond the mere existence of the fact was thought to be required to justify the disabilities of women, people seldom assigned as a reason their inferior mental capacity; which, in times when there was a real trial of personal faculties (from which all women were not excluded) in the struggles of public life, no one really believed in. The reason given in those days was not women's unfitness, but the interest of society, by which was meant the interest of men: just as the *raison d'état*, meaning the convenience of the government, and the support of existing authority, was deemed a sufficient explanation and excuse for the most flagitious crimes. In the present day, power holds a smoother language, and whomsoever it oppresses, always pretends to do so for their own good: accordingly, when anything is forbidden to women, it is thought necessary to say, and desirable to believe, that they are incapable of doing it, and that they depart from their real path of success and happiness when they aspire to it. But to make this reason plausible (I do not say valid), those by whom it is urged must be prepared to carry it to a much greater length than any one ventures to do in the face of present experience. It is not sufficient to maintain that women on the average are less gifted than men on the average, with certain of the higher mental faculties, or that a smaller number of women than of men are fit for occupations and functions of the highest intellectual character. It is necessary to maintain that no women at all are fit for them, and that the most eminent women are inferior in mental faculties to the most mediocre of the men on whom those functions at present devolve. For if the performance of the function is decided either by competition, or by any mode of choice which secures regard to the public interest, there needs to be no apprehension that any important employments will fall into the hands of women inferior to average men, or to the average of their male competitors. The only result would be that there would be fewer women than men in such employments; a result certain to happen in any case, if only from the preference always likely to be felt by the majority of women for the one vocation in which there is nobody to compete with them. Now, the most determined depreciator of women will not venture to deny, that when we add the experience of recent times to that of ages past, women, and not a few merely, but many women, have proved themselves capable of everything, perhaps without a single exception, which is done by men, and of doing it successfully and creditably. The utmost that can be said is, that there are many things which none of them have succeeded in doing as well as they have been done by some men — many in which they have not reached the very highest rank. But there are extremely few, dependent only on mental faculties, in which they have not attained the rank next to the highest. Is not this enough, and much more than enough, to make it a tyranny to them, and a detriment to society, that they should not be allowed to compete with men for the exercise of these functions? Is it not a mere truism to say, that such functions are often filled by men far less fit for them than numbers of women, and who would be beaten by women in any fair field of competition? What difference does it make that there may be men somewhere, fully employed about other things, who may be still better qualified for the things in question than these women? Does not this take place in all competitions? Is there so great a superfluity of men fit for high duties, that society can afford to reject the service of any competent person? Are we so certain of always finding a man made to our hands for any duty or function of social importance which falls vacant, that we lose nothing by putting a ban upon one-half of mankind, and refusing beforehand to make their faculties available, however distinguished they may be? And even if we could do without them, would it be consistent with justice to refuse to them their fair share of honor and distinction, or to deny to them the equal moral right of all human beings to choose their occupation (short of injury to others) according to their own preferences, at their own risk? Nor is the injustice confined to them: it is shared by those who are in a position to benefit by their services. To ordain that any kind of persons shall not be physicians, or shall not be advocates, or shall not be members of parliament, is to injure not them only, but all who employ physicians or advocates, or elect members of parliament, and who are deprived of the stimulating effect of greater competition on the exertions of the competitors, as well as restricted to a narrower range of individual choice.

It will perhaps be sufficient if I confine myself, in the details of my argument, to functions of a public nature: since, if I am successful as to those, it probably will be readily granted that women should be admissible to all other occupations to which it is at all material whether they are admitted or not. And here let me begin by marking out one function, broadly distinguished from all others, their right to which is entirely independent of any question which can be raised concerning their faculties. I mean the suffrage, both parliamentary and municipal. The right to share in the choice of those who are to exercise a public trust, is altogether a distinct thing from that of competing for the trust itself. If no one could vote for a member of parliament who was not fit to be a candidate, the government would be a narrow oligarchy indeed. To have a voice in choosing those by whom one is to be governed, is a means of self-protection due to every one, though he were to remain for ever excluded from the function of governing: and that women are considered fit to have such a choice, may be presumed from the fact, that the law already gives it to women in the most important of all cases to themselves: for the choice of the man who is to govern a woman to the end of life, is always supposed to be voluntarily made by herself. In the case of election to public trusts, it is the business of constitutional law to surround the right of suffrage with all needful securities and limitations; but whatever securities are sufficient in the case of the male sex, no others need be required in the case of women. Under whatever conditions, and within whatever limits, men are admitted to the suffrage, there is not a shadow of justification for not admitting women under the same. The majority of the women of any class are not likely to differ in political opinion from the majority of the men of the same class, unless the question be one in which the interests of women, as such, are in some way involved; and if they are so, women require the suffrage, as their guarantee of just and equal consideration. This ought to be obvious even to those who coincide in no other of the doctrines for which I contend. Even if every woman were a wife, and if every wife ought to be a slave, all the more would these slaves stand in need of legal protection: and we know what legal protection the slaves have, where the laws are made by their masters.

With regard to the fitness of women, not only to participate in elections, but themselves to hold offices or practice professions involving important public responsibilities; I have already observed that this consideration is not essential to the practical question in dispute: since any woman, who succeeds in an open profession, proves by that very fact that she is qualified for it. And in the case of public offices, if the political system of the country is such as to exclude unfit men, it will equally exclude unfit women: while if it is not, there is no additional evil in the fact that the unfit persons whom it admits may be either women or men. As long therefore as it is acknowledged that even a few women may be fit for these duties, the laws which shut the door on those exceptions cannot be justified by any opinion which can be held respecting the capacities of women in general. But, though this last consideration is not essential, it is far from being irrelevant. An unprejudiced view of it gives additional strength to the arguments against the disabilities of women, and reinforces them by high considerations of practical utility.

Let us at first make entire abstraction of all psychological considerations tending to show, that any of the mental differences supposed to exist between women and men are but the natural effect of the differences in their education and circumstances, and indicate no radical difference, far less radical inferiority, of nature. Let us consider women only as they already are, or as they are known to have been; and the capacities which they have already practically shown. What they have done, that at least, if nothing else, it is proved that they can do. When we consider how sedulously they are all trained away from, instead of being trained towards, any of the occupations or objects reserved for men, it is evident that I am taking a very humble ground for them, when I rest their case on what they have actually achieved. For, in this case, negative evidence is worth little, while any positive evidence is conclusive. It cannot be inferred to be impossible that a woman should be a Homer, or an Aristotle, or a Michael Angelo, or a Beethoven, because no woman has yet actually produced works comparable to theirs in any of those lines of excellence. This negative fact at most leaves the question uncertain, and open to psychological discussion. But it is quite certain that a woman can be a Queen Elizabeth, or a Deborah,[3] or a Joan of Arc, since this is not inference, but fact. Now it is a curious consideration, that the only things which the existing law excludes women from doing, are the things which they have proved that they are able to do. There is no law to prevent a woman from having written all the plays of Shakespeare, or composed all the operas of Mozart. But Queen Elizabeth or Queen Victoria, had they not inherited the throne, could not have been intrusted with the smallest of the political duties, of which the former showed herself equal to the greatest.

If anything conclusive could be inferred from experience, without psychological analysis, it would be that the things which women are not allowed to do are the very ones for which they are peculiarly qualified; since their vocation for government has made its way, and become conspicuous, through the very few opportunities which have been given; while in the lines of distinction which apparently were freely open to them, they have by no means so eminently distinguished themselves. We know how small a number of reigning queens history presents, in comparison with that of kings. Of this smaller number a far larger proportion have shown talents for rule; though many of them

3. Old Testament heroine who led the Israelites to victory over the Canaanites (Judges 4–5).

have occupied the throne in difficult periods. It is remarkable, too, that they have, in a great number of instances, been distinguished by merits the most opposite to the imaginary and conventional character of women: they have been as much remarked for the firmness and vigour of their rule, as for its intelligence. When, to queens and empresses, we add regents, and viceroys of provinces, the list of women who have been eminent rulers of mankind swells to a great length.[4] This fact is so undeniable, that some one, long ago, tried to retort the argument, and turned the admitted truth into an additional insult, by saying that queens are better than kings, because under kings women govern, but under queens, men.

It may seem a waste of reasoning to argue against a bad joke; but such things do affect people's minds; and I have heard men quote this saying, with an air as if they thought that there was something in it. At any rate, it will serve as well as anything else for a starting point in discussion. I say, then, that it is not true that under kings, women govern. Such cases are entirely exceptional: and weak kings have quite as often governed ill through the influence of male favourites, as of female. When a king is governed by a woman merely through his amatory propensities, good government is not probable, though even then there are exceptions. But French history counts two kings who have voluntarily given the direction of affairs during many years, the one to his mother, the other to his sister: one of them, Charles VIII, was a mere boy, but in doing so he followed the intentions of his father Louis XI,[5] the ablest monarch of his age. The other, Saint Louis, was the best, and one of the most vigorous rulers, since the time of Charlemagne. Both these princesses ruled in a manner hardly equaled by any prince among their contemporaries. The emperor Charles the Fifth, the most politic prince of his time, who had as great a number of able men in his service as a ruler ever had, and was one of the least likely of all sovereigns to sacrifice his interest to personal feelings, made two princesses of his family successively Governors of the Netherlands, and kept one or other of them in that post during his whole life (they were afterwards succeeded by a third). Both ruled very successfully, and one

---

4. Especially is this true if we take into consideration Asia as well as Europe. If a Hindoo principality is strongly, vigilantly, and economically governed; if order is preserved without oppression; if cultivation is extending, and the people prosperous, in three cases out of four that principality is under a woman's rule. This fact, to me an entirely unexpected one, I have collected from a long official knowledge of Hindoo governments. There are many such instances: for though, by Hindoo institutions, a woman cannot reign, she is the legal regent of a kingdom during the minority of the heir; and minorities are frequent, the lives of the male rulers being so often prematurely terminated through the effect of inactivity and sensual excesses. When we consider that these princesses have never been seen in public, have never conversed with any man not of their own family except from behind a curtain, that they do not read, and if they did, there is no book in their languages which can give them the smallest instruction on political affairs; the example they afford of the natural capacity of women for government is very striking [Mill's note].

5. Louis XI (1423–1483), king of France and the most important figure in the nation's recovery from the Hundred Years' War. Charles VIII (1470–1498), only thirteen at the time of his accession, was notoriously dull witted. Until 1491, his sister Anne was the regent.

of them, Margaret of Austria,[6] was one of the ablest politicians of the age. So much for one side of the question. Now as to the other. When it is said that under queens men govern, is the same meaning to be understood as when kings are said to be governed by women? Is it meant that queens choose as their instruments of government, the associates of their personal pleasures? The case is rare even with those who are as unscrupulous on the latter point as Catherine II:[7] and it is not in these cases that the good government, alleged to arise from male influence, is to be found. If it be true, then, that the administration is in the hands of better men under a queen than under an average king, it must be that queens have a superior capacity for choosing them; and women must be better qualified than men both for the position of sovereign, and for that of chief minister; for the principal business of a prime minister is not to govern in person, but to find the fittest persons to conduct every department of public affairs. The more rapid insight into character, which is one of the admitted points of superiority in women over men, must certainly make them, with anything like parity of qualifications in other respects, more apt than men in that choice of instruments, which is nearly the most important business of every one who has to do with governing mankind. Even the unprincipled Catherine de' Medici could feel the value of a Chancellor de l'Hôpital.[8] But it is also true that most great queens have been great by their own talents for government, and have been well served precisely for that reason. They retained the supreme direction of affairs in their own hands: and if they listened to good advisers, they gave by that fact the strongest proof that their judgment fitted them for dealing with the great questions of government.

Is it reasonable to think that those who are fit for the greater functions of politics, are incapable of qualifying themselves for the less? Is there any reason in the nature of things, that the wives and sisters of princes should, whenever called on, be found as competent as the princes themselves to *their* business, but that the wives and sisters of statesmen, and administrators, and directors of companies, and managers of public institutions, should be unable to do what is done by their brothers and husbands? The real reason is plain enough; it is that princesses, being more raised above the generality of men by their rank than placed below them by their sex, have never been taught that it was improper for them to concern themselves with politics; but have been allowed to feel the liberal interest natural to any cultivated human being, in the

6. Charles V (1500–1558), Holy Roman emperor and king of Spain, was brought up by his aunt Margaret of Austria, who acted as regent of The Netherlands. Her successor was Charles's sister, Mary of Hungary. She, in turn, was succeeded by her daughter, Margaret of Parma.
7. The Empress Catherine the Great of Russia (1729–1796), notorious for her love of handsome soldiers.
8. Michel de l'Hôpital (1507–1573), Catherine's chief minister when she tried to avert a civil war between the Catholics and the Protestants. Catherine de' Medicis (1519–1589), wife of King Henri II of France (1547–59).

great transactions which took place around them, and in which they might be called on to take a part. The ladies of reigning families are the only women who are allowed the same range of interests and freedom of development as men; and it is precisely in their case that there is not found to be any inferiority. Exactly where and in proportion as women's capacities for government have been tried, in that proportion have they been found adequate.

This fact is in accordance with the best general conclusions which the world's imperfect experience seems as yet to suggest, concerning the peculiar tendencies and aptitudes characteristic of women, as women have hitherto been. I do not say, as they will continue to be; for, as I have already said more than once, I consider it presumption in any one to pretend to decide what women are or are not, can or cannot be, by natural constitution. They have always hitherto been kept, as far as regards spontaneous development, in so unnatural a state, that their nature cannot but have been greatly distorted and disguised; and no one can safely pronounce that if women's nature were left to choose its direction as freely as men's, and if no artificial bent were attempted to be given to it except that required by the conditions of human society, and given to both sexes alike, there would be any material difference, or perhaps any difference at all, in the character and capacities which would unfold themselves. I shall presently show, that even the least contestable of the differences which now exist, are such as may very well have been produced merely by circumstances, without any difference of natural capacity. But, looking at women as they are known in experience, it may be said of them, with more truth than belongs to most other generalizations on the subject, that the general bent of their talents is towards the practical. This statement is conformable to all the public history of women, in the present and the past. It is no less borne out by common and daily experience. Let us consider the special nature of the mental capacities most characteristic of a woman of talent. They are all of a kind which fits them for practice, and makes them tend towards it. What is meant by a woman's capacity of intuitive perception? It means, a rapid and correct insight into present fact. It has nothing to do with general principles. Nobody ever perceived a scientific law of nature by intuition, nor arrived at a general rule of duty or prudence by it. These are results of slow and careful collection and comparison of experience; and neither the men nor the women of intuition usually shine in this department, unless, indeed, the experience necessary is such as they can acquire by themselves. For what is called their intuitive sagacity makes them peculiarly apt in gathering such general truths as can be collected from their individual means of observation. When, consequently, they chance to be as well provided as men are with the results of other people's experience, by reading and education, (I use the word chance advisedly, for, in respect to the knowledge that tends to fit them for the greater concerns of life, the only educated women

are the self-educated) they are better furnished than men in general
with the essential requisites of skillful and successful practice. Men who
have been much taught, are apt to be deficient in the sense of present
fact; they do not see, in the facts which they are called upon to deal
with, what is really there, but what they have been taught to expect.
This is seldom the case with women of any ability. Their capacity of
"intuition" preserves them from it. With equality of experience and of
general faculties, a woman usually sees much more than a man of what
is immediately before her. Now this sensibility to the present, is the
main quality on which the capacity for practice, as distinguished from
theory, depends. To discover general principles, belongs to the speculative faculty: to discern and discriminate the particular cases in which
they are and are not applicable, constitutes practical talent: and for this,
women as they now are have a peculiar aptitude. I admit that there
can be no good practice without principles, and that the predominant
place which quickness of observation holds among a woman's faculties,
makes her particularly apt to build over-hasty generalizations upon her
own observation; though at the same time no less ready in rectifying
those generalizations, as her observation takes a wider range. But the
corrective to this defect, is access to the experience of the human race;
general knowledge — exactly the thing which education can best supply.
A woman's mistakes are specifically those of a clever self-educated man,
who often sees what men trained in routine do not see, but falls into
errors for want of knowing things which have long been known. Of
course he has acquired much of the pre-existing knowledge, or he could
not have got on at all; but what he knows of it he has picked up in
fragments and at random, as women do.

But this gravitation of women's minds to the present, to the real, to
actual fact, while in its exclusiveness it is a source of errors, is also a
most useful counteractive of the contrary error. The principal and most
characteristic aberration of speculative minds as such, consists precisely
in the deficiency of this lively perception and ever-present sense of
objective fact. For want of this, they often not only overlook the contradiction which outward facts oppose to their theories, but lose sight
of the legitimate purpose of speculation altogether, and let their speculative faculties go astray into regions not peopled with real beings,
animate or inanimate, even idealized, but with personified shadows
created by the illusions of metaphysics or by the mere entanglement of
words, and think these shadows the proper objects of the highest, the
most transcendant, philosophy. Hardly anything can be of greater value
to a man of theory and speculation who employs himself not in col-
lecting materials of knowledge by observation, but in working them up
by processes of thought into comprehensive truths of science and laws
of conduct, than to carry on his speculations in the companionship,
and under the criticism, of a really superior woman. There is nothing
comparable to it for keeping his thoughts within the limits of real

things, and the actual facts of nature. A woman seldom runs wild after an abstraction. The habitual direction of her mind to dealing with things as individuals rather than in groups, and (what is closely connected with it) her more lively interest in the present feelings of persons, which makes her consider first of all, in anything which claims to be applied to practice, in what manner persons will be affected by it — these two things make her extremely unlikely to put faith in any speculation which loses sight of individuals, and deals with things as if they existed for the benefit of some imaginary entity, some mere creation of the mind, not resolvable into the feelings of living beings. Women's thoughts are thus as useful in giving reality to those of thinking men, as men's thoughts in giving width and largeness to those of women. In depth, as distinguished from breadth, I greatly doubt if even now, women, compared with men, are at any disadvantage.

If the existing mental characteristics of women are thus valuable even in aid of speculation, they are still more important, when speculation has done its work, for carrying out the results of speculation into practice. For the reasons already given, women are comparatively unlikely to fall into the common error of men, that of sticking to their rules in a case whose specialties either take it out of the class to which the rules are applicable, or require a special adaptation of them. Let us now consider another of the admitted superiorities of clever women, greater quickness of apprehension. Is not this preeminently a quality which fits a person for practice? In action, everything continually depends upon deciding promptly. In speculation, nothing does. A mere thinker can wait, can take time to consider, can collect additional evidence; he is not obliged to complete his philosophy at once, lest the opportunity should go by. The power of drawing the best conclusion possible from insufficient data is not indeed useless in philosophy; the construction of a provisional hypothesis consistent with all known facts is often the needful basis for further inquiry. But this faculty is rather serviceable in philosophy, than the main qualification for it: and, for the auxiliary as well as for the main operation, the philosopher can allow himself any time he pleases. He is in no need of the capacity of doing rapidly what he does; what he rather needs is patience, to work on slowly until imperfect lights have become perfect, and a conjecture has ripened into a theorem. For those, on the contrary, whose business is with the fugitive and perishable — with individual facts, not kinds of facts — rapidity of thought is a qualification next only in importance to the power of thought itself. He who has not his faculties under immediate command, in the contingencies of action, might as well not have them at all. He may be fit to criticize, but he is not fit to act. Now it is in this that women, and the men who are most like women, confessedly excel. The other sort of man, however pre-eminent may be his faculties, arrives slowly at complete command of them: rapidity of judgment and promptitude of judicious action, even in the things he knows best, are the gradual and late result of strenuous effort grown into habit.

It will be said, perhaps, that the greater nervous susceptibility of women is a disqualification for practice, in anything but domestic life, by rendering them mobile, changeable, too vehemently under the influence of the moment, incapable of dogged perseverance, unequal and uncertain in the power of using their faculties. I think that these phrases sum up the greater part of the objections commonly made to the fitness of women for the higher class of serious business. Much of all this is the mere overflow of nervous energy run to waste, and would cease when the energy was directed to a definite end. Much is also the result of conscious or unconscious cultivation; as we see by the almost total disappearance of "hysterics" and fainting fits, since they have gone out of fashion. Moreover, when people are brought up, like many women of the higher classes (though less so in our own country than in any other) a kind of hothouse plants, shielded from the wholesome vicissitudes of air and temperature, and untrained in any of the occupations and exercises which give stimulus and development to the circulatory and muscular system, while their nervous system, especially in its emotional department, is kept in unnaturally active play; it is no wonder if those of them who do not die of consumption, grow up with constitutions liable to derangement from slight causes, both internal and external, and without stamina to support any task, physical or mental, requiring continuity of effort. But women brought up to work for their livelihood show none of these morbid characteristics, unless indeed they are chained to an excess of sedentary work in confined and unhealthy rooms. Women who in their early years have shared in the healthful physical education and bodily freedom of their brothers, and who obtain a sufficiency of pure air and exercise in after-life, very rarely have any excessive susceptibility of nerves which can disqualify them for active pursuits. There is indeed a certain proportion of persons, in both sexes, in whom an unusual degree of nervous sensibility is constitutional, and of so marked a character as to be the feature of their organization which exercises the greatest influence over the whole character of the vital phenomena. This constitution, like other physical conformations, is hereditary, and is transmitted to sons as well as daughters; but it is possible, and probable, that the nervous temperament (as it is called) is inherited by a greater number of women than of men. We will assume this as a fact: and let me then ask, are men of nervous temperament found to be unfit for the duties and pursuits usually followed by men? If not, why should women of the same temperament be unfit for them? The peculiarities of the temperament are, no doubt, within certain limits, an obstacle to success in some employments, though an aid to it in others. But when the occupation is suitable to the temperament, and sometimes even when it is unsuitable, the most

brilliant examples of success are continually given by the men of high
nervous sensibility. They are distinguished in their practical manifestations chiefly by this, that being susceptible of a higher degree of excitement than those of another physical constitution, their powers when
excited differ more than in the case of other people, from those shown
in their ordinary state: they are raised, as it were, above themselves, and
do things with ease which they are wholly incapable of at other times.
But this lofty excitement is not, except in weak bodily constitutions, a
mere flash, which passes away immediately, leaving no permanent
traces, and incompatible with persistent and steady pursuit of an object.
It is the character of the nervous temperament to be capable of *sustained* excitement, holding out through long continued efforts. It is
what is meant by *spirit*. It is what makes the highbred racehorse run
without slackening speed till he drops down dead. It is what has enabled
so many delicate women to maintain the most sublime constancy not
only at the stake, but through a long preliminary succession of mental
and bodily tortures. It is evident that people of this temperament are
particularly apt for what may be called the executive department of the
leadership of mankind. They are the material of great orators, great
preachers, impressive diffusers of moral influences. Their constitution
might be deemed less favourable to the qualities required from a statesman in the cabinet, or from a judge. It would be so, if the consequence
necessarily followed that because people are excitable they must always
be in a state of excitement. But this is wholly a question of training.
Strong feeling is the instrument and element of strong self-control: but
it requires to be cultivated in that direction. When it is, it forms not
the heroes of impulse only, but those also of self-conquest. History and
experience prove that the most passionate characters are the most fa-
natically rigid in their feelings of duty, when their passion has been
trained to act in that direction. The judge who gives a just decision in
a case where his feelings are intensely interested on the other side,
derives from that same strength of feeling the determined sense of the
obligation of justice, which enables him to achieve this victory over
himself. The capability of that lofty enthusiasm which takes the human
being out of his every-day character, reacts upon the daily character
itself. His aspirations and powers when he is in this exceptional state,
become the type with which he compares, and by which he estimates,
his sentiments and proceedings at other times: and his habitual purposes assume a character molded by and assimilated to the moments
of lofty excitement, although those, from the physical nature of a human being, can only be transient. Experience of races, as well as of
individuals, does not show those of excitable temperament to be less
fit, on the average, either for speculation or practice, than the more
unexcitable. The French, and the Italians, are undoubtedly by nature
more nervously excitable than the Teutonic races, and, compared at
least with the English, they have a much greater habitual and daily

emotional life: but have they been less great in science, in public business, in legal and judicial eminence, or in war? There is abundant evidence that the Greeks were of old, as their descendants and successors still are, one of the most excitable of the races of mankind. It is superfluous to ask, what among the achievements of men they did not excel in. The Romans, probably, as an equally southern people, had the same original temperament: but the stern character of their national discipline, like that of the Spartans, made them an example of the opposite type of national character; the greater strength of their natural feelings being chiefly apparent in the intensity which the same original temperament made it possible to give to the artificial. If these cases exemplify what a naturally excitable people may be made, the Irish Celts afford one of the aptest examples of what they are when left to themselves; (if those can be said to be left to themselves who have been for centuries under the indirect influence of bad government, and the direct training of a Catholic hierarchy and of a sincere belief in the Catholic religion.) The Irish character must be considered, therefore, as an unfavorable case: yet, whenever the circumstances of the individual have been at all favorable, what people have shown greater capacity for the most varied and multifarious individual eminence? Like the French compared with the English, the Irish with the Swiss, the Greeks or Italians compared with the German races, so women compared with men may be found, on the average, to do the same things with some variety in the particular kind of excellence. But, that they would do them fully as well on the whole, if their education and cultivation were adapted to correcting instead of aggravating the infirmities incident to their temperament, I see not the smallest reason to doubt.

Supposing it, however, to be true that women's minds are by nature more mobile than those of men, less capable of persisting long in the same continuous effort, more fitted for dividing their faculties among many things than for traveling in any one path to the highest point which can be reached by it: this may be true of women as they now are (though not without great and numerous exceptions), and may account for their having remained behind the highest order of men in precisely the things in which this absorption of the whole mind in one set of ideas and occupations may seem to be most requisite. Still, this difference is one which can only affect the kind of excellence, not the excellence itself, or its practical worth: and it remains to be shown whether this exclusive working of a part of the mind, this absorption of the whole thinking faculty in a single subject, and concentration of it on a single work, is the normal and healthful condition of the human faculties, even for speculative uses. I believe that what is gained in special development by this concentration, is lost in the capacity of the mind for the other purposes of life; and even in abstract thought, it is my decided opinion that the mind does more by frequently returning to a difficult problem, than by sticking to it without interruption. For the purposes, at all events, of practice, from its highest to its humblest departments, the capacity of passing promptly from one subject of consideration to another, without letting the active spring of the intellect run down between the two, is a power far more valuable; and this power women pre-eminently possess, by virtue of the very mobility of which they are accused. They perhaps have it from nature, but they certainly have it by training and education; for nearly the whole of the occupations of women consist in the management of small but multitudinous details, on each of which the mind cannot dwell even for a minute, but must pass on to other things, and if anything requires longer thought, must steal time at odd moments for thinking of it. The capacity indeed which women show for doing their thinking in circumstances and at times which almost any man would make an excuse to himself for not attempting it, has often been noticed: and a woman's mind, though it may be occupied only with small things, can hardly ever permit itself to be vacant, as a man's so often is when not engaged in what he chooses to consider the business of his life. The business of a woman's ordinary life is things in general, and can as little cease to go on as the world to go round.

But (it is said) there is anatomical evidence of the superior mental capacity of men compared with women: they have a larger brain. I reply, that in the first place the fact itself is doubtful. It is by no means established that the brain of a woman is smaller than that of a man. If it is inferred merely because a woman's bodily frame generally is of less dimensions than a man's, this criterion would lead to strange consequences. A tall and large-boned man must on this showing be wonderfully superior in intelligence to a small man, and an elephant or a whale must prodigiously excel mankind. The size of the brain in human beings, anatomists say, varies much less than the size of the body, or even of the head, and the one cannot be at all inferred from the other. It is certain that some women have as large a brain as any man. It is within my knowledge that a man who had weighed many human brains, said that the heaviest he knew of, heavier even than Cuvier's (the heaviest previously recorded,) was that of a woman. Next, I must observe that the precise relation which exists between the brain and the intellectual powers is not yet well understood, but is a subject of great dispute. That there is a very close relation we cannot doubt. The brain is certainly the material organ of thought and feeling: and (making abstraction of the great unsettled controversy respecting the appropriation of different parts of the brain to different mental faculties) I admit that it would be an anomaly, and an exception to all we know of the general laws of life and organization, if the size of the organ were wholly indifferent to the function; if no accession of power were derived from the greater magnitude of the instrument. But the exception and the anomaly would be fully as great if the organ exercised influence by its magnitude *only*. In all the more delicate operations of nature — of which those of the animated creation are the most delicate, and those of the nervous system by far the most delicate of these — differences in the effect depend as much on differences of quality in the physical agents, as on their quantity: and if the quality of an instrument is to be tested by the nicety and delicacy of the work it can do, the indications point to a greater average fineness of quality in the brain and nervous system of women than of men. Dismissing abstract difference of quality, a thing difficult to verify, the efficiency of an organ is known to depend not solely on its size but on its activity: and of this we have an approximate measure in the energy with which the blood circulates through it, both the stimulus and the reparative force being mainly dependent on the circulation. It would not be surprising — it is indeed an hypothesis which accords well with the differences actually observed between the mental operations of the two sexes — if men on the average should have the advantage in the size of the brain, and women in activity of cerebral circulation. The results which conjecture, founded on analogy, would lead us to expect from this difference of organization, would correspond to some of those which we most commonly see. In the first place, the mental operations of men might be expected to be slower. They would neither be so prompt as women in thinking, nor so quick to feel. Large bodies take more time to get into full action. On the other hand, when once got thoroughly into play, men's brain would bear more work. It would be more persistent in the line first taken; it would have more difficulty in changing from one mode of action to another, but, in the one thing it was doing, it could go on longer without loss of power or sense of fatigue. And do we not find that the things in which men most excel women are those which require most plodding and long hammering at a single thought, while women do best what must be done rapidly? A woman's brain is sooner fatigued, sooner exhausted; but given the degree of exhaustion, we should expect to find that it would recover itself sooner. I repeat that this speculation is entirely hypothetical; it pretends to no more than to suggest a line of enquiry. I have before repudiated the notion of its being yet certainly known that there is any natural difference at all in the average strength or direction of the mental capacities of the two sexes, much less what that difference is. Nor is it possible that this should be known, so long as the psychological laws of the formation of character have been so little studied, even in a general way, and in the particular case never scientifically applied at all; so long as the most obvious external causes of difference of character are habitually disregarded — left unnoticed by the observer, and looked down upon with a kind of supercilious contempt by the prevalent schools both of natural history and of mental philosophy: who, whether they look for the source of what mainly distinguishes human beings from one another, in the world of matter or in that of spirit, agree in running down those who prefer to explain these differences by the different relations of human beings to society and life.

To so ridiculous an extent are the notions formed of the nature of women, mere empirical generalizations, framed, without philosophy or analysis, upon the first instances which present themselves, that the popular idea of it is different in different countries, according as the opinions and social circumstances of the country have given to the women living in it any specialty of development or non-development. An Oriental thinks that women are by nature peculiarly voluptuous; see the violent abuse of them on this ground in Hindoo writings. An Englishman usually thinks that they are by nature cold. The sayings about women's fickleness are mostly of French origin; from the famous distich of Francis the First,[9] upward and downward.

In England it is a common remark, how much more constant women are than men. Inconstancy has been longer reckoned discreditable to a woman, in England than in France; and Englishwomen are besides, in their inmost nature, much more subdued to opinion. It may be remarked by the way, that Englishmen are in peculiarly unfavorable circumstances for attempting to judge what is or is not natural, not merely to women, but to men, or to human beings altogether, at least if they have only English experience to go upon: because there is no place where human nature shows so little of its original lineaments. Both in a good and a bad sense, the English are farther from a state of nature than any other modern people. They are, more than any other people, a product of civilization and discipline. England is the country in which social discipline has most succeeded, not so much in con-quering, as in suppressing, whatever is liable to conflict with it. The English, more than any other people, not only act but feel according to rule. In other countries, the taught opinion, or the requirement of society, may be the stronger power, but the promptings of the individual nature are always visible under it, and often resisting it: rule may be stronger than nature, but nature is still there. In England, rule has to a great degree substituted itself for nature. The greater part of life is carried on, not by following inclination under the control of rule, but by having no inclination but that of following a rule. Now this has its good side doubtless, though it has also a wretchedly bad one; but it must render an Englishman peculiarly ill-qualified to pass a judgment on the original tendencies of human nature from his own experience. The errors to which observers elsewhere are liable on the subject, are of a different character. An Englishman is ignorant respecting human nature, a Frenchman is prejudiced. An Englishman's errors are nega-tive, a Frenchman's positive. An Englishman fancies that things do not

---

9. Francis I (1494–1547), king of France, was known for the phrase — not a "distich" — *toute femme varie* ("all women are inconsistent").

exist, because he never sees them; a Frenchman thinks they must always and necessarily exist, because he does see them. An Englishman does not know nature, because he has had no opportunity of observing it; a Frenchman generally knows a great deal of it, but often mistakes it, because he has only seen it sophisticated and distorted. For the artificial state superinduced by society disguises the natural tendencies of the thing which is the subject of observation, in two different ways: by extinguishing the nature, or by transforming it. In the one case there is but a starved residuum of nature remaining to be studied; in the other case there is much, but it may have expanded in any direction rather than that in which it would spontaneously grow.

I have said that it cannot now be known how much of the existing mental differences between men and women is natural, and how much artificial; whether there are any natural differences at all; or, supposing all artificial causes of difference to be withdrawn, what natural character would be revealed. I am not about to attempt what I have pronounced impossible: but doubt does not forbid conjecture, and where certainty is unattainable, there may yet be the means of arriving at some degree of probability. The first point, the origin of the differences actually observed, is the one most accessible to speculation; and I shall attempt to approach it, by the only path by which it can be reached; by tracing the mental consequences of external influences. We cannot isolate a human being from the circumstances of his condition, so as to ascertain experimentally what he would have been by nature; but we can consider what he is, and what his circumstances have been, and whether the one would have been capable of producing the other.

Let us take, then, the only marked case which observation affords, of apparent inferiority of women to men, if we except the merely physical one of bodily strength. No production in philosophy, science, or art, entitled to the first rank, has been the work of a woman. Is there any mode of accounting for this, without supposing that women are naturally incapable of producing them?

In the first place, we may fairly question whether experience has afforded sufficient grounds for an induction. It is scarcely three generations since women, saving very rare exceptions, have begun to try their capacity in philosophy, science, or art. It is only in the present generation that their attempts have been at all numerous; and they are even now extremely few, everywhere but in England and France. It is a relevant question, whether a mind possessing the requisites of first-rate eminence in speculation or creative art could have been expected, on the mere calculation of chances, to turn up during that lapse of time, among the women whose tastes and personal position admitted of their devoting themselves to these pursuits. In all things which there has yet been time for — in all but the very highest grades in the scale of excellence, especially in the department in which they have been longest engaged, literature (both prose and poetry) — women have done quite as much, have obtained fully as high prizes as many of them, as could be expected from the length of time and the number of competitors. If we go back to the earlier period when very few women made the attempt, yet some of those few made it with distinguished success. The Greeks always accounted Sappho among their great poets; and we may well suppose that Myrtis, said to have been the teacher of Pindar, and Corinna, who five times bore away from him the prize of poetry, must at least have had sufficient merit to admit of being compared with that great name. Aspasia[1] did not leave any philosophical writings; but it is an admitted fact that Socrates resorted to her for instruction, and avowed himself to have obtained it.

If we consider the works of women in modern times, and contrast them with those of men, either in the literary or the artistic department, such inferiority as may be observed resolves itself essentially into one thing: but that is a most material one; deficiency of originality. Not total deficiency; for every production of mind which is of any substantive value, has an originality of its own — is a conception of the mind itself, not a copy of something else. Thoughts original, in the sense of being unborrowed — of being derived from the thinker's own observations or intellectual processes — are abundant in the writings of women. But they have not yet produced any of those great and luminous new ideas which form an era in thought, nor those fundamentally new conceptions in art, which open a vista of possible effects not before thought of, and found a new school. Their compositions are mostly grounded on the existing fund of thought, and their creations do not deviate widely from existing types. This is the sort of inferiority which their works manifest: for in point of execution, in the detailed application of thought, and the perfection of style, there is no inferiority. Our best novelists in point of composition, and of the management of detail, have mostly been women; and there is not in all modern literature a more eloquent vehicle of thought than the style of Madame de Stael, nor, as a specimen of purely artistic excellence, anything superior to the prose of Madame Sand,[2] whose style acts upon the nervous system like a symphony of Haydn or Mozart. High originality of conception is, as I have said, what is chiefly wanting. And now to examine if there is any manner in which this deficiency can be accounted for.

Let us remember, then, so far as regards mere thought, that during all that period in the world's existence, and in the progress of culti-

1. Famous in fifth-century Athens as the mistress of the city's greatest general, Pericles, with whom she lived from 445 B.C. until his death in 429. Sappho (c. 610–580 B.C.), Greek poet, famous for her love poems. Myrtis, a near contemporary of Pindar, and Corinna, his rival as Mill suggests, were women poets from the region of Beotia. Pindar (c. 518–438 B.C.), was a great lyric poet.
2. George Sand (1804–1876), the pseudonym for Amandine Dupin, French novelist; she was as famous for her affairs, with Chopin especially, as for her novels. Germain de Stäel (1766–1817), distinguished woman of letters and liberal politician.

vation, in which great and fruitful new truths could be arrived at by
mere force of genius, with little previous study and accumulation of
knowledge — during all that time women did not concern themselves
with speculation at all. From the days of Hypatia to those of the Reformation, the illustrious Heloisa[3] is almost the only woman to whom
any such achievement might have been possible; and we know not how
great a capacity of speculation in her may have been lost to mankind
by the misfortunes of her life. Never since any considerable number of
women have begun to cultivate serious thought, has originality been
possible on easy terms. Nearly all the thoughts which can be reached
by mere strength of original faculties, have long since been arrived at;
and originality, in any high sense of the word, is now scarcely ever
attained but by minds which have undergone elaborate discipline, and
are deeply versed in the results of previous thinking. It is Mr. Maurice,[4]
I think, who has remarked on the present age, that its most original
thinkers are those who have known most thoroughly what had been
thought by their predecessors: and this will always henceforth be the
case. Every fresh stone in the edifice has now to be placed on the top
of so many others, that a long process of climbing, and of carrying up
materials, has to be gone through by whoever aspires to take a share in
the present stage of the work. How many women are there who have
gone through any such process? Mrs. Somerville,[5] alone perhaps of
women, knows as much of mathematics as is now needful for making
any considerable mathematical discovery: is it any proof of inferiority
in women, that she has not happened to be one of the two or three
persons who in her lifetime have associated their names with some
striking advancement of the science? Two women, since political economy has been made a science, have known enough of it to write usefully on the subject: of how many of the innumerable men who have
written on it during the same time, is it possible with truth to say more?
If no woman has hitherto been a great historian, what woman has had
the necessary erudition? If no woman is a great philologist, what woman
has studied Sanscrit and Slavonic, the Gothic of Ulphila and the Persic
of the Zendavesta?[6] Even in practical matters we all know what is the
value of the originality of untaught geniuses. It means, inventing over
again in its rudimentary form something already invented and improved
upon by many successive inventors. When women have had the prep-

3. Héloise (c. 1098–1164), the lover of Peter Abelard, prioress at the Paraclete, renowned as a
   teacher. Hypatia (c. 370–415), an Egyptian philosopher and the first notable woman
   mathematician.
4. F. D. Maurice (1805–1872), a friend of Mill's from youth; later well known as a Christian
   Socialist.
5. Mary Somerville (1780–1872), after whom Somerville College, Oxford, was named, wrote on
   geometry and mechanics and was the leading woman theorist of her day.
6. The nineteenth-century rendering of Avestan, the archaic Iranian language in which the
   sacred texts of Zoroastrianism were written. "Ulphila": an alphabet devised by Ulfilas (fourth
   century), a bishop, to record the language of the Goths.

aration which all men now require to be eminently original, it will be time enough to begin judging by experience of their capacity for originality.

It no doubt often happens that a person, who has not widely and accurately studied the thoughts of others on a subject, has by natural sagacity a happy intuition, which he can suggest, but cannot prove, which yet when matured may be an important addition to knowledge: but even then, no justice can be done to it until some other person, who does possess the previous acquirements, takes it in hand, tests it, gives it a scientific or practical form, and fits it into its place among the existing truths of philosophy or science. Is it supposed that such felicitous thoughts do not occur to women? They occur by hundreds to every woman of intellect. But they are mostly lost, for want of a husband or friend who has the other knowledge which can enable him to estimate them properly and bring them before the world: and even when they are brought before it, they generally appear as his ideas, not their real author's. Who can tell how many of the most original thoughts put forth by male writers, belong to a woman by suggestion, to themselves only by verifying and working out? If I may judge by my own case, a very large proportion indeed.

If we turn from pure speculation to literature in the narrow sense of the term, and the fine arts, there is a very obvious reason why women's literature is, in its general conception and in its main features, an imitation of men's. Why is the Roman literature, as critics proclaim to satiety, not original, but an imitation of the Greek? Simply because the Greeks came first. If women lived in a different country from men, and had never read any of their writings, they would have had a literature of their own. As it is, they have not created one, because they found a highly advanced literature already created. If there had been no suspension of the knowledge of antiquity, or if the Renaissance had occurred before the Gothic cathedrals were built, they never would have been built. We see that, in France and Italy, imitation of the ancient literature stopped the original development even after it had commenced. All women who write are pupils of the great male writers. A painter's early pictures, even if he be a Raffaelle,[7] are undistinguishable in style from those of his master. Even a Mozart does not display his powerful originality in his earliest pieces. What years are to a gifted individual, generations are to a mass. If women's literature is destined to have a different collective character from that of men, depending on any difference of natural tendencies, much longer time is necessary than has yet elapsed, before it can emancipate itself from the influence of accepted models, and guide itself by its own impulses. But if, as I believe, there will not prove to be any natural tendencies common to

7. Raffaello Sangio (1483–1520), known as Raphael, one of the greatest painters of the High Renaissance.

women, and distinguishing their genius from that of men, yet every individual writer among them has her individual tendencies, which at present are still subdued by the influence of precedent and example: and it will require generations more, before their individuality is sufficiently developed to make head against the influence.

It is in the fine arts, properly so called, that the *primâ facie* evidence of inferior original powers in women at first sight appears the strongest: since opinion (it may be said) does not exclude them from these, but rather encourages them, and their education, instead of passing over this department, is in the affluent classes mainly composed of it. Yet in this line of exertion they have fallen still more short than in many others, of the highest eminence attained by men. This shortcoming, however, needs no other explanation than the familiar fact, more universally true in the fine arts than in anything else; the vast superiority of professional persons over amateurs. Women in the educated classes are almost universally taught more or less of some branch or other of the fine arts, but not that they may gain their living or their social consequence by it. Women artists are all amateurs. The exceptions are only of the kind which confirm the general truth. Women are taught music, but not for the purpose of composing, only of executing it: and accordingly it is only as composers, that men, in music, are superior to women. The only one of the fine arts which women do follow, to any extent, as a profession, and an occupation for life, is the histrionic; and in that they are confessedly equal, if not superior, to men. To make the comparison fair, it should be made between the productions of women in any branch of art, and those of men not following it as a profession. In musical composition, for example, women surely have produced fully as good things as have ever been produced by male amateurs. There are now a few women, a very few, who practice painting as a profession, and these are already beginning to show quite as much talent as could be expected. Even male painters (*pace* Mr. Ruskin)[8] have not made any very remarkable figure these last centuries, and it will be long before they do so. The reason why the old painters were so greatly superior to the modern, is that a greatly superior class of men applied themselves to the art. In the fourteenth and fifteenth centuries the Italian printers were the most accomplished men of their age. The greatest of them were men of encyclopedical acquirements and powers, like the great men of Greece. But in their times fine art was, to men's feelings and conceptions, among the grandest things in which a human being could excel; and by it men were made, what only political or military distinction now makes them, the companions of sovereigns, and the equals of the highest nobility. In the present age, men of anything like similar caliber find something more important to do, for their own fame and the uses of the modern world, than painting:

8. John Ruskin (1818–1900), author of *Modern Painters* (1843).

and it is only now and then that a Reynolds or a Turner[9] (of whose relative rank among eminent men I do not pretend to an opinion) applies himself to that art. Music belongs to a different order of things; it does not require the same general powers of mind, but seems more dependant on a natural gift: and it may be thought surprising that no one of the great musical composers has been a woman. But even this natural gift, to be made available for great creations, requires study, and professional devotion to the pursuit. The only countries which have produced first-rate composers, even of the male sex, are Germany and Italy — countries in which, both in point of special and of general cultivation, women have remained far behind France and England, being generally (it may be said without exaggeration) very little educated, and having scarcely cultivated at all any of the higher faculties of mind. And in those countries the men who are acquainted with the principles of musical composition must be counted by hundreds, or more probably by thousands, the women barely by scores: so that here again, on the doctrine of averages, we cannot reasonably expect to see more than one eminent woman to fifty eminent men; and the last three centuries have not produced fifty eminent male composers either in Germany or in Italy.

There are other reasons, besides those which we have now given, that help to explain why women remain behind men, even in the pursuits which are open to both. For one thing, very few women have time for them. This may seem a paradox; it is an undoubted social fact. The time and thoughts of every woman have to satisfy great previous demands on them for things practical. There is, first, the superintendence of the family and the domestic expenditure, which occupies at least one woman in every family, generally the one of mature years and acquired experience; unless the family is so rich as to admit of delegating that task to hired agency, and submitting to all the waste and malversation inseparable from that mode of conducting it. The superintendence of a household, even when not in other respects laborious, is extremely onerous to the thoughts; it requires incessant vigilance, an eye which no detail escapes, and presents questions for consideration and solution, foreseen and unforeseen, at every hour of the day, from which the person responsible for them can hardly ever shake herself free. If a woman is of a rank and circumstances which relieve her in a measure from these cares, she has still devolving on her the management for the whole family of its intercourse with others — of what is called society, and the less the call made on her by the former duty, the greater is always the development of the latter: the dinner parties, concerts, evening parties, morning visits, letter writing, and all that goes with them. All this is over and above the engrossing duty which society

9. J. W. M. Turner (1775–1851), perhaps the most original British painter of all time; Ruskin was a passionate defender of his work. Sir Joshua Reynolds (1723–1792), among the most famous portrait painters of the later eighteenth century.

imposes exclusively on women, of making themselves charming. A clever woman of the higher ranks finds nearly a sufficient employment of her talents in cultivating the graces of manner and the arts of conversation. To look only at the outward side of the subject: the great and continual exercise of thought which all women who attach any value to dressing well (I do not mean expensively, but with taste, and perception of natural and of artificial *convenance*) must bestow upon their own dress, perhaps also upon that of their daughters, would alone go a great way towards achieving respectable results in art, or science, or literature, and does actually exhaust much of the time and mental power they might have to spare for either.[1] If it were possible that all this number of little practical interests (which are made great to them) should leave them either much leisure, or much energy and freedom of mind, to be devoted to art or speculation, they must have a much greater original supply of active faculty than the vast majority of men. But this is not all. Independently of the regular offices of life which devolve upon a woman, she is expected to have her time and faculties always at the disposal of everybody. If a man has not a profession to exempt him from such demands, still, if he has a pursuit, he offends nobody by devoting his time to it; occupation is received as a valid excuse for his not answering to every casual demand which may be made on him. Are a woman's occupations, especially her chosen and voluntary ones, ever regarded as excusing her from any of what are termed the calls of society? Scarcely are her most necessary and recognised duties allowed as an exemption. It requires an illness in the family, or something else out of the common way, to entitle her to give her own business the precedence over other people's amusement. She must always be at the beck and call of somebody, generally of everybody. If she has a study or a pursuit, she must snatch any short interval which accidentally occurs to be employed in it. A celebrated woman, in a work which I hope will some day be published, remarks truly that everything a woman does is done at odd times. Is it wonderful, then, if she does not attain the highest eminence in things which require consecutive attention, and the concentration on them of the chief interest of life? Such is philosophy, and such, above all, is art, in which, besides the devotion of the thoughts and feelings, the hand also must be kept in constant exercise to attain high skill.

There is another consideration to be added to all these. In the various

1. "It appears to be the same right turn of mind which enables a man to acquire the *truth*, or the just idea of what is right, in the ornaments, as in the more stable principles of art. It has still the same centre of perfection, though it is the centre of a smaller circle. — To illustrate this by the fashion of dress, in which there is allowed to be a good or bad taste. The component parts of dress are continually changing from great to little, from short to long; but the general form still remains: it is still the same general dress which is comparatively fixed, though on a very slender foundation; but it is on this which fashion must rest. He who invents with the most success, or dresses in the best taste, would probably, from the same sagacity employed to greater purposes, have discovered equal skill, or have formed the same correct taste, in the highest labours of art." — *Sir Joshua Reynolds' Discourses*, Disc. vii [Mill's note].

arts and intellectual occupations, there is a degree of proficiency sufficient for living by it, and there is a higher degree on which depend the great productions which immortalize a name. To the attainment of the former, there are adequate motives in the case of all who follow the pursuit professionally: the other is hardly ever attained where there is not, or where there has not been at some period of life, an ardent desire of celebrity. Nothing less is commonly a sufficient stimulus to undergo the long and patient drudgery, which, in the case even of the greatest natural gifts, is absolutely required for great eminence in pursuits in which we already possess so many splendid memorials of the highest genius. Now, whether the cause be natural or artificial, women seldom have this eagerness for fame. Their ambition is generally confined within narrower bounds. The influence they seek is over those who immediately surround them. Their desire is to be liked, loved, or admired, by those whom they see with their eyes: and the proficiency in knowledge, arts, and accomplishments, which is sufficient for that, almost always contents them. This is a trait of character which cannot be left out of the account in judging of women as they are. I do not at all believe that it is inherent in women. It is only the natural result of their circumstances. The love of fame in men is encouraged by education and opinion: to "scorn delights and live laborious days" for its sake, is accounted the part of "noble minds," even if spoken of as their "last infirmity,"[2] and is stimulated by the access which fame gives to all objects of ambition, including even the favor of women; while to women themselves all these objects are closed, and the desire of fame itself considered daring and unfeminine. Besides, how could it be that a woman's interests should not be all concentrated upon the impressions made on those who come into her daily life, when society has ordained that all her duties should be to them, and has contrived that all her comforts should depend on them? The natural desire of consideration from our fellow creatures is as strong in a woman as in a man; but society has so ordered things that public consideration is, in all ordinary cases, only attainable by her through the consideration of her husband or of her male relations, while her private consideration is forfeited by making herself individually prominent, or appearing in any other character than that of an appendage to men. Whoever is in the least capable of estimating the influence on the mind of the entire domestic and social position and the whole habit of a life, must easily recognize in that influence a complete explanation of nearly all the apparent differences between women and men, including the whole of those which imply any inferiority.

As for moral differences, considered as distinguished from intellectual, the distinction commonly drawn is to the advantage of women. They are declared to be better than men; an empty compliment, which

2. Mill quotes from John Milton's *Lycidas* (1638).

must provoke a bitter smile from every woman of spirit, since there is no other situation in life in which it is the established order, and considered quite natural and suitable, that the better should obey the worse. If this piece of idle talk is good for anything, it is only as an admission by men, of the corrupting influence of power; for that is certainly the only truth which the fact, if it be a fact, either proves or illustrates. And it *is* true that servitude, except when it actually brutalizes, though corrupting to both, is less so to the slaves than to the slave-masters. It is wholesomer for the moral nature to be restrained, even by arbitrary power, than to be allowed to exercise arbitrary power without restraint. Women, it is said, seldomer fall under the penal law — contribute a much smaller number of offenders to the criminal calendar, than men. I doubt not that the same thing may be said, with the same truth, of negro slaves. Those who are under the control of others cannot often commit crimes, unless at the command and for the purposes of their masters. I do not know a more signal instance of the blindness with which the world, including the herd of studious men, ignore and pass over all the influences of social circumstances, than their silly depreciation of the intellectual, and silly panegyrics on the moral, nature of women.

The complimentary dictum about women's superior moral goodness may be allowed to pair off with the disparaging one respecting their greater liability to moral bias. Women, we are told, are not capable of resisting their personal partialities: their judgment in grave affairs is warped by their sympathies and antipathies. Assuming it to be so, it is still to be proved that women are oftener misled by their personal feelings than men by their personal interests. The chief difference would seem in that case to be, that men are led from the course of duty and the public interest by their regard for themselves, women (not being allowed to have private interests of their own) by their regard for somebody else. It is also to be considered, that all the education which women receive from society inculcates on them the feeling that the individuals connected with them are the only ones to whom they owe any duty — the only ones whose interest they are called upon to care for; while, as far as education is concerned, they are left strangers even to the elementary ideas which are presupposed in any intelligent regard for larger interests or higher moral objects. The complaint against them resolves itself merely into this, that they fulfil only too faithfully the sole duty which they are taught, and almost the only one which they are permitted to practice.

The concessions of the privileged to the unprivileged are so seldom brought about by any better motive than the power of the unprivileged to extort them, that any arguments against the prerogative of sex are likely to be little attended to by the generality, as long as they are able to say to themselves that women do not complain of it. That fact certainly enables men to retain the unjust privilege some time longer; but does not render it less unjust. Exactly the same thing may be said of the women in the harem of an Oriental: they do not complain of not being allowed the freedom of European women. They think our women insufferably bold and unfeminine. How rarely it is that even men complain of the general order of society; and how much rarer still would such complaint be, if they did not know of any different order existing anywhere else. Women do not complain of the general lot of women; or rather they do, for plaintive elegies on it are very common in the writings of women, and were still more so as long as the lamentations could not be suspected of having any practical object. Their complaints are like the complaints which men make of the general unsatisfactoriness of human life; they are not meant to imply blame, or to plead for any change. But though women do not complain of the power of husbands, each complains of her own husband, or of the husbands of her friends. It is the same in all other cases of servitude, at least in the commencement of the emancipatory movement. The serfs did not at first complain of the power of their lords, but only of their tyranny. The Commons began by claiming a few municipal privileges; they next asked an exemption for themselves from being taxed without their own consent; but they would at that time have thought it a great presumption to claim any share in the king's sovereign authority. The case of women is now the only case in which to rebel against established rules is still looked upon with the same eyes as was formerly a subject's claim to the right of rebelling against his king. A woman who joins in any movement which her husband disapproves, makes herself a martyr, without even being able to be an apostle, for the husband can legally put a stop to her apostleship. Women cannot be expected to devote themselves to the emancipation of women, until men in considerable number are prepared to join with them in the undertaking.

4

There remains a question, not of less importance than those already discussed, and which will be asked the most importunately by those opponents whose conviction is somewhat shaken on the main point. What good are we to expect from the changes proposed in our customs and institutions? Would mankind be at all better off if women were free? If not, why disturb their minds, and attempt to make a social revolution in the name of an abstract right?

It is hardly to be expected that this question will be asked in respect to the change proposed in the condition of women in marriage. The sufferings, immoralities, evils of all sorts, produced in innumerable cases by the subjection of individual women to individual men, are far too terrible to be overlooked. Unthinking or uncandid persons, counting those cases alone which are extreme, or which attain publicity, may say that the evils are exceptional; but no one can be blind to their existence, nor, in many cases, to their intensity. And it is perfectly obvious that the abuse of the power cannot be very much checked while the power remains. It is a power given, or offered, not to good men, or to decently respectable men, but to all men; the most brutal, and the most criminal. There is no check but that of opinion, and such men are in general within the reach of no opinion but that of men like themselves. If such men did not brutally tyrannize over the one human being whom the law compels to bear everything from them, society must already have reached a paradisiacal state. There could be no need any longer to curb men's vicious propensities. Astraea must not only have returned to earth, but the heart of the worst man must have become her temple. The law of servitude in marriage is a monstrous contradiction to all the principles of the modern world, and to all the experience through which those principles have been slowly and painfully worked out. It is the sole case, now that negro slavery has been abolished, in which a human being in the plenitude of every faculty is delivered up to the tender mercies of another human being, in the hope forsooth that this other will use the power solely for the good of the person subjected to it. Marriage is the only actual bondage known to our law. There remain no legal slaves, except the mistress of every house.

It is not, therefore, on this part of the subject, that the question is likely to be asked, *Cui bono?*[3] We may be told that the evil would outweigh the good, but the reality of the good admits of no dispute. In regard, however, to the larger question, the removal of women's disabilities — their recognition as the equals of men in all that belongs to citizenship — the opening to them of all honorable employments, and of the training and education which qualifies for those employments — there are many persons for whom it is not enough that the inequality has no just or legitimate defence; they require to be told what express advantage would be obtained by abolishing it.

To which let me first answer, the advantage of having the most universal and pervading of all human relations regulated by justice instead of injustice. The vast amount of this gain to human nature, it is hardly possible, by any explanation or illustration, to place in a stronger light than it is placed by the bare statement, to any one who attaches a moral meaning to words. All the selfish propensities, the self-worship, the unjust self-preference, which exist among mankind, have their source and root in, and derive their principal nourishment from, the present constitution of the relation between men and women. Think what it is to a boy, to grow up to manhood in the belief that without any merit or any exertion of his own, though he may be the most frivolous and empty or the most ignorant and stolid of mankind, by the mere fact of being

3. For whose benefit? (Latin)

born a male he is by right the superior of all and every one of an entire half of the human race: including probably some whose real superiority to himself he has daily or hourly occasion to feel; but even if in his whole conduct he habitually follows a woman's guidance, still, if he is a fool, she thinks that of course she is not, and cannot be, equal in ability and judgment to himself; and if he is not a fool, he does worse — he sees that she is superior to him, and believes that, notwithstanding her superiority, he is entitled to command and she is bound to obey. What must be the effect on his character, of this lesson? And men of the cultivated classes are often not aware how deeply it sinks into the immense majority of male minds. For, among right-feeling and well-bred people, the inequality is kept as much as possible out of sight; above all, out of sight of the children. As much obedience is required from boys to their mother as to their father: they are not permitted to domineer over their sisters, nor are they accustomed to see these postponed to them, but the contrary; the compensations of the chivalrous feeling being made prominent, while the servitude which requires them is kept in the background. Well brought-up youths in the higher classes thus often escape the bad influences of the situation in their early years, and only experience them when, arrived at manhood, they fall under the dominion of facts as they really exist. Such people are little aware, when a boy is differently brought up, how early the notion of his inherent superiority to a girl arises in his mind; how it grows with his growth and strengthens with his strength; how it is inoculated by one schoolboy upon another; how early the youth thinks himself superior to his mother, owing her perhaps forbearance, but no real respect; and how sublime and sultan-like a sense of superiority he feels, above all, over the woman whom he honours by admitting her to a partnership of his life. Is it imagined that all this does not pervert the whole manner of existence of the man, both as an individual and as a social being? It is an exact parallel to the feeling of a hereditary king that he is excellent above others by being born a king, or a noble by being born a noble. The relation between husband and wife is very like that between lord and vassal, except that the wife is held to more unlimited obedience than the vassal was. However the vassal's character may have been affected, for better and for worse, by his subordination, who can help seeing that the lord's was affected greatly for the worse? whether he was led to believe that his vassals were really superior to himself, or to feel that he was placed in command over people as good as himself, for no merits or labors of his own, but merely for having, as Figaro[4] says, taken the trouble to be born. The self-worship of the monarch, or of the feudal superior, is matched by the self-worship of the male. Human beings do not grow up from childhood in the possession of unearned distinctions, without pluming themselves upon them. Those whom

4. The servant, Figaro in Beaumarchais's satirical play *The Marriage of Figaro* (1784).

privileges not acquired by their merit, and which they feel to be disproportioned to it, inspire with additional humility, are always the few, and the best few. The rest are only inspired with pride, and the worst sort of pride, that which values itself upon accidental advantages, not of its own achieving. Above all, when the feeling of being raised above the whole of the other sex is combined with personal authority over one individual among them; the situation, if a school of conscientious and affectionate forbearance to those whose strongest points of character are conscience and affection, is to men of another quality a regularly constituted Academy or Gymnasium for training them in arrogance and overbearingness; which vices, if curbed by the certainty of resistance in their intercourse with other men, their equals, break out towards all who are in a position to be obliged to tolerate them, and often revenge themselves upon the unfortunate wife for the involuntary restraint which they are obliged to submit to elsewhere.

The example afforded, and the education given to the sentiments, by laying the foundation of domestic existence upon a relation contradictory to the first principles of social justice, must, from the very nature of man, have a perverting influence of such magnitude, that it is hardly possible with our present experience to raise our imaginations to the conception of so great a change for the better as would be made by its removal. All that education and civilization are doing to efface the influences on character of the law of force, and replace them by those of justice, remains merely on the surface, as long as the citadel of the enemy is not attacked. The principle of the modern movement in morals and politics, is that conduct, and conduct alone, entitles to respect: that not what men are, but what they do, constitutes their claim to deference; that, above all, merit, and not birth, is the only rightful claim to power and authority. If no authority, not in its nature temporary, were allowed to one human being over another, society would not be employed in building up propensities with one hand which it has to curb with the other. The child would really, for the first time in man's existence on earth, be trained in the way he should go, and when he was old there would be a chance that he would not depart from it. But so long as the right of the strong to power over the weak rules in the very heart of society, the attempt to make the equal right of the weak the principle of its outward actions will always be an uphill struggle; for the law of justice, which is also that of Christianity, will never get possession of men's inmost sentiments; they will be working against it, even when bending to it.

The second benefit to be expected from giving to women the free use of their faculties, by leaving them the free choice of their employments, and opening to them the same field of occupation and the same prizes and encouragements as to other human beings, would be that of doubling the mass of mental faculties available for the higher service of humanity. Where there is now one person qualified to benefit mankind and promote the general improvement, as a public teacher, or an administrator of some branch of public or social affairs, there would then be a chance of two. Mental superiority of any kind is at present everywhere so much below the demand; there is such a deficiency of persons competent to do excellently anything which it requires any considerable amount of ability to do; that the loss to the world, by refusing to make use of one-half of the whole quantity of talent it possesses, is extremely serious. It is true that this amount of mental power is not totally lost. Much of it is employed, and would in any case be employed, in domestic management, and in the few other occupations open to women and from the remainder indirect benefit is in many individual cases obtained, through the personal influence of individual women over individual men. But these benefits are partial; their range is extremely circumscribed; and if they must be admitted, on the one hand, as a deduction from the amount of fresh social power that would be acquired by giving freedom to one-half of the whole sum of human intellect, there must be added, on the other, the benefit of the stimulus that would be given to the intellect of men by the competition; or (to use a more true expression) by the necessity that would be imposed on them of deserving precedency before they could expect to obtain it.

This great accession to the intellectual power of the species, and to the amount of intellect available for the good management of its affairs, would be obtained, partly, through the better and more complete intellectual education of women, which would then improve *pari passu*[5] with that of men. Women in general would be brought up equally capable of understanding business, public affairs, and the higher matters of speculation, with men in the same class of society; and the select few of the one as well as of the other sex, who were qualified not only to comprehend what is done or thought by others, but to think or do something considerable themselves, would meet with the same facilities for improving and training their capacities in the one sex as in the other. In this way, the widening of the sphere of action for women would operate for good, by raising their education to the level of that of men, and making the one participate in all improvements made in the other. But independently of this, the mere breaking down of the barrier would of itself have an educational virtue of the highest worth. The mere getting rid of the idea that all the wider subjects of thought and action, all the things which are of general and not solely of private interest, are men's business, from which women are to be warned off —positively interdicted from most of it, coldly tolerated in the little which is allowed them—the mere consciousness a woman would then have of being a human being like any other, entitled to choose her pursuits, urged or invited by the same inducements as any one else to

5. With equal steps (Latin, literal trans.); i.e., simultaneously.

interest herself in whatever is interesting to human beings, entitled to exert the share of influence on all human concerns which belongs to an individual opinion, whether she attempted actual participation in them or not—this alone would effect an immense expansion of the faculties of women, as well as enlargement of the range of their moral sentiments.

Besides the addition to the amount of individual talent available for the conduct of human affairs, which certainly are not at present so abundantly provided in that respect that they can afford to dispense with one-half of what nature proffers; the opinion of women would then possess a more beneficial, rather than a greater, influence upon the general mass of human belief and sentiment. I say a more beneficial, rather than a greater influence; for the influence of women over the general tone of opinion has always, or at least from the earliest known period, been very considerable. The influence of mothers on the early character of their sons, and the desire of young men to recommend themselves to young women, have in all recorded times been important agencies in the formation of character, and have determined some of the chief steps in the progress of civilization. Even in the Homeric age, αιδως towards the Τρωαδας ελκεσιπεπλσυς[6] is an acknowledged and powerful motive of action in the great Hector.[7] The moral influence of women has had two modes of operation. First, it has been a softening influence. Those who were most liable to be the victims of violence, have naturally tended as much as they could towards limiting its sphere and mitigating its excesses. Those who were not taught to fight, have naturally inclined in favour of any other mode of settling differences rather than that of fighting. In general, those who have been the greatest sufferers by the indulgence of selfish passion, have been the most earnest supporters of any moral law which offered a means of bridling passion. Women were powerfully instrumental in inducing the northern conquerors to adopt the creed of Christianity, a creed so much more favourable to women than any that preceded it. The conversion of the Anglo-Saxons and of the Franks may be said to have been begun by the wives of Ethelbert and Clovis.[8] The other mode in which the effect of women's opinion has been conspicuous, is by giving a powerful stimulus to those qualities in men, which, not being themselves trained in, it was necessary for them that they should find in their protectors. Courage, and the military virtues generally, have at all times been greatly indebted to the desire which men felt of being admired by women: and the stimulus reaches far beyond this one class

6. Reverence to the gowns of the women of Troy (Greek).
7. Son of King Priam and Queen Hecuba, the hero who led the Trojan forces in the Trojan War.
8. Clovis I, the first Merovingian king of France, was married to Clotilda, who urged him to accept Christianity; victory at Tolbiacum in 496 when he pushed back invading German tribes finally persuaded him. Aethelbert of Kent was married to Bertha, who encouraged him to welcome St. Augustine's mission in 597.

of eminent qualities, since, by a very natural effect of their position, the best passport to the admiration and favour of women has always been to be thought highly of by men. From the combination of the two kinds of moral influence thus exercised by women, arose the spirit of chivalry: the peculiarity of which is, to aim at combining the highest standard of the warlike qualities with the cultivation of a totally different class of virtues — those of gentleness, generosity, and self-abnegation, towards the nonmilitary and defenceless classes generally, and a special submission and worship directed towards women; who were distinguished from the other defenceless classes by the high rewards which they had it in their power voluntarily to bestow on those who endeavored to earn their favor, instead of extorting their subjection. Though the practice of chivalry fell even more sadly short of its theoretic standard than practice generally falls below theory, it remains one of the most precious monuments of the moral history of our race; as a remarkable instance of a concerted and organized attempt by a most disorganized and distracted society, to raise up and carry into practice a moral ideal greatly in advance of its social condition and institutions; so much so as to have been completely frustrated in the main object, yet never entirely inefficacious, and which has left a most sensible, and for the most part a highly valuable impress on the ideas and feelings of all subsequent times.

The chivalrous ideal is the acme of the influence of women's sentiments on the moral cultivation of mankind: and if women are to remain in their subordinate situation, it were greatly to be lamented that the chivalrous standard should have passed away, for it is the only one at all capable of mitigating the demoralizing influences of that position. But the changes in the general state of the species rendered inevitable the substitution of a totally different ideal of morality for the chivalrous one. Chivalry was the attempt to infuse moral elements into a state of society in which everything depended for good or evil on individual prowess, under the softening influences of individual delicacy and generosity. In modern societies, all things, even in the military department of affairs, are decided, not by individual effort, but by the combined operations of numbers; while the main occupation of society has changed from fighting to business, from military to industrial life. The exigencies of the new life are no more exclusive of the virtues of generosity than those of the old, but it no longer entirely depends on them. The main foundations of the moral life of modern times must be justice and prudence; the respect of each for the rights of every other, and the ability of each to take care of himself. Chivalry left without legal check all forms of wrong which reigned unpunished throughout society; it only encouraged a few to do right in preference to wrong, by the direction it gave to the instruments of praise and admiration. But the real dependence of morality must always be upon its penal sanctions — its power to deter from evil. The security of society cannot rest on merely rendering honor to right, a motive so comparatively weak in all but a few, and which on very many does not operate at all. Modern society is able to repress wrong through all departments of life, by a fit exertion of the superior strength which civilization has given it, and thus to render the existence of the weaker members of society (no longer defenceless but protected by law) tolerable to them, without reliance on the chivalrous feelings of those who are in a position to tyrannize. The beauties and graces of the chivalrous character are still what they were, but the rights of the weak, and the general comfort of human life, now rest on a far surer and steadier support; or rather, they do so in every relation of life except the conjugal.

At present the moral influence of women is no less real, but it is no longer of so marked and definite a character: it has more nearly merged in the general influence of public opinion. Both through the contagion of sympathy, and through the desire of men to shine in the eyes of women, their feelings have great effect in keeping alive what remains of the chivalrous ideal — in fostering the sentiments and continuing the traditions of spirit and generosity. In these points of character, their standard is higher than that of men; in the quality of justice, somewhat lower. As regards the relations of private life it may be said generally, that their influence is, on the whole, encouraging to the softer virtues, discouraging to the sterner: though the statement must be taken with all the modifications dependent on individual character. In the chief of the greater trials to which virtue is subject in the concerns of life — the conflict between interest and principle — the tendency of women's influence is of a very mixed character. When the principle involved happens to be one of the very few which the course of their religious or moral education has strongly impressed upon themselves, they are potent auxiliaries to virtue: and their husbands and sons are often prompted by them to acts of abnegation which they never would have been capable of without that stimulus. But, with the present education and position of women, the moral principles which have been impressed on them cover but a comparatively small part of the field of virtue, and are, moreover, principally negative; forbidding particular acts, but having little to do with the general direction of the thoughts and purposes. I am afraid it must be said, that disinterestedness in the general conduct of life — the devotion of the energies to purposes which hold out no promise of private advantages to the family — is very seldom encouraged or supported by women's influence. It is small blame to them that they discourage objects of which they have not learnt to see the advantage, and which withdraw their men from them, and from the interests of the family. But the consequence is that women's influence is often anything but favorable to public virtue.

Women have, however, some share of influence in giving the tone to public moralities since their sphere of action has been a little widened, and since a considerable number of them have occupied themselves practically in the promotion of objects reaching beyond their own family and household. The influence of women counts for a great deal in two of the most marked features of modern European life — its aversion to war, and its addiction to philanthropy. Excellent characteristics both; but unhappily, if the influence of women is valuable in the encouragement it gives to these feelings in general, in the particular applications the direction it gives to them is at least as often mischievous as useful. In the philanthropic department more particularly, the two provinces chiefly cultivated by women are religious proselytism and charity. Religious proselytism at home, is but another word for embittering of religious animosities: abroad, it is usually a blind running at an object, without either knowing or heeding the fatal mischiefs — fatal to the religious object itself as well as to all other desirable objects — which may be produced by the means employed. As for charity, it is a matter in which the immediate effect on the persons directly concerned, and the ultimate consequence to the general good, are apt to be at complete war with one another: while the education given to women — an education of the sentiments rather than of the understanding — and the habit inculcated by their whole life, of looking to immediate effects on persons, and not to remote effects on classes of persons — make them both unable to see, and unwilling to admit, the ultimate evil tendency of any form of charity or philanthropy which commends itself to their sympathetic feelings. The great and continually increasing mass of unenlightened and shortsighted benevolence, which, taking the care of people's lives out of their own hands, and relieving them from the disagreeable consequences of their own acts, saps the very foundations of the self-respect, self-help, and self-control which are the essential conditions both of individual prosperity and of social virtue — this waste of resources and of benevolent feelings in doing harm instead of good, is immensely swelled by women's contributions, and stimulated by their influence. Not that this is a mistake likely to be made by women, where they have actually the practical management of schemes of beneficence. It sometimes happens that women who administer public charities — with that insight into present fact, and especially into the minds and feelings of those with whom they are in immediate contact, in which women generally excel men — recognise in the clearest manner the demoralizing influence of the alms given or the help afforded, and could give lessons on the subject to many a male political economist. But women who only give their money, and are not brought face to face with the effects it produces, how can they be expected to foresee them? A woman born to the present lot of women, and content with it, how should she appreciate the value of self-dependence? She is not self-dependent; she is not taught self-dependence; her destiny is to receive everything from others, and why should what is good enough for her be bad for the poor? Her familiar notions of good are of blessings descending from a superior.

She forgets that she is not free, and that the poor are; that if what they need is given to them unearned, they cannot be compelled to earn it: that everybody cannot be taken care of by everybody, but there must be some motive to induce people to take care of themselves; and that to be helped to help themselves, if they are physically capable of it, is the only charity which proves to be charity in the end.

These considerations show how usefully the part which women take in the formation of general opinion, would be modified for the better by that more enlarged instruction, and practical conversancy with the things which their opinions influence, that would necessarily arise from their social and political emancipation. But the improvement it would work through the influence they exercise, each in her own family, would be still more remarkable.

It is often said that in the classes most exposed to temptation, a man's wife and children tend to keep him honest and respectable, both by the wife's direct influence, and by the concern he feels for their future welfare. This may be so, and no doubt often is so, with those who are more weak than wicked; and this beneficial influence would be preserved and strengthened under equal laws; it does not depend on the woman's servitude, but is, on the contrary, diminished by the disrespect which the inferior class of men always at heart feel towards those who are subject to their power. But when we ascend higher in the scale, we come among a totally different set of moving forces. The wife's influence tends, as far as it goes, to prevent the husband from falling below the common standard of approbation of the country. It tends quite as strongly to hinder him from rising above it. The wife is the auxiliary of the common public opinion. A man who is married to a woman his inferior in intelligence, finds her a perpetual dead weight, or, worse than a dead weight, a drag, upon every aspiration of his to be better than public opinion requires him to be. It is hardly possible for one who is in these bonds, to attain exalted virtue. If he differs in his opinion from the mass — if he sees truths which have not yet dawned upon them, or if, feeling in his heart truths which they nominally recognize, he would like to act up to those truths more conscientiously than the generality of mankind — to all such thoughts and desires, marriage is the heaviest of drawbacks, unless he be so fortunate as to have a wife as much above the common level as he himself is.

For, in the first place, there is always some sacrifice of personal interest required; either of social consequence, or of pecuniary means; perhaps the risk of even the means of subsistence. These sacrifices and risks he may be willing to encounter for himself; but he will pause before he imposes them on his family. And his family in this case means his wife and daughters; for he always hopes that his sons will feel as he feels himself, and that what he can do without, they will do without, willingly, in the same cause. But his daughters — their marriage may depend upon it: and his wife, who is unable to enter into or understand the objects for which these sacrifices are made — who, if she thought them worth any sacrifice, would think so on trust, and solely for his sake — who can participate in none of the enthusiasm or the self-approbation he himself may feel, while the things which he is disposed to sacrifice are all in all to her; will not the best and most unselfish man hesitate the longest before bringing on her this consequence? If it be not the comforts of life, but only social consideration, that is at stake, the burthen upon his conscience and feelings is still very severe. Whoever has a wife and children has given hostages to Mrs. Grundy.[9] The approbation of that potentate may be a matter of indifference to him, but it is of great importance to his wife. The man himself may be above opinion, or may find sufficient compensation in the opinion of those of his own way of thinking. But to the women connected with him, he can offer no compensation. The almost invariable tendency of the wife to place her influence in the same scale with social consideration, is sometimes made a reproach to women, and represented as a peculiar trait of feebleness and childishness of character in them: surely with great injustice. Society makes the whole life of a woman, in the easy classes, a continued self-sacrifice; it exacts from her an unremitting restraint of the whole of her natural inclinations, and the sole return it makes to her for what often deserves the name of a martyrdom, is consideration. Her consideration is inseparably connected with that of her husband, and after paying the full price for it, she finds that she is to lose it, for no reason of which she can feel the cogency. She has sacrificed her whole life to it, and her husband will not sacrifice to it a whim, a freak, an eccentricity; something not recognised or allowed for by the world, and which the world will agree with her in thinking a folly, if it thinks no worse! The dilemma is hardest upon that very meritorious class of men, who, without possessing talents which qualify them to make a figure among those with whom they agree in opinion, hold their opinion from conviction, and feel bound in honor and conscience to serve it, by making profession of their belief, and giving their time, labour, and means, to anything undertaken in its behalf. The worst case of all is when such men happen to be of a rank and position which of itself neither gives them, nor excludes them from, what is considered the best society; when their admission to it depends mainly on what is thought of them personally — and however unexceptionable their breeding and habits, their being identified with opinions and public conduct unacceptable to those who give the tone to society would operate as an effectual exclusion. Many a woman flatters herself (nine times out of ten quite erroneously) that nothing prevents her and her husband from moving in the highest society of her neighborhood — society in which others well known to her, and in the same class of

9. A figure in Thomas Morton's play *Speed the Plough* (1798). She never appeared; the name was that of a neighbor. The expression then took on a life of its own.

life, mix freely — except that her husband is unfortunately a Dissenter, or has the reputation of mingling in low radical politics. That it is, she thinks, which hinders George from getting a commission or a place, Caroline from making an advantageous match, and prevents her and her husband from obtaining invitations, perhaps honors, which, for aught she sees, they are as well entitled to as some folks. With such an influence in every house, either exerted actively, or operating all the more powerfully for not being asserted, is it any wonder that people in general are kept down in that mediocrity of respectability which is becoming a marked characteristic of modern times?

There is another very injurious aspect in which the effect, not of women's disabilities directly, but of the broad line of difference which those disabilities create between the education and character of a woman and that of a man, requires to be considered. Nothing can be more unfavorable to that union of thoughts and inclinations which is the ideal of married life. Intimate society between people radically dissimilar to one another, is an idle dream. Unlikeness may attract, but it is likeness which retains; and in proportion to the likeness is the suitability of the individuals to give each other a happy life. While women are so unlike men, it is not wonderful that selfish men should feel the need of arbitrary power in their own hands, to arrest *in limine*[1] the lifelong conflict of inclinations, by deciding every question on the side of their own preference. When people are extremely unlike, there can be no real identity of interest. Very often there is conscientious difference of opinion between married people, on the highest points of duty. Is there any reality in the marriage union where this takes place? Yet it is not uncommon anywhere, when the woman has any earnestness of character; and it is a very general case indeed in Catholic countries, when she is supported in her dissent by the only other authority to which she is taught to bow, the priest. With the usual barefacedness of power not accustomed to find itself disputed, the influence of priests over women is attacked by Protestant and Liberal writers, less for being bad in itself, than because it is a rival authority to the husband, and raises up a revolt against his infallibility. In England, similar differences occasionally exist when an Evangelical wife has allied herself with a husband of a different quality; but in general this source at least of dissension is got rid of, by reducing the minds of women to such a nullity, that they have no opinions but those of Mrs. Grundy, or those which the husband tells them to have. When there is no difference of opinion, differences merely of taste may be sufficient to detract greatly from the happiness of married life. And though it may stimulate the amatory propensities of men, it does not conduce to married happiness, to exaggerate by differences of education whatever may be the native differences of the sexes. If the married pair are well-bred and well-

1. On the threshold (Latin).

behaved people, they tolerate each other's tastes; but is mutual toleration what people look forward to, when they enter into marriage? These differences of inclination will naturally make their wishes different, if not restrained by affection or duty, as to almost all domestic questions which arise. What a difference there must be in the society which the two persons will wish to frequent, or be frequented by! Each will desire associates who share their own tastes: the persons agreeable to one, will be indifferent or positively disagreeable to the other; yet there can be none who are not common to both, for married people do not now live in different parts of the house and have totally different visiting lists, as in the reign of Louis XV.[2] They cannot help having different wishes as to the bringing up of the children: each will wish to see reproduced in them their own tastes and sentiments: and there is either a compromise, and only a half-satisfaction to either, or the wife has to yield — often with bitter suffering; and, with or without intention, her occult influence continues to counterwork the husband's purposes.

It would of course be extreme folly to suppose that these differences of feeling and inclination only exist because women are brought up differently from men, and that there would not be differences of taste under any imaginable circumstances. But there is nothing beyond the mark in saying that the distinction in bringing-up immensely aggravates those differences, and renders them wholly inevitable. While women are brought up as they are, a man and a woman will but rarely find in one another real agreement of tastes and wishes as to daily life. They will generally have to give it up as hopeless, and renounce the attempt to have, in the intimate associate of their daily life, that *idem velle, idem nolle*,[3] which is the recognized bond of any society that is really such: or if the man succeeds in obtaining it, he does so by choosing a woman who is so complete a nullity that she has no *velle* or *nolle* at all, and is as ready to comply with one thing as another if anybody tells her to do so. Even this calculation is apt to fail; dulness and want of spirit are not always a guarantee of the submission which is so confidently expected from them. But if they were, is this the ideal of marriage? What, in this case, does the man obtain by it, except an upper servant, a nurse, or a mistress? On the contrary, when each of two persons, instead of being a nothing, is a something; when they are attached to one another, and are not too much unlike to begin with; the constant partaking in the same things, assisted by their sympathy, draws out the latent capacities of each for being interested in the things which were at first interesting only to the other; and works a gradual assimilation of the tastes and characters to one another, partly by the insensible modification of each, but more by a real enriching of the two natures, each acquiring the tastes and capacities of the other in addition to its own. This often

2. Born in 1710, he was king of France from 1715 until his death in 1774.
3. Want the same thing; reject the same thing (Latin).

happens between two friends of the same sex, who are much associated in their daily life: and it would be a common, if not the commonest, case in marriage, did not the totally different bringing-up of the two sexes make it next to an impossibility to form a really well-assorted union. Were this remedied, whatever differences there might still be in individual tastes, there would at least be, as a general rule, complete unity and unanimity as to the great objects of life. When the two persons both care for great objects, and are a help and encouragement to each other in whatever regards these, the minor matters on which their tastes may differ are not all-important to them; and there is a foundation for solid friendship, of an enduring character, more likely than anything else to make it, through the whole of life, a greater pleasure to each to give pleasure to the other, than to receive it.

I have considered, thus far, the effects on the pleasures and benefits of the marriage union which depend on the mere unlikeness between the wife and the husband: but the evil tendency is prodigiously aggravated when the unlikeness is inferiority. Mere unlikeness, when it only means difference of good qualities, may be more a benefit in the way of mutual improvement, than a drawback from comfort. When each emulates, and desires and endeavors to acquire, the other's peculiar qualities, the difference does not produce diversity of interest, but increased identity of it, and makes each still more valuable to the other. But when one is much the inferior of the two in mental ability and cultivation, and is not actively attempting by the other's aid to rise to the other's level, the whole influence of the connection upon the development of the superior of the two is deteriorating: and still more so in a tolerably happy marriage than in an unhappy one. It is not with impunity that the superior in intellect shuts himself up with an inferior, and elects that inferior for his chosen, and sole completely intimate, associate. Any society which is not improving, is deteriorating: and the more so, the closer and more familiar it is. Even a really superior man almost always begins to deteriorate when he is habitually (as the phrase is) king of his company: and in his most habitual company the husband who has a wife inferior to him is always so. While his self-satisfaction is incessantly ministered to on the one hand, on the other he insensibly imbibes the modes of feeling, and of looking at things, which belong to a more vulgar or a more limited mind than his own. This evil differs from many of those which have hitherto been dwelt on, by being an increasing one. The association of men with women in daily life is much closer and more complete than it ever was before. Men's life is more domestic. Formerly, their pleasures and chosen occupations were among men, and in men's company: their wives had but a fragment of their lives. At the present time, the progress of civilization, and the turn of opinion against the rough amusements and convivial excesses which formerly occupied most men in their hours of relaxation—together with (it must be said) the improved tone of modern feeling as to the reciprocity of duty which binds the husband towards the wife — have thrown the man very much more upon home and its inmates, for his personal and social pleasures: while the kind and degree of improvement which has been made in women's education, has made them in some degree capable of being his companions in ideas and mental tastes, while leaving them, in most cases, still hopelessly inferior to him. His desire of mental communion is thus in general satisfied by a communion from which he learns nothing. An unimproving and unstimulating companionship is substituted for (what he might otherwise have been obliged to seek) the society of his equals in powers and his fellows in the higher pursuits. We see, accordingly, that young men of the greatest promise generally cease to improve as soon as they marry, and, not improving, inevitably degenerate. If the wife does not push the husband forward, she always holds him back. He ceases to care for what she does not care for; he no longer desires, and ends by disliking and shunning, society congenial to his former aspirations, and which would now shame his falling-off from them; his higher faculties both of mind and heart cease to be called into activity. And this change coinciding with the new and selfish interests which are created by the family, after a few years he differs in no material respect from those who have never had wishes for anything but the common vanities and the common pecuniary objects.

What marriage may be in the case of two persons of cultivated faculties, identical in opinions and purposes, between whom there exists that best kind of equality, similarity of powers and capacities with reciprocal superiority in them — so that each can enjoy the luxury of looking up to the other, and can have alternately the pleasure of leading and of being led in the path of development — I will not attempt to describe. To those who can conceive it, there is no need; to those who cannot, it would appear the dream of an enthusiast. But I maintain, with the profoundest conviction, that this, and this only, is the ideal of marriage; and that all opinions, customs, and institutions which favor any other notion of it, or turn the conceptions and aspirations connected with it into any other direction, by whatever pretences they may be colored, are relics of primitive barbarism. The moral regeneration of mankind will only really commence, when the most fundamental of the social relations is placed under the rule of equal justice, and when human beings learn to cultivate their strongest sympathy with an equal in rights and in cultivation.

Thus far, the benefits which it has appeared that the world would gain by ceasing to make sex a disqualification for privileges and a badge of subjection, are social rather than individual; consisting in an increase of the general fund of thinking and acting power, and an improvement in the general conditions of the association of men with women. But it would be a grievous understatement of the case to omit the most direct benefit of all, the unspeakable gain in private happiness to the liberated half of the species; the difference to them between a life of subjection to the will of others, and a life of rational freedom. After the primary necessities of food and raiment, freedom is the first and strongest want of human nature. While mankind are lawless, their desire is for lawless freedom. When they have learnt to understand the meaning of duty and the value of reason, they incline more and more to be guided and restrained by these in the exercise of their freedom; but they do not therefore desire freedom less; they do not become disposed to accept the will of other people as the representative and interpreter of those guiding principles. On the contrary, the communities in which the reason has been most cultivated, and in which the idea of social duty has been most powerful, are those which have most strongly asserted the freedom of action of the individual—the liberty of each to govern his conduct by his own feelings of duty, and by such laws and social restraints as his own conscience can subscribe to.

He who would rightly appreciate the worth of personal independence as an element of happiness, should consider the value he himself puts upon it as an ingredient of his own. There is no subject on which there is a greater habitual difference of judgment between a man judging for himself, and the same man judging for other people. When he hears others complaining that they are not allowed freedom of action—that their own will has not sufficient influence in the regulation of their affairs—his inclination is, to ask, what are their grievances? what positive damage they sustain? and in what respect they consider their affairs to be mismanaged? and if they fail to make out, in answer to these questions, what appears to him a sufficient case, he turns a deaf ear, and regards their complaint as the fanciful querulousness of people whom nothing reasonable will satisfy. But he has a quite different standard of judgment when he is deciding for himself. Then, the most unexceptionable administration of his interests by a tutor set over him, does not satisfy his feelings: his personal exclusion from the deciding authority appears itself the greatest grievance of all, rendering it superfluous even to enter into the question of mismanagement. It is the same with nations. What citizen of a free country would listen to any offers of good and skilful administration, in return for the abdication of freedom? Even if he could believe that good and skilful administration can exist among a people ruled by a will not their own, would not the consciousness of working out their own destiny under their own moral responsibility be a compensation to his feelings for great rudeness and imperfection in the details of public affairs? Let him rest assured that whatever he feels on this point, women feel in a fully equal degree. Whatever has been said or written, from the time of Herodotus[4] to the present, of the ennobling influence of free government—the nerve and

---

4. Greek historian of the Persian Wars; little is known of his life. He was born around 480 B.C. and died between 430 and 420 B.C.

spring which it gives to all the faculties, the larger and higher objects which it presents to the intellect and feelings, the more unselfish public spirit, and calmer and broader views of duty, that it engenders, and the generally loftier platform on which it elevates the individual as a moral, spiritual, and social being — is every particle as true of women as of men. Are these things no important part of individual happiness? Let any man call to mind what he himself felt on emerging from boyhood — from the tutelage and control of even loved and affectionate elders — and entering upon the responsibilities of manhood. Was it not like the physical effect of taking off a heavy weight, or releasing him from obstructive, even if not otherwise painful, bonds? Did he not feel twice as much alive, twice as much a human being, as before? And does he imagine that women have none of these feelings? But it is a striking fact, that the satisfactions and mortifications of personal pride, though all in all to most men when the case is their own, have less allowance made for them in the case of other people, and are less listened to as a ground or a justification of conduct, than any other natural human feelings; perhaps because men compliment them in their own case with the names of so many other qualities, that they are seldom conscious how mighty an influence these feelings exercise in their own lives. No less large and powerful is their part, we may assure ourselves, in the lives and feelings of women. Women are schooled into suppressing them in their most natural and most healthy direction, but the internal principle remains, in a different outward form. An active and energetic mind, if denied liberty, will seek for power: refused the command of itself, it will assert its personality by attempting to control others. To allow to any human beings no existence of their own but what depends on others, is giving far too high a premium on bending others to their purposes. Where liberty cannot be hoped for, and power can, power becomes the grand object of human desire; those to whom others will not leave the undisturbed management of their own affairs, will compensate themselves, if they can, by meddling for their own purposes with the affairs of others. Hence also women's passion for personal beauty, and dress and display; and all the evils that flow from it, in the way of mischievous luxury and social immorality. The love of power and the love of liberty are in eternal antagonism. Where there is least liberty, the passion for power is the most ardent and unscrupulous. The desire of power over others can only cease to be a depraving agency among mankind, when each of them individually is able to do without it: which can only be where respect for liberty in the personal concerns of each is an established principle.

But it is not only through the sentiment of personal dignity, that the free direction and disposal of their own faculties is a source of individual happiness, and to be fettered and restricted in it, a source of unhappiness, to human beings, and not least to women. There is nothing, after disease, indigence, and guilt, so fatal to the pleasurable enjoyment of life as the want of a worthy outlet for the active faculties. Women who have the cares of a family, and while they have the cares of a family, have this outlet, and it generally suffices for them: but what of the greatly increasing number of women, who have had no opportunity of exercising the vocation which they are mocked by telling them is their proper one? What of the women whose children have been lost to them by death or distance, or have grown up, married, and formed homes of their own? There are abundant examples of men who, after a life engrossed by business, retire with a competency to the enjoyment, as they hope, of rest, but to whom, as they are unable to acquire new interests and excitements that can replace the old, the change to a life of inactivity brings ennui, melancholy, and premature death. Yet no one thinks of the parallel case of so many worthy and devoted women, who, having paid what they are told is their debt to society — having brought up a family blamelessly to manhood and womanhood — having kept a house as long as they had a house needing to be kept — are deserted by the sole occupation for which they have fitted themselves; and remain with undiminished activity but with no employment for it, unless perhaps a daughter or daughter-in-law is willing to abdicate in their favour the discharge of the same functions in her younger household. Surely a hard lot for the old age of those who have worthily discharged, as long as it was given to them to discharge, what the world accounts their only social duty. Of such women, and of those others to whom this duty has not been committed at all — many of whom pine through life with the consciousness of thwarted vocations, and activities which are not suffered to expand — the only resources, speaking generally, are religion and charity. But their religion, though it may be one of feeling, and of ceremonial observance, cannot be a religion of action, unless in the form of charity. For charity many of them are by nature admirably fitted; but to practise it usefully, or even without doing mischief, requires the education, the manifold preparation, the knowledge and the thinking powers, of a skilful administrator. There are few of the administrative functions of government for which a person would not be fit, who is fit to bestow charity usefully. In this as in other cases (pre-eminently in that of the education of children), the duties permitted to women cannot be performed properly, without their being trained for duties which, to the great loss of society, are not permitted to them. And here let me notice the singular way in which the question of women's disabilities is frequently presented to view, by those who find it easier to draw a ludicrous picture of what they do not like, than to answer the arguments for it. When it is suggested that women's executive capacities and prudent counsels might sometimes be found valuable in affairs of state, these lovers of fun hold up to the ridicule of the world, as sitting in parliament or in the cabinet, girls in their teens, or young wives of two or three and twenty, transported bodily, exactly as they are, from the drawing-room to the House of Commons.

They forget that males are not usually selected at this early age for a seat in Parliament, or for responsible political functions. Common sense would tell them that if such trusts were confided to women, it would be to such as having no special vocation for married life, or preferring another employment of their faculties (as many women even now prefer to marriage some of the few honorable occupations within their reach), have spent the best years of their youth in attempting to qualify themselves for the pursuits in which they desire to engage; or still more frequently perhaps, widows or wives of forty or fifty, by whom the knowledge of life and faculty of government which they have acquired in their families, could by the aid of appropriate studies be made available on a less contracted scale. There is no country of Europe in which the ablest men have not frequently experienced, and keenly appreciated, the value of the advice and help of clever and experienced women of the world, in the attainment both of private and of public objects; and there are important matters of public administration to which few men are equally competent with such women; among others, the detailed control of expenditure. But what we are now discussing is not the need which society has of the services of women in public business, but the dull and hopeless life to which it so often condemns them, by forbidding them to exercise the practical abilities which many of them are conscious of, in any wider field than one which to some of them never was, and to others is no longer, open. If there is anything vitally important to the happiness of human beings, it is that they should relish their habitual pursuit. This requisite of an enjoyable life is very imperfectly granted, or altogether denied, to a large part of mankind; and by its absence many a life is a failure, which is provided, in appearance, with every requisite of success. But if circumstances which society is not yet skilful enough to overcome, render such failures often for the present inevitable, society need not itself inflict them. The injudiciousness of parents, a youth's own inexperience, or the absence of external opportunities for the congenial vocation, and their presence for an uncongenial, condemn numbers of men to pass their lives in doing one thing reluctantly and ill, when there are other things which they could have done well and happily. But on women this sentence is imposed by actual law, and by customs equivalent to law. What, in unenlightened societies, color, race, religion, or in the case of a conquered country, nationality, are to some men, sex is to all women; a peremptory exclusion from almost all honorable occupations, but either such as cannot be fulfilled by others, or such as those others do not think worthy of their acceptance. Sufferings arising from causes of this nature usually meet with so little sympathy, that few persons are aware of the great amount of unhappiness even now produced by the feeling of a wasted life. The case will be even more frequent, as increased cultivation creates a greater and greater disproportion between the ideas and faculties of women, and the scope which society allows to their activity.

When we consider the positive evil caused to the disqualified half of the human race by their disqualification — first in the loss of the most inspiriting and elevating kind of personal enjoyment, and next in the weariness, disappointment, and profound dissatisfaction with life, which are so often the substitute for it; one feels that among all the lessons which men require for carrying on the struggle against the inevitable imperfections of their lot on earth, there is no lesson which they more need, than not to add to the evils which nature inflicts, by their jealous and prejudiced restrictions on one another. Their vain fears only substitute other and worse evils for those which they are idly apprehensive of: while every restraint on the freedom of conduct of any of their human fellow creatures, (otherwise than by making them responsible for any evil actually caused by it), dries up *pro tanto*[5] the principal fountain of human happiness, and leaves the species less rich, to an inappreciable degree, in all that makes life valuable to the individual human being.

---

5. To that extent (Latin).

[The Composition of the Essays]

In his *Autobiography*, Mill described his methods of composition and revision and gave an account of the origins of the essays reprinted in this volume. *The Subjection of Women* appeared after he finished composing his *Autobiography* — it ends with his departure from Parliament in 1868 — and receives only a passing mention in the text and a footnote that discusses Harriet Taylor's role in its doctrines. Mill wrote *Subjection* after Harriet's death on the suggestion of Helen Taylor, his stepdaughter, as a way of keeping Harriet's memory fresh. He published it several years later when he judged the time ripe for it. It is something of a paradox that Mill treats his writing of "The Spirit of the Age" as the occasion to insist on his wife's superiority to Carlyle and insists on the centrality of her contribution to *On Liberty*, but he has to take full responsibility for *The Subjection of Women*.

For the next few years I wrote copiously in newspapers.[1] It was about this time that Fonblanque, who had for some time written the political articles in the *Examiner*, became the proprietor and editor of the paper. It is not forgotten with what verve and talent, as well as fine wit, he carried it on, during the whole period of Lord Grey's ministry, and what importance it assumed as the principal representative, in the newspaper press, of radical opinions. The distinguishing character of the paper was given to it entirely by his own articles, which formed at least three fourths of all the original writing contained in it: but of the remaining fourth I contributed during those years a much larger share than any one else. I wrote nearly all the articles on French subjects, including a weekly summary of French politics, often extending to considerable length; together with many leading articles on general politics, commercial and financial legislation, and any miscellaneous subjects in which I felt interested, and which were suitable to the paper, including occasional reviews of books. Mere newspaper articles on the occurrences or questions of the moment gave no opportunity for the development of any general mode of thought; but I attempted, in the beginning of 1831, to embody in a series of articles, headed "The Spirit of the Age," some of my new opinions, and especially to point out in the character of the present age, the anomalies and evils characteristic of the transition from a system of opinions which had worn out, to another only in process of being formed. These articles were, I fancy, lumbering in style, and not lively or striking enough to be at any time acceptable to newspaper readers; but had they been far more at-

1. From July 1830 to September 1834, Mill wrote some two hundred articles for the *Examiner*. This selection is from CW, vol. 1, 179–83. Mill went to Paris after the July Revolution of 1830, and on his return to England, he started work on "The Spirit of the Age."

tractive, still, at that particular moment, when great political changes were impending, and engrossing all minds, these discussions were ill timed, and missed fire altogether. The only effect which I know to have been produced by them, was that Carlyle, then living in a secluded part of Scotland, read them in his solitude, and saying to himself (as he afterwards told me) "here is a new Mystic," enquired on coming to London that autumn respecting their authorship; an enquiry which was the immediate cause of our becoming personally acquainted.

I have already mentioned Carlyle's earlier writings as one of the channels through which I received the influences which enlarged my early narrow creed; but I do not think that those writings, by themselves, would ever have had any effect on my opinions. What truths they contained, though of the very kind which I was already receiving from other quarters, were presented in a form and vesture less suited than any other to give them access to a mind trained as mine had been. They seemed a haze of poetry and German metaphysics, in which almost the only clear thing was a strong animosity to most of the opinions which were the basis of my mode of thought; religious scepticism, utilitarianism, the doctrine of circumstances, and the attaching any importance to democracy, logic, or political economy. Instead of my having been taught anything, in the first instance, by Carlyle, it was only in proportion as I came to see the same truths, through media more suited to my mental constitution, that I recognized them in his writings. Then, indeed, the wonderful power with which he put them forth made a deep impression upon me, and I was during a long period one of his most fervent admirers; but the good his writings did me, was not as philosophy to instruct, but as poetry to animate. Even at the time when our acquaintance commenced, I was not sufficiently advanced in my new modes of thought, to appreciate him fully; a proof of which is, that on his shewing me the manuscript of *Sartor Resartus*, his best and greatest work, which he had just then finished, I made little of it; though when it came out about two years afterwards in *Fraser's Magazine*, I read it with enthusiastic admiration and the keenest delight. I did not seek and cultivate Carlyle less on account of the fundamental differences in our philosophy. He soon found out that I was not "another mystic," and when for the sake of my own integrity I wrote to him a distinct profession of all those of my opinions which I knew he most disliked, he replied that the chief difference between us was that I "was as yet consciously nothing of a mystic." I do not know at what period he gave up the expectation that I was destined to become one; but though both his and my opinions underwent in subsequent years considerable changes, we never approached much nearer to each other's modes of thought than we were in the first years of our acquaintance. I did not, however, deem myself a competent judge of Carlyle. I felt that he was a poet, and that I was not; that he was a man of intuition, which I was not; and that as such, he not only saw many things long before me, which I could only, when they were pointed out to me, hobble after and prove, but that it was highly probable he could see many things which were not visible to me even after they were pointed out. I knew that I could not see round him, and could never be certain that I saw over him; and I never presumed to judge him with any definiteness, until he was interpreted to me by one greatly the superior of us both[2] — who was more a poet than he, and more a thinker than I — whose own mind and nature included his, and infinitely more.

＊　＊　＊

During the two years which immediately preceded the cessation of my official life, my wife and I were working together at the *Liberty*.[3] I had first planned and written it as a short essay, in 1854. It was in mounting the steps of the Capitol, in January 1855, that the thought first arose of converting it into a volume. None of my writings have been either so carefully composed, or so sedulously corrected as this. After it had been written as usual twice over, we kept it by us, bringing it out from time to time and going through it *de novo*, reading, weighing and criticizing every sentence. Its final revision was to have been a work of the winter of 1858/59, the first after my retirement, which we had arranged to pass in the South of Europe. That hope and every other were frustrated by the most unexpected and bitter calamity of her death — at Avignon, on our way to Montpellier, from a sudden attack of pulmonary congestion.

＊　＊　＊

The *Liberty* was more directly and literally our joint production than anything else which bears my name, for there was not a sentence of it that was not several times gone through by us together, turned over in many ways, and carefully weeded of any faults, either in thought or expression, that we detected in it. It is in consequence of this that, although it never underwent her final revision, it far surpasses, as a mere specimen of composition, anything which has proceeded from me either before or since. With regard to the thoughts, it is difficult to identify any particular part or element as being more hers than all the rest. The whole mode of thinking of which the book was the expression, was emphatically hers. But I also was so thoroughly imbued with it that the same thoughts naturally occurred to us both. That I was thus penetrated with it, however, I owe in a great degree to her. There was a moment in my mental progress when I might easily have fallen into a tendency towards over-government, both social and political; as there

2. Harriet Taylor.
3. This and the following selection are from CW, vol. 1, 249 and 257–61. Mill retired from the East India Company in 1858. He was in Rome in 1855 on the journey he took to recover his health after discovering that he was consumptive.

was also a moment when, by reaction from a contrary excess, I might have become a less thorough radical and democrat than I am. In both these points as in many others, she benefitted me as much by keeping me right where I was right, as by leading me to new truths and ridding me of errors. My great readiness and eagerness to learn from everybody, and to make room in my opinions for every new acquisition by adjusting the old and the new to one another, might, but for her steadying influence, have seduced me into modifying my early opinions too much. She was in nothing more valuable to my mental development than by her just measure of the relative importance of different considerations, which often protected me from allowing to truths I had only recently learnt to see, a more important place in my thoughts than was properly their due.

The *Liberty* is likely to survive longer than anything else that I have written (with the possible exception of the *Logic*), because the conjunction of her mind with mine has rendered it a kind of philosophic text-book of a single truth, which the changes progressively taking place in modern society tend to bring out into ever stronger relief: the importance, to man and society, of a large variety in types of character, and of giving full freedom to human nature to expand itself in innumerable and conflicting directions. Nothing can better shew how deep are the foundations of this truth, than the great impression made by the exposition of it at a time which, to superficial observation, did not seem to stand much in need of such a lesson. The fears we expressed lest the inevitable growth of social equality and of the government of public opinion should impose on mankind an oppressive yoke of uniformity in opinion and practice, might easily have appeared chimerical to those who looked more at present facts than at tendencies; for the gradual revolution that is taking place in society and institutions has thus far been decidedly favourable to the development of new opinions, and has procured for them a much more unprejudiced hearing than they previously met with. But this is a feature belonging to periods of transition, when old notions and feelings have been unsettled and no new doctrines have yet succeeded to their ascendancy. At such times people of any mental activity, having given up many of their old beliefs, and not feeling quite sure that those they still retain can stand unmodified, listen eagerly to new opinions. But this state of things is necessarily transitory: some particular body of my name claimed no originality for any of its doctrines, and was not intended to write their history, the only author who had preceded me in their assertion of whom I thought it appropriate to say anything, was Humboldt, who furnished the motto to the work; although in one passage I borrowed from the Warrenites their phrase, the sovereignty of the individual. It is hardly necessary here to remark that there are abundant differences in detail, between the conception of the doctrine by any of the predecessors I have mentioned, and that set forth in the book.

After my irreparable loss one of my earliest cares was to print and publish the treatise, so much of which was the work of her whom I had lost, and consecrate it to her memory. I have made no alteration or addition to it, nor shall I ever. Though it wants the last touch of her hand, no substitute for that touch shall ever be attempted by mine.

*   *   *

The steps in my mental growth for which I was indebted to her were far from being those which a person wholly uninformed on the subject would probably suspect.[4] It might be supposed, for instance, that my strong convictions on the complete equality in all legal, political, social and domestic relations, which ought to exist between men and women, may have been adopted or learnt from her. This was so far from being the fact, that those convictions were among the earliest results of the application of my mind to political subjects, and the strength with which I held them was, as I believe, more than anything else, the originating cause of the interest she felt in me. What is true is, that until I knew her, the opinion was, in my mind, little more than an abstract principle. I saw no more reason why women should be held in legal subjection to other people, than why men should. I was certain that their interests required fully as much protection as those of men, and were quite as little likely to obtain it without an equal voice in making the laws by which they are to be bound. But that perception of the vast practical bearings of women's disabilities which found expression in the book on *The Subjection of Women* was acquired mainly through her teaching. But for her rare knowledge of human nature and comprehension of moral and social influences, though I should doubtless have held my present opinions I should have had a very insufficient perception of the mode in which the consequences of the inferior position of women intertwine themselves with all the evils of existing society and with all the difficulties of human improvement. I am indeed painfully conscious how much of her best thoughts on the subject I have failed to reproduce, and how greatly that little treatise falls short of what would have been given to the world if she had put on paper her entire mind on this question, or had lived to revise and improve, as she certainly would have done, my imperfect statement of the case.

4. This selection appeared as a footnote in CW, vol. 1, 253.

COMMENTARIES

R. H. HUTTON

Mill on Liberty†

Mr. John Stuart Mill's essay on Liberty is a very melancholy book on a great subject. It is written in the sincere foreboding that the strong individualities of the old types of English character are in imminent danger of being swallowed up in those political and social influences which emanate from large masses of men. It might almost, indeed, have come from the prison-cell of some persecuted thinker bent on making one last protest against the growing tyranny of the public mind, though conscious that his appeal will be in vain, — instead of from the pen of a writer who has perhaps exercised more influence over the formation of the philosophical and social principles of cultivated Englishmen than any other man of his generation. While agreeing with Mr. Mill, as most thoughtful politicians must, in some at least of the most important practical conclusions at which he eventually arrives as to the fitting limits of legislative interference, and the proper bounds to the jurisdiction of that secondary tribunal which we call public opinion, we differ from him widely and fundamentally with regard to the leading assumptions from which he starts, and the main principle which he takes with him as his clue in the inquiry. * * * But before we follow him into his political philosophy, we must explain why we think him totally wrong in the most important of his preliminary assumptions.

We differ widely from Mr. Mill as to the *truth* of the painful conviction which has evidently given rise to this essay. We do not for a moment doubt that English "public opinion" is a much more intelligible and homogeneous thing in our own day than it has ever been at any previous time; that it comprehends much fewer conflicting types of thought, much fewer distinctly divergent social tendencies, much less honest and sturdy controversy between diametrical opposites in intellectual theory. Sectarian lines are fading away, political bonds are sundering, even social attractions and repulsions are less marked than they used to be; and to this extent we willingly concede to Mr. Mill that considerable progress is rapidly making towards that universal assimilation of the social conditions of life. * * * But to what do these facts point? Mr. Mill believes that they point to an increasing despotism of social and political masses over the moral and intellectual freedom of individuals. To us his conclusion appears singularly hasty, and utterly unsustained by the premises he lays down. If, indeed, Mr. Mill still

† From *The National Review* 8 (1859), 393–424.

holds, as many passages in his earlier works would seem to indicate, that there is no such thing as an inherent difference in the original constitution of human minds, — that the varieties in the characters of men are due entirely to the varieties of physical, moral, and social influence to which they are exposed, — then, no doubt, he must argue that the great assimilation of outward circumstances which civilisation necessarily brings, will naturally end in producing a fatal monotony in human character. But * * * we would suggest that any moral monotony which springs exclusively from the assimilation of social conditions is not only inevitable, but a necessary result of social and political *liberty*, instead of a menace to it.

And what *are* the varieties of character which disappear as the process of social assimilation goes on? Surely *not* individual varieties of character, — varieties, that is, proper to the natural development of an individual character; but simply class types, — the varieties due to well-marked sectional groups, — to widely-severed phases of custom, — to the exclusive occupations of separate *castes*, — in short, to some local or social organisation, the sharp boundary of which is gradually becoming softened or altogether dissolved by the blending and fusing influences of civilisation. That this process has been going on very rapidly during the last century, we believe. But so far from holding, with Mr. Mill, that it is a process fatal to the due development of individualities of character, we conceive that it has not contracted, but rather enlarged, the sphere of individual freedom. The country gentleman stands out no longer in that marked contrast to the tradesman or the man of letters which was observable in the days of Sir Robert Walpole; the dissenter is no longer a moral foil to the churchman; and the different shades of English religious opinion can not any more be mapped out as distinctly as the different counties in a map of England. But what individual freedom has any one lost by the fading away of those well-defined local and moral groups? That there has been a loss of social *intensity* of character in consequence, we admit. The exclusive association of people of the same habits of life and thought has no doubt a tendency to intensify the peculiarities thus associated, and to steep the character thoroughly with that one influence, to the exclusion of all others. But this intensification of local, or social, or religious one-sidedness is as far as possible from the development of that individuality of character for which Mr. Mill pleads so eagerly. Rather must the impressed force of such social moulds or stamps have tended to overpower all forms of individual originality which were not consistent with those special moulds or stamps. No doubt if there were any remarkable element of character in the individual which also belongs specially to the group or caste, we might expect that it would be fostered by such association into excessive energy. But any peculiarly individual element of character, on the other hand, would have been in danger of being overwhelmed. And it is therefore mere assumption to say that because there are now fewer striking varieties of type and class than there were in former generations, there is less scope for individual freedom. The very reverse must be the case, unless the assimilated public opinion of a whole nation be supposed to be more minute, more exigeant and irritating in its despotism, than the sectarian opinion of small local bodies or social castes.

* * *

But Mr. Mill may perhaps say that there is much more danger of tyranny from the unchecked power of a single homogeneous body of "public opinion" than there is from the local prejudices or conflicting political sects which formerly contended for the mastery. But this depends entirely on the mode in which this body of public opinion is generated, — whether it arise, as in England, from the genuine assimilation of opposite schools of thought, or, as in the United States, from the mere forcible triumph of a single class-creed, which in consequence of democratic institutions, is unhappily able to drown by sheer violence the voice of all higher and more cultivated schools of thought. When people come to think more and more alike, simply because the same influences are extending from class to class, and the same set of reasons recommend themselves to the intellects of moderate men in all classes, — when this is the way in which a "public opinion" is formed, it is obvious that the restraint exercised by such public opinion, gathered up as it is from a *very wide social range*, is far less oppressive than the narrower and intenser type of opinion which pervades a single social class or political sect. In the United States, on the other hand, there has been nothing of this gradual assimilation of the different political convictions of different classes. Knowledge and civilising influences have not been the agents in giving predominance to that tyrannical type of thought which there goes by the name of "public opinion." The despotism of public opinion in America is not due to the gradual disappearance of local types of opinion and sectional habits of mind, and the natural fusion of political creeds which thus results, — but to the complete political victory which a false constitutional system has given to the largest and most ignorant class of the community over all those whose wishes and judgment were entitled to greater weight. A public opinion which is really only a special class-opinion, accidentally enabled to *silence* all higher elements of thought *instead of* assimilating them, is no fair specimen of that assimilation of view which is confessedly due mainly to the freer interchange of thought between class and class. And yet it is a public opinion formed, as he admits, in the latter fashion, which Mr. Mill thinks so much more menacing to individual liberty than those narrower and straiter forms of class-opinion and conviction which preceded it, and have been absorbed into it.

* * * Though we believe that never at any previous time were Englishmen at large so free to think and act as they deem right in all important matters, without even the necessity of rendering any account

of their actions to the social circles in which they move, — we believe
also that the intensity of character lost in this process is sometimes not
counterbalanced by the gain in freedom. Mr. Mill has got into inextri-
cable confusion between the strength or intensity of a well-marked type
of character encouraged by every social influence to grow *out* prominently in certain directions, — and that individuality which is simply left
at liberty to find and follow out its own perhaps not very defined bent.
Massiveness and strong outline in character are certainly less promoted
by the *laissez-faire* system Mr. Mill recommends than by the predominance of certain tyrannical and one-sided customs, and motives, and
restraints, and schools of thought, in the moral atmosphere by which
men are surrounded. Mr. Mill is probably right when he complains
that the character of the present age is to be "without any marked
character;" but for our parts, instead of ascribing it to that exigeant
commonplace with which our author wages so internecine a war, we
ascribe it in the main to the exactly opposite cause, — the dissolution
of various stringent codes of social opinion and custom, which extended
the variety of well-marked types of character *at the expense* of the individuality of those who were subject to their influence. * * *

Holding as we do that Mr. Mill ascribes this dead level of character
to a cause nearly the reverse of the true cause, it is not surprising that
we differ from him still more widely when he suggests his remedy. Mr.
Mill sees no means of stimulating the individual mind to assert its own
right to rebel against the tyrannous desire of average men "that all other
people shall resemble" themselves. And so he sets himself to persuade
average men that, whether with regard to their influence over legislation, or with regard to their share in forming the public opinion of the
day, they must steadily resist the temptation of interfering at all to regulate the standard of individual morality, except so far as it touches
social rights. This is the one object of his essay. It is not at present half
so important, he says, to purify the public conscience, as to break down
once and for ever its right to intrude its impressions on individuals.
* * * He is so anxious to secure free action for human individualities,
that he would interdict the "public mind" from expressing any opinion
at all on some of the gravest topics that can be submitted to human
discussion. He would, in short, emasculate public opinion, in order to
remove one principal stumbling-block in the way of those who tremble
to assert their own individual convictions in the face of that terrible
tribunal.

Now we are far from denying that the power of public opinion is
often a real and painful stumbling-block to men in the discharge of
their duty. It is often hasty, and often ignorant, and often cruel. It
sometimes crushes the weak, while it spares altogether the strong and
the shameless. It continually "judges according to appearance and not
righteous judgment." Its standard is conventional, and is yet generally
applied with most rigour where it is, in fact, inapplicable altogether.

All this is true, but is certainly no truer of that section of public opinion which regards individual duty than of that which regards social duty; and the remedy does not lie in the artificial proposal to warn Government and Society off the former field altogether. This, however, is exactly the position which Mr. Mill has written his book to defend. * * * His essay is an inquiry into the "nature and limits of the power which can be legitimately exercised by society over the individual;" and he does not confine it to investigating the legitimate degree of *State* interference, but, assuming that the principle on which society may claim to interfere with individual self-government by the infliction of social penalties is identical in kind, though not necessarily equally applicable in all cases, with that which warrants legislative interference, he makes it his object to establish that "the sole end for which mankind are warranted, individually or collectively, in interfering with the liberty of action of any of their number is self-protection," or "to prevent harm to others."

Before we follow Mr. Mill into his able exposition and defence of this principle, we wish to call attention to the new light thrown upon it by the position we have attempted to establish. We have affirmed that the loss of power and intensity which is observable in the typical characters of the present day arises not, as Mr. Mill affirms, from that galling slavery to Commonplace, under the name of Public Opinion, into which men, as it is said, have recently fallen; but from the partial disappearance of those narrow religious, social, and political organisations which formerly gave a more definite outline, and lent a more constant sustaining power, in the shape of strong class-sympathy, to the minds of those who were formed under their influence. But if this be so, * * * then it would seem that the effect of even much stricter codes of social custom, and much narrower sectarian and political prejudices, than any now prevalent tended to sharpen rather than obliterate that edge, and flavour, and intensity which Mr. Mill so much admires and which he misnames "individuality." Suppose for a moment Mr. Mill could have emasculated the various petty "public opinions," confined to special castes and classes, which produced the well-marked characters of the last century, as he would now emasculate the wider and less definite public opinion of modern English society, what would have been the result? The very pith of every strong class-opinion was and is its ideal of *personal* excellence, that touchstone by which it proves the mettle of all its members, and by reference to which it accords its popular judgment of favour or censure. And not only is this true, but it is equally true that no qualities of character enter more deeply into such class-ideals of excellence than those termed by Mr. Mill purely "self-regarding qualities,"—self-possession, courage, firmness, self-restraint,—which, according to our author, should be confined to the most solitary chambers of the imagination. Moreover, once admit that such virtues may and must enter into the very essence of popular standards of character, and you cannot prevent that severity of popular condemnation on the corresponding vices which Mr. Mill regards as a violation of the principle of individual freedom. Suppose, for instance, the country gentlemen of the last century had been induced, in anticipation of Mr. Mill's philosophy, sternly to discourage all tyrannical social prejudices as to the so-called "self-regarding" excellences of the country gentleman; they would of course have discouraged any attempt to affix a social stigma on avarice, meanness, timidity in field-sports, and so forth. But how could this have been possible without destroying entirely the strength, freshness, and clearness of outline, which has engraved that type of character so deeply in the English imagination? * * * In fact, nothing is more remarkable as regards popular English standards of character than a certain undue esteem for purely personal gifts and excellences, and a deeper detestation of those deformities which imply a want of self-respect than even of those which imply a want of respect for others.

* * * Mr. Mill's proposal to encourage the growth of moral individuality by entirely warning off the conscience of a society or a class from any responsible criticism of this interior world, would have exactly the opposite effect to that which he desires. A strong type of character may be the result either of vivid sympathy or keen collision with the social morality it finds around it; but where the social conscience practically ignores altogether any sphere of universal morality, it will seldom be the case that individual characters will dwell with any intensity upon it. Social indifference will result, not in individual vitality, but in individual indifference. Personal morality, once conscious that society has suspended its judgment, will grow up as colourless as a flower excluded from the light. And if society do not suspend its judgment, it cannot but take leave to mark its approval and disapproval, to praise its heroes and to brand its outlaws. In spite of Mr. Mill's authority, we hold that if his object be, as he states, to encourage the growth of those more bold and massive types of character which he mourns over as extinct, it will be more wise, as well as more practicable, to select as his means to that end the purifying of social judgments from their one-sidedness than to attempt the complete suspension of them on certain tabooed subjects; to seek to infuse into them a truer justice and a deeper charity in estimating individual principles of conduct than to lecture society on the impropriety of passing any opinion on them at all. The "liberty of indifference" is the only kind of liberty which Mr. Mill's proposal would be likely to confer; and that is scarcely consistent with the massive and defined strength of purpose he wishes to restore.

* * * Mr. Mill begins by disclaiming, as a utilitarian must, any appeal to abstract right. "I regard utility," he says, "as the ultimate appeal on all ethical questions; but it must be utility in the largest sense, grounded on the permanent interests of man as a progressive being." And the influence of this theory is marked throughout the book. For, starting

with the assumption that there is no inward standard of right or wrong, no standard except that which is attained by studying the *results* of conduct, he is led to divide actions into two great classes, — those which affect exclusively or mainly the agents, which are therefore beyond the reach of any external criticism, since no one can know the full consequences except the agent; and actions which affect directly or at least necessarily the interests of others, which can be classified into right and wrong according as they would, if generally permitted, satisfy or interfere with the claims of others.

*   *   *

Accordingly he classes cruelty, malice, envy, dissimulation, insincerity, love of domineering, as *immoral*; while cowardice, self-conceit, prodigality, and sensuality, so long as they infringe no one else's rights, he regards as beyond the bounds of morality proper. Their evil, he maintains, depends on their evil consequences. Those consequences, we may think, indeed, that we discern, but they are really experienced only by the mind of the agent; while the evil consequences of the former class of dispositions, on the other hand, are directly measurable by the disturbing influence they exert on the well-being of others. Mr. Mill is consistent, therefore, as a utilitarian, in drawing the broadest distinction between the faults and crimes which aggrieve others, and those which directly hurt, or are supposed to hurt, none except those who commit them.

Mr. Mill is perfectly consistent, we say; but what conscience can acquiesce? Insincerity, he says, is an immorality; lying is a *vice* properly visited by an extreme social penalty; and a fraud is a *crime* properly requited by a severe legal penalty; for lying and fraud invade the rights of others; it is an obligation to others to tell the truth and to act the truth, for others are relying upon you. But sensuality, unless it trespasses on the rights of others, is a "folly," a "want of self-respect," a carelessness as to "self-development;" but, "to whatever pitch" it may be carried, it "does not constitute wickedness." We cannot wonder at this inference from the utilitarian ethics; but we do wonder that so marvellous a result should not stagger any great thinker as to the justice of his premises. The truth is, that Mr. Mill is deceived by the epithet of "self-regarding," which he assigns to the various evil dispositions and actions thus intended to be exempted from social criticism. "Prudence," "self-respect," and "self-development," against which alone he considers them to be transgressions, convey no sense of obligation. A man may sacrifice his own good, indulge little in self-respect, or even have erroneous notions as to the best direction of self-development, without any sense of guilt. None of these phrases in the least describe the origin of the self-reproach which accompanies any kind of evil self-indulgence, moral or sensual. The reason why the term "self-regarding" is so misleading, is not because there is any error in supposing that these things do primarily affect ourselves, but because it seems to indicate that there

is a real distinction in kind, which there is not, between the inward
moral conditions of this kind of evil disposition or action and those of
dispositions or actions which affect primarily others than ourselves.
Were Mr. Mill's theory, and the special epithet of "self-regarding"
which represents it, a copy of any characteristic inward feeling, — then
any habit of self-indulgence, such as that of anger or envy for example,
which directly tends to infringe the rights of others, would be separated
by a broad moral chasm in our own minds from any other habit of
self-indulgence, moral or sensual, which directly tends only to affect
our own nature. But this, as Mr. Mill knows, is not the case. The
consideration as to whom any guilty act will mainly strike is an *arrière
pensée* of the mind, not the least involved in the primary sense of guilt.
The classification may be important to the politician, but to the moralist
it is utterly artificial. There is as much, and usually far more, sense of
a violated claim in the first impurity of thought, which does not seem
to go forth into the external world at all, than in the first passionate
blow or the first malignant insinuation, which are clear self-indulgences
at the expense of another. However important, therefore, may be the
distinction between what Mr. Mill calls "self-regarding" faults and what
he calls immoralities affecting others in result, it is simply an error to
suppose that it is a *natural* distinction, which is recognised by the self-
accusing and self-condemning power in man. In both classes of moral
evils alike the sting of self-reproach is entirely inward; and is not removed by any demonstration that no *injury* to society has resulted, or
is likely to result. Of neither class of evils, again, is it a true account of
the matter to say that they lie absolutely within us; for, quite apart from
any theological conviction, in both classes of offences alike there is the
same sense of transgression of some deep invisible claim on us, which
we have no power to release as we can release any mere right of property of our own. * * * Mr. Mill's classification is in no sense a classification of wrong dispositions and actions according to the kind, or even
degree, of guilt with which they universally impress men, in no sense
a moral, but only a political classification. In this, of course, we are at
direct issue with Mr. Mill; since, as we have seen, he applies the word
"immoral" to the one class, and entirely excludes the other class from
any share in that epithet.

But notwithstanding this broad distinction in our ethical theory, it is
clear that Mr. Mill's case may be argued, as, indeed, he generally argues
it, without any explicit logical reference to his utilitarian creed. For the
object of the essay is not to discuss the amount of moral penalty to the
individual which different classes of faults ought to entail, but only that
portion of it which social custom or political law is justified in *inflicting*
for the purpose either of retribution or restraint. Now, even for those
who hold that Mr. Mill's classification of "self-regarding" and non-self-
regarding faults is morally an artificial one, it is quite a tenable position
that the only legitimate ground for social or political penalty ought to

be an injury to society or the state. This, accordingly, is Mr. Mill's position; he denies to society the right to intimidate by any intentional combination, even by the combined expression of moral opinion, those whose practice evinces a great divergence of moral principle from the accepted standard, so long as the practice at issue has no bearing on the rights of any other than the offending persons. We have a right, he says, to choose our own society according to our own tastes, and we may therefore avoid the society of a man who offends those tastes; but we have no right to inflict any social penalty upon him by inducing others to do the same, unless his offence be one which threatens the social rights of others.

*   *   *

This contains, we believe, the substance of Mr. Mill's argument. First, an injury to society is the only legitimate ground of social or political punishment; since any other fault or vice expiates itself, and we can only claim to inflict penalty from that principle of social resentment which is implied in the right to self-protection. Next, if society does transgress this rule at all, the chances are that it will be on the wrong side; since society is some judge of its own interests, but will judge simply by accidental liking or prejudice as to things which do not affect its own interests. Again, the individual is the best judge of his own self-development; and to fetter him by social restraints in what does not affect society is to menace the principle of free self-government. And finally, to the argument that every thing which hurts the inward life and purity of the individual necessarily reacts on society, Mr. Mill replies that he does not deny it, but that the principle of mere authority has had at least an adequate trial during the period of early education, when no one would argue for absolute liberty, even in "self-regarding" acts: but there must be some limit to interference; and if society is to interfere with the self-government of the mature, on the ground only of the infectious nature of all moral evil, there will be no secure sphere of individual freedom at all.

We must keep in mind, in discussing this argument, that Mr. Mill applies it as much to any combination of social opinion which tends to prevent or to render painful the assertion of individual freedom as to political legislation. His tests of what such social combination is, seems to be this: any act of which it is the intention to discourage a social heresy of this kind, is a social persecution if the heresy menace the rights of no one but the heretics. Individual disapproval may show itself, as a mere offended taste would show itself; but if you try to put an end to it at all, if you do more than simply withdraw your own countenance, and express your own opinion when natural occasion offers, you are guilty of a social persecution. You may disapprove of gambling or fornication, — you may even perhaps punish those who live by offering inducements to these vices, for that is a social act, which may possibly, at least, trench on the rights of others; but you may not (even socially) punish those who commit them in the exercise of their mature discretion; for the evil falls on themselves, and not (except through the moral infection) on society. You may avoid them yourself; you are bound not to do any thing with the intention of discouraging such a life, except by expressing temperately your individual opinion and regulating your individual conduct. You may not try to excite public censure against these things, — to bring them under the ban of society; as you might a furious temper or an envious and dishonest tongue. In the latter case, the heavier the social penalty you bring down the better. Society must be protected against it. But the evil of "errors" which are visited exclusively on the head of those who commit them ought not to be increased, but if possible alleviated, by lookers-on: and they may not be errors, after all; there is no worse judge than a society on whose rights they do not trench, and which is actuated only by prejudiced "likings" or "dislikings" of its own.

We have done our best to state Mr. Mill's case. * * * Still it seems to us to fail miserably in furnishing even the ground-plan of a sound political philosophy. * * * There is no element so utterly absent, from the first page to the last, as any indication of sympathy with the free play of a national or social character in its natural organic action. Mr. Mill's essay regards "liberty" from first to last in its negative rather than its positive significance. But in that sense in which the very word "liberty" is apt to excite the deepest enthusiasm of which human nature is capable, it means a great deal more than the mere absence of restraints on the individual; it implies that fresh and unconstrained play of national character, that fullness of social life and vivacity of public energy, which it is one of the worst results of such constraint to subdue or extinguish. But any sympathy with a full social life or fresh popular impulses is exactly the element in which Mr. Mill's book is most deficient. The only liberty he would deny the nation is the liberty to be a nation. He distrusts social and political freedom. There is a depressed and melancholy air about his essay in treating of social and political organisms. He thinks strongly that individuals should be let alone, but virtually on condition that they shall not coalesce into a society and have a social or political life that may react strongly on the principles of individual action. * * * An aggregate of individually free minds, if they are to be held asunder from natural social combinations by the stiff framework of such a doctrine as Mr. Mill's, would not make in any true or deep sense a free society or a free nation. For any thing this essay contains to the contrary, a nation might be held to possess the truest freedom though there were no indication in it of a common life, no sign of a united society, no vestige of a national will. It is strange that, while Mr. Mill lays so much and such just stress on the liberty of individual thought and expression, he should quite ignore the equally sacred liberty of social and national thought and expression, and even invent a canon for the express purpose of discouraging any action of society at all on topics where he would think it dangerous to the liberty of the individual. In England we should regard the mere absence of interference with individual opinions and actions as a poor sort of liberty, unless there were also due provision for the free play of social opinion, a suitable organ for the expression of those characteristic thoughts which elicit a response from the whole nation, a fit instrument for the timely assertion of England's antipathies and sympathies, hopes and will. If it be in reality a far truer mode of thinking to conceive individuals as members of a society, rather than society as pieced together of individuals, it is certain that true liberty demands for the deepest forms of social thought and life as free and characteristic an expression as it demands for the deepest forms of individual thought and life.

But, says Mr. Mill, what business has society to interfere with actions which do not in any way infringe on the rights of others? * * * We reply that, even if the consequences of what Mr. Mill calls "self-regarding errors" can be admitted to be individual only, yet that it is not by the consequences that even the agent himself judges his own action, and therefore not by the consequences that the society of which he is a member can judge it. Both the individual and society feel that the inward principle which is violated in many of these "self-regarding errors" is of infinitely more importance in estimating their relation both to the individual character and to the constitution of society, than the immediate consequences can ever be. The distinction between "self-regarding" consequences and consequences to society is not usually a distinction naturally suggested to the agent, but a distinction taken afterwards on his behalf by astute advocates. And if not a distinction which the individual conscience can always recognise as morally important, then also not a distinction which the social conscience — if a society may be permitted a conscience — can recognise either. Mr. Mill speaks as if those who violate the laws of social morality could properly be conceived as *outside* the social body, as mere invaders of society, and their guilt estimated by the amount of immediate social confusion it tends to produce upon others than themselves. * * * Now this is a completely artificial and deceptive mode of thought. Individuals who in any special point reject the moral authority of the society in which they live, are none the less members of that society. Their act is not an invasion, but a rebellion. In other words, it has a double influence, which the aggressive acts of mere invaders never have, — the external and the internal, — the directly injurious results, which, even though they fall exclusively upon their own heads, still fall upon living members of a society who cannot suffer without injury to the whole; and again, the still more important influence of the practical protest put forth by living members of a society against the social principle they have violated. If that principle be one really essential either to social unity or social purity, it is clear that society cannot treat either the immediate ill consequences or the practical protest as if it came from an external source.

If there be any transgressions of social morality which are conceived, as well by the individual as the social conscience, as momentous, not nearly so much because of their immediate results as because they soon extinguish that sense of the inviolable sanctity of social life which is its best and most distinctly religious bond, then surely society, if it have an inward life and constitution and conscience at all, has even more right to express itself in open resentment and displeasure, than in the case of offences which happen to affect the external lot of others of its members. Mr. Mill will not deny that there are offences not trenching on the rights of any other member of society, which yet do more to relax the strength of that spiritual tie which holds society together, than many offences which are direct aggressions upon the rights of others. * * * Yet because offences of the former class are, in the first instance, sins only against that hidden conscience, or rather that overshadowing power, which constitutes the true spiritual bond of society, while offences of the latter class are also visibly traced in unjust violence or defrauded claims, Mr. Mill would call an organic expression of social displeasure towards sins of the one class a tyranny, and towards sins of the other class a needful and justifiable resentment. It is, we suppose, because Mr. Mill denies the existence of any moral standard of action, except consequences, in the individual, that he is also unwilling to admit the existence of any inward social principles apart from consequences against which members of a society can offend. Were it not so, he would see as clearly as we see that the danger of severing the spiritual roots of social purity and unity is the true danger to society, and needs even more sedulous and organised protest in cases where there is no one person specially interested in raising it, than even in those cases where some one is directly wronged, and therefore certain to call in the aid of others in his own behalf. Social liberty, or liberty for the free play of social character, is quite as sacred as individual liberty; and it cannot exist at all if the deepest principles which form that character are to be kept in abeyance out of respect for the liberty of those who infringe them. How far the individual should be compelled, *otherwise* than by the free expression of social opinion, to respect such moral laws, is quite another question, which involves a large class of new considerations. But to propose that social opinion should spontaneously put itself under unnatural restrictions, with regard to principles which go to the very root of social life, in deference to individual liberty, is to ask that society should renounce its best impulses, in order that individuals may indulge their worst.

We shall not, we trust, be understood to deny that such a thing as social tyranny — quite apart from legislative enactment — is very common and very dangerous. No doubt society often does interfere with the proper sphere of private individual liberty. We only maintain that

Mr. Mill's principle altogether fails properly to distinguish the two spheres, and practically denies any inward life and character to society altogether; turning it into a mere *arbiter* between individuals, instead of regarding it as an organised body, in the common life of which all its members partake. Mr. Mill thinks society a competent judge of its own *external interests*; but that its moral likings and dislikings are mere tyrannical sentiments, which it will impose at pleasure on any unfortunate minority within its control. No doubt societies, like individuals, are disposed to bigotry. No doubt majorities will at times strive to impose their coarser tastes and poor commonplace thoughts on minorities, instead of desiring to know and try the principle opposed to theirs. But what is the true check upon social bigotry? According to Mr. Mill, the only guarantee against it is to erect, by common consent, every individual human mind into an impregnable and independent fortress, within the walls of which social authority shall have no jurisdiction; the functions of the latter being strictly limited to arbitrating questions at issue between all such independent lords, and prohibiting mutual encroachments. Now we do not deny that such a total withdrawal of individual duty and morality from the circle of social questions might secure against bigotry; but at what expense? At the sacrifice, we believe, of that mediating body of social faith and conviction which connects together the more marked individualities of different minds, interprets them, and renders them mutually intelligible and useful, — at the cost of that social unity of spirit which alone renders the diversity of individual gifts capable of profiting by each other. Mr. Mill's essay may be said to be one long *éloge* on individuality — its importance in itself, and its paramount importance to society. This we accept as strongly as Mr. Mill. But individuality may suffer in either of two ways: from the too great rigour or from the too great looseness of the social bond, — from the tyrannical domination of custom and commonplace over the individual; or from that paralysis of social life which permits individual modes of thought and conduct to diverge too widely for mutual influence and aid. What is it that really makes strong individualities of character and thought so important to society, but their real power of increasing the moral and intellectual experience of general society? And how could this be, if they were not kept constantly in living relation with general society by the sense of social authority over them? It is this moral authority exercised by social opinion, and this alone, which obliges the innovator to remember, and, if he can, to appreciate, the body of diffused social conviction, even while modifying, deviating from, and expanding it. People of strong one-sided individualities are always in danger of losing their full and fair influence on society; nay, of losing even the full advantage of their special characteristics, from want of adequate sympathy with the society which they wish to influence. * * *

And what is true of intellectual characteristics is far more uniformly true of moral characteristics. Those who ignore entirely the restraints of the code of social morality under which they live, are never likely to deepen, widen, or elevate it. Moral heretics may often render a great service to the world, but only where they feel acutely where it is that their creed diverges from that of the world, and on what grounds it thus diverges; only if they recognise the moral authority of the social creed to the full so far as it is sound, and dispute it on the one point on which they have tested its unsoundness. Mere groundless eccentricity,—which Mr. Mill, with less than his usual good sense, goes into a special digression to extol,—has more effect, we believe, in aggravating the social bigotry of Commonplace, and rendering men suspicious of all genuine individuality, than any other influence. Proper individuality is any thing but eccentricity; it is a development—one-sided perhaps, but still a development—of convictions and characteristics the germs of which are common to all men. * * *

If now Mr. Mill asks us what we regard as the true check upon that oppressive social bigotry which so often gives rise to weakness and moral cowardice on the one hand, and to unjust social excommunications on the other, we should reply, that there is the same check on the tyrannical treatment by society of what he calls "self-regarding" heresies as there is on similar social tyrannies towards what he admits to be justly punishable social immoralities. * * * That society is an imperfect judge of right and wrong, is true enough. Is it likely to improve under the exhortation to give up thinking of right and wrong altogether, and to calculate instead the tendency of human actions to produce external social disturbance? Is it likely to be more charitable and less unjust when told that it must no longer try human action by a practical human standard; that it must take pains to distinguish between actions with evil social consequences and actions with evil individual consequences only; and while disregarding the latter altogether, it should administer the unwritten law of social instinct upon the former with all the deterrent rigour it can command? * * * He thinks that if society would but confess that is has no social right to set up any concrete standard of moral duty, if it could but be persuaded to confine its criticisms to that abstract idea of his, "social man," and to plead absolute incompetence to deal with the "self-regarding" duties of human life,—that then individual minds would begin to play freely, and health to return to the whole social system. We believe, on the contrary, that if Mr. Mill's prescription could be carried out at all, which it cannot, the result would be exactly opposite. The individuality of individual life would be paralysed by this artificial indifference on the part of Society to its proceedings. The social morality of social life would lose all depth and seriousness by being thus unnaturally dissevered from the deeper judgments of the individual conscience. Social morality, striving to judge of actions simply by their effects on the rights of others, and ostentatiously excluding all the natural canons of moral criticism, would become arbitrary, conventional, formal. In proportion as it relaxed its hold on the individual conscience, it would become pharisaic in its anxiety about the rights of others. Professing to judge men only by this rigid test-formula, 'What is the net social result of your action?' instead of by any natural human conception of good or evil, social morality would wander farther and farther from the natural principles of justice, and soon substitute a *doctrinaire* social bigotry of its own, in the place of that moral bigotry in judging of individual conduct from which Mr. Mill hopes to redeem it.

*   *   *

Mr. Mill is well aware that the principal recommendation of his social theory to ordinary minds is not likely to consist in its inherent strength half so much as in its inviting logical affinity to one very important and very direct application, which English thought has already, on other grounds, heartily accepted; we mean the perfect liberty of individual opinion, and the evil of any sort of social excommunication of mere heresy. * * * Accordingly he spends the first half of his essay on reconsidering this principle, and developing it beyond its already familiar political aspects into its purely social bearings. He sees that there is much chronic social intolerance left which ought to be eradicated, and he perhaps justly thinks his theory of society well adapted to educe an extension of this principle, to prove the inadmissibility of those social excommunications which religious heresy still frequently draws down. If society has no further right than to protect itself against practical transgressors of social duties and claims, how clear that it has no right to stir up any sort of social resentment or arm prejudice against a man who has simply used his own individual liberty of thought to form his own individual convictions! And what theory of society but that of self-protection would be likely to leave the sphere of individual thought so inviolable? * * *

Unfortunately, however, for his social theory, he ought to separate the right to form individual convictions from the right to *propagate* them. The two rights, he freely concedes, are practically inseparable; yet the two certainly do not bear the same relation to his social theory. So long, indeed, as the convictions formed have no direct bearing on the admitted rights of others, — so long as they are religious, or belong only to the "self-regarding" class of moral duties, — so long his theory would justify their free propagation as well as their free formation. But once let them have a revolutionary tendency in their bearing on social life, — once let their adoption have evil consequence which would fall primarily on *others*, — and he feels at once that the "self-protecting" theory of society would justify both government and social opinion in interfering to punish or to excommunicate the propagandist. Mr. Mill does not attempt to get over this difficulty. He knows that government ought to interfere only with evil actions, not with dangerous opinions. He knows that social feeling itself ought to draw a broad distinction between evil actions and those opinions which merely encourage and impel to evil actions; but his theory will not admit this distinction. If "self-protection" be the duty of society, it ought surely to discourage in the germ those views which endanger its existence, and not to wait till the risk has borne fruits of serious evil.

Mr. Mill is obliged to draw a distinction between opinions so expressed "as to constitute a positive instigation to some mischievous act," and abstract opinions with the same tendency: "An opinion that corn-dealers are starvers of the poor, or that private property is robbery, ought to be unmolested when simply circulated through the press; but may justly incur punishment when delivered orally to an excited mob assembled before the house of a corn-dealer, or when handed about by the same mob in the form of a placard."

With this doctrine we entirely agree; but if it be taken absolutely, what does it really amount to except a complete abandonment of Mr. Mill's own theory, and a virtual admission of our position that, after all, it is the judgment of the social conscience, and not any technical formula derived from a right to protect itself against external disorders, which justifies society in the infliction of political and social penalties, and the expression of social resentment? For if, as Mr. Mill contends, society is the best and only proper judge of what is inimical to its own interest, and is bound to watch over and protect them without regard to the principles of individual morality involved, how can he regard as any thing but positively praiseworthy its attempt to stifle at once, — if not by law, at least by the expression of stern displeasure on the part of the public, — all teaching that would directly tend to subversive actions? On the principle that prevention is better than cure, * * * no one can deny that to brand the propagation of opinions dangerous to the constitution of society with social opprobrium would be a much safer measure than to punish those who act them out. If an opinion is advocated "that corn-dealers are starvers of the poor," and it is possible, by uniformly frowning upon and, if needful, excommunicating the advocates of such subversive opinions, to prevent the assemblage of that unruly mob before the corn-dealer's door altogether, how much more merciful this course would be than to let the doctrine reach that degree of influence and then punish its propounders! Mr. Mill makes reply, as we understand him, that he admits this consequence; that, strictly speaking, society has the right to guard itself against revolutionary opinions, even while only abstract; but that it wisely waives this right for the chance which always exists that by habitually listening to all abstract opinions, it may occasionally be induced to reconsider its own view, and give in its adhesion to what it at first erroneously deemed subversive doctrine. In short, society, he thinks, properly runs the risk of delaying for a while to protect itself against many really dangerous opinions which may gain ground and become practically threatening, in order that it may protect itself against the alternative and worse risk of overlooking the truth contained in some seemingly but not really dangerous opinions. This is, however, practically leaving it to the discretion of society whether in any given case it regards the practical risk or the chance of new light as the greater. The right of self-protection always exists; and if it is waived, it is only because society does not fear so much as it hopes. * * * Accordingly political and social intolerance is certainly clearly admissible, — on the theory that the only duty of society is to protect itself, — in the case of all opinions which seem to threaten, in the opinion of the majority, much more social danger than their investigation could possibly bring new light. * * *

Moreover, Mr. Mill's theory does not only leave large room for social and political intolerance, but in those cases where it does admit intolerance at all, it admits it in the highest degree. Suppose society convinced — say by bitter experience, such as that of revolutionary France — that it had far more danger to apprehend from the spread of exciting doctrine on any particular subject than enlightenment to look for from the discussion, it will be warranted in using the most effective social measures for its extinction. That is but poor "self-protection" that only half does its work. The earlier the blow is struck, the more entirely theoretic the stage in which the social heresy is extinguished, the farther it is from any actual criminal intention at the time, the better. So far from waiting till the mob is before the corn-dealer's door, according to the true principle of self-protection, society would raise a hue and cry against the social heretic when first he began to intimate that to destroy granaries of corn in order to raise the price of the remainder is a selfish and unprincipled act. Once let the teaching take the form of a popular cry, — once let selfish ends become interwoven with it, — and it might be too late. The theory of self-protection, then, will not only justify intolerance to social heresies in given cases, but in those cases will justify it at the point farthest removed from practical action; while the intellectual error, and that alone, is the danger to be feared.

* * *

We hold, then, that Mr. Mill's own theory does not permit nearly so clear a distinction between opinions and actions as is absolutely necessary for any true guarantee of social tolerance. Measure Wrong by the mere amount of tendency to imperil the admitted rights of others, and you cannot draw any satisfactory distinction between the intellectual and the practical tendencies which imperil them. Measure it, on the other hand, by a practical standard, the purpose and circumstances of the wrong-doer, and there is the broadest distinction between a theory and an instigation, — an impersonal conclusion of the intellect, and a practical recommendation which realises the whole actual significance of the injurious theory. * * *

How, then, Mr. Mill will ask, do we provide against that religious and social intolerance which, as his own essay most eloquently shows, is still so deadly a poison in English society? If we contend that the social conscience should be as free to judge and speak as the individual conscience, how are we to protest with any force against that miserable bigotry which *always* professes to speak from the impulses of a pure moral zeal, and very generally really is closely connected with the moral nature? * * * The way to convince society that it is in error is, not to deny that its conscience has any right to judge of individual conduct, but to exhibit the many great complexities of intellectual constitution which have prevented, and do prevent, men of pure life and stainless integrity from accepting these faiths; and to point out, moreover, that one of the greatest obstacles in their way is the uncharitable excommunication to which society in its pharisaism dooms them. This would be a victory over the social conscience gained by an appeal to the social conscience, and therefore, we believe, would be much more likely to be firm and permanent than one gained by merely persuading society —which it would be hard to do—that it has no concern with the individual principles of life and action, as such, at all. We always mistrust these indirect victories over either individual or social opinion. The social conscience, like the individual conscience, will not submit to be merely out-manœuvred; it takes the liberty, after all, of forming its judgments, with reference to the rights of a question, on those rights.

* * *

If Society is to be made to feel that it is to have no social judgment, no social conviction, no social likings and dislikings, on individual morals and creeds at all,—if the social mind is simply to *abstain* from all corporate acts of conviction which might carry the weak along with it, or intimidate the cowardly into base compliance,—how could we have any thing but "heresies smouldering in the narrow circle of studious persons among whom they originate"? What is it that makes opinions "blaze out far and wide," and "light up the affairs of mankind with either a true or a deceptive light," except a profound conviction on the part of the social conscience that it *is* concerned in those convictions, and *has* a real relation to them, either in the way of cordial belief or of as cordial rejection? If Mr. Mill had looked for a theory of society which, if adopted, might have the effect of prolonging so undesirable a condition of things, he could not have invented any so excellently adapted to that purpose as his own. It is the belief that society, as society, has a common life, liable to be vitally influenced by the acceptance or rejection of religious and moral faiths; it is this true belief that favours those hearty battles between conflicting sections which are so much better and healthier a sign of the times than "smouldering" orthodoxies and equally smouldering heterodoxies. If, as Mr. Mill believes, society has no such common life, it is impossible that the enunciation of truths or errors could stir up in it these elevated moods of social emotion. If common opinions are to be debarred all active expression, all signs of either approval or censure, for fear they may subdue the cowardly or silence the timid, it is impossible that the conflict between truth and error can be any thing but a weak and dropping fire carried on by individual marksmen. Mr. Mill uniformly advocates an unsocial conception of liberty which exactly corresponds to the condition of things he so eloquently condemns. * * *

JAMES FITZJAMES STEPHEN

[Mill's Fallacies]†

There is hardly anything in the whole essay which can properly be called proof as distinguished from enunciation or assertion of the general principles quoted. I think, however, that it will not be difficult to show that the principle stands in much need of proof. In order to make this clear it will be desirable in the first place to point out the meaning of the word liberty according to principles which I think are common to Mr Mill and to myself. I do not think Mr Mill would have disputed the following statement of the theory of human actions. All voluntary acts are caused by motives. All motives may be placed in one of two categories—hope and fear, pleasure and pain. Voluntary acts of which hope is the motive are said to be free. Voluntary acts of which fear is the motive are said to be done under compulsion, or omitted under restraint. A woman marries. This in every case is a voluntary action. If she regards the marriage with the ordinary feelings and acts from the ordinary motives, she is said to act freely. If she regards it as a necessity, to which she submits in order to avoid greater evil, she is said to act under compulsion and not freely.

If this is the true theory of liberty—and, though many persons would deny this, I think they would have been accepted by Mr Mill—the propositions already stated will in a condensed form amount to this: 'No one is ever justified in trying to affect any one's conduct by exciting his fears, except for the sake of self-protection;' or, making another substitution which he would also approve—'It can never promote the general happiness of mankind that the conduct of any persons should be affected by an appeal to their fears, except in the cases excepted.'

Surely these are not assertions which can be regarded as self-evident, or even as otherwise than paradoxical. What is all morality, and what are all existing religions in so far as they aim at affecting human conduct, except an appeal either to hope or fear, and to fear far more commonly and far more emphatically than to hope? Criminal legislation proper may be regarded as an engine of prohibition unimportant in comparison with morals and the forms of morality sanctioned by theology. For one act from which one person is restrained by the fear

† From James Fitzjames Stephen, *Liberty, Equality, Fraternity* (London, 1873), pp. 8–15, 22–23, 26–27, 43–44, 46–48, 76–79, 123, 130–31, 145–49, 153, 154, 184–85.

of the law of the land, many persons are restrained from innumerable acts by the fear of the disapprobation of their neighbours, which is the moral sanction; or by the fear of punishment in a future state of existence, which is the religious sanction; or by the fear of their own disapprobation, which may be called the conscientious sanction, and may be regarded as a compound case of the other two. Now, in the innumerable majority of cases, disapprobation, or the moral sanction, has nothing whatever to do with self-protection. The religious sanction is by its nature independent of it. Whatever special forms it may assume, the fundamental condition of it is a being intolerant of evil in the highest degree, and inexorably determined to punish it wherever it exists, except upon certain terms. I do not say that this doctrine is true, but I do say that no one is entitled to assume it without proof to be essentially immoral and mischievous. Mr Mill does not draw this inference, but I think his theory involves it, for I know not what can be a greater infringement of his theory of liberty, a more complete and formal contradiction to it, than the doctrine that there are a court and a judge in which, and before whom, every man must give an account of every work done in the body, whether self-regarding or not. According to Mr Mill's theory, it ought to be a good plea in the day of judgment to say 'I pleased myself and hurt nobody else.' Whether or not there will ever be a day of judgment is not the question, but upon his principles the conception of a day of judgment is fundamentally immoral. A God who punished any one at all, except for the purpose of protecting others, would, upon his principles, be a tyrant trampling on liberty.

The application of the principle in question to the moral sanction would be just as subversive of all that people commonly regard as morality. The only moral system which would comply with the principle stated by Mr Mill would be one capable of being summed up as follows: 'Let every man please himself without hurting his neighbour;' and every moral system which aimed at more than this, either to obtain benefits for society at large other than protection against injury or to do good to the persons affected, would be wrong in principle. This would condemn every existing system of morals. Positive morality is nothing but a body of principles and rules more or less vaguely expressed, and more or less left to be understood, by which certain lines of conduct are forbidden under the penalty of general disapprobation, and that quite irrespectively of self-protection. Mr Mill himself admits this to a certain extent. In the early part of his fourth chapter he says that a man grossly deficient in the qualities which conduce to his own good is 'necessarily and properly a subject of distaste, or in extreme cases even of contempt,' and he enumerates various inconveniences to which this would expose such a person. He adds, however: 'The inconveniences which are strictly inseparable from the unfavourable judgment of others are the only ones to which a person should ever be subjected for that portion of his conduct and character which concerns his own good, but which does not affect the interests of others in their relation with him.' This no doubt weakens the effect of the admission; but be this how it may, the fact still remains that morality is and must be a prohibitive system, one of the main objects of which is to impose upon every one a standard of conduct and of sentiment to which few persons would conform if it were not for the constraint thus put upon them. In nearly every instance the effects of such a system reach far beyond anything that can be described as the purposes of self-protection.

Mr Mill's system is violated not only by every system of theology which concerns itself with morals, and by every known system of positive morality, but by the constitution of human nature itself. There is hardly a habit which men in general regard as good which is not acquired by a series of more or less painful and laborious acts. The condition of human life is such that we must of necessity be restrained and compelled by circumstances in nearly every action of our lives. Why, then, is liberty, defined as Mr Mill defines it, to be regarded as so precious? What, after all, is done by the legislator or by the person who sets public opinion in motion to control conduct of which he disapproves — or, if the expression is preferred, which he dislikes — which is not done for us all at every instant of our lives by circumstances? The laws which punish murder or theft are substitutes for private vengeance, which, in the absence of law, would punish those crimes more severely, though in a less regular manner. If there were laws which punished incontinence, gluttony, or drunkenness, the same might be said of them. Mr Mill admits in so many words that there are 'inconveniences which are strictly inseparable from the unfavourable judgment of others.' What is the distinction in principle between such inconveniences and similar ones organized, defined, and inflicted upon proof that the circumstances which call for their infliction exist? This organization, definition, and procedure make all the difference between the restraints which Mr Mill would permit and the restraints to which he objects. I cannot see on what the distinction rests. I cannot understand why it must always be wrong to punish habitual drunkenness by fine, imprisonment, or deprivation of civil rights, and always be right to punish it by the infliction of those consequences which are 'strictly inseparable from the unfavourable judgment of others.' It may be said that these consequences follow, not because we think them desirable, but in the common order of nature. This answer only suggests the further question, whether nature is in this instance to be regarded as a friend or as an enemy? Every reasonable man would answer that the restraint which the fear of the disapprobation of others imposes on our conduct is the part of the constitution of nature which we could least afford to dispense with. But if this is so, why draw the line where Mr Mill draws it? Why treat the penal consequences of disapprobation as things to be minimized and restrained within the narrowest limits?

What 'inconvenience,' after all, is 'strictly inseparable from the unfavourable judgment of others'? If society at large adopted fully Mr Mill's theory of liberty, it would be easy to diminish very greatly the inconveniences in question. Strenuously preach and rigorously practise the doctrine that our neighbour's private character is nothing to us, and the number of unfavourable judgments formed, and therefore the number of inconveniences inflicted by them, can be reduced as much as we please, and the province of liberty can be enlarged in a corresponding ratio. Does any reasonable man wish for this? Could any one desire gross licentiousness, monstrous extravagance, ridiculous vanity, or the like, to be unnoticed, or, being known, to inflict no inconveniences?

If, however, the restraints on immorality are the main safeguards of society against influences which might be fatal to it, why treat them as if they were bad? Why draw so strongly marked a line between social and legal penalties? Mr Mill asserts the existence of the distinction in every form of speech. He makes his meaning perfectly clear. Yet from one end of his essay to the other I find no proof and no attempt to give the proper and appropriate proof of it. His doctrine could have been proved if it had been true. It was not proved because it was not true.

*　　*　　*

Not only is an appeal to facts and experience opposed to Mr Mill's principle, but his essay contains exceptions and qualifications which are really inconsistent with it. He says that his principle 'is meant to apply to human beings only in the maturity of their faculties,' and, he adds, 'we may leave out of account those backward states of society in which the race itself may be considered in its nonage.' Despotism, he says, 'is a legitimate mode of government in dealing with barbarians, provided the end be their improvement, and the means justified by actually effecting that end. Liberty as a principle has no application to any state of things anterior to the time when mankind have become capable of being improved by free and equal discussion. Until then there is nothing for them but implicit obedience to an Akbar or a Charlemagne if they are so fortunate as to find one. But as soon as mankind have attained the capacity of being guided to their own improvement by conviction or persuasion (a period long since reached in all nations with whom we need here concern ourselves), compulsion is no longer admissible as a means to their own good, and is justifiable only for the security of others.'

It seems to me that this qualification either reduces the doctrine qualified to an empty commonplace which no one would care to dispute, or makes an incredible assertion about the state of human society. No one, I suppose, ever denied either in theory or in practice that there is a sphere within which the tastes of people of mature age ought not to be interfered with, and within which differences must be regarded as natural and inevitable — in which better or worse means that which the individual prefers or dislikes. On the other hand, no one ever suggested that it was or could be good for anyone to be compelled to do what he did not like, unless the person compelling was not only stronger but wiser than the person compelled, at all events in reference to the matter to which the compulsion applied.

⁕   ⁕   ⁕

A narrower interpretation would be as follows. There is a period, now generally reached all over Europe and America, at which discussion takes the place of compulsion, and in which people when they know what is good for them generally do it. When this period is reached, compulsion may be laid aside. To this I should say that no such period has as yet been reached anywhere, and that there is no prospect of its being reached anywhere within any assignable time.

Where, in the very most advanced and civilised communities, will you find any class of persons whose views or whose conduct on subjects on which they are interested are regulated even in the main by the results of free discussion? What proportion of human misconduct in any department in life is due to ignorance, and what to wickedness or weakness? Of ten thousand people who get drunk, is there one who could say with truth that he did so because he had been brought to think on full deliberation and after free discussion that it was wise to get drunk? Would not every one of the ten thousand, if he told the real truth, say in some dialect or other — 'I got drunk because I was weak and a fool, because I could not resist the immediate pleasure for the sake of future and indefinite advantage'?

⁕   ⁕   ⁕

The great defect of Mr Mill's later writings seems to me to be that he has formed too favourable an estimate of human nature. This displays itself in the chapter ["Of Individuality, as One of the Elements of Well-Being"] by the tacit assumption which pervades every part of it that the removal of restraints usually tends to invigorate character. Surely the very opposite of this is the truth. Habitual exertion is the greatest of all invigorators of character, and restraint and coercion in one form or another is the great stimulus to exertion. If you wish to destroy originality and vigour of character, no way to do so is so sure as to put a high level of comfort easily within the reach of moderate and commonplace exertion. A life made up of danger, vicissitude, and exposure is the sort of life which produces originality and resource. A soldier or sailor on active service lives in an atmosphere of coercion by the elements, by enemies, by disease, by the discipline to which he is subjected. Is he usually a tamer and less original person than a comfortable London shopkeeper or a man with just such an income as enables him to do exactly as he likes? A young man who is educated and so kept under close and continuous discipline till he is twenty-two or twenty-three years of age will generally have a much more vigorous and more original character than one who is left entirely to his own devices at an age when his mind and his tastes are unformed. Almost every human being requires more or less coercion and restraint as astringents to give him the maximum of power which he is capable of attaining. The maximum attainable in particular cases depends upon something altogether independent of social arrangements — namely, the nature of the human being himself who is subjected to them; and what this is or how it is to be affected are questions which no one has yet answered.

＊　＊　＊

There is one more point in this curious chapter which I must notice in conclusion. Nothing can exceed Mr Mill's enthusiasm for individual greatness. The mass, he says, in all countries constitute collective mediocrity. They never think at all, and never rise above mediocrity, 'except in so far as the sovereign many have let themselves be guided and influenced (which in their best times they always have done) by the counsels and influence of a more highly gifted or instructed one or few. The initiation of all wise or noble things comes and must come from individuals; generally at first from some one individual.' The natural inference would be that these individuals are the born rulers of the world, and that the world should acknowledge and obey them as such. Mr Mill will not admit this. All that the man of genius can claim is 'freedom to point out the way. The power of compelling others into it is not only inconsistent with the freedom and development of all the rest, but corrupting to the strong man himself.' This would be perfectly true if the compulsion consisted in a simple exertion of blind force, like striking a nail with a hammer; but who ever acted so on others to any extent worth mentioning? The way in which the man of genius rules is by persuading an efficient minority to coerce an indifferent and self-indulgent majority, which is quite a different process.

The odd manner in which Mr Mill worships mere variety, and confounds the proposition that variety is good with the proposition that goodness is various, is well illustrated by the lines which follow this passage: 'Exceptional individuals . . . should be encouraged in acting differently from the mass' — in order that there may be enough of them to 'point out the way.' Eccentricity is much required in these days. Precisely because the tyranny of opinion is such as to make eccentricity a reproach, it is desirable, in order to break through that tyranny, that people should be eccentric. Eccentricity has always abounded when and where strength of character has abounded, and the amount of eccentricity in a society has generally been proportioned to the amount of genius, mental vigour, and moral courage it contained. That so few now dare to be eccentric makes the chief danger of the time.

If this advice were followed, we should have as many little oddities in manner and behaviour as we have people who wish to pass for men of genius. Eccentricity is far more often a mark of weakness than a mark of strength. Weakness wishes, as a rule, to attract attention by trifling distinctions, and strength wishes to avoid it. Originality consists in thinking for yourself, not in thinking differently from other people.

*   *   *

The real question is as to social intolerance. Has a man who believes in God and a future state a moral right to disapprove of those who do not, and to try by the expression of that disapproval to deter them from publishing, and to deter others from adopting, their views? I think that he has if and in so far as his opinions are true. Mr Mill thinks otherwise.

*   *   *

The heretics, says Mr Mill, are grievously injured by this, and are much to be pitied, but 'the greatest harm is done to those who are not heretics, and whose whole mental development is cramped and their reason cowed by the fear of heresy. Who can compute what the world loses in the multitude of promising intellects combined with timid characters, who dare not follow out any bold, vigorous, independent train of thought lest it should land them in something which would admit of being considered irreligious or immoral?'

On this point I am utterly unable to agree with Mr Mill. It seems to me that to publish opinions upon morals, politics, and religion is an act as important as any which any man can possibly do; that to attack opinions on which the framework of society rests is a proceeding which both is and ought to be dangerous. I do not say that it ought not to be done in many cases, but it should be done sword in hand, and a man who does it has no more right to be surprised at being fiercely resisted than a soldier who attacks a breach. Mr Mill's whole charge against social intolerance is that it makes timid people afraid to express unpopular opinions. An old ballad tells how a man, losing his way on a hill-side, strayed into a chamber full of enchanted knights, each lying motionless in complete armour, with his war-horse standing motionless beside him. On a rock lay a sword and a horn, and the intruder was told that if he wanted to lead the army, he must choose between them. He chose the horn and blew a loud blast, upon which the knights and their horses vanished in a whirlwind and their visitor was blown back into common life, these words sounding after him on the wind:

> Cursed be the coward that ever he was born
> Who did not draw the sword before he blew the horn.

No man has a right to give the signal for such a battle by blowing the horn, unless he has first drawn the sword and knows how to make his hands guard his head with it. Then let him blow as loud and long as he likes, and if his tune is worth hearing he will not want followers. Till a man has carefully formed his opinions on these subjects, thought them out, assured himself of their value, and decided to take the risk of proclaiming them, the strong probability is that they are not much worth having. Speculation on government, morals, and religion is a matter of vital practical importance, and not mere food for curiosity. Curiosity, no doubt, is generally the motive which leads a man to study them; but, till he has formed opinions on them for which he is prepared to fight, there is no hardship in his being compelled by social intolerance to keep them to himself and to those who sympathise with him. It should never be forgotten that opinions have a moral side to them. The opinions of a bad and a good man, the opinions of an honest and a dishonest man, upon these subjects are very unlikely to be the same.

❊   ❊   ❊

So far I have considered the theoretical grounds of Mr Mill's principle and its practical application to liberty of thought and discussion. I now proceed to consider its application to morals.

❊   ❊   ❊

First, there is no principle on which the cases in which Mr Mill admits the justice of legal punishment can be distinguished from those in which he denies it. The principle is that private vices which are injurious to others may justly be punished, if the injury be specific and the persons injured distinctly assignable, but not otherwise. If the question were as to the possibility in most cases of drawing an indictment against such persons I should agree with him. Criminal law is an extremely rough engine, and must be worked with great caution; but it is one thing to point out a practical difficulty which limits the application of a principle and quite another to refute the principle itself. Mr Mill's proviso deserves attention in considering the question whether a given act should be punished by law, but he applies it to 'the moral coercion of public opinion,' as well as to legal coercion, and to this the practical difficulty which he points out does not apply. A set of young noblemen of great fortune and hereditary influence, the representatives of ancient names, the natural leaders of the society of large districts, pass their whole time and employ all their means in gross debauchery. Such people are far more injurious to society than common pickpockets, but Mr Mill says that if any one having the opportunity of making them ashamed of themselves uses it in order to coerce them into decency, he sins against liberty, unless their example does assignable harm to specific people. It might be right to say, 'You, the Duke of A, by extravagantly keeping four mistresses—to wit, B and C in London, and D and E in Paris—set an example which induced your friend F to elope with Mrs G at — on —, and you are a great blackguard for your pains, and all the more because you are a duke.' It could never be right to say, 'You, the Duke of A, are scandalously immoral and ought to be made to smart for it, though the law cannot touch you.' The distinction is more likely to be overlooked than to be misunderstood.

❊   ❊   ❊

The object of morally intolerant legislation ❊ ❊ ❊ is to establish, to maintain, and to give power to that which the legislator regards as a good moral system or standard. ❊ ❊ ❊ I think that this object is good if and in so far as the system so established and maintained is good. How far any particular system is good or not is a question which probably does not admit of any peremptory final decision; but I may observe that there are a considerable number of things which appear good and bad, though no doubt in different degrees, to all mankind. For the practical purpose of legislation refinements are of little importance. In any given age and nation virtue and vice have meanings which for that purpose are quite definite enough.

* * *

If this is so, the only remaining questions will be as to the efficiency of the means at the disposal of society for this purpose, and the cost of their application. Society has at its disposal two great instruments by which vice may be prevented and virtue promoted — namely, law and public opinion; and law is either criminal or civil. The use of each of these instruments is subject to certain limits and conditions, and the wisdom of attempting to make men good either by Act of Parliament or by the action of public opinion depends entirely upon the degree in which those limits and conditions are recognized and acted upon.

First, I will take the case of criminal law. What are the conditions under which and the limitations within which it can be applied with success to the object of making men better? In considering this question it must be borne in mind that criminal law is at once by far the most powerful and by far the roughest engine which society can use for any purpose. Its power is shown by the fact that it can and does render crime exceedingly difficult and dangerous. Indeed, in civilized society it absolutely prevents avowed open crime committed with the strong hand, except in cases where crime rises to the magnitude of civil war. Its roughness hardly needs illustration. It strikes so hard that it can be enforced only on the gravest occasions, and with every sort of precaution against abuse or mistake. Before an act can be treated as a crime, it ought to be capable of distinct definition and of specific proof, and it ought also to be of such a nature that it is worth while to prevent it at the risk of inflicting great damage, direct and indirect, upon those who commit it. These conditions are seldom, if ever, fulfilled by mere vices. It would obviously be impossible to indict a man for ingratitude or perfidy. Such charges are too vague for specific discussion and distinct proof on the one side, and disproof on the other. Moreover, the expense of the investigations necessary for the legal punishment of such conduct would be enormous. It would be necessary to go into an infinite number of delicate and subtle inquiries which would tear off all privacy from the lives of a large number of persons. These considerations are, I think, conclusive reasons against treating vice in general as a crime.

The excessive harshness of criminal law is also a circumstance which very greatly narrows the range of its application. It is the *ratio ultima* of the majority against persons whom its application assumes to have renounced the common bonds which connect men together. When a man is subjected to legal punishment, society appeals directly and exclusively to his fears. It renounces the attempt to work upon his affections or feelings. In other words, it puts itself into distinct, harsh, and undisguised opposition to his wishes; and the effect of this will be to make him rebel against the law. The violence of the rebellion will be measured partly by the violence of the passion the indulgence of which is forbidden, and partly by the degree to which the law can count upon an ally in the man's own conscience. A law which enters into a direct contest with a fierce imperious passion, which the person who feels it does not admit to be bad, and which is not directly injurious to others, will generally do more harm than good; and this is perhaps the principal reason why it is impossible to legislate directly against unchastity, unless it takes forms which every one regards as monstrous and horrible. The subject is not one for detailed discussion, but any one who will follow out the reflections which this hint suggests will find that they supply a striking illustration of the limits which the harshness of criminal law imposes upon its range.

If we now look at the different acts which satisfy the conditions specified, it will, I think, be found that criminal law in this country actually is applied to the suppression of vice and so to the promotion of virtue to a very considerable extent; and this I say is right.

The punishment of common crimes, the gross forms of force and fraud, is no doubt ambiguous. It may be justified on the principle of self-protection, and apart from any question as to their moral character. It is not, however, difficult to show that these acts have in fact been forbidden and subjected to punishment not only because they are dangerous to society, and so ought to be prevented, but also for the sake of gratifying the feeling of hatred — call it revenge, resentment, or what you will — which the contemplation of such conduct excites in healthily constituted minds. If this can be shown, it will follow that criminal law is in the nature of a persecution of the grosser forms of vice, and an emphatic assertion of the principle that the feeling of hatred and the desire of vengeance above-mentioned are important elements of human nature which ought in such cases to be satisfied in a regular public and legal manner.

*   *   *

I now pass to the manner in which civil law may and does, and as I say properly, promote virtue and prevent vice. This is a subject so wide that I prefer indicating its nature by a few illustrations to attempting to deal with it systematically. It would, however, be easy to show that nearly every branch of civil law assumes the existence of a standard of moral good and evil which the public at large have an interest in maintaining, and in many cases enforcing — a proceeding which is diametrically opposed to Mr Mill's fundamental principles.

*   *   *

Perhaps the most pointed of all illustrations of the moral character of civil law is to be found in the laws relating to marriage and inheritance. They all proceed upon an essentially moral theory as to the relation of the sexes. Take the case of illegitimate children. A bastard is *filius nullius* — he inherits nothing, he has no claim on his putative father. What is all this except the expression of the strongest possible determination on the part of the Legislature to recognize, maintain, and favour marriage in every possible manner as the foundation of civilized society? It has been plausibly maintained that these laws bear hardly upon bastards, punishing them for the sins of their parents. It is not necessary to my purpose to go into this, though it appears to me that the law is right. I make the remark merely for the sake of showing to what lengths the law does habitually go for the purpose of maintaining the most important of all moral principles, the principle upon which one great department of it is entirely founded. It is a case in which a good object is promoted by efficient and adequate means.

*   *   *

I have now said what I had to say about liberty, and I may briefly sum up the result. It is that, if the word 'liberty' has any definite sense attached to it, and if it is consistently used in that sense, it is almost impossible to make any true general assertion whatever about it, and quite impossible to regard it either as a good thing or a bad one. If, on the other hand, the word is used merely in a general popular way without attaching any distinct signification to it, it is easy to make almost any general assertion you please about it; but these assertions will be incapable of either proof or disproof as they will have no definite meaning. Thus the word is either a misleading appeal to passion, or else it embodies or rather hints at an exceedingly complicated assertion, the truth of which can be proved only by elaborate historical investigations.

ISAIAH BERLIN

John Stuart Mill and the Ends of Life†

> the importance, to man and society . . . of giving full freedom to human nature to expand itself in innumerable and conflicting directions.
>
> J.S. MILL, *Autobiography*

I must begin by thanking you for the honour that you have done me, in inviting me to address you on the subject to which the Robert Waley

† A Robert Waley Cohen Memorial Lecture, delivered at The Conference Hall, London, on December 2, 1959; first published by The Council of Christians and Jews, Kingsway Chambers, 162a Strand, London WC2, in the same year. Reprinted by permission of Oxford University Press.

Cohen Memorial Lectures are dedicated—tolerance. In a world in which human rights were never trampled on, and men did not perse- cute each other for what they believed or what they were, this Council would have no reason for existence. This, however, is not our world. We are a good deal remoter from this desirable condition than some of our more civilized ancestors, and, in this respect, unfortunately con- form only too well to the common pattern of human experience. The periods and societies in which civil liberties were respected, and variety of opinion and faith tolerated, have been very few and far between — oases in the desert of human uniformity, intolerance, and oppression. Among the great Victorian preachers, Carlyle and Marx have turned out to be better prophets than Macaulay and the Whigs, but not nec- essarily better friends to mankind; sceptical, to put it at its lowest, of the principles which this Council exists to promote. Their greatest champion, the man who formulated these principles most clearly and thereby founded modern liberalism, was, as everyone knows, the author of the *Essay on Liberty*, John Stuart Mill. This book—this great short book, as Sir Richard Livingstone has justly called it in his own lecture in this series—was published 100 years ago. The subject was then in the forefront of discussion. The year 1859 saw the death of the two best-known champions of individual liberty in Europe, Macaulay and Tocqueville. It marked the centenary of the birth of Friedrich Schiller, who was acclaimed as the poet of the free and creative personality fighting against great odds. The individual was seen by some as the victim of, by others as rising to his apotheosis in, the new and trium- phant forces of nationalism and industrialism which exalted the power and the glory of great disciplined human masses that were transforming the world in factories or battlefields or political assemblies. The predic- ament of the individual versus the state or the nation or the industrial organization or the social or political group was becoming an acute personal and public problem. In the same year there appeared Darwin's *On the Origin of Species*, probably the most influential work of science of its century, which at once did much to destroy the ancient accu- mulation of dogma and prejudice, and, in its misapplication to psy- chology, ethics, and politics, was used to justify violent imperialism and naked competition. Almost simultaneously with it there appeared an essay, written by an obscure economist expounding a doctrine which has had a decisive influence on mankind. The author was Karl Marx, the book was the *Critique of Political Economy*, the preface to which contained the clearest statement of the materialist interpretation of history—the heart of all that goes under the name of Marxism today. But the impact made upon political thought by Mill's treatise was more immediate, and perhaps no less permanent. It superseded earlier for- mulations of the case for individualism and toleration, from Milton and Locke to Montesquieu and Voltaire, and, despite its outdated psychol- ogy and lack of logical cogency, it remains the classic statement of the case for individual liberty. We are sometimes told that a man's behaviour is a more genuine expression of his beliefs than his words. In Mill's case there is no conflict. His life embodied his beliefs. His single-minded devotion to the cause of toleration and reason was unique even among the dedicated lives of the nineteenth century. The centenary of his profession of faith should not, therefore, be allowed to pass without a word before this Council.

I

Everyone knows the story of John Stuart Mill's extraordinary education. His father, James Mill, was the last of the great *raisonneurs* of the eighteenth century, and remained completely unaffected by the new romantic currents of the time in which he lived. Like his teacher Bentham and the French philosophical materialists, he saw man as a natural object and considered that a systematic study of the human species — conducted on lines similar to those of zoology or botany or physics — could and should be established on firm empirical foundations. He believed himself to have grasped the principles of the new science of man, and was firmly convinced that any man educated in the light of it, brought up as a rational being by other rational beings, would thereby be preserved from ignorance and weakness, the two great sources of unreason in thought and action, which were alone responsible for the miseries and vices of mankind. He brought up his son, John Stuart, in isolation from other — less rationally educated — children; his own brothers and sisters were virtually his only companions. The boy knew Greek by the age of five, algebra and Latin by the age of nine. He was fed on a carefully distilled intellectual diet, prepared by his father, compounded of natural science and the classical literatures. No religion, no metaphysics, little poetry — nothing that Bentham had stigmatized as the accumulation of human idiocy and error — were permitted to reach him. Music, perhaps because it was supposed that it could not easily misrepresent the real world, was the only art in which he could indulge himself freely. The experiment was, in a sense, an appalling success. John Mill, by the time he reached the age of twelve, possessed the learning of an exceptionally erudite man of thirty. In his own sober, clear, literal-minded, painfully honest account of himself, he says that his emotions were starved while his mind was violently over-developed. His father had no doubt of the value of his experiment. He had succeeded in producing an excellently informed and perfectly rational being. The truth of Bentham's views on education had been thoroughly vindicated.

The results of such treatment will astonish no one in our psychologically less naïve age. In his early manhood John Mill went through his first agonizing crisis. He felt lack of purpose, a paralysis of the will, and terrible despair. With his well trained and, indeed, ineradicable habit of reducing emotional dissatisfaction to a clearly formulated problem, he asked himself a simple question: supposing that the noble Benthamite ideal of universal happiness which he had been taught to believe, and to the best of his ability did believe, were realized, would this, in fact, fulfil all his desires? He admitted to himself, to his horror, that it would not. What, then, was the true end of life? He saw no purpose in existence: everything in his world now seemed dry and bleak. He tried to analyse his condition. Was he perhaps totally devoid of feeling — was he a monster with a large part of normal human nature atrophied? He felt that he had no motives for continuing to live, and wished for death. One day, as he was reading a pathetic story in the memoirs of the now almost forgotten French writer Marmontel, he was suddenly moved to tears. This convinced him that he was capable of emotion, and with this his recovery began. It took the form of a revolt, slow, concealed, reluctant, but profound and irresistible, against the view of life inculcated by his father and the Benthamites. He read the poetry of Wordsworth, he read and met Coleridge; his view of the nature of man, his history and his destiny, was transformed. John Mill was not by temperament rebellious. He loved and deeply admired his father, and was convinced of the validity of his main philosophical tenets. He stood with Bentham against dogmatism, transcendentalism, obscurantism, all that resisted the march of reason, analysis, and empirical science. To these beliefs he held firmly all his life. Nevertheless, his conception of man, and therefore of much else, suffered a great change. He became not so much an open heretic from the original utilitarian movement, as a disciple who quietly left the fold, preserving what he thought true or valuable, but feeling bound by none of the rules and principles of the movement. He continued to profess that happiness was the sole end of human existence, but his conception of what contributed to it changed into something very different from that of his mentors, for what he came to value most was neither rationality nor contentment, but diversity, versatility, fullness of life — the unaccountable leap of individual genius, the spontaneity and uniqueness of a man, a group, a civilization. What he hated and feared was narrowness, uniformity, the crippling effect of persecution, the crushing of individuals by the weight of authority or of custom or of public opinion; he set himself against the worship of order or tidiness, or even peace, if they were bought at the price of obliterating the variety and colour of untamed human beings with unextinguished passions and untrammelled imaginations. This was, perhaps, a natural enough compensation for his own drilled, emotionally shrivelled, warped, childhood and adolescence.

By the time he was seventeen he was mentally fully formed. John Mill's intellectual equipment was probably unique in that or any other age. He was clear-headed, candid, highly articulate, intensely serious, and without any trace of fear, vanity, or humour. During the next ten years he wrote articles and reviews, with all the weight of the official heir presumptive of the whole utilitarian movement upon his shoulders; and although his articles made him a great name, and he grew to be a formidable publicist and a source of pride to his mentors and allies, yet the note of his writings is not theirs. He praised what his father had praised — rationality, empirical method, democracy, equality, and he attacked what the utilitarians attacked — religion, belief in intuitive and undemonstrable truths and their dogmatic consequences, which, in their view and in his, led to the abandonment of reason, hierarchical societies, vested interests, intolerance of free criticism, prejudice, reaction, injustice, depotism, misery. Yet the emphasis had shifted. James Mill and Bentham had wanted literally nothing but pleasure obtained by whatever means were the most effective. If someone had offered them a medicine which could scientifically be shown to put those who took it into a state of permanent contentment, their premises would have bound them to accept this as the panacea for all that they thought evil. Provided that the largest possible number of men receive lasting happiness, or even freedom from pain, it should not matter how this is achieved. Bentham and Mill believed in education and legislation as the roads to happiness. But, if a shorter way had been discovered, in the form of pills to swallow, techniques of subliminal suggestion, or other means of conditioning human beings in which our century has made such strides, then, being men of fanatical consistency, they might well have accepted this as a better, because more effective and perhaps less costly, alternative than the means that they had advocated. John Stuart Mill, as he made plain both by his life and by his writings, would have rejected with both hands any such solution. He would have condemned it as degrading the nature of man. For him man differs from animals primarily neither as the possessor of reason, nor as an inventor of tools and methods, but as a being capable of choice, one who is most himself in choosing and not being chosen for; the rider and not the horse; the seeker of ends, and not merely of means, ends that he pursues, each in his own fashion: with the corollary that the more various these fashions, the richer the lives of men become; the larger the field of interplay between individuals, the greater the opportunities of the new and the unexpected; the more numerous the possibilities for altering his own character in some fresh or unexplored direction, the more paths open before each individual, and the wider will be his freedom of action and thought.

   In the last analysis, all appearances to the contrary, this is what Mill seems to me to have cared about most of all. He is officially committed to the exclusive pursuit of happiness. He believes deeply in justice, but his voice is most his own when he describes the glories of individual freedom, or denounces whatever seeks to curtail or extinguish it. Bentham, too, unlike his French predecessors who trusted in moral and scientific experts, had laid it down that each man is the best judge of his own happiness. Nevertheless, this principle would remain valid for

Bentham even after every living man had swallowed the happiness-inducing pill and society was thereby lifted or reduced to a condition of unbroken and uniform bliss. For Bentham individualism is a psychological datum; for Mill it is an ideal. Mill likes dissent, independence, solitary thinkers, those who defy the establishment. In an article written at the age of seventeen (demanding toleration for a now almost forgotten atheist named Carlyle), he strikes a note which sounds and resounds in his writings throughout the rest of his life:

> Christians, whose reformers perished in the dungeon or at the stake as heretics, as apostates, as blasphemers — Christians, whose religion breathes charity, liberty and mercy in every line . . . that they, having gained the power of which they were the victims, should employ it in the self same way . . . in vindictive persecution . . . is most monstrous.[1]

He remained the champion of heretics, apostates, and blasphemers, of liberty and mercy, for the rest of his life.

His acts were in harmony with his professions. The public policies with which Mill's name was associated as a journalist, a reformer, and a politician, were seldom connected with the typically utilitarian projects advocated by Bentham and successfully realized by many of his disciples: great industrial, financial, educational schemes, reforms of public health or the organization of labour or leisure. The issues to which Mill was dedicated, whether in his published views or his actions, were concerned with something different: the extension of individual freedom, especially freedom of speech: seldom with anything else. When Mill declared that war was better than oppression, or that a revolution that would kill all men with an income of more than £500 per annum might improve things greatly, or that the Emperor Napoleon III of France was the vilest man alive; when he expressed delight at Palmerston's fall over the Bill that sought to make conspiracy against foreign despots a criminal offence in England; when he denounced the Southern States in the American Civil War, or made himself violently unpopular by speaking in the House of Commons in defence of Fenian assassins (and thereby probably saving their lives), or for the rights of women, or of workers, or of colonial peoples, and thereby made himself the most passionate and best-known champion in England of the insulted and the oppressed, it is difficult to suppose that it was not liberty and justice (at whatever cost) but utility (which counts the cost) that were uppermost in his mind. His articles and his political support saved Durham and his Report, when both were in danger of being defeated by the combination of right and left-wing adversaries, and thereby did much to ensure self-government in the British Commonwealth. He

1. From a tribute to John Stuart Mill by James Bain, quoted in the full and interesting *Life of John Stuart Mill* by Michael St John Packe (London, Secker & Warburg, 1954), 54.

helped to destroy the reputation of Governor Eyre who had perpetrated brutalities in Jamaica. He saved the right of public meeting and of free speech in Hyde Park, against a government that wished to destroy it. He wrote and spoke for proportional representation because this alone, in his view, would allow minorities (not necessarily virtuous or rational ones) to make their voices heard. When, to the surprise of radicals, he opposed the dissolution of the East India Company for which he, like his father before him, had worked so devotedly, he did this because he feared the dead hand of the government more than the paternalist and not inhumane rule of the Company's officials. On the other hand he did not oppose state intervention as such; he welcomed it in education or labour legislation because he thought that without it the weakest would be enslaved and crushed; and because it would increase the range of choices for the great majority of men, even if it restrained some. What is common to all these causes is not any direct connexion they might have with the 'greater happiness' principle but the fact that they turn on the issue of human rights — that is to say, of liberty and toleration.

I do not, of course, mean to suggest that there was no such connexion in Mill's own mind. He often seems to advocate freedom on the ground that without it the truth cannot be discovered — we cannot perform those experiments either in thought or 'in living' which alone reveal to us new, unthought-of ways of maximizing pleasure and minimizing pain — the only ultimate source of value. Freedom, then, is valuable as a means, not as an end. But when we ask what Mill meant either by pleasure or by happiness, the answer is far from clear. Whatever happiness may be, it is, according to Mill, not what Bentham took it to be: for his conception of human nature is pronounced too narrow and altogether inadequate; he has no imaginative grasp of history or society or individual psychology; he does not understand either what holds, or what should hold, society together — common ideals, loyalties, national character; he is not aware of honour, dignity, self-culture, or the love of beauty, order, power, action; he understands only the 'business' aspects of life. Are these goals, which Mill rightly regards as central, so many means to a single universal goal — happiness? Or are they species of it? Mill never clearly tells us. He says that happiness — or utility — is of no use as a criterion of conduct — destroying at one blow the proudest claim, and indeed the central doctrine, of the Benthamite system. 'We think', he says in his essay on Bentham (published only after his father's death), 'utility or happiness much too complex or indefinite at end to be sought except through the medium of various secondary ends, concerning which there may be, and often is, agreement among persons who differ in the ultimate standard.' This is simple and definite enough in Bentham; but Mill rejects his formula because it rests on a false view of human nature. It is 'complex and indefinite' in Mill because he packs into it the many diverse (and, perhaps, not always compatible) ends which men in fact pursue for their own sake, and which Bentham had either ignored or falsely classified under the head of pleasure: love, hatred, desire for justice, for action, for freedom, for power, for beauty, for knowledge, for self-sacrifice. In J.S. Mill's writings happiness comes to mean something very like 'realization of one's wishes', whatever they may be. This stretches its meaning to the point of vacuity. The letter remains; but the spirit—the old, tough-minded Benthamite view for which happiness, if it was not a clear and concrete criterion of action, was nothing at all, as worthless as the 'transcendental' intuitionist moonshine it was meant to replace—the true utilitarian spirit—has fled. Mill does indeed add that 'when two or more of the secondary principles conflict, direct appeal to some first principle becomes necessary'; this principle is utility; but he gives no indication how this notion, drained of its old, materialistic but intelligible content, is to be applied. It is this tendency of Mill's to escape into what Bentham called 'vague generality' that leads one to ask what, in fact, was Mill's real scale of values as shown in his writings and actions. If his life and the causes he advocated are any evidence, then it seems clear that in public life the highest values for him—whether or not he calls them 'secondary ends'—were individual liberty, variety, and justice. If challenged about variety Mill would have defended it on the ground that without a sufficient degree of it many, at present wholly unforeseeable, forms of human happiness (or satisfaction, or fulfilment, or higher levels of life—however the degrees of these were to be determined and compared) would be left unknown, untried, unrealized; among them happier lives than any yet experienced. This is his thesis and he chooses to call it utilitarianism. But if anyone were to argue that a given, actual or attainable, social arrangement yielded enough happiness—that given the virtually impassable limitations of the nature of men and their environment (e.g. the very high improbability of men's becoming immortal or growing as tall as Everest) it were better to concentrate on the best that we have, since change would, in all empirical likelihood, lead to lowering of general happiness, and should therefore be avoided, we may be sure that Mill would have rejected this argument out of hand. He was committed to the answer that we can never tell (until we have tried) where greater truth or happiness (or any other form of experience) may lie. Finality is therefore in principle impossible: all solutions must be tentative and provisional. This is the voice of a disciple of both Saint-Simon and Constant or Humboldt. It runs directly counter to traditional—that is, eighteenth-century—utilitarianism, which rested on the view that there exists an unalterable nature of things, and answers to social, as to other, problems, can, at least in principle, be scientifically discovered once and for all. It is this perhaps, that, despite his fear of ignorant and irrational democracy and consequent craving for government by the enlightened and the expert (and insistence, early and late in his life, on the importance of objects of common, even uncritical, worship) checked his Saint-Simonism, turned him against Comte, and preserved him from the elitist tendency of his Fabian disciples.

There was a spontaneous and uncalculating idealism in his mind and his actions that was wholly alien to the dispassionate and pene-trating irony of Bentham, or the vain and stubborn rationalism of James Mill. He tells us that his father's educational methods had turned him into a desiccated calculating machine, not too far removed from the popular image of the inhuman utilitarian philosopher; his very aware-ness of this makes one wonder whether it can ever have been wholly true. Despite the solemn bald head, the black clothes, the grave ex-pression, the measured phrases, the total lack of humour, Mill's life is an unceasing revolt against his father's outlook and ideals, the greater for being subterranean and unacknowledged.

Mill had scarcely any prophetic gift. Unlike his contemporaries, Marx, Burckhardt, Tocqueville, he had no vision of what the twentieth century would bring, neither of the political and social consequences of industrialization, nor of the discovery of the strength of irrational and unconscious factors in human behaviour, nor of the terrifying tech-niques to which this knowledge has led and is leading. The transfor-mation of society which has resulted — the rise of dominant secular ideologies and the wars between them, the awakening of Africa and Asia, the peculiar combination of nationalism and socialism in our day — these were outside Mill's horizon. But if he was not sensitive to the contours of the future, he was acutely aware of the destructive factors at work in his own world. He detested and feared standardiza-tion. He perceived that in the name of philanthropy, democracy, and equality a society was being created in which human objectives were artificially made narrower and smaller and the majority of men were being converted, to use his admired friend Tocqueville's phrase, into mere 'industrious sheep', in which, in his own words, 'collective me-diocrity' was gradually strangling originality and individual gifts. He was against what have been called 'organization men', a class of persons to whom Bentham could have had in principle no rational objection. He knew, feared, and hated timidity, mildness, natural conformity, lack of interest in human issues. This was common ground between him and his friend, his suspicious and disloyal friend, Thomas Carlyle. Above all he was on his guard against those who, for the sake of being left in peace to cultivate their gardens, were ready to sell their fundamental human right to self-government in the public spheres of life; these characteristics of our lives today he would have recognized with horror. He took human solidarity for granted, perhaps altogether too much for granted. He did not fear the isolation of individuals or groups, the factors that make for the alienation and disintegration of individuals

and societies. He was preoccupied with the opposite evils of socialization and uniformity.[2] He longed for the widest variety of human life
and character. He saw that this could not be obtained without protecting individuals from each other, and, above all, from the terrible weight
of social pressure; this led to his insistent and persistent demands for
toleration.

Toleration, Professor Butterfield has told us in his own lecture in
this series, implies a certain disrespect. I tolerate your absurd beliefs
and your foolish acts, though I know them to be absurd and foolish.
Mill would, I think, have agreed. He believed that to hold an opinion
deeply is to throw our feelings into it. He once declared[3] that when we
deeply care, we must dislike those who hold the opposite views. He
preferred this to cold temperaments and opinions. He asked us not
necessarily to respect the views of others — very far from it — only to try
to understand and tolerate them; only tolerate; disapprove, think ill of,
if need be mock or despise, but tolerate; for without conviction, without
some antipathetic feeling, there was, he thought, no deep conviction;
and without deep conviction there were no ends of life, and then the
awful abyss on the edge of which he had himself once stood would
yawn before us. But without tolerance the conditions for rational criticism, rational condemnation, are destroyed. He therefore pleads for
reason and toleration at all costs. To understand is not necessarily to
forgive. We may argue, attack, reject, condemn with passion and hatred.
But we may not suppress or stifle: for that is to destroy the bad and the
good, and is tantamount to collective moral and intellectual suicide.
Sceptical respect for the opinions of our opponents seems to him preferable to indifference or cynicism. But even these attitudes are less
harmful than intolerance, or an imposed orthodoxy which kills rational
discussion. This is Mill's faith. It obtained its classical formulation in
the tract on Liberty, which he began writing in 1855 in collaboration
with his wife, who, after his father, was the dominant figure in his life.
Until his dying day he believed her to be endowed with a genius vastly
superior to his own. He published the essay after her death in 1859
without those improvements which he was sure that her unique gifts
would have brought to it. It is this event that I venture to invite you to
celebrate today.

---

2. He did not seem to look on socialism, which under the influence of Mrs Taylor he advocated
    in the *Political Economy* and later, as a danger to individual liberty in the way in which
    democracy, for example, might be so. This is not the place to examine the very peculiar
    relationship of Mill's socialist to his individualist convictions. Despite his socialist professions,
    none of the socialist leaders of his time — neither Louis Blanc nor Proudhon nor Lassalle nor
    Herzen — not to speak of Marx, appears to have regarded him even as a fellow traveller. He
    was to them the very embodiment of a mild reformist liberal or bourgeois radical. Only the
    Fabians claimed him as an ancestor.
3. Mill, *CW*, 1:51–3.

II

I shall not impose upon your patience by giving you an abstract of Mill's argument. I should like to remind you only of those salient ideas to which Mill attached the greatest importance — beliefs which his opponents attacked in his lifetime, and attack even more vehemently today. These propostitions are still far from self-evident; time has not turned them to platitudes; they are not even now undisputed assumptions of a civilized outlook. Let me attempt to consider them briefly.

Men want to curtail the liberties of other men, either (*a*) because they wish to impose their power on others; or (*b*) because they want conformity — they do not wish to think differently from others, or others to think differently from themselves; or, finally, (*c*) because they believe that to the question of how one should live there can be (as with any genuine question) one true answer and one only; this answer is discoverable by means of reason, or intuition, or direct revelation, or a form of life or 'unity of theory and practice'; its authority is identifiable with one of these avenues to final knowledge; all deviation from it is error which imperils human salvation; this justifies legislation against, or even extirpation of, those who lead away from the truth, whatever their character or intentions. Mill dismisses the first two motives as being irrational, since they stake out no intellectually argued claim, and are therefore incapable of being answered by rational argument. The only motive which he is prepared to take seriously is the last, namely, that if the true ends of life can be discovered, those who oppose these truths are spreading pernicious falsehood, and must be repressed. To this he replies that men are not infallible; that the supposedly pernicious view might turn out to be true after all; that those who killed Socrates and Christ sincerely believed them to be purveyors of wicked falsehoods, and were themselves men as worthy of respect as any to be found today; that Marcus Aurelius, 'the gentlest and most amiable of rulers', known as the most enlightened man of his time and one of the noblest, nevertheless authorized the persecution of Christianity as a moral and social danger, and that no argument ever used by any other persecutor had not been equally open to him. We cannot suppose that persecution never kills the truth. 'It is a piece of idle sentimentality', Mill observes, 'that truth, merely as truth, has any inherent power denied to error, of prevailing against the dungeon and the stake' (p. 63).[4] Persecution is historically only too effective.

> To speak only of religious opinions: the Reformation broke out at least twenty times before Luther, and was put down. Arnold of Brescia was put down. Fra Dolcino was put down. Savonarola was put down. The Albigeois were put down. The Vaudois were put

4. Mill, *On Liberty*; all page references in the text refer to [the Norton Critical Edition of] this volume.

down. The Lollards were put down. The Hussites were put down
. . . In Spain, Italy, Flanders, the Austrian Empire, Protestantism
was rooted out; and most likely would have been so in England
had Queen Mary lived or Queen Elizabeth died . . . No reasonable
person can doubt that Christianity might have been extirpated in
the Roman Empire. (pp. 62–63)

And if it be said against this that, just because we have erred in the
past, it is mere cowardice to refrain from striking down evil when we
see it in the present in case we may be mistaken again; or, to put it in
another way, that, even if we are not infallible, yet, if we are to live at
all, we must make decisions and act, and must do so on nothing better
than probability, according to our lights, with constant risk of error; for
all living involves risk, and what alternative have we? Mill answers that
'There is the greatest difference between presuming an opinion to be
true, because with every opportunity for contesting it, it has not been
refuted, and assuming its truth for the purpose of not permitting its
refutation' (p. 55). You can indeed stop 'bad men from perverting society with false or pernicious views' (p. 55), but only if you give men
liberty to deny that what you yourself call bad, or pernicious, or per-
verted, or false, is such; otherwise your conviction is founded on mere
dogma and is not rational, and cannot be analysed or altered in the
light of any new facts and ideas. Without infallibility how can truth
emerge save in discussion? there is no *a priori* road towards it; a new
experience, a new argument, can in principle always alter our views,
no matter how strongly held. To shut doors is to blind yourself to the
truth deliberately, to condemn yourself to incorrigible error.

   Mill had a strong and subtle brain and his arguments are never neg-
ligible. But it is, in this case, plain that his conclusion only follows from
premises which he does not make explicit. He was an empiricist; that
is, he believed that no truths are — or could be — rationally established,
except on the evidence of observation. New observations could in principle always upset a conclusion founded on earlier ones. He believed
this rule to be true of the laws of physics, even of the laws of logic and
mathematics; how much more, therefore, in 'ideological' fields where
no scientific certainty prevailed — in ethics, politics, religion, history,
the entire field of human affairs, where only probability reigns; here,
unless full liberty of opinion and argument is permitted, nothing can
ever be rationally established. But those who disagree with him, and
believe in intuited truths, in principle not corrigible by experience, will
disregard this argument. Mill can write them off as obscurantists, dog-
matists, irrationalists. Yet something more is needed than mere contemptuous dismissal if their views, more powerful today perhaps than
even in Mill's own century, are to be rationally contested. Again, it may
well be that without full freedom of discussion the truth cannot emerge.
But this may be only a necessary, not a sufficient, condition of its

discovery; the truth may, for all our efforts, remain at the bottom of a well, and in the meantime the worse cause may win, and do enormous damage to mankind. Is it so clear that we must permit opinions advocating, say, race hatred to be uttered freely, because Milton has said that 'though all the winds of doctrine are let loose upon the earth . . . whoever knew truth put to the worse in a free and open encounter?' because 'the truth must always prevail in a fair fight with falsehood'? These are brave and optimistic judgments, but how good is the empirical evidence for them today? Are demagogues and liars, scoundrels and blind fanatics, always, in liberal societies, stopped in time, or refuted in the end? How high a price is it right to pay for the great boon of freedom of discussion? A very high one, no doubt; but is it limitless? And if not, who shall say what sacrifice is, or is not, too great? Mill goes on to say that an opinion believed to be false may yet be partially true; for there is no absolute truth, only different roads towards it; the suppression of an apparent falsehood may also suppress what is true in it, to the loss of mankind. This argument, again, will not tell with those who believe that absolute truth is discoverable once and for all, whether by metaphysical or theological argument, or by some direct insight, or by leading a certain kind of life, or, as Mill's own mentors believed, by scientific or empirical methods.

His argument is plausible only on the assumption which, whether he knew it or not, Mill all too obviously made, that human knowledge was in principle never complete, and always fallible; that there was no single, universally visible, truth; that each man, each nation, each civilization might take its own road towards its own goal, not necessarily harmonious with those of others; that men are altered, and the truths in which they believe are altered, by new experiences and their own actions — what he calls 'experiments in living'; that consequently the conviction, common to Aristotelians and a good many Christian scholastics and atheistical materialists alike, that there exists a basic knowable human nature, one and the same, at all times, in all places, in all men — a static, unchanging substance underneath the altering appearances, with permanent needs, dictated by a single, discoverable goal, or pattern of goals, the same for all mankind — is mistaken; and so, too, is the notion that is bound up with it, of a single true doctrine carrying salvation to all men everywhere, contained in natural law, or the revelation of a sacred book, or the insight of a man of genius, or the natural wisdom of ordinary men, or the calculations made by an elite of utilitarian scientists set up to govern mankind.

Mill — bravely for a professed utilitarian — observes that the human (that is the social) sciences are too confused and uncertain to be properly called sciences at all — there are in them no valid generalizations, no laws, and therefore no predictions or rules of action can properly be deduced from them. He honoured the memory of his father, whose whole philosophy was based on the opposite assumption; he respected

Auguste Comte, and subsidized Herbert Spencer, both of whom claimed to have laid the foundations for just such a science of society. Yet his own half-articulate assumption contradicts this. Mill believes that man is spontaneous, that he has freedom of choice, that he moulds his own character, that as a result of the interplay of men with nature and with other men something novel continually arises, and that this novelty is precisely what is most characteristic and most human in men. Because Mill's entire view of human nature turns out to rest not on the notion of the repetition of an identical pattern, but on his perception of human lives as subject to perpetual incompleteness, self-transformation, and novelty, his words are today alive and relevant to our own problems; whereas the works of James Mill, and of Buckle and Comte and Spencer, remain huge half-forgotten hulks in the river of nineteenth-century thought. He does not demand or predict ideal conditions for the final solution of human problems or for obtaining universal agreement on all crucial issues. He assumes that finality is impossible, and implies that it is undesirable too. He does not demonstrate this. Rigour in argument is not among his accomplishments. Yet it is this belief, which undermines the foundations on which Helvétius, Bentham, and James Mill built their doctrines — a system never formally repudiated by him — that gives his case both its plausibility and its humanity.

His remaining arguments are weaker still. He says that unless it is contested, truth is liable to degenerate into dogma or prejudice; men would no longer feel it as a living truth; opposition is needed to keep it alive. 'Both teachers and learners go to sleep at their post, as soon as there is no enemy in the field', overcome as they are by 'the deep slumber of a decided opinion' (p. 74). So deeply did Mill believe this, that he declared that if there were no genuine dissenters, we had an obligation to invent arguments against ourselves, in order to keep ourselves in a state of intellectual fitness. This resembles nothing so much as Hegel's argument for war as keeping human society from stagnation. Yet if the truth about human affairs were in principle demonstrable, as it is, say, in arithmetic, the invention of false propositions in order to be knocked down would scarcely be needed to preserve our understanding of it. What Mill seems really to be asking for is diversity of opinion for its own sake. He speaks of the need for 'fair play to all sides of the truth' (p. 78) — a phrase that a man would scarcely employ if he believed in simple, complete truths as the earlier utilitarians did; and he makes use of bad arguments to conceal this scepticism, perhaps even from himself. 'In an imperfect state of the human mind', he says, 'the interests of the truth require a diversity of opinions' (p. 81). Or again, 'Do we really accept the logic of the persecutors [and say] we may persecute others because we are right, and they may not persecute us because they are wrong?' (p. 108) Catholics, Protestants, Jews, Muslims have all justified persecution by this argument in their day; and on their premisses there may be nothing logically amiss with it. It is these premisses that Mill rejects, and rejects not, it seems to me, as a result of a chain of reasoning, but because he believes — even if he never, so far as I know, admits this explicitly — that there are no final truths not corrigible by experience, at any rate in what is now called the ideological sphere — that of value judgements and of general outlook and attitude to life. Yet within this framework of ideas and values, despite all the stress on the value of 'experiments in living' and what they may reveal, Mill is ready to stake a very great deal on the truth of his convictions about what he thinks to be the deepest and most permanent interests of men. Although his reasons are drawn from experience and not *a priori* knowledge, the propositions themselves are very like those defended on metaphysical grounds by the traditional upholders of the doctrine of natural rights. Mill believes in liberty, that is, the rigid limitation of the right to coerce, because he is sure that men cannot develop and flourish and become fully human unless they are left free from interference by other men within a certain minimum area of their lives, which he regards as — or wishes to make — inviolable. This is his view of what men are, and therefore of their basic moral and intellectual needs, and he formulates his conclusions in the celebrated maxims according to which 'The individual is not accountable to society for his actions, in so far as these concern the interests of no person but himself' (p. 114), and that

> The only reason for which power can be rightfully exercised over any member of a civilised community against his will is to prevent harm to others. His own good, either physical or moral, is not a sufficient warrant. He cannot rightfully be compelled to do or to forbear . . . because in the opinion of others to do so would be wise or even right. (p. 48)

This is Mill's profession of faith, and the ultimate basis of political liberalism, and therefore the proper target of attack — both on psychological and moral (and social) grounds — by its opponents during Mill's lifetime and after. Carlyle reacted with characteristic fury in a letter to his brother Alexander: 'As if it were a sin to control or coerce into better methods human swine in any way . . . Ach Gott in Himmel!'[5]

Milder and more rational critics have not failed to point out that the limits of private and public domain are difficult to demarcate, that anything a man does could, in principle, frustrate others; that no man is an island; that the social and the individual aspects of human beings often cannot, in practice, be disentangled. Mill was told that when men look upon forms of worship in which other men persist as being not merely 'abominable' in themselves, but as an offence to them or to their God, they may be irrational and bigoted, but they are not nec-

---

5. A. Carlyle, ed., *New Letters of Thomas Carlyle*, 2 vols (London, John Lane, 1904), 2:196.

essarily lying; and that when he asks rhetorically why Muslims should not forbid the eating of pork to everyone, since they are genuinely disgusted by it, the answer, on utilitarian premisses, is by no means self-evident. It might be argued that there is no *a priori* reason for supposing that most men would not be happier — if that is the goal — in a wholly socialized world where private life and personal freedom are reduced to vanishing point, that in Mill's individualist order; and that whether this is so or not is a matter for experimental verification. Mill constantly protests against the fact that social and legal rules are too often determined merely by 'the likings and dislikings of society', and correctly points out that these are often irrational or are founded on ignorance. But if damage to others is what concerns him most (as he professes), then the fact that their resistance to this or that belief is instinctive, or intuitive, or founded on no rational ground, does not make it the less painful, and, to that extent, damaging to them. Why should rational men be entitled to the satisfaction of their ends more than the irrational? Why not the irrational, if the greatest happiness of the greatest number (and the greatest number are seldom rational) is the sole justified purpose of action? Only a competent social psychologist can tell what will make a given society happiest. If happiness is the sole criterion, then human sacrifice, or the burning of witches, at times when such practices had strong public feeling behind them, did doubtless, in their day, contribute to the happiness of the majority. If there is no other moral criterion, then the question whether the slaughter of innocent old women (together with the ignorance and prejudice which made this acceptable) or the advance in knowledge and rationality (which ended such abominations but robbed men of comforting illusions) — which of these yielded a higher balance of happiness is only a matter of actuarial calculation. Mill paid no attention to such considerations: nothing could go more violently against all that he felt and believed. At the centre of Mill's thought and feeling lies, not his utilitarianism, nor the concern about enlightenment, nor about dividing the private from the public domain — for he himself at times concedes that the state may invade the private domain, in order to promote education, hygiene, or social security or justice — but his passionate belief that men are made human by their capacity for choice — choice of evil and good equally. Fallibility, the right to err, as a corollary of the capacity for self-improvement; distrust of symmetry and finality as enemies of freedom — these are the principles which Mill never abandons. He is acutely aware of the many-sidedness of the truth and of the irreducible complexity of life, which rules out the very possibility of any simple solution, or the idea of a final answer to any concrete problem. Greatly daring, and without looking back at the stern intellectual puritanism in which he was brought up, he preaches the necessity of understanding and gaining illumination from doctrines that are incompatible with one another — say those of Coleridge and Bentham; he explained in his autobiography the need to understand and learn from both.[6]

III

Kant once remarked that 'out of the crooked timber of humanity no straight thing was ever made'. Mill believed this deeply. This, and his almost Hegelian distrust of simple models and of cut-and-dried formulae to cover complex, contradictory, and changing situations, made him a very hesitant and uncertain adherent of organized parties and programmes. Despite his father's advocacy, despite Mrs Taylor's passionate faith in the ultimate solution of all social evils by some great institutional change (in her case that of socialism), he could not rest in the notion of a clearly discernible final goal, because he saw that men differed and evolved, not merely as a result of natural causes, but also because of what they themselves did to alter their own characters, at times in unintended ways. This alone makes their conduct unpredictable, and renders laws or theories, whether inspired by analogies with mechanics or with biology, nevertheless incapable of embracing the complexity and qualitative properties of even an individual character, let alone of a group of men. Hence the imposition of any such construction upon a living society is bound, in his favourite words of warning, to dwarf, maim, cramp, wither the human faculties.

His greatest break with his father was brought about by this conviction: by his belief (which he never explicitly admitted) that particular predicaments required each its own specific treatment; that the application of correct judgement, in curing a social malady, mattered at least as much as knowledge of the laws of anatomy or pharmacology. He was a British empiricist and not a French rationalist, or a German metaphysician, sensitive to day-to-day play of circumstances, differences of 'climate', as well as to the individual nature of each case, as Helvétius or Saint-Simon or Fichte, concerned as they were with the *grandes lignes* of development, were not. Hence his unceasing anxiety, as great as Tocqueville's and greater than Montesquieu's, to preserve variety, to keep doors open to change, to resist the dangers of social pressure, and above all his hatred of the human pack in full cry against a victim, his desire to protect dissidents and heretics as such. The whole burden of his charge against the 'progressives' (he means utilitarians and perhaps socialists) is that, as a rule, they do no more than try to alter social opinion in order to make it more favourable to this or that scheme or reform, instead of assailing the monstrous principle itself which says that social opinion 'should be a law for individuals' (p. 46).

Mill's overmastering desire for variety and individuality for their own

6. And in the essays on 'Coleridge' and 'Bentham', CW, 10.

sake emerges in many shapes. He notes that 'Mankind are greater gainers by suffering each other to live as seems good to themselves, than
by compelling each to live as seems good to the rest' (pp. 50–51) — a
truism which, he declares, 'stands opposed to the general tendency of
existing opinion and practice'. At other times he speaks in sharper
terms. He remarks that

> it is the habit of our time to desire nothing strongly. Its ideal of
> character is to be without any marked character; to maim by com-
> pression, like a Chinese lady's foot, every part of human nature
> which stands out prominently, and tends to make the person mark-
> edly dissimilar in outline to commonplace humanity (p. 95).

And again:

> The greatness of England is now all collective; individually small,
> we only appear capable of anything great by combining; and with
> this our moral and religious philanthropists are perfectly content.
> But it was men of another stamp that made England what it has
> been; and men of another stamp will be needed to prevent its
> decline (p. 95).

The tone of this, if not the content, would have shocked Bentham; so
indeed would this bitter echo of Tocqueville:

> Comparatively speaking, they now read the same things, listen to
> the same things, see the same things, go to the same places, have
> their hopes and fears directed to the same objects, have the same
> rights and liberties and the same means of asserting them . . . All
> the political changes of the age promote it, since they all tend to
> raise the low and lower the high. Every extension of education
> promotes it, because education brings people under common in-
> fluences. Improvement in the means of communication promotes
> it . . . Increase of commerce and manufacture promotes it . . .
> The ascendancy of public opinion . . . forms so great a mass of
> influence hostile to individuality (p. 98) [that] in this age the
> mere example of non-conformity, the mere refusal to bend the
> knee to custom, is itself a service (p. 93).

We have come to such a pass that mere differences, resistance for its
own sake, protest as such, is now enough. Conformity, and the intolerance which is its offensive and defensive arm, are for Mill always
detestable, and peculiarly horrifying in an age which thinks itself enlightened; in which, nevertheless, a man can be .sent to prison for
twenty-one months for atheism; jurymen are rejected and foreigners
denied justice because they hold no recognized religious beliefs; no
public money is given for Hindu or Muslim schools because an 'imbecile display' (p. 65n) is made by an Under-Secretary, who declares that
toleration is desirable only among Christians but not for unbelievers.

It is no better when workers employ 'moral police' to prevent some members of their trade union being paid higher wages earned by superior skill or industry than the wages paid to those who lack these attributes. Such conduct is even more loathsome when it interferes with private relations between individuals. He declared that 'what any person might freely do with respect to sexual relations' should be deemed to be an unimportant and purely private matter which concerns no one but themselves; that to have held any human being responsible to other people, and to the world, for the fact itself (apart from such of its consequences as the birth of children, which clearly created duties which should be socially enforced) would one day be thought one of the superstitions and barbarisms of the infancy of the human race. The same seemed to him to apply to the enforcement of temperance or Sabbath observance, or any of the matters on which 'intrusively pious members of society should be told to mind their own business' (p. 109). No doubt the gossip to which Mill was exposed during his relationship with Mrs Taylor before his marriage to her — the relationship which Carlyle mocked at as platonic — made him peculiarly sensitive to this form of social persecution. But it is of a piece with his deepest and most permanent convictions.

Mill's suspicion of democracy as the only just, and yet potentially the most oppressive, form of government, springs from the same roots. He wondered uneasily whether centralization of authority and the inevitable dependence of each on all and 'surveillance of each by all' would not end by grinding all down into 'a tame uniformity of thought, dealings and actions', and produce 'automatons in human form' and 'liberticide'. Tocqueville had written pessimistically about the moral and intellectual effects of democracy in America. Mill agreed. He said that even if such power did not destroy, it prevented existence; it compressed, enervated, extinguished, and stupefied a people; and turned them into a flock of 'timid and industrious animals of whom the government is a shepherd'. Yet the only cure for this, as Tocqueville himself maintained (it may be a little half-heartedly), is more democracy,[7] which can alone educate a sufficient number of individuals to independence, resistance, and strength. Men's disposition to impose their own views on others is so strong that, in Mill's view, only want of power restricts it; this power is growing; hence unless further barriers are erected it will increase, leading to a proliferation of 'conformers, time servers, hyprocrites, created by silencing opinion',[8] and finally to a society where timidity has killed independent thought, and men confine themselves to safe subjects. Yet if we make the barriers too high, and do not interfere with opinion at all, will this not end, as Burke or the

7. Which in any case he regarded as inevitable and, perhaps, to a vision wider than his own time-bound one, ultimately more just and more generous.
8. Packe, *The Life of John Stuart Mill*, 203.

Hegelians have warned in the dissolution of the social texture, atomization of society — anarchy? To this Mill replies that 'the inconvenience arising from conduct which neither violates specific duty to the public, nor hurts any assignable individual, is one which society can afford to bear for the sake of the greater good of human freedom' (p. 105). This is tantamount to saying that if society, despite the need for social cohesion, has itself failed to educate its citizens to be civilized men, it has no right to punish them for irritating others, or being misfits, or not conforming to some standard which the majority accepts. A smooth and harmonious society could perhaps be created, at any rate for a time, but it would be purchased at too high a price. Plato saw correctly that if a frictionless society is to emerge the poets must be driven out; what horrifies those who revolt against this policy is not so much the expulsion of the fantasy-mongering poets as such, but the underlying desire for an end to variety, movement, individuality of any kind; a craving for a fixed pattern of life and thought, timeless, changeless, and uniform. Without the right of protest, and the capacity for it, there is for Mill no justice, there are no ends worth pursuing.

> If all mankind minus one were of one opinion, and only one person were of a contrary opinion, mankind would be no more justified in silencing that one person than he, if he had the power, would be justified in silencing mankind. (p. 53)

In his lecture in this series, to which I have already referred, Sir Richard Livingstone, whose sympathy with Mill is not in doubt, charges him with attributing too much rationality to human beings: the ideal of untrammelled freedom may be the right of those who have reached the maturity of their faculties, but of how many men today, or at most times, is this true? Surely Mill asks far too much and is far too optimistic? There is certainly an important sense in which Sir Richard is right: Mill was no prophet. Many social developments caused him grief, but he had no inkling of the mounting strength of the irrational forces that have moulded the history of the twentieth century. Burckhardt and Marx, Pareto and Freud, were more sensitive to the deeper currents of their own times, and saw a good deal more deeply into the springs of individual and social behaviour. But I know of no evidence that Mill overestimated the enlightenment of his own age, or that he supposed that the majority of men of his own time were mature or rational or likely soon to become so. What he did see before him was the spectacle of some men, civilized by any standards, who were kept down, or discriminated against, or persecuted by prejudice, stupidity, 'collective mediocrity'; he saw such men deprived of what he regarded as their most essential rights, and he protested. He believed that all human progress, all human greatness and virtue and freedom, depended chiefly on the preservation of such men and the clearing of paths before them. But he did not[9] want them appointed Platonic Guardians. He thought that others like them could be educated, and, when they were educated, would be entitled to make choices, and that these choices must not, within certain limits, be blocked or directed by others. He did not merely advocate education and forget the freedom to which it would entitle the educated (as communists have), or press for total freedom of choice, and forget that without adequate education it would lead to chaos and, as a reaction to it, a new slavery (as anarchists do). He demanded both. But he did not think that this process would be rapid, or easy, or universal; he was on the whole a pessimistic man, and consequently at once defended and distrusted democracy, for which he has been duly attacked, and is still sharply criticized. Sir Richard has observed that Mill was acutely conscious of the circumstances of his age, and saw no further than that. This seems to me a just comment. The disease of Victorian England was claustrophobia—there was a sense of suffocation, and the best and most gifted men of the period, Mill and Carlyle, Nietzsche and Ibsen, men both of the left and of the right—demanded more air and more light. The mass neurosis of our age is agoraphobia; men are terrified of disintegration and of too little direction: they ask, like Hobbes's masterless men in a state of nature, for walls to keep out the raging ocean, for order, security, organization, clear and recognizable authority, and are alarmed by the prospect of too much freedom, which leaves them lost in a vast, friendless vacuum, a desert without paths or landmarks or goals. Our situation is different from that of the nineteenth century, and so are our problems: the area of irrationality is seen to be vaster and more complex than any that Mill had dreamed of. Mill's psychology has become antiquated and grows more so with every discovery that is made. He is justly criticized for paying too much attention to purely spiritual obstacles to the fruitful use of freedom—lack of moral and intellectual light; and too little (although nothing like as little as his detractors have maintained) to poverty, disease, and their causes, and to the common sources and the interaction of both, and for concentrating too narrowly on freedom of thought and expression. All this is true. Yet what solutions have we found, with all our new technological and psychological knowledge and great new powers, save the ancient prescription advocated by the creators of humanism—Erasmus and Spinoza, Locke and Montesquieu, Lessing and Diderot—reason, education, self-knowledge, responsibility—above all, self-knowledge? What other hope is there for men, or has there ever been?

9. This is the line which divides him from Saint-Simon and Comte, and from H.G. Wells and the technocrats.

IV

Mill's ideal is not original. It is an attempt to fuse rationalism and romanticism: the aim of Goethe and Wilhelm Humboldt, a rich, spontaneous, many-sided, fearless, free, and yet rational, self-directed character. Mill notes that Europeans owe much to 'plurality of paths.' From sheer differences and disagreements sprang toleration, variety, humanity. In a sudden outburst of anti-egalitarian feeling, he praises the Middle Ages because men were then more individual and more responsible: men died for ideas, and women were equal to men. 'The poor Middle Ages, its Papacy, its chivalry, its feudality, under what hands did they perish? Under that of the attorney, and fraudulent bankrupt, the false coiner.'[1] This is the language not of a philosophical radical, but of Burke, or Carlyle, or Chesterton. In his passion for the colour and the texture of life Mill has forgotten his list of martyrs, he has forgotten the teachings of his father, of Bentham, or Condorcet. He remembers only Coleridge, only the horrors of a levelling, middle-class society—the grey, conformist, congregation that worships the wicked principle that 'it is the absolute social right of every individual that every other individual should act in every respect exactly as he ought' (p. 111) or, worse still, 'that it is one man's duty that another should be religious', for 'God not only abominates the acts of the mis-believer, but will not hold us guiltless if we leave them unmolested' (p. 112). These are the shibboleths of Victorian England, and if that is its conception of social justice, it were better dead. In a similar, earlier moment of acute indignation with the self-righteous defences of the exploitation of the poor, Mill had expressed his enthusiasm for revolution and slaughter, since justice was more precious than life. He was twenty-five years old when he wrote that. A quarter of a century later, he declared that a civilization which had not the inner strength to resist barbarism had better succumb (p. 114). This may not be the voice of Kant, but it is not that of utilitarianism; rather that of Rousseau or Mazzini.

But Mill seldom continues in this tone. His solution is not revolutionary. If human life is to be made tolerable, information must be centralized and power disseminated. If everyone knows as much as possible, and has not too much power, then we may yet avoid a state which 'dwarfs its men', in which 'there is the absolute rule of the head of the executive over a congregation of isolated individuals, all equals but all slaves'. With small men 'no great thing can really be accomplished' (p. 131). There is a terrible danger in creeds and forms of life which 'compress', 'stunt', 'dwarf' men. The acute consciousness in our day of the dehumanizing effect of mass culture; of the destruction of genuine purposes, both individual and communal, by the treatment of

---

1. Packe, *The Life of John Stuart Mill*, 294–5.

men as irrational creatures to be deluded and manipulated by the media of mass advertising, and mass communication — and so 'alienated' from the basic purposes of human beings by being left exposed to the play of the forces of nature interacting with human ignorance, vice, stupidity, tradition, and above all self-deception and institutional blindness — all this was as deeply and painfully felt by Mill as by Ruskin or William Morris. In this matter he differs from them only in his clearer awareness of the dilemma created by the simultaneous needs for individual self-expression and for human community. It is on this theme that the tract on Liberty was composed. 'It is to be feared', Mill added gloomily, 'that the teachings' of his essay 'will retain their value for a long time.'

It was, I think, Bertrand Russell — Mill's godson — who remarked somewhere that the deepest convictions of philosophers are seldom contained in their formal arguments: fundamental beliefs, comprehensive views of life, are like citadels which must be guarded against the enemy. Philosophers expend their intellectual power in arguments against actual and possible objections to their doctrines, and although the reasons they find, and the logic that they use, may be complex, ingenious, and formidable, they are defensive weapons; the inner fortress itself — the vision of life for the sake of which the war is being waged — will, as a rule, turn out to be relatively simple and unsophisticated. Mill's defence of his position in the tract on Liberty is not, as has often been pointed out, of the highest intellectual quality: most of his arguments can be turned against him; certainly none is conclusive, or such as would convince a determined or unsympathetic opponent. From the days of James Stephen, whose powerful attack on Mill's position appeared in the year of Mill's death, to the conservatives and socialists and authoritarians and totalitarians of our day, the critics of Mill have, on the whole, exceeded the number of his defenders. Nevertheless, the inner citadel — the central thesis — has stood the test. It may need elaboration or qualification, but it is still the clearest, most candid, persuasive, and moving exposition of the point of view of those who desire an open and tolerant society. The reason for this is not merely the honesty of Mill's mind, or the moral and intellectual charm of his prose, but the fact that he is saying something true and important about some of the most fundamental characteristics and aspirations of human beings. Mill is not merely uttering a string of clear propositions (each of which, viewed by itself, is of doubtful plausibility) connected by such logical links as he can supply. He perceived something profound and essential about the destructive effect of man's most successful efforts at self-improvement in modern society; about the unintended consequences of modern democracy, and the fallaciousness and practical dangers of the theories by which some of the worst of these consequences were (and still are) defended. That is why, despite the weakness of the argument, the loose ends, the dated examples, the touch of the finishing governess that Disraeli so maliciously noted, de-spite the total lack of that boldness of conception which only men of original genius possess, his essay educated his generation, and is con-troversial still. Mill's central propositions are not truisms, they are not at all self-evident. They are statements of a position which has been resisted and rejected by the modern descendants of his most notable contemporaries, Marx, Carlyle, Dostoevsky, Newman, Comte, and they are still assailed because they are still contemporary. The *Essay on Liberty* deals with specific social issues in terms of examples drawn from genuine and disturbing issues of its day, and its principles and conclu-sions are alive in part because they spring from acute moral crises in a man's life, and thereafter from a life spent in working for concrete causes and taking genuine — and therefore at times dangerous — deci-sions. Mill looked at the questions that puzzled him directly, and not through spectacles provided by any orthodoxy. His revolt against his father's education, his bold avowal of the values of Coleridge and the Romantics was the liberating act that dashed these spectacles to the ground. From these half-truths, too, he liberated himself in turn, and became a thinker in his own right. For this reason, while Spencer and Comte, Taine and Buckle — even Carlyle and Ruskin, figures who loomed very large in their generation — are fast receding into (or have been swallowed by) the shadows of the past, Mill himself remains real.

One of the symptoms of this kind of three-dimensional, rounded, authentic quality is that we feel sure that we can tell where he would have stood on the issues of our own day. Can anyone doubt what position he would have taken on the Dreyfus case, or the Boer War, or fascism, or communism? Or, for that matter, on Munich, or Suez, or Budapest, or Apartheid, or colonialism, or the Wolfenden report? Can we be so certain with regard to other eminent Victorian moralists? Carlyle or Ruskin or Dickens? or even Kingsley or Wilberforce or New-man? Surely that alone is some evidence of the permanence of the issues with which Mill dealt and the degree of his insight into them.

V

Mill is usually represented as a just and high-souled Victorian school-master, honourable, sensitive, humane, but 'sober, censorious and sad'; something of a goose, something of a prig, a good and noble man, but bleak, sententious, and desiccated; a waxwork among other waxworks in an age now dead and gone and stiff with such effigies. His autobiography — one of the most moving accounts of a human life — modifies this impression. Mill was certainly an intellectual, and was well aware, and not at all ashamed, of this fact. He knew that his main interest lay in general ideas in a society largely distrustful of them: 'the English', he wrote to his friend d'Eichthal, 'invariably mistrust the most evident truths if he who propounds them is suspected of having general

ideas'. He was excited by ideas and wanted them to be as interesting
as possible. He admired the French for respecting intellectuals as the
English did not. He noted that there was a good deal of talk in England
abut the march of intellect at home, but he remained sceptical. He
wondered whether 'our march of intellect be not rather a march towards doing without intellect, and supplying our deficiency in giants
by the united effort of the constantly increasing multitude of dwarfs'.
The word 'dwarfs', and the fear of smallness, pervades all his writings.

Because he believed in the importance of ideas, he was prepared to
change his own if others could convince him of their inadequacy, or
when a new vision was revealed to him, as it was by Coleridge or Saint-
Simon, or, as he believed, by the transcendent genius of Mrs Taylor.
He liked criticism for its own sake. He detested adulation, even praise
of his own work. He attacked dogmatism in others and was genuinely
free from it himself. Despite the efforts of his father and his mentors,
he retained an unusually open mind, and his 'still and cold appearance'
and 'the head that reasons as a great steam engine works'[2] were united
(to quote his friend Stirling) with a 'warm, upright and really lofty soul'
and a touching and pure-hearted readiness to learn from anyone, at
any time. He lacked vanity and cared little for his reputation, and therefore did not cling to consistency for its own sake, nor to his own personal dignity, if a human issue was at stake. He was loyal to movements,
to causes, and to parties, but could not be prevailed upon to support
them at the price of saying what he did not think to be true. A characteristic instance of this is his attitude to religion. His father brought
him up in the strictest and narrowest atheist dogma. He rebelled against
it. He embraced no recognized faith, but he did not dismiss religion,
as the French encyclopaedists or the Benthamites had done, as a tissue
of childish fantasies and emotions, comforting illusions, mystical gib-
berish and deliberate lies. He held that the existence of God was possible, indeed probable, but unproven, but that if God was good he
could not be omnipotent, since he permitted evil to exist. He would
not hear of a being at once wholly good and omnipotent whose nature
defied the canons of human logic, since he rejected belief in mysteries
as mere attempts to evade agonizing issues. If he did not understand
(this must have happened often), he did not pretend to understand.
Although he was prepared to fight for the rights of others to hold a faith
detached from logic, he rejected it himself. He revered Christ as the
best man who ever lived, and regarded theism as a noble, though to
him unintelligible, set of beliefs. He regarded immortality as possible,
but rated its probability very low. He was, in fact, a Victorian agnostic
who was uncomfortable with atheism and regarded religion as something that was exclusively the individual's own affair. When he was
invited to stand for parliament, to which he was duly elected, he de-

2. Ibid., 222.

clared that he was prepared to answer any questions that the electors of Westminster might choose to put to him, save those on his religious views. This was not cowardice — his behaviour throughout the election was so candid and imprudently fearless, that someone remarked that on Mill's platform God Almighty Himself could not expect to be elected. His reason was that a man had an indefeasible right to keep his private life to himself and to fight for this right, if need be. When, at a later date, his stepdaughter Helen Taylor and others upbraided him for not aligning himself more firmly with the atheists, and accused him of temporizing and shilly-shallying, he remained unshaken. His doubts were his own property: no one was entitled to extort a confession of faith from him, unless it could be shown that his silence harmed others; since this could not be shown, he saw no reason for publicly committing himself. Like Acton after him, he regarded liberty and religious toleration as the indispensable protection of all true religion, and the distinction made by the Church between spiritual and temporal realms as one of the great achievements of Christianity, inasmuch as it had made possible freedom of opinion. This last he valued beyond all things, and he defended Bradlaugh passionately, although, and because, he did not agree with his opinions.

He was the teacher of a generation, of a nation, but still no more than a teacher, not a creator or an innovator. He is known for no lasting discovery or invention. He made scarcely any significant advance in logic or philosophy or economics or political thought. Yet his range, and his capacity for applying ideas to fields in which they would bear fruit was unexampled. He was not original, yet he transformed the structure of the human knowledge of his age.

Because he had an exceptionally honest, open, and civilized mind, which found natural expression in lucid and admirable prose; because he combined an unswerving pursuit of the truth with the belief that its house had many mansions, so that even 'one-eyed men like Bentham might see what men with normal vision would not'[3] because, despite his inhibited emotions and his overdeveloped intellect, despite his humourless, cerebral, solemn character, his conception of man was deeper, and his vision of history and life wider and less simple than that of his utilitarian predecessors or liberal followers, he has emerged as a major political thinker in our own day. He broke with the pseudo-scientific model, inherited from the classical world and the age of reason, of a determined human nature, endowed at all times, everywhere, with the same unaltering needs, emotions, motives, responding differently only to differences of situation and stimulus, or evolving according to some unaltering pattern. For this he substituted (not altogether consciously) the image of man as creative, incapable of self-completion,

---

3. He goes on: 'Almost all rich veins of original and striking speculation have been opened by systematic half-thinkers'. 'Bentham', CW, 10:94.

and therefore never wholly predictable: fallible, a complex combination of opposites, some reconcilable, others incapable of being resolved or harmonized; unable to cease from his search for truth, happiness, novelty, freedom, but with no guarantee, theological or logical or scientific, of being able to attain them: a free, imperfect being, capable of determining his own destiny in circumstances favourable to the development of his reason and his gifts. He was tormented by the problem of free will, and found no better solution for it than anyone else, although at times he thought he had solved it. He believed that it is neither rational thought, nor domination over nature, but freedom to choose and to experiment that distinguishes men from the rest of nature; of all his ideas it is this view that has ensured his lasting fame.[4] By freedom he meant a condition in which men were not prevented from choosing both the object and the manner of their worship. For him only a society in which this condition was realized could be called fully human. No man deserves commemoration by this Council more than Mill, for it was created to serve an ideal which he regarded as more precious than life itself.

GERTRUDE HIMMELFARB

From Liberty of Thought and Discussion†

The principle of absolute freedom of discussion, and its corollary, the dependence of truth upon absolute freedom, are so prominent a part of *On Liberty* and so commonly associated with Mill that it may come as a surprise to find him expressing, on other occasions, a quite different view of the matter.

One might not care to make too much of Mill's first essay on the

---

4. It will be seen from the general tenor of this essay that I am not in agreement with those who wish to represent Mill as favouring some kind of hegemony of right-minded intellectuals. I do not see how this can be regarded as Mill's considered conclusion; not merely in view of the considerations that I have urged, but of his own warnings against Comtian despotism, which contemplated precisely such a hierarchy. At the same time, he was, in common with a good many other liberals in the nineteenth century both in England and elsewhere, not merely hostile to the influence of uncriticized traditionalism, or the sheer power of inertia, but apprehensive of the rule of the uneducated democratic majority, consequently he tried to insert into his system some guarantees against the vices of uncontrolled democracy, plainly hoping that, at any rate while ignorance and irrationality were still widespread (he was not over-optimistic about the rate of the growth of education), authority would tend to be exercised by the more rational, just, and well-informed persons in the community. It is, however, one thing to say that Mill was nervous of majorities as such, and another to accuse him of authoritarian tendencies, of favouring the rule of a rational élite, whatever the Fabians may or may not have derived from him. He was not responsible for the views of his disciples, particularly of those whom he himself had not chosen and never knew. Mill was the last man to be guilty of advocating what Bakunin, in the course of an attack on Marx, described as *la pédantocratie*, the government by professors, which he regarded as one of the most oppressive of all forms of despotism.

† From Gertrude Himmelfarb, *On Liberty and Liberalism* (New York: Knopf, 1974), 33–56. Reprinted by permission of the author.

subject, an article on the liberty of the press in the *Westminster Review* in 1825. For anyone else, an essay written before the age of nineteen would qualify as juvenilia. This essay, however, is as mature a piece of writing as anything that appeared in that sophisticated journal. It is, in fact, quite as mature as anything Bentham or James Mill had written on the subject—perhaps because it derived so largely from them.

Bentham's earlier essay "On the Liberty of the Press and Public Discussion," written in 1820–21 in the form of a letter to the Spanish people, had put the utilitarian argument in its sharpest form. Liberty of the press was an essential security for good government, a means of resistance against a despotic government and a check against abuse in an "undespotic" one. (Bentham could not bring himself to speak of a "free" government because in his view no government was free, government being an exercise of power and every power being a limitation on freedom.[1] James Mill elaborated upon this doctrine in an article written shortly after this for the Supplement to the *Encyclopaedia Britannica*. In the course of this essay he raised one point Bentham had not dwelt upon: the relation of opinion and truth.

> We have then arrived at the following important conclusions,— that there is no safety to the people in allowing any body to choose opinions for them; that there are no marks by which it can be decided beforehand, what opinions are true and what are false; that there must, therefore, be equal freedom of declaring all opinions, both true and false; and that, when all opinions, true and false, are equally declared, the assent of the greater number, when their interests are not opposed to them, may always be expected to be given to the true. These principles, the foundation of which appears to be impregnable, suffice for the speedy determination of every practical question.[2]

In 1825, when John Stuart Mill undertook to write about the same subject, he consciously assumed the same role in relation to his father that James Mill had towards Bentham—that of disciple and popularizer. Unlike James Mill, however, who necessarily transmitted Bentham's ideas in an *übersetzt und verbessert* form (Bentham's own writings being often abstruse and nearly incoherent), John Mill had little to do but quote and paraphrase. The burden of his argument was the familiar one: the necessity of free speech as a security for good government. A minor theme was the importance of free opinion for the emergence of truth: "Truth, if it has fair play, always in the end triumphs over error, and becomes the opinion of the world"—a proposition, he added, which "rests upon the broadest principles of human

---

1. Bentham, *Collected Works*, II, 287–88. Bentham did at one point use the expression "free government," but he hastily added that the more precise term was "non-despotic government."
2. James Mill, *Essays on Government, Jurisprudence, Liberty of the Press, and Law of Nations* (New York, 1967), p. 23.

nature."[3] It is not clear whether Mill intentionally altered his father's argument at this point; perhaps after all he too was not above a bit of *übersetzung und verbesserung*. Whatever the case, it is interesting to compare the two formulations. Where James Mill expected only that the "greater number" would give their assent to the truth, John Mill was confident that the "opinion of the world" would coincide with the truth. And where James had predicted that truth would prevail only if the "interests" of the majority were not opposed to it, John derived his universal assent from the "principles of human nature." Perhaps even at this early period, the son was beginning to exhibit the first symptoms of deviation from the utilitarian faith. But even then, he was not prepared to make an absolute of freedom, not even of the freedom of press. Facts, he said, belonged to a different category from that of opinion and therefore did not require the same freedom.

> False opinions must be tolerated for the sake of the true: since it is impossible to draw any line by which true and false opinions can be separated from one another. There is no corresponding reason for permitting the publication of false statements of fact. The truth or falsehood of an alleged fact, is matter, not of opinion, but of evidence; and may be safely left to be decided by those, on whom the business of deciding upon evidence in other cases devolves.[4]

This article was written a year before the fateful "crisis" that profoundly altered Mill's life and thought. By 1831, when he had occasion to return to the theme of liberty — liberty of discussion rather than merely the liberty of the press — he treated it in a quite different manner. In a series of articles called "The Spirit of the Age," published anonymously in the *Examiner*, Mill singled out freedom of discussion as one of the chief characteristics of his age. He described this freedom as inevitable and in many respects desirable, but he also dwelt at some length upon its unfortunate consequences. It is no wonder that he later chose not to include these articles among his collected essays, for no amount of editing would have brought them into conformity with the central thesis of *On Liberty*. He had not, however, forgotten them. For while he was writing *On Liberty*, he was also rereading these articles with a view to their possible republication; and at the same time he was explaining, in his *Autobiography*, why he decided not to reprint them. The articles, he said, had made little impression when they were first published. Apart from attracting Carlyle, who saw in them the work of a fellow spirit, a "new Mystic," and made a point of seeking out Mill's acquaintance, they had been generally ignored. As newspaper articles, they were too "lumbering in style" to be effective. They were, moreover, peculiarly ill-timed, having appeared just at the height of

---

3. "Law of Libel and Liberty of the Press," *Westminster Review*, III (1825), 291.
4. *Ibid.*, p. 299.

the Reform Bill crisis, when men were more preoccupied with the task of enlarging democracy than with guarding against the dangers of democracy.[5]

Mill may well have been right about their lack of impact at the time, but his explanations do not account for his refusal to reprint them almost thirty years later. If their style was inappropriate to a newspaper audience (it was in fact, no more "lumbering" than most of his writings), it was certainly lively enough for the readers of his collected essays. And if it was premature in 1831, it was not so (again by his own standards) in 1859. For "The Spirit of the Age" was based upon exactly the same premise as *On Liberty*: both assumed that democratic society, if not democratic government, was the salient fact of contemporary life and that the gravest evil was the overweening influence of public opinion. It is all the more interesting, therefore, to see how the two works, starting from the same point, arrived at quite different conclusions.

"The Spirit of the Age" derived its theme from Saint-Simon and Comte: the alternation in history between "natural" and "transitional" periods.[6] England was then, as Mill saw it, in a transitional stage, the old institutions and doctrines having fallen into disrepute and no new ones having acquired the authority to replace them. It was a time of "intellectual anarchy," a time for the "*diffusion* of superficial *knowledge*" rather than the acquisition of sound knowledge, a time witnessing a great "increase of discussion" without an "increase of wisdom." Men reasoned more about the great questions of the day, but not necessarily better. More men had opinions, but few, "except the very penetrating, or the very presumptuous," had full confidence in their opinions. The current condition, therefore, was "not a state of health, but, at the best, of convalescence," a necessary but temporary transition to a new "natural" state.[7]

Discussion flourished in such a transitional age, Mill explained, because it was a more effective means of exposing error than of establishing truth. A single, simple fact thrown up by discussion could prove a doctrine false. But the truth of a doctrine depended not upon mere discussion but upon analysis: the examination and weighing of an immense number and variety of facts. Indeed, the mood generated by discussion, which was so propitious for the uncovering of error, was least propitious for the investigation and discovery of truth. Men who

---

5. *Autobiography*, p. 122 [pp. 217–18]. [Page references to this Norton Critical Edition are in brackets, throughout.]
6. These were Mill's terms. Saint-Simon's were "organic" and "critical," Comte's "static" and "dynamic." Mill's choice of words is revealing. To the English ear, "natural" has a more favorable connotation than "organic" or "static"; conversely, "transitional" is more pejorative than "critical" or "dynamic."
7. Mill, *Essays on Politics and Culture*, ed. Gertrude Himmelfarb (Anchor edn.; New York, 1963), pp. 5–6 [pp. 10–11]. (All references are to this edition. Italics in quotations are in the original.)

were eager to discuss were also inclined to settle too readily for half or less than half of the truth; they were impatient and unequipped for the careful reasoning and slow accumulation of fact by which truth is established. Above all, they were too attached to "the exercise of private judgment," to which discussion had accustomed them, to heed the judgments of those who were wiser or better instructed than they. In the physical sciences, no one invoked the "right" of private judgment unless he had first qualified himself as a man of science — and in the process had come to accept, on the basis of the evidence, the "received opinion." The moral and social sciences, no less than the physical sciences, were "systems of connected truth" in which many propositions had to be understood and agreed upon; yet here "every dabbler . . . thinks his opinion as good as another's." Most political discussions were of an order which one might expect "if the binomial theorem were propounded for argument in a debating society none of whose members had completely made up their minds upon the Rule of Three." Men engaged in discussion with minds "in no degree fitted, by previous acquirements, to understand and appreciate the true arguments: . . . truth, they think, is under a peremptory obligation of being intelligible to them, whether they take the right means of understanding or no."[8]

The "right means of understanding," moreover, were not accessible to all men. Even if there were a great growth of intelligence among the mass of the people — and Mill expected the advance of civilization would lead to such a growth — something more was required, which most people, because of the necessary circumstances of their lives, could not attain.

> I yield to no one in the degree of intelligence of which I believe them to be capable. But I do not believe that, along with this intelligence, they will ever have sufficient opportunities of study and experience, to become themselves familiarly conversant with all the inquiries which lead to the truths by which it is good that they should regulate their conduct, and to receive into their own minds the whole of the evidence from which those truths have been collected, and which is necessary for their establishment.
> . . . Those persons whom the circumstances of society, and their own position in it, permit to dedicate themselves to the investigation and study of physical, moral, and social truths, as their peculiar calling, can alone be expected to make the evidences of such truths a subject of profound meditation, and to make themselves thorough masters of the philosophical grounds of those opinions of which it is desirable that all should be firmly *persuaded*, but which they alone can entirely and philosophically *know*. The remainder of mankind must, and, except in periods of transition

8. *Ibid.*, pp. 9–11 [pp. 11–13].

like the present, always do, take the far greater part of their opinions on all extensive subjects upon the authority of those who have studied them.[9]

The real question, therefore, was not whether to pursue truth or rely on authority, but whether to put confidence in one's own judgment or in that of an authority. The answer to this question depended upon the person asking it: "There are some persons in whom disregard of authority is a virtue, and others in whom it is both an absurdity and a vice."[1] Most men fall into the latter category.

If you once persuade an ignorant or a half-instructed person, that he ought to assert his liberty of thought, discard all authority, and — I do not say use his own judgment, for that he never can do too much — but trust solely to his own judgment, and receive or reject opinions according to his own views of the evidence . . . the merest trifle will suffice to unsettle and perplex their minds. There is not a truth in the whole range of human affairs, however obvious and simple, the evidence of which an ingenious and artful sophist may not succeed in rendering doubtful to minds not very highly cultivated, if those minds insist upon judging of all things exclusively by their own lights. . . . You may prevail on them to repudiate the authority of the best-instructed, but each will full surely be a mere slave to the authority of the person next to him, who has greatest facilities for continually forcing upon his attention considerations favourable to the conclusion he himself wishes to be drawn.

It is, therefore, one of the necessary conditions of humanity, that the majority must either have wrong opinions, or no fixed opinions, or must place the degree of reliance warranted by reason, in the authority of those who have made moral and social philosophy their peculiar study. It is right that every man should attempt to understand his interest and his duty. It is right that he should follow his reason as far as his reason will carry him, and cultivate the faculty as highly as possible. But reason itself will teach most men that they must, in the last resort, fall back upon the authority of still more cultivated minds, as the ultimate sanction of the convictions of their reason itself.[2]

This, Mill judged, was one of the unfortunate qualities of a transitional age: the lack of that essential "condition of humanity" which would ensure the "authority of the best-instructed." But such a transitional period could not long prevail and would ultimately give way to a "natural state of society . . . — namely, the state in which the opinions and feelings of the people are, with their voluntary acquiescence,

9. *Ibid.*, pp. 12–13 [pp. 12–13].
1. *Ibid.*, p. 14 [p. 14].
2. *Ibid.*, p. 15 [pp. 14–15].

formed *for* them, by the most cultivated minds, which the intelligence and morality of the times call into existence."[3] And this would happen, Mill predicted, when the present possessors of wordly power were divested of their monopoly of power, a monopoly they had used to prevent uncongenial opinions from becoming established as the "received doctrine." Once that monopoly was broken up, a true moral and intellectual authority would reassert itself: "The most virtuous and best-instructed of the nation will acquire that ascendancy over the opinions and feelings of the rest, by which alone England can emerge from this crisis of transition and enter once again into a natural state of society."[4]

"The Spirit of the Age" has been quoted at such length because one might not otherwise believe that Mill was capable of expressing and sustaining views so antithetical to those of *On Liberty*. So far from being an absolute good, freedom of discussion appeared, in these articles, as at best a very mixed good, at worst a necessary evil; and rather than furthering the advance of truth, it was seen as hindering, as often as not, the acquisition of truth and, still more, of wisdom. Nor were men encouraged to rely on their "private judgment"; on the contrary, they were urged to recognize the natural moral and intellectual authority of their betters. Finally — and this is a more subtle point of difference but a profoundly important one — there is the question of "received opinion." Whereas in *On Liberty* such opinion was implicitly equated with "public opinion" and, like everything "received," was to be resisted by enlightened and independent individuals, here it represented the best thought of the best minds, a consensus of truth which the educated could arrive at by a process of reasoning and the uneducated by accepting the authority of the educated. In short, where *On Liberty* was confident and unequivocal in its faith in liberty, "The Spirit of the Age" was questioning and ambivalent.

"The Spirit of the Age" was among Mill's earliest writings. But it must not be supposed that it was an aberration of mind or immature fancy which he soon outgrew. On the contrary, themes from this series reappear in almost all his later work, sometimes alluded to casually, at other times developed at some length.

On one occasion, in the course of a discussion of the concepts of "delegate" and "representative," Mill commented on the argument that if legislators were regarded as delegates who merely executed the will of their constituencies, philosophers would be under an obligation to enlighten the multitude so that they would be capable of wise judgments. No one, he protested, was more desirous than he of this kind of popular education. But he was also acutely aware of the limitations of such an education. Political truths were as difficult to understand as

3. *Ibid.*, p. 36 [p. 33].
4. *Ibid.*, p. 44 [p. 40].

they were to discover; they were the result of a "concatenation of propositions," some of which required an entire course of study, others a long process of meditation and much experience of human nature. How could philosophers convey these to the multitude? "Can they enable common sense to judge of science, or inexperience of experience?" In political philosophy, the false view was, as often as not, more plausible than the true one, and most truths were paradoxical to all except those who made a special study of them. The most that could be hoped for would be a growing consensus among the "instructed classes" so that "the many will not only defer to their authority, but cheerfully acknowledge them as their superiors in wisdom, and the fittest to rule."[5]

The following year, in the essay "Civilization," he returned more explicitly to the problems posed by "The Spirit of the Age." The essay opened with a diagnosis of the malady of the times: the increased power of the masses and a corresponding decrease in the power of individuals. The diffusion of property and knowledge, together with the growth of habits and instruments of combination, had conferred upon the masses a formidable amount of physical and intellectual power. Individuals, however, had experienced no similar accession of power, indeed, had suffered a visible decline of moral power. The same qualities that made this a more amiable and humane age also made it a less heroic one. Great vices had become less common, but so had great virtues. The outward decencies of life were better preserved, but at the considerable sacrifice of personal energy and character. The superior refinement of life was accompanied by a growing "moral effeminacy, an inaptitude for every kind of struggle."[6] The individual was thus doubly weakened: as his power was eroded by a mass society, so his character was enervated by the progress of civilization.

So far, in the diagnosis of the malady, "Civilization" resembled *On Liberty*. In one crucial respect, however, the diagnosis — and with it the prescription — differed. In "Civilization" Mill attributed part of the decline of the influence of individuals, especially of superior individuals, to the vast increase of literature in modern times and the large number of competing ideas in circulation. He quoted a passage from one of his earlier reviews to suggest the inverse relationship between the quantity and quality of intellectual activity.

> This is a reading age; and precisely because it is so reading an age, any book which is the result of profound meditation is, perhaps, less likely to be duly and profitably read than at a former period. The world reads too much and too quickly to read well. When books were few, to get through one was a work of time and labour:

---

5. Review of vol. I of Tocqueville, *Democracy in America*, in *London and Westminster Review*, October 1835; reprinted in *Essays on Politics and Culture*, pp. 196–97.
6. "Civilization," *London and Westminster Review*, April 1836; reprinted in *Essays on Politics and Culture*, p. 58.

what was written with thought was read with thought, and with a desire to extract from it as much of the materials of knowledge as possible. But when almost every person who can spell, can and will write, what is to be done? . . . The world, in consequence, gorges itself with intellectual food, and in order to swallow the more, bolts it. . . . The public is in the predicament of an indolent man, who cannot bring himself to apply his mind vigorously to his own affairs, and over whom, therefore, not he who speaks most wisely, but he who speaks most frequently, obtains the influence.[7]

Thus the quantity and competition of ideas, which in *On Liberty* figured as part of the cure for the modern malady, appeared in "Civilization" as a cause and symptom of the malady itself. Similarly, instead of seeking to stimulate discussion and competition, as he did in *On Liberty*, in this earlier essay he sought rather to encourage a "greater and more perfect combination among individuals," a greater "spirit of cooperation." In literature especially such a system of cooperation and combination was required, for there "the system of individual competition has fairly worked itself out." The public, presently at the mercy of self-serving advertisements and reviews, had to have some better guidance "to direct them in distinguishing what is not worth reading from what is."[8] Mill suggested that something like a "collective guild" of authors might perform that function: "The resource must in time be, some organized co-operation among the leading intellects of the age, whereby works of first-rate merit, of whatever class, and of whatever tendency in point of opinion, might come forth with the stamp on them, from the first, of the approval of those whose name would carry authority."[9]

In his famous essay on Coleridge, written four years later, Mill went much further in the same direction. Here it was not a collective guild of authors that he recommended but something much more ambitious: a "clerisy" comprehending the learned of all denominations, roughly corresponding to Coleridge's idea of a "national church." This clerisy was to be supported and maintained by the state as an "endowed establishment" with the purpose of cultivating and transmitting not religion (as the common view of the establishment had it) but rather the national culture.[1] A small part of this order, its more distinguished members representing the "fountain heads of the humanities," was charged with preserving and enlarging the stock of knowledge as well as instructing their lesser colleagues. The latter, the ordinary professionals distributed throughout the country, would provide each locality

---

7. *Ibid.*, pp. 61–62. (The quotation is from Mill's review of John Austin, *Lectures on Jurisprudence*, in *Tait's Magazine*, December 1832.)
8. *Ibid.*, pp. 63–65.
9. *Ibid.*, pp. 65–66.
1. "Coleridge," *London and Westminster Review*, March 1840; reprinted in *Essays on Politics and Culture*, p. 157.

with its "resident guide, guardian, and instructor." Thus knowledge would be diffused to every person in the community.[2]

This essay also contained a memorable account of the nature of political society, which had important implications for freedom of discussion. One of the preconditions for a permanent polity, Mill said, was a sense of "allegiance" or "loyalty." The constitution of every state had to make provision for "*something* which is settled, something permanent and not to be called in question."[3] By "constitution" Mill, like Coleridge, meant not a written constitution but rather the "idea" underlying the state. And it was some part of that idea, whether represented by a God, or person, or system of laws, or political principle, which had to be regarded as "*above* discussion."

> In all political societies which have had a durable existence, there has been some fixed point; something which men agreed in holding sacred; which it might or might not be lawful to contest in theory, but which no one could either fear or hope to see shaken in practice; which, in short (except perhaps during some temporary crisis), was in the common estimation placed above discussion. And the necessity of this may easily be made evident. A state never is, nor, until mankind are vastly improved, can hope to be, for any long time exempt from internal dissension; for there neither is nor has ever been any state of society in which collisions did not occur between the immediate interests and passions of powerful sections of the people. What, then, enables society to weather these storms, and pass through turbulent times without any permanent weakening of the ties which hold it together? Precisely this — that however important the interests about which men fall out, the conflict does not affect the fundamental principles of the system of social union which happen to exist; nor threaten large portions of the community with the subversion of that on which they have built their calculations, and with which their hopes and aims have become identified. But when the questioning of these fundamental principles is (not an occasional disease, but) the habitual condition of the body politic; and when all the violent animosities are called forth, which spring naturally from such a situation, the state is virtually in a position of civil war; and can never long remain free from it in act and fact.[4]

2. *Ibid.*, p. 152.
3. *Ibid.*, p. 137.
4. *Ibid.*, pp. 137–38. This is the passage as it originally appeared in the *London and Westminster Review*, March 1840. The passage was quoted in this form in the first two editions of Mill's *A System of Logic* (1843 and 1846). For the third edition of the *Logic* (1851), Mill made small but significant changes in it, and these were reproduced in the essay as it was eventually reprinted in *Dissertations and Discussions*. In the revised version the clause in the first sentence, "which it might or might not be lawful to contest in theory," was altered to read "which, wherever freedom of discussion was a recognized principle, it was of course lawful to contest in theory." And in the parenthetical clause in the last sentence, the words "or salutary medicine" followed "not an occasional disease." (*Essays on Politics and Culture*, p. 138.) The effect was to weaken slightly Mill's original argument and make some concessions to the doctrine of *On Liberty*.

The last sentence of this passage might have been written by a critic of *On Liberty* anticipating a state of affairs in which the doctrine of that work—the deliberate and constant "questioning of these fundamental principles"—would have become the "habitual condition of the body politic."

On less formal occasions, in private letters and in his diary, Mill voiced opinions which were even more dramatically opposed to *On Liberty*. Here too the evidence ranges over a longer span of time than might be supposed. One passage, from a letter to Carlyle in 1833, could have been written by Carlyle himself: "I have not any great notion of the advantage of what the 'free discussion' men call the 'collision of opinions,' it being my creed that Truth is *sown* and germinates in the mind itself, and is not to be struck *out* suddenly like fire from a flint by knocking another hard body against it."[5]

A short-lived diary of 1854 reverted to the theme of "The Spirit of the Age" written almost a quarter of a century earlier. While Mill was now convinced, as he had not been before, of the intellectual superiority of the present over the past, he was also convinced of its moral and spiritual inferiority—a deficiency of conviction, character, feeling, and the sense of truth. As in those earlier articles, he attributed these defects to the "multitude of thoughts," the variety of opinions which bred uncertainty and a lack of conviction. "Those who should be the guides of the rest, see too many sides to every question. They hear so much said, or find that so much can be said, about everything, that they feel no assurance of the truth of anything. But where there are no strong opinions there are (unless, perhaps, in private matters) no strong feelings, nor strong characters."[6] Where *On Liberty* assumed a continuum of opinion and truth—the vitality of truth dependent upon the freest circulation of opinions—in his diary he testified to exactly the opposite experience: a radical discontinuity between truth and opinion, the very variety and accessibility of opinions undermining any certainty of truth and therefore any strength of feeling and character.

Shortly after this diary entry, at about the time he was writing the first draft of *On Liberty*, Mill was involved in a curious episode which put the doctrine of that work to a practical test. He had been invited to join the "Neophyte Writer's Society," the function of which, as Mill understood it, was not to "promote any opinions in particular" but rather to bring together writers of "conflicting opinions" so that they would become better writers. Mill declined the invitation with some acerbity, protesting that he was not interested in "aiding the diffusion of opinions contrary to my own," but only in promoting those which he considered "true and just."

5. *Earlier Letters*, I, 153 (May 18, 1833).
6. *The Letters of John Stuart Mill*, ed. Hugh S. R. Elliot (London, 1910), II, 359 (Diary, Jan. 13, 1854).

Now, I set no value whatever on writing for its own sake, and have much less respect for the literary craftsman than for the manual labourer, except so far as he uses his powers in promoting what I consider true and just. I have, on most of the subjects interesting to mankind, opinions to which I attach importance, and which I earnestly desire to diffuse, but I am not desirous of aiding the diffusion of opinions contrary to my own; and with respect to the mere faculty of expression, independently of what is to be expressed, it does not appear to me to require any encouragement. There is already an abundance, not to say superabundance, of writers who are able to express in an effective manner the mischievous commonplaces which they have got to say. I would gladly give any aid in my power towards improving their opinions, but I have no fear that any opinions they have will not be sufficiently well expressed, nor in any way should I be disposed to aid in sharpening weapons when I know not in what cause they will be used.[7]

One would also have difficulty in recognizing the author of *On Liberty* in an episode precipitated by him shortly after the publication of that work. Mrs. Gaskell, in her biography of Charlotte Brontë, had quoted a letter written by Brontë about "Enfranchisement of Women." "When I first read the paper," Brontë had written, "I thought it was the work of a powerful minded, clear-headed woman, who had a hard, jealous heart, muscles of iron, and nerves of bend leather; of a woman who longed for power and had never felt affection." Finding out that the essay was by Mill, Brontë conceded its "admirable sense," although she thought Mill would make a "hard, dry, dismal world of it." His head, she concluded, "is, I dare say, very good, but I feel disposed to scorn his heart."[8]
Although the biography had been published two years earlier, Mill came upon this letter only after his wife's death and after he himself had publicly attributed to her this particular essay. He was, therefore, dismayed to read Brontë's remarks about the kind of woman who might have written it, and he was outraged that the letter should have been published. He charged Mrs. Gaskell with disregarding the "obligation which custom founded on reason has imposed, of omitting what would be offensive to the feelings and perhaps injurious to the moral reputation of individuals." He attributed to her the idea that a biographer was justified in publishing whatever might throw light on his subject—a notion, he said, that "the world, and those who are higher and better than the world, would, I believe, perfectly unite in condemning."[9]
Upon receiving this rebuke, Mrs. Gaskell abjectly apologized, de-

7. *Later Letters*, I, 205 (Apr. 23, 1854).
8. E. C. Gaskell, *The Life of Charlotte Brontë* (New York, 1857), II, 189–90 (quoting a letter by Brontë, Sept. 20, 1851).
9. *Later Letters*, II, 628–29 (JSM to Mrs. Gaskell, July 1859).

nying that she had ever held so misguided a view of the function of the biographer. After reading the dedication to *On Liberty*, she said, she could well understand how deeply wounded Mill would be by any sentiment derogatory of his wife. The answer, however, only incensed Mill more, since it sounded as if he were merely being sensitive on his wife's behalf, whereas his objection, he insisted, was a matter of principle. He then repeated his initial charge that she had "neglected the usual and indispensable duties which custom (founded on reason) has imposed of omitting all that might be offensive to the feeling of individuals."[1]

If Mrs. Gaskell had read beyond the dedication to *On Liberty*, she might have been amused — she was a good-natured woman — by the very different tone of that book. Mill did, at one point, grant that "opinion" ought to condemn those who were guilty of "want of candour, or malignity, bigotry, or intolerance of feeling."[2] But in the context in which this phrase appears, it is difficult to believe that Mill intended to prevent the publication of anything that might offend the feelings of any single individual; what he clearly meant to discourage was an intolerance of the order of bigotry — a want of respect for religious, national, racial, or moral sensibilities. Anything else would have been an invitation to censorship on the largest scale. This had been Mill's argument when he rejected the idea that discussion be free only on condition that it be "temperate" and "fair"; any strong statement, he then pointed out, was bound to seem intemperate and unfair, to give "offence," to anyone who disagreed with it.[3] If Mrs. Gaskell were duty-bound to omit the Brontë letter on the grounds that it was "offensive to the feelings or injurious to the reputation" of Mrs. Mill, regardless of how revealing it might be of Brontë's attitude toward a most important subject (Mill implicitly admitted the intrinsic importance of the letter), one wonders what remains of the central argument of *On Liberty* — the need for fearless, frank, candid, bold discussion, uninhibited by conventional opinions and feelings.

Only a few weeks after this affair, Mill expressed himself on another matter in a fashion that was similarly inconsistent with *On Liberty*; and here there was no personal involvement to obscure the issue. When his old friend (and future biographer) Alexander Bain wrote that he thought *On Liberty* was meant to convert not the world but only an "intellectual aristocracy," Mill disavowed such an elitist intention. On the contrary, he said, he wanted to make "the many more accessible to all the truth by making them more open minded." But he then went on to say that if Bain's remark applied only to the subject of religion, there was some truth in it: "On that, certainly I am not anxious to bring over any but really superior intellects and characters to the whole of

1. *Ibid.*, pp. 629–30 (July 1859).
2. *On Liberty*, p. 113 [p. 83].
3. *Ibid.*, p. 112 [p. 82].

my own opinions—in the case of all others I would much rather, as things now are, try to improve their religion than to destroy it."[4]

The reservation was an important one—and appears nowhere in *On Liberty*. If religion enjoyed the special immunity Mill was now giving it, it could only have been because, whatever its other defects, it still functioned as a support for morality. But this implied that something less than the whole truth was more desirable than the whole truth, that a religion based upon intellectual error was preferable to an agnosticism which may have been intellectually sounder. This suggestion is so at odds with the entire argument of *On Liberty* that one can only attribute it to the "other" Mill, a Mill who was sensible of the complexity of the moral life and was aware that prudence was as much a moral imperative as truth.

Mill's *Autobiography* reveals something of the tension of thought under which he labored while he was writing *On Liberty*. In a revised version of the *Autobiography* (revised in the late 1850s while he was working on *On Liberty*), he purported to describe his state of mind at the time of "The Spirit of the Age":

> I looked forward, through the present age of loud disputes but generally weak convictions, to a future which will unite the best qualities of the critical with the best of the organic periods; unchecked liberty of thought, perfect freedom of individual action in things not hurtful to others; but along with this, firm convictions as to right and wrong, useful and pernicious, deeply engraven on the feelings by early education and general unanimity of sentiment, and so well grounded in reason and in the real exigencies of life, that they shall not, like all former and present creeds, religious, ethical and political, require to be periodically thrown off and replaced by others.[5]

Here, as in so much of the *Autobiography*, Mill was trying to straddle two positions that were further apart than he cared to admit, to have the best of two worlds that were, if not mutually exclusive, at least in important respects antithetical. There is something almost pathetic in his retrospective attempt to superimpose the principles of *On Liberty* —"unchecked liberty of thought, perfect freedom of individual action in things not hurtful to others" (the wording is almost identical with that of *On Liberty*)—upon the Comtean vision of an organic society so firmly based upon reason, morality, and a "general unanimity of sentiment" as to preclude any further change.

The original draft of this portion of the *Autobiography* reflected more

4. *Later Letters*, II, 631 (JSM to Alexander Bain, Aug. 6, 1859).
5. *The Early Draft of John Stuart Mill's Autobiography*, ed. Jack Stillinger (Urbana, Ill., 1961), p. 139. With some minor changes, this passage is essentially the same as in the final version of the *Autobiography* (Columbia Univ. Press edn., pp. 116–17).

faithfully the state of mind that had produced "The Spirit of the Age."
In place of the passage quoted above, with its unconvincing synthesis
of the critical and the organic, Mill described the logic of ideas which
had led him to the vision of an organic society. The organic nature of
the physical sciences, he explained, had been familiar enough.

> In mathematics and physics what is called the liberty of conscience
> or the right of private judgment, is merely nominal: though in no
> way restrained by law, the liberty is not exercised: those who have
> studied the subject are all of the same opinion; if any one rejected
> what has been proved by demonstration or experiment he would
> be thought to be asserting no right but the right of being a fool:
> those who have not studied these sciences take their conclusions
> on trust from those who have, and the practical world goes on
> incessantly applying laws of nature and conclusions of reasoning
> which it receives on the faith not of its own reason but of the
> authority of the instructed.[6]

What had not been generally appreciated, and what he himself had
first learned from Comte, was the extent to which the "moral, social,
and political sciences" shared the same organic quality—the quality of
objective, certain knowledge. When these moral sciences would have
advanced to the point presently occupied by the physical sciences, the
attitudes appropriate to a critical age—"liberty of conscience or the
right of private judgment"—would become as irrelevant as they now
were in the case of mathematics or physics.

Prior to his reading of Comte, Mill continued (with a barely veiled
allusion to the teachings of Bentham and James Mill), he had "always
identified deference to authority with mental slavery and the repression
of individual thought." And so it was, in those cases where at least a
minority of "thinking and instructed persons" privately disbelieved what
they were publicly obliged to avow. But when all such persons would
have become as nearly unanimous in their moral, social, and political
beliefs as they presently were in regard to physics or mathematics, they
would naturally and properly exercise their "authority" and "ascendancy"
over the multitude. It was the desirability of this "united authority"
that Comte had impressed upon him.

> I did not become one atom less zealous for increasing the knowl-
> edge and improving the understanding of the man; but I no longer
> believed that the fate of mankind depended on the possibility of
> making all of them competent judges of questions of government
> and legislation. From this time my hopes of improvement rested
> less on the reason of the multitude, than on the possibility of
> effecting such an improvement in the methods of political and
> social philosophy, as should enable all thinking and instructed

6. *Early Draft*, p. 188. This is not part of the final version of the *Early Draft* but of a still earlier
version—what the editor calls the "rejected leaves."

persons who have no sinister interest to be so nearly of one mind on these subjects, as to carry the multitude with them by their united authority.[7]

Few critics of *On Liberty* have gone so far as Mill himself, on other occasions, in disputing the absolute value of absolute freedom of discussion. Even more startling is the fact that at the very time he was writing *On Liberty*, he was mindful of everything that could be said, that he himself had said, in qualification of that view. His argument for an intellectual "clerisy" is most familiar in the form he gave it in his essay on Coleridge. But many of his other writings testify to the same conviction that some intellectual authority and consensus were necessary for the sake both of truth and of the well-being of society. If public opinion was ill-informed, he repeatedly argued, it could be enlightened and elevated only under the guidance of the well-informed. Left to its own devices, it could only multiply opinions without providing the means for judging between good and bad opinions, between truth and error. Nor was it only reason that suffered from this indiscriminate profusion of opinion. Society suffered as well, for in a natural order of society consensus rather than dissension was the normal state of affairs, and the wise were acknowledged to be the superiors of the ignorant.

It is in contrast to this conception of a natural, organic age that *On Liberty* emerges more sharply than ever as the credo of a critical age. And not of a critical age *faute de mieux*, an age of transition which in the normal and natural course of events would give way to a new organic age; but of a critical age in perpetuity, an age which was represented as both the natural and the ideal condition for mankind. In his other writings Mill analyzed and criticized the critical spirit. In *On Liberty* he celebrated and glorified it.

JOHN C. REES

The Principle of Liberty†

I

My aim in this chapter is to discuss what Mill was trying to do in his essay *On Liberty*. Or, to put it more precisely, to consider whether the commonly accepted version of 'the very simple principle' asserted in the essay is a fair account of Mill's intentions. Before setting out what I take to be the traditional version and giving my reasons for questioning

---

7. *Ibid.*, pp. 188–89.
† This chapter first appeared as "A Re-reading of Mill on Liberty," *Political Studies* (1960), 113–29. Reprinted by permission of the Political Studies Association and Blackwell Publishers.

it, we ought to remind ourselves of the general purpose Mill had in publishing his work.

In his *Autobiography* Mill describes the essay as 'a philosophic text-book of a single truth . . . the importance, to man and society, of a large variety in types of character, and of giving full freedom to human nature to expand itself in innumerable and conflicting directions'.[1] The book deals with one of the recurring questions of politics but was written in circumstances which gave that question a new significance. For behind Mill's question—'What is the nature and extent of the power which society ought to exercise over the individual?'—was his anxiety lest the tendencies which he claimed to see at work in the civilized world would eventually extinguish spontaneity in all the important branches of human conduct. 'Society has now [the manuscript was completed in 1857] fairly got the better of individuality . . . in our times, from the highest class of society down to the lowest, every one lives as under the eye of a hostile and dreaded censorship.'[2] The essay had, therefore, the practical aim of helping to ward off the dangers which the trends of the age seemed to carry with them and, in particular, to counter 'the general tendency of things throughout the world to render mediocrity the ascendant power among mankind'.[3] The work, Mill tells us, was conceived and written as a short essay in 1854.[4] In a letter to Harriet from Rome in January 1855 he wrote:

> On my way here cogitating thereon I came back to an idea we have talked about, and thought that the best thing to write and publish at present would be a volume on Liberty. So many things might be brought into it and nothing seems more to be needed—it is a growing need too, for opinion tends to encroach more and more on liberty, and almost all the projects of social reformers of these days are really liberticide—Comte's particularly so.[5]

But Mill's fears and anxieties go back long before this period. They were clearly expressed in an essay on 'Civilization' published in 1836 and there are definite signs that they were taking root in even earlier years.[6]

One of the tasks Mill set himself in *On Liberty* was to fix a limit 'to the legitimate interference of collective opinion with individual independence'.[7] This seemed to him to be at least as important as 'protection against political despotism', for the 'yoke of opinion in England is perhaps heavier, that of the law is lighter, than in most other countries

---

1. *Autobiography*, p. 215.
2. *On Liberty*, p. 119 [p. 88]. [Page references to this Norton Critical Edition are in brackets, throughout.]
3. Ibid., p. 123 [p. 92].
4. *Autobiography*, p. 212.
5. *Collected Works*, Vol. XIV, p. 294.
6. As well as the essay on 'Civilization', *Collected Works*, Vol. XVIII, see the essay on 'Genius' (1832), *Collected Works*, Vol. I, and Chapter II above.
7. *On Liberty*, p. 68 [p. 44].

of Europe'.[8] The preservation of individuality and variety of character was possible, he believed, if a principle were observed whereby every person was accorded an area of liberty in thought and action. His father and Bentham had argued the case for representative government, but its practical consequences, whether in the United States as revealed by Tocqueville or experienced in England since the Reform Act, were in his view by no means wholly favourable to liberty.[9] And even more menacing than the now apparent weaknesses of a system of government whose establishment was the great aim of the orthodox Utilitarians were the informal pressures of society that the coming of democracy tended to strengthen and make still more relentless. Progress and the attainment of the truth were, as Mill saw it, the work of a select few; and to promote and safeguard the conditions for the distinctive activity of this élite in face of the growing power of the mediocre mass was a result he hoped his essay would help to achieve. Yet to a number who have shared his aspirations the specific principle he offered has always seemed defective. Mill's attachment to liberty has been admired on all sides and the many eloquent and moving passages he dedicates to its virtues have been widely acclaimed as classic utterances on behalf of one of the most cherished of western ideals, but, it has been generally said, the principle he advances for its protection cannot do what is expected of it. My purpose here is to look again at that principle and to discuss whether it has been properly understood by its critics.

II

The object of this Essay [says Mill] is to assert one very simple principle . . . that the sole end for which mankind are warranted,

8. Ibid., pp. 71–2 [p. 47].
9. Before the publication of the first part of Tocqueville's work in 1835 the American Unitarian preacher and writer, William Ellery Channing, had uttered warnings similar to Tocqueville's at a number of points. Channing's writings were known in England and there were reviews of some of them in the *Edinburgh Review* and the *Westminster Review* in 1829 and 1830. I argued in Chapter II that Mill was influenced by Channing's views. Apart from the 'Remarks on the Formation of Associations', which Mill certainly knew, there is the election sermon of 1880. The latter was reprinted in a two-volume edition of Channing's works published in Britain in 1835 (see Vol. II, pp. 255ff.). One or two passages are worth quoting.

'The advantages of civilization have their peril. In such a state of society, opinion and law impose salutary restraint, and produce general order and security. But the power of opinion grows into a despotism, which, more than all things, represses original and free thought, subverts individuality of character, reduces the community to a spiritless monotony, and chills the love of perfection' [p. 268]. 'An espionage of bigotry may as effectually close our lips and chill our hearts, as an armed and hundred-eyed police' [p. 271]. 'Our great error as a people, is, that we put an idolatrous trust in free institutions; as if these, by some magic power, must secure our rights, however we enslave ourselves to evil passions. We need to learn that forms of liberty are not its essence; that whilst the letter of a free constitution is preserved, its spirit may be lost; that even its wisest provisions and most guarded powers may be made weapons of tyranny. In a country called free, a majority may become a faction, and a proscribed minority may be insulted, robbed, and oppressed. Under elective governments, a dominant party may become as truly a usurper, and as treasonably conspire against the state, as an individual who forces his way by arms to the throne' [p. 278].

individually or collectively, in interfering with the liberty of action of any of their number is self-protection . . . to prevent harm to others. . . . His own good, either physical or moral, is not a sufficient warrant. . . . The only part of the conduct of any one, for which he is amenable to society, is that which concerns others. In the part which merely concerns himself, his independence is, of right, absolute.[1]

This passage appears in the first chapter of the essay. In the last chapter, where Mill offers some examples of how his principle might be applied in practical cases, he restates

the two maxims which together form the entire doctrine of this Essay . . . first, that the individual is not accountable to society for his actions, in so far as these concern the interests of no person but himself. . . . Secondly, that for such actions as are prejudicial to the interests of others, the individual is accountable, and may be subjected either to social or to legal punishment, if society is of opinion that the one or the other is requisite for its protection.[2]

A study of the comments on Mill's essay during the century since its publication shows that the principle just stated has been widely criticized because it appears to rest on the possibility of classifying human actions into two categories — actions which concern only the agent and actions that concern others besides the agent. The distinction between these two categories, it has been repeatedly argued, is impossible to sustain. As one of the critics has put it: 'The greater part of English history since his day has been a practical commentary on the fallacy of this distinction. No action, however intimate, is free from social consequences. No human being can say that what he is, still less what he does, affects no one but himself.[3] The crucial point in this criticism is clearly the supposition that Mill's principle depends for its validity on there being some actions, including some important ones, which are free from social consequences, i.e. that they affect no one but the agent himself.[4] I shall argue that this assumption on the part of the critics is false and that it derives from a failure to observe the form of words which Mill often employs in the text and to take at its full value Mill's firm assertion that actions of the so-called 'self-regarding' variety may

1. *On Liberty*, pp. 72–3 [p. 48].
2. Ibid., pp. 149–50 [p. 114].
3. Leading article in the *Times Literary Supplement*, 10 July 1948. Reprinted as part of a pamphlet, *Western Values*, published by *The Times*.
4. 'Including some important ones' is necessary here in order to prevent the issue from being trivialized. When Mill's critics say that no action is free from social consequences they must be assumed to be ignoring many petty acts which are obviously free from social effects, or else they are mistaken in refusing to admit their existence. For example, if I shave in a well-lit room before a mirror that reflects the face with uniform clarity and I can, in these conditions, shave equally well no matter which side I begin to shave, then starting with the left or the right is a matter which cannot be considered to have any effects on other persons. Hence it is of no concern to society how I, or anyone else, begins to shave each morning. The debate between Mill and his critics clearly does not hinge on trivial acts of this kind.

frequently affect, even harmfully, persons other than the agent. Before elaborating this claim I want to pass briefly in review the evidence for my contention that the traditional account of Mill's principle makes just this assumption about his classification of human actions.

I begin with a commonly made criticism, drawn from among the first reviews of *On Liberty*. There is no conduct whose impact is confined to the agent, said the *London Review* in 1859, because 'no moral quality is limited in its action to the sphere of its possessor's own history and doings . . . society has an interest, over and above that of mere self-defence, in the conduct of everyone of its members'.[5] Fourteen years later, Fitzjames Stephen, whose *Liberty, Equality, Fraternity* has set the pattern for much of the criticism directed against Mill up to the present time, asserted with characteristic vigour that 'the attempt to distinguish between self-regarding acts and acts which regard others, is like an attempt to distinguish between acts which happen in time and acts which happen in space. Every act happens at some time and in some place, and in like manner every act that we do either does or may affect both ourselves and others . . . the distinction is altogether fallacious and unfounded.[6] Further, in defence of the attitude of a temperance reformer whom Mill had attacked in the *Liberty*, Stephen remarks: 'It is surely a simple matter of fact that every human creature is deeply interested not only in the conduct, but in the thoughts, feelings, and opinions of millions of persons who stand in no other assignable relation to him than that of being his fellow-creatures. . . . A man would no more be a man if he was alone in the world than a hand would be a hand without the rest of the body.'[7] The view of human relations expressed in this last passage was, of course, shared by the Oxford Idealists, and we should expect from them too a decided lack of sympathy with Mill's principle. Thus Ritchie considers the conception of the individual implied in Mill's doctrine to be abstract and negative, for the individual finds his true self 'not in distinction and separation from others, but in community with them'.

> We may very well doubt [he continues] whether any acts, nay, even thoughts, of the individual can, in the strictest sense, be merely self-regarding, and so matter of indifference to other individuals. . . . The more we learn of human society, the more we discover that there are no absolute divisions, but that every atom influences and is influenced by every other. It may be very inexpedient to meddle with particular acts, or it may be practically impossible to do so; but we can lay down no hard and fast line, separating self-regarding acts from acts which affect others.[8]

5. *London Review*, Vol. XIII, p. 274.
6. J. F. Stephen, p. x, preface to the 2nd edn., 1874.
7. Ibid., p. 128 (1st edn., 1873). Mill's remarks appear in *On Liberty*, pp. 145–6 [pp. 111–12].
8. D. G. Ritchie, pp. 96–8.

And Bosanquet: '. . . every act of mine affects both myself and others. . . . It may safely be said that no demarcation between self-regarding and other-regarding action can possibly hold good.'[9]

Closer to our own day, MacIver in his *Modern State* remarks of Mill's principle:

> This statement has a form which suggests that the full significance of the interdependence of social beings is hardly realized by Mill . . . he thinks of man as in certain categories social, but in others wholly 'individual'. But if we realize that the nature of man is a unity, that in every *aspect* he is a social being at the same time that he is also autonomous and self-legislating, so that his sociality and his individuality cannot belong to two different spheres . . . we can no longer be content with an abstract doctrine of liberty.[1]

In similar vein Sir Ernest Barker says that Mill's assumption of the existence of two different spheres of conduct is open to the criticism that Mill separates the inseparable. 'The conduct of any man', maintains Sir Ernest, 'is a single whole: there can be nothing in it that concerns himself only, and does not concern other men: whatever he is, and whatever he does, affects others and therefore concerns them.'[2] Finally, to conclude with a quotation from one of the best studies of Mill's philosophy that has appeared in recent decades, here is the view of Professor R. P. Anschutz. He is commenting on Mill's principle of self-protection ('the argument for insulation' as Anschutz calls it) and says: 'It is a completely untenable as well as a completely impracticable doctrine. It is quite impossible to distinguish between that part of a person's behaviour which affects himself and that part which also affects others; and there is nothing to be gained by attempting to make the distinction.'[3]

This, then, is the case which has been built up against Mill over the last hundred years. The essential point in the criticism is, as I have said, that Mill wrongly assumes some human actions to be free of social consequences. But if we look carefully at the two passages quoted at the beginning of this section, where Mill is explicitly stating his principle, it will be noticed that, although in the first case he writes of conduct which 'merely concerns' the agent and of conduct which 'concerns others', he introduces the word 'interests' in the second passage.

9. B. Bosanquet, *Philosophical Theory of the State* (London, 1899) p. 60. Writing about the same time Frederic Harrison (*Tennyson, Ruskin, Mill*) states: 'The attempt to distinguish between conduct which concerns oneself, and conduct that may remotely concern others, is quite fallacious. No distinction can be drawn, for human acts are organically inseparable' (p. 300). See also F. C. Montague's *The Limits of Individual Liberty*, pp. 185–8: Mill's distinction, says Montague, is an offshoot of the doctrine of the social contract and 'is impossible to those who look upon man as receiving from society his whole character and his whole endowment, and as reacting upon society at every moment of his life'.
1. MacIver, *Modern State* (Oxford, 1926) pp. 457 and 459.
2. E. Barker, *Principles of Social and Political Theory* (Oxford, 1951) p. 217.
3. R. P. Anschutz, p. 48.

He says that the individual is to be held accountable only for those actions which 'are prejudicial to the *interests* of others'.[4] Elsewhere in the essay both types of phrase appear, with a number of variations within each type. Thus we find on the one hand: 'what only regards himself', 'conduct which affects only himself', 'which concerns only himself', 'things wherein the individual alone is concerned'; and on the other: 'concern the interests of others', 'affects the interests of no one but himself', 'affect the interests of others', 'damage to the interests of others'. Traditional commentary has assumed that all these expressions were intended to convey the same meaning and that Mill's distinction was simply between actions which affect no one but the agent and actions which affect others. My case in this chapter is that we ought not to gloss over these different modes of expression, that there is an important difference between just 'affecting others' and 'affecting the interests of others', and that there are passages in the essay which lend support to the view that Mill was thinking of 'interests' and not merely 'effects'. As a first step I wish to support my claim that there is a significant difference between saying, on the one hand, that an action affects another person and, on the other, that it affects his interests.

It seems to me quite clear that a person may be affected by another's behaviour without his interests being affected. For example, when we speak of a man's equilibrium not being affected in trying circumstances we are not thinking of his interests. Indeed a man's interests may well be seriously injured without his equilibrium being affected to any marked degree. And even if it were, there would be two things affected, not one. Similarly, if we heard of someone's outlook on life being fundamentally affected by an event such as a religious experience we should not have to conclude that his interests had likewise been affected. True, a religious convert has an interest in religion that he did not have before, but we are not speaking of interests in that sense. My interests in literature can undergo a radical change without anything like business, professional, or property interests being affected to the slightest extent. To bring out the distinction I am trying to make between interests and effects, but with no pretence at offering a definitive account of the nature of interests, one might say that interests — and I do not wish to imply that they are necessarily legal — depend for their existence on social recognition and are closely connected with prevailing standards about the sort of behaviour a man can legitimately expect from others. A claim that something should be recognized as an interest is one we should require to be supported by reasons and one capable of being made the subject of discussion. On the other hand I could be very seriously affected by the action of another person merely because I had an extraordinarily sensitive nature and no claim to have others respect these tender spots would be recognized as amounting to an

4. My italics.

interest. How one is affected by a theatrical performance depends partly on one's tastes, but the interests of a businessman would be affected by a tax on business property no matter what his tastes or susceptibilities; just as the interests of a university are affected by a scheme to establish a research institute in the same area (in a common subject of course) whether the university authorities welcome the idea or not. Moreover, 'effects' is a concept applicable to plants and animals as well as human beings, but no one talks about the interests of plants. Crops are affected by fertilizers or drought in much the same way as a certain drug would have an effect on, say, chronic lassitude. And dogs are affected by thunder in the kind of way that I might be affected by the news that my favourite football team had been beaten in the cup-final. There are no interests necessarily at stake here, though drought could affect my interests as well as the crops, and gamblers stand to win or lose by a result that could also leave them dismayed. Apart from really trivial actions —which we can ignore in this context—it is probably true that what I do or am like affects other people.[5] Any principle which rested on the assumption that other people are not (or may not be) affected would be open to precisely the objections brought against Mill. But deciding whether interests are affected is another matter and a principle that seeks to limit social interference to cases where interests are involved cannot be attacked because it fails to recognize the truth that 'every atom influences and is influenced by every other' or to realize that 'the nature of man is a unity'.

It might be objected at this stage that Mill does not consistently adhere to the term 'interests' and that one is not entitled to assume from its appearance in some passages, coupled with the employment of such phrases as 'conduct which concerns only himself', that there is one unambiguous doctrine running through the entire essay. Our objector might well concede the distinction between a principle based on interests and one based on mere effects, but he feels we are not justified in attempting to produce a coherent theory when, from the variety of the terms used in the relevant passages, there is clearly not one there to extract. My answer to this objection, for the moment at least (whether one can find a single consistent principle running through the whole work I discuss below), is that if Mill is really trying to maintain two (possibly more) principles, and moves from one to the other at different points of the essay without really knowing what he is doing and hence with no warning to his readers of what he is about, then to recognize this fact is at least to notice something which commentators on Mill have, so far as I know, failed to discern in the past. But it need not necessarily follow that because Mill uses phrases like 'conduct which concerns only himself' along with 'conduct which affects the interests of no persons besides himself' this must be regarded as conclusive evidence of an unwitting affirmation of two distinct and potentially incompatible principles. For though the word 'concerns' has sometimes no more force than 'has reference to' or 'affects', with no implication that interests are being referred to or affected, it can also mean 'is of importance to' and could in some contexts carry with it the suggestion that interests are involved. Thus when Mill says that social control is permissible only in cases when one's conduct 'concerns others' we are not compelled to assume that he means actions which just have 'effects' on others. Hence it may well be that the ambiguity of the word 'concerns' is responsible for concealing a coherent theory based on 'interests' rather than 'effects' and that we can so interpret the passages where the term 'interests' is not specifically used as to yield a single consistent principle.

However that may be, it should be observed that there are statements in the essay suggesting that Mill was quite aware of the manner in which individuals are constantly affecting one another. And so forthright are they that one wonders how it ever came to be thought of Mill that he wished to declare a whole area of human behaviour 'self-regarding' because the actions so named had no 'effects' on others (as opposed to 'affecting their interests'). Thus in the fourth chapter of the essay Mill discusses a possible objection to his principle in these terms: 'How (it may be asked) can any part of the conduct of a member of society be a matter of indifference to the other members? No person is an entirely isolated being; it is impossible for a person to do anything seriously or permanently hurtful to himself, without mischief reaching at least to his near connections, and often far beyond them . . . '. And Mill concedes to this objection 'that the mischief which a person does to himself may *seriously affect*, both through their sympathies and their interests, those nearly connected with him and, in a minor degree, society at large'. But he goes on to insist that only when conduct of this sort (i.e. conduct affecting others) violates 'a distinct and assignable obligation to any other person or persons' is 'the case taken out of the self-regarding class, and becomes amenable to moral disapprobation'. A little farther on in the same chapter Mill speaks of a person preventing himself 'by conduct purely self-regarding, from the performance of some definite duty incumbent on him to the public' and thus being guilty of a social offence, but where the conduct 'neither violates any specific duty to the public, nor occasions perceptible hurt to any assignable individual except himself; the inconvenience is one which society can afford to bear, for the sake of the greater good of human freedom'.[6] It is surely obvious that Mill would be contradicting himself here in the most flagrant manner if we were to interpret 'purely self-regarding' to mean those actions which have no impact (i.e. no 'effects') on other members of society. And the case against this interpretation

6. The quotations in this paragraph are from *On Liberty*, pp. 136–8 [pp. 103–05].

becomes even more conclusive if we consider Mill's remarks in the opening chapter where he is elaborating the central principle of the essay. He writes: '. . . there is a sphere of action in which society, as distinguished from the individual, has if any, only an indirect interest; comprehending all that portion of a person's life and conduct which affects only himself . . . when I say only himself, I mean directly, and in the first instance; for whatever affects himself, may affect others through himself . . .'.[7] Further, in the fourth chapter, Mill talks of the 'self-regarding deficiencies' which a person may manifest and which 'render him necessarily and properly a subject of distaste, or, in extreme cases, even of contempt'. For vices of this kind, he says, a man may 'suffer very severe penalties at the hands of others for faults which directly concern only himself'. Here, then, is a clear affirmation that what he calls, perhaps misleadingly, 'self-regarding conduct' can have effects on others. Even to the extent that those affected can retaliate with '*very severe penalties*'!

Mill's critics, Fitzjames Stephen among them, have wondered how the division of human conduct into two spheres could be sustained if self-regarding actions might suffer severe penalties at the hands of others. Mill attempted to maintain the distinction, which is, of course, crucial for the viability of his principle, in these words: '. . . the inconveniences which are strictly inseparable from the unfavourable judgment of others, are the only ones to which a person should ever be subjected for that portion of his conduct and character which concerns his own good, but which does not affect the interests of others in their relations with him. Acts injurious to others require a totally different treatment . . . these are fit objects of moral reprobation, and, in grave cases, of moral retribution and punishment.' And as if to meet the objections of the sceptical Stephen, who could not see how 'inconveniences strictly inseparable from the unfavourable judgment of others' could be differentiated from the 'moral retribution' to be visited when other people's interests were harmed, Mill went on to show why this distinction was not merely nominal, in his eyes at least. In the former case the offender incurs a loss of consideration by reason of his imprudence or lack of dignity, whereas in the latter reprobation is due to him 'for an offence against the rights of others'.[8] And, claims Mill, people will react differently if the conduct of which they disapprove is such that they think that they have a right to control the agent. Whether Mill makes his point or not I do not wish to discuss further, but the words 'for an offence against the *rights* of others' raise a very important question and seem to introduce a new element into the principle. Nor is this the sole occasion when 'rights' are mentioned.[9] In the same chapter from which I have just been quoting, specifically devoted to

7. Ibid., p. 75 [p. 50].
8. Ibid., pp. 134–6 [pp. 101–03].
9. Ibid., pp. 120 [p. 90] and 135 [p. 102] (my italics).

discussing 'the limits to the authority of society over the individual', and therefore concerned to elaborate and give more detailed consideration to the principle mentioned and briefly treated in the opening chapter — it is in this fourth chapter that we should, I think, look for pointers to Mill's intentions — Mill attempts to demarcate the area of conduct for which we are to be made responsible to society. 'This conduct', he says, 'consists in not injuring the interests of one another; or rather certain interests which, either by express legal provision or by tacit understanding, ought to be considered as *rights*.' Nor is this the complete extent of social control, for conduct may harm others 'without going to the length of violating any of their *constituted rights*'. In those cases punishment is inflicted by opinion rather than the law. Then, to sum up, Mill adds: 'As soon as any part of a person's conduct affects prejudicially the interests of others, society has jurisdiction over it', but no such question can arise 'when a person's conduct affects the interests of no persons besides himself . . .'[1]

The paragraph from which these extracts have been taken, coming as it does at a crucial stage in Mill's argument, is of some significance for the interpretation of his leading principle. It serves, incidentally, as further proof of my claim that it is 'interests' rather than 'effects' with which Mill is concerned. But its main significance for us at this stage is the appearance in it of the term 'rights' and the relationship Mill seems to suppose that term to have to the idea of 'interests'. From Mill's wording it is certain that the rights he has in mind are legal rights ('constituted rights'), for he envisages the law, rather than opinion, protecting some interests and these interests are then to be considered as rights. Other interests will not receive legal protection, though Mill does not exclude the possibility that these might be regarded as rights, though not legal ('constituted') rights. Certainly Mill is not saying that rights and interests are the same things, synonymous terms (and of course they are not), but he does seem to imply that they are very closely related to each other. It would be consistent with what he says here to suppose that when a person can be thought to have interests he is thereby possessed of a right, though not necessarily a right to the unqualified protection of his interests; perhaps only a right to have his interests taken into account. Moreover, by linking interests to rights in this way Mill leaves us with no excuse for confusing the notions of 'interests' and 'effects', which must now be seen as belonging to quite different categories. It may be true that because of the element of vagueness attaching to rights and interests (i.e. as to what a man may legitimately, I do not mean *legally*, account his rights or interests) the concepts would be much more difficult to operate as part of a principle of liberty than the relatively simple notion of effects, but that ought not

1. These last quotations are from ibid., p. 132 [p. 99].

to blind us to the difference it makes to a principle to have the one rather than the other type of concept as a component.

III

The case I have been trying to make out is that Mill's principle of self-protection rests on a division of conduct into actions which either do or do not affect the interests of other persons rather than on what has generally been supposed to have been the division, namely, into conduct having or not having effects on others. This interpretation does not rely on the evidence of only one or two isolated passages where the word 'interests' appears. In fact the word appears at least fifteen times in the course of the essay and some of the passages where it is used are of the greatest importance in assessing Mill's intentions.[2] Furthermore, there is also the evidence I have already cited which shows how freely Mill admitted that what have commonly been thought of as literally self-regarding actions did have their effects on other persons. But having said that, I would be seriously misleading the reader if I failed to mention a number of difficulties which stand in the way of this interpretation, or at least suggest that Mill was not always clear in his own mind as to what he wanted to say. The first difficulty arises out of a passage previously quoted in another context: '. . . there is a sphere of action in which society, as distinguished from the individual, has, if any, only an indirect interest; comprehending all that portion of a person's life and conduct which affects only himself. . . . When I say only himself, I mean *directly, and in the first instance*; for whatever affects himself, may affect others through himself . . .'.[3] And we find phrases similar to the one italicized here in other parts of the essay; for example, 'things which do not *primarily* concern others' and 'the part of life in which it is *chiefly* the individual that is interested . . . [as opposed to] the part which *chiefly* interests society'.[4] This seems to me a difficulty because if we are to take this passage seriously (and the repetition of like phrases elsewhere suggests it is not merely a case of careless writing) we should, on the account I have been giving, have to say that when Mill writes here of 'conduct which affects only himself' he means to say 'conduct which affects only his own interests'.[5] Further, since what affects my

2. I have found the word on the following pages: 74 [p. 49] (twice), 75 [p. 50], 120 [p. 89], 132 [pp. 99–100] (four times), 135 [p. 101], 138 [p. 103], 142 [p. 108], 149 [pp. 114–115] (twice), and 150 [p. 115] (twice).
3. Ibid., p. 75 [p. 50] (my italics).
4. Ibid., pp. 115 [p. 85] and 132 [p. 99]. It should be noted, however, that 'primarily' and 'chiefly' are not equivalent to 'directly' or 'in the first instance'.
5. In my draft of this the words 'to say' did not appear. I have inserted them in response to a remark made by Mr J. M. Brown in some very valuable comments he kindly sent me on the draft. Mr Brown pointed out that to allow 'conduct which affects only himself' to mean 'conduct which only affects his own interests' would undermine the distinction I have sought to make between these two types of statement.

interests may also affect the interests of others, we should have to allow that 'self-regarding' conduct could affect the interests of others, though not 'directly' or 'primarily'. Hence the distinction Mill was attempting to make in his use of the self-regarding and other-regarding categories would seem to resolve itself into a division between (i) actions which primarily affect the interests of the agent but may affect the interests of others too, and (ii) actions which primarily affect the interests of others, though the agent's own interests may also be involved. It requires little imagination to foresee the immense complications that would be bound to arise in the application of such a formula. Nothing could be less appropriately described as a 'very simple principle' — Mill's own characterization in his opening chapter. Yet we should have to interpret these passages in some such manner or else admit, which is quite possible, that Mill falls occasionally into the language of 'effects', without realizing that he thereby allows a second principle to peep through from time to time while adhering mainly to a doctrine based on 'interests'.

IV

Assuming, then, that Mill's doctrine involves the idea of 'interests' rather than 'effects', is it, interpreted thus, a useful working principle of liberty in the way that the traditional version is patently not? The revised version would read something like this: 'Social control of individual actions ought to be exercised only in cases where the interests of others are either threatened or actually affected.'[6] But how to decide when interests are affected? What are interests? Is there any commonly accepted criterion, or set of criteria, of an interest? Mill's principle, as reformulated, must inevitably provoke questions like these and its value will obviously depend on the answers to be given to them. They cannot be fully treated here and all I shall attempt are some preliminary and tentative remarks.

As it is commonly used, the concept of 'interests' is an elusive one. There is no precise and generally acceptable definition. As Mr Plamenatz observed, the idea of 'interest', compared with notions like 'right' or 'duty', is extremely vague.[7] But there are many important concepts in our language which evade exact description and they remain none the less indispensable. Failure to bring the notion within the confines of a neat definition ought not to be a sufficient reason for rejecting out of hand a theory to which the concept is central. Moreover, there are sociologists and jurists for whom the term occupies an important place in their theories. MacIver, for example, conceives human activity through the two concepts 'interest' and 'will'. There is, he says, 'no will without an interest and no interest apart from a will'. And

6. I am leaving out the complications connected with 'primarily', 'chiefly', and 'directly'.
7. *Political Studies*, Vol. II, 1954.

by an interest he means 'some object which determines activity', though it is more than mere desire; it has 'a certain permanence and stability'.[8] Another definition of interest he offers is, 'the object of consciousness . . . anything, material or immaterial, factual or conceptual, to which we devote our attention'.[9] Roscoe Pound, too, employs the word with the same kind of wide meaning. For him an interest is a *de facto* claim and he draws up a comprehensive classification of interests which covers a vast field, ranging from individual claims to privacy to the social interest in free science and cultural progress. Among other writers the term is confined to certain kinds of consciousness or a particular class of attitudes such as, for example, those based on needs; and an appropriate list is provided of the bodily and spiritual needs which are to count for this purpose.[1] How are these uses of the word related to the normal sense of the term? Indeed, is it possible to identify an 'ordinary' use of the word? There would seem to be some grounds for saying that in a normal context an interest should not be construed as just a claim, far less any sort of claim. Rather it seems to be the condition in which a person's claim to, or title to, or share in something is recognized as valid by others, or at least is regarded as worthy of consideration. That is to say, there is an objective element about it which precludes any fanciful demand from being an interest. For interests are things we would generally look upon as deserving protection, to be prejudicially affected only by advantages likely to accrue in another direction. Certainly we feel that they ought not to be ignored even if there are compelling reasons for subordinating them to what we think are more important considerations. Interests, then, are not just arbitrary wishes, fleeting fancies, or capricious demands, though some of them may well have developed from forms to which these terms might have been particularly apposite at the time.

Mill does not say much to indicate how he understood the notion of interest, but there is nothing in the essay to suggest that he uses the term in any exceptional manner. There is a passage, however, which points to some of the problems inseparably connected with the idea of interests. The secretary of an association formed to secure prohibition had claimed a right to be protected from the consequences of the liquor trade which, he argued, 'destroys my primary right of security, by constantly creating and stimulating social disorder. . . . It impedes my right to free moral and intellectual development, by surrounding my path with dangers, and by weakening and demoralising society, from which I have a right to claim mutual aid and intercourse.' Mill repudiates with indignation such a sweeping claim, amounting, as he saw it, to 'the absolute social right of every individual, that every other individual shall act in every respect exactly as he ought' and conferring on ev-

8. R. M. MacIver, *Community* (London, 1917) 3rd edn., pp. 98–101.
9. R. M. MacIver, *Society* (London, 1937) pp. 20–1.
1. See A. Ross, *On Law and Justice* (London, 1958), pp. 358–9.

eryone 'a vested interest in each other's moral, intellectual, and even physical perfection'.[2] Mill and the prohibitionist are disputing what may legitimately be claimed as rights and what is to count as an injury to a person's interests. According to the standards prevailing in Mill's day, and certainly by those current in our own time, the secretary's claims appear ludicrously excessive and there would be no point in taking his case seriously. But what is of importance is the very fact of disagreement as to what a man may hold to be his interests. The prohibitionist could have submitted the relatively modest claim that a man's interests are prejudicially affected by the noisy behaviour of groups of people gathering outside a public house adjoining, or close to, his home. If the noise became such a nuisance as to lower the value of the property it could not be denied that interests had been affected. But apart from depreciation of value, has a man's interest been adversely affected by the mere fact of disturbance of his privacy? He could be the tenant of the house and suffer no personal pecuniary loss, yet he might find the behaviour of the publican's clients extremely annoying and might set a high monetary value on its cessation. Is it part of a man's interests to be free from interference of this sort? From the noise of the radio in his neighbour's flat or from the machines on the airfield near his house? If we are going to say 'no' to the claim that interests are affected by interference such as noise, as opposed to monetary loss caused by noise, then this would seem to prevent Mill's principle from operating in spheres in which he clearly wanted it to work. But it is obvious that people can differ about what are to be regarded as interests, since standards and values enter into what will be recognized as interests (or what will *not* be recognized) at any given time in a way that they do not in the case of 'effects'.[3] Consequently, whether one takes a wide or narrow view of interests, the principle of self-protection must necessarily harbour value-ingredients which will inevitably render its use a controversial operation. That a drug affects a certain disease is a strictly empirical matter. There are objective procedures for tracing its 'effects'. It is true that there are also cases when it would be a relatively simple matter to decide if my interests have been affected: legal interests for example. But there are also occasions when, because standards differ, people will disagree about what their interests are. And this is likely to make a principle based on 'interests' rather than 'effects' difficult to apply in many situations. For not only is the concept 'interest' in itself vague: what are to count as interests, even supposing there were a commonly accepted definition, would be an open question in an indeterminate number of cases. Had Mill formulated his principle in terms of rights

2. *On Liberty*, pp. 145–6 [110–11].
3. And even if it came to be accepted that a man's interests were affected by the noisy interruption of his privacy there is still the question of whether these interests should be protected against other claims, such as, for example, freedom to converse outside public houses, the demand for air travel, or the desire to listen to music.

rather than interests he would have met the same difficulty precisely because what a man's rights are is a question which can be reasonably answered in more than one way.

Mill's principle raises yet another problem. Social interference, he says, is justifiable only when the interests of others are affected but, he adds, 'it must by no means be supposed, because damage, or probability of damage, to the interests of others, can alone justify the interference of society, that therefore it always does justify such interference'.[4] Evidently the principle is not intended to absolve us from deciding cases on their merits even when interests have actually been affected. We should have to weigh up the advantages and disadvantages of social interference on each occasion. As Mill puts it: '. . . the question whether the general welfare will or will not be promoted by interfering with [another person's conduct], becomes open to discussion'.[5] One of the examples he gives is the unsuccessful candidate in a competitive examination.[6] Others have gained at his expense, but no one would have it otherwise. A recent example would be the publicity given to statements warning of the harmful effects of heavy smoking. No one would wish to suppress information about the relation between smoking and lung cancer merely because it affected the interests of the tobacco firms. However, says Mill, in the case of conduct which affects no person's interests but one's own there can be no question of permitting social control and restraint: 'in all such cases, there should be perfect freedom, legal and social, to do the action and stand the consequences'.[7] So the principle provides us with a clear directive only when we can be sure that other people's interests are *not* involved; where interests *are* affected we are left with a margin of discretion and are advised to consider whether the general welfare is or is not likely to be promoted by interference in each particular instance. Hence the range of matters covered by the 'automatic' application of the rule is limited to those occasions on which it can be said that no one's interests have been injured. And it seems to be assumed that the question of interests being injured or not is one that can be readily determined.

It would be uncharitable to reject Mill's principle out of hand merely because it fails to provide an automatic and definite solution in an extensive range of cases (i.e. actions which *do* affect the interests of others). For how many of the principles we constantly wield in everyday life supply us with quick and certain answers? From Mill's point of view the important thing was to check the growing tendency to interfere in cases where intervention should be totally banned, and for this purpose what had to be done was to demarcate the area of non-intervention from that in which a prima facie right to control could only be

---

4. *On Liberty*, p. 150 [114].
5. Ibid., p. 132 [p. 99].
6. Ibid., p. 150 [p. 115].
7. Ibid., p. 132 [p. 99].

overridden by an appeal to the 'general welfare'. We have seen that with all its indefiniteness Mill's principle is emphatic on one point, namely, that when the interests of others have *not* been affected society should not intervene. But even here a serious doubt emerges. Are there not some actions we should want to control or prohibit which do not seem to injure the interests of others? Take the case of obscenity. It may be that some acts and some kinds of publications which the present law in the United Kingdom prohibits would be permitted in a more enlightened society, but there are certainly many which are, and ought to continue to be, prevented. Mill, too, seems to take this view. He refers to 'offences against decency', acts which, when done publicly, violate good manners, and places them 'within the category of offences against others' and therefore to be prohibited. But he remarks that offences of this nature 'are only connected indirectly with our subject'.[8] Why this should be so he does not explain and it is difficult to see what reasons he could have for saying it. Perhaps he realized that to prohibit offences against decency on the ground that they caused harm to other people's interests would involve a dangerous extension of the conception of 'interests'. For whose interests are threatened or injured by the appearance of obscene publications (or the sale of opium, to take an example from a related field)? The interests of those who concern themselves with public morality? Or the social interest in maintaining standards of public decency? But if we are allowed to bring in considerations of this sort, how could Mill have maintained his opposition to a prohibition on the eating of pork in a predominantly Muslim country?[9] Measures against the dropping of litter or the emission of black smoke from chimneys in specified areas are taken in order to protect the *public interest*, not because they affect the interests of particular persons. That Mill recognized the claims of the general interest is clear enough from his discussion of the case of the person who instigates or counsels others to do acts which if done of one's own free and unaided will would be 'blameable' but not subject to social penalties because 'the evil directly resulting falls wholly on the agent.'[1] On the one hand, argues Mill, people must be allowed 'to consult with one another . . . to exchange opinions, and give and receive suggestions', but the question becomes 'doubtful only when the instigator derives a personal benefit from his advice' and is gainfully occupied in promoting 'what society and the State consider to be an evil'; for we would then be faced with a class of persons having an interest 'opposed to what is considered

---

8. Ibid., p. 153 [p. 118].
9. This is one of Mill's examples (pp. 141–2). 'There are few acts which Christians and Europeans regard with more unaffected disgust than Mussulmans regard this particular mode of satisfying hunger', says Mill. He goes on to argue that the only good reason for condemning an attempt to ban the eating of pork in a country where the Mussulmans were a majority would be 'that with the personal tastes and self-regarding concerns of individuals the public has no business to interfere'.
1. *On Liberty*, pp. 153–5 [pp. 118–19].

as the public weal'. Mill has in mind such people as the pimp and the
keeper of a gambling house. He fails to come to a definite conclusion
about the justifiability of prohibiting these activities, remarking that
'there are arguments on both sides'. What is interesting in Mill's discussion here is — apart from the confirmation that his principle can
yield no clear directive in questions of this kind — his appeal to 'the
public weal' as a factor we have to take into account before deciding
on the legitimacy of social control. Does he intend that we should
classify actions as being harmful to the interests of others if it could be
shown that they are contrary to 'the public weal'? We are thus led back
to the problem of how widely (or narrowly) we are to construe the
notion of interests. Are we to interpret interests so narrowly as to exclude
the public interest or so widely as to involve consideration of the general
interest and social morality? On the former interpretation we should
find ourselves unable to prohibit activity we should want to prohibit;
on the latter we should be able to prohibit actions that Mill would
certainly wish to be left unrestrained. And if standards and values enter
into what we conceive to be a man's interests even in a restricted sense
of the term, *a fortiori* they will shape what we take the public interest
to require.

JEREMY WALDRON

Mill and the Value of Moral Distress†

I

In the modern discussion of pornography and obscenity — and in the
perennial liberal debates about freedom, toleration, and neutrality — it
remains unclear what or how much should be made of the fact that
people in one group find the views, the tastes, or the life-style of others
in their community *disturbing*. Even if an action (or a book or a film)
is not directly harmful, in the sense that it does not actually contribute
to the causation of injury, loss, or damage, still it may be perceived as
indecent, insulting, degrading, threatening, or distressing in less tangi-
ble ways. In the pornography debate, in particular, there is much to be
said for the view that politicians and philosophers have concentrated
too long on what pornography *does* (what it causes) and too little on
what it *is* or what it represents, especially as far as women are concerned. That balance is now gradually being redressed, but further consideration of the issues involved in this shift of concerns is certainly

† Reprinted from *Political Studies*, 35 (1987), 310–423, by permission of the Political Studies
Association and Blackwell Publishers.

necessary.[1] Undoubtedly one of the main characteristics of pornography (though one which it shares with the best art and literature) is that it *disturbs* us and makes us uneasy. That, I suppose, can be regarded as one of its *effects*, and, to the extent that people do not like being disturbed, to the extent that being disturbed in this way *hurts*, such an effect may be regarded as one of the *harmful* consequences of pornography and therefore as a basis for part of the case in favor of its prohibition. Alternatively, it may be argued that these negative effects accrue only because of moral views and prejudices that are held already by those who suffer from them, and therefore that they provide no distinct basis for prohibition apart from whatever arguments can be constructed out of the moral views and prejudices themselves.[2]

A full consideration of the issues here would involve untangling the various ideas that come together when we talk about a person being *disturbed* by another's behavior: the perception of threat, the perception of insult, the perception of symbol or representation, the vehemence of moral condemnation, the feeling of outrage, the elements of pity, contempt, sublimated guilt, shame, and so on. These need to be distinguished and their connections with one another carefully investigated in order to be able to deal sensitively with the variety of cases that can be accumulated under this general heading.[3] A full consideration would also mean exploring the way in which each of these strands is perceived in the various traditions of liberal and nonliberal argument: we must not assume, for example, that the Kantian argument for toleration and the Millian argument for toleration treat *moral outrage* or *threat* or *perceived insult* in the same way. On the contrary, these elements will be assigned different roles in different arguments, even when those arguments are driving toward substantially the same conclusion. There is, then, a lot to be done before we have anything like a satisfactory account of the relation between the fact that something is disturbing and a proposal that it ought to be prohibited.

My aims in the present chapter are very modest. I want to concentrate on what I shall call the element of moral distress — the fact that someone is distressed because of what he takes to be the immorality or the depravity of another's behavior. (Think, for example, of the distress many citizens experience when they see two men kissing passionately or when they consider what those two get up to in their bedroom at night.) I want to consider the place of this sort of distress, this element of disturbance, in what is perhaps the most influential of the modern

1. See, e.g., Beverley Brown, "A Feminist Interest in Pornography — Some Modest Proposals," *m/f*, nos. 5–6 (1981); Andrea Dworkin, *Pornography: Men Possessing Women* (London, 1981); Susan Griffin, *Pornography and Silence* (London, 1981).
2. See Richard Wollheim, "John Stuart Mill and the Limits of State Action," *Social Research*, 7 (1973), pp. 1–30; also Ronald Dworkin, "Is There a Right to Pornography?," *Oxford Journal of Legal Studies*, 1 (1981), pp. 177–212.
3. Phenomenologically, an excellent starting point is the author's postscript in A. Dworkin, *Pornography*, op. cit., pp. 302–4.

liberal arguments for toleration—the argument in John Stuart Mill's essay, *On Liberty*.

If we approach the issue of the social enforcement of ethical and religious standards in terms of Mill's famous Harm Principle — the principle which holds that "the only purpose for which power can be rightfully exercised over any member of a civilized community, against his will, is to prevent harm to others"[4]—we face the following question. Does moral distress of the kind I have mentioned count as *harm* for the purposes of Mill's principle?

Theoretically, at least, the question is an important one. It is true that moral conservatives and perfectionists have not usually relied on the existence of these harms to justify the enforcement of their moral views. From their perspective, that would be a rather sordid and self-interested approach; they prefer to attack the Harm Principle directly rather than squeeze out an interpretation of it congenial to their commitments.[5] Instead, Mill's critics make use of the problem to *discredit* the Harm Principle, and to show the folly of imagining that there can be a sphere of individual morality and immorality which in principle does not affect the interests of other people.[6] The liberal, then, for his part, is interested in the problem not because he imagines that conservatives will try to justify the moralistic use of power on this basis, but because of the implicit challenge posed to the meaning and point of the principle he has invoked to protect individual liberty.

One possible approach that the liberal might take is to concede that moral distress falls within the scope of the Harm Principle, but to insist that it is, on the whole, outweighed by the pain that would be involved in the prohibition of the conduct that occasions it.[7] After all, the fact that one's conduct harms another is, on Mill's account, only a necessary not a sufficient justification for intervention; once harm is established, everything depends on a calculation of the costs and the benefits of preventing it.[8] The point of the Harm Principle is to establish a threshold which must be crossed before utilitarian calculations of that sort are even in order, not to elevate every little incident of harm into a pretext for prohibition. But this approach seems unsatisfactory, from a liberal point of view, for two reasons. First, it makes the case against the enforcement of ethical and religious standards rather more precarious than liberals have usually been willing to concede. On this approach the liberty, for example, of a religious minority will depend on

4. J. S. Mill, *On Liberty* (Indianapolis, 1955), Ch. 1, p. 13 [p. 48]. [Page references to this Norton Critical Edition are in brackets, throughout.]
5. See, e.g., Roger Scruton, *The Meaning of Conservatism* (Harmondsworth, 1980), pp. 76–9.
6. This appears to be the intention in R. P. Wolff, *The Poverty of Liberalism* (Boston, 1968), Ch. 1, and in Patrick Devlin, *The Enforcement of Morals* (Oxford, 1965), Ch. 6.
7. Cf. Ted Honderich, "*On Liberty* and morality-dependent harm," *Political Studies*, 30 (1982), pp. 507 and 510. I will discuss Honderich's article further in Section VI.
8. Mill, op. cit., Ch. 5, pp. 114–15 [p. 114]. (See also C. L. Ten, *Mill on Liberty* [Oxford, 1980], p. 4.)

how large the opposing majority is and on the intensity of the popular feeling directed against them. If the majority is very large and the feeling very intense, then the "harm" (to the "interests" of the majority) that could be prevented by persecution might greatly outweigh the harm that persecution would cause. But one's liberal instincts suggest that the case for toleration becomes *more* not less compelling the smaller and less popular the group whose liberty is in question. Second, if we agree that ethical and religious conviction is in part a matter of feeling and that everyone who takes his convictions seriously is to some degree upset when he discovers that others do not share them, it seems odd that the mere existence of moral distress should be sufficient to cross the threshold test established by the Harm Principle. For then what work is the principle doing? What cases of the enforcement of morals could it possibly exclude? The answer is: only those cases which are not really taken seriously by the moralists anyway. That is why I suggest that the problem of morality-dependent harm poses a threat not just to the operation, but to the very coherence, of the Harm Principle. If a moralist's *natural* and *predictable* response to deviance is sufficient to count as his being harmed, then the idea of deploying a *Harm* Principle to limit the enforcement of conventional morals seems hopelessly ill-conceived.

The question of moral distress has been considered many times in the vast literature that has accumulated around Mill's essay.[9] I want to argue that if we approach it in terms of Mill's *arguments* for the Harm Principle, we get an answer which is clear, unequivocal, and surprising: far from providing the basis of an argument for prohibition, moral distress on Mill's account is actually a *positive* feature of deviant actions and life-styles; the outrage and disturbance that deviance evokes is something to be welcomed, nurtured, and encouraged in the free society that Mill is arguing for.

II

Let me begin with one or two comments about methodology and interpretation. The problem of whether moral distress should be regarded as *harm* for the purposes of Mill's principle is not one that can be resolved by a logical analysis of the concept of harm or by looking up "harm" in a dictionary. There is at least one sense of the term in which anyone who is discomforted and distressed by an activity is *eo ipso* harmed by it (he experiences what feels from the inside remarkably like pain), even if there are other narrower senses, which an analytically minded liberal might want to invoke, which do not cover this type of experience. When we are faced, in this way, with rival conceptions of

9. For a helpful review and discussion, see Ten, op. cit., Ch. 2.

harm, the question is then not what "harm" *really* means, but what reasons of principle there are for preferring one conception to another in the present context. A similar point can be made about the maneuver, common among Mill scholars, which insists that his principle was concerned only with harm to individual *interests*.[1] The concept of interest is also a contested one. There are conceptions in terms of which moral distress has an indubitably adverse effect on one's interests:

> Suppose that Jones is a devout Calvinist or a principled vegetarian. The very presence in his community of a Catholic or a meat-eater may cause him fully as much pain as a blow in the face or theft of his purse. . . . If the existence of ungodly persons in my community tortures my soul and destroys my sleep, who is to say that my interests are not affected?[2]

And there are, as I shall argue, conceptions in terms of which one's interests should be said to be promoted rather than disserved by the experience of moral distress.[3] Once again, the question is not what "interests" *really* means, but rather what reasons of principle there are for preferring one conception of interests to another in this context.

When we are considering a text like *On Liberty*, we need to remember that a doctrine such as the Harm Principle is not a piece of legislation, and questions posed in jurisprudence and political philosophy about how it is to be understood are not questions of statutory construction. As a pronouncement it has no authority in itself. The principle is presented in Chapter 1 of *On Liberty* as the upshot of an argument which Mill is about to present, and the only meaning or interest it can possibly have for us lies in its relation to that justificatory argument.[4] If we accept, as I think we must, that terms such as "harm" and "interests" (like "power," "liberty," and "law") have no clear or indisputable meaning awaiting our analysis, and that they rather pick out concepts whose nature it is to be contested from different evaluative standpoints, then the question is not simply which is the better conception of harm, but which conception answers more adequately to the purposes for which the concept is deployed. In the context of *On Liberty*, those purposes are established by Mill's *arguments* for freedom of opinion and lifestyle, that is, by his account of what we have to lose if liberty in those areas is withheld.

1. See, e.g., J. C. Rees, "A re-reading of Mill on liberty," *Political Studies*, 7 (1960), pp. 113–20 [p. 294ff.]
2. Wolff, op. cit., p. 24. See also Bernard Williams (ed.), *Obscenity and Film Censorship: An Abridgement of the Williams Report* (Cambridge, 1981), p. 99, and Joel Feinberg, *Rights, Justice and the Bounds of Liberty: Essays in Social Philosophy* (Princeton, 1980), p. 71.
3. See the discussion in Section VI, below.
4. This heuristic is also adopted in Anthony Ellis, "Offense and the liberal conceptions of the law," *Philosophy and Public Affairs*, 13 (1984), p. 5, though Ellis pursues rather different lines of argument. A less satisfactory analytical strategy is pursued in Joel Feinberg, *Harm to Others: The Moral Limits of the Criminal Law* (New York, 1984), pp. 31 ff. and 65.

III

On Liberty contains several arguments in favor of individual freedom of thought, discussion, and life-style. The most important of these are based on the desirability of what I am going to refer to as *ethical confrontation* — the open clash between earnestly held ideals and opinions about the nature and basis of the good life. Ethical confrontation should be understood to include conflicts on all sorts of issues — moral, philosophical, political, and religious — and to range from verbal debate on the one hand to the demonstration and flaunting of rival life-styles on the other. On Mill's view, the main argument against interference with individual liberty was that it diminished the occasion and opportunity for ethical confrontation in this sense.

Mill's attitude to confrontation was far from nihilistic; he did not take any satanic delight in the prospect of a *bellum omnium contra omnes* in the ethical realm. Although he denied the existence of any *one* solution to the problem of the good life, he certainly believed that there were objectively better and worse solutions.[5] As much as any of his perfectionist critics, he believed that genuine moral progress was possible. But progress, Mill insisted, was certainly not *guaranteed* under modern conditions; he rejected as a "pleasant falsehood" the dictum that truth always triumphs and that the good will come out on top in the end.[6] He saw a real danger that contemporary society might become stuck in a mire of prejudice and mediocrity, a danger of its becoming "another China"[7] — a more worrying analogue to the "stationary society" that he foresaw in the realm of economics.[8] If we want our society to remain progressive, Mill said, we must work at it, and the disappearance of ethical confrontation would be alarming evidence that we were failing in that task.

What contribution does ethical confrontation make to progress? The contribution, on Mill's account, is of two sorts. First, it contributes to the emergence of new and better ideas. Second, it makes an important contribution to the way ideas are held in society.

The first argument depends on a roughly dialectical account of ethical progress. It is a safe assumption that neither the prevailing doctrines in a society (if there are any) nor their main rivals express the whole truth about the human condition and the good life; most current doctrines contain elements of the truth and moral progress is a matter of the development of new doctrines that take up half-truths from here and there, and generate syntheses which have somewhat greater verisimilitude than the views out of which they grew. Mill does not believe

---

5. See, e.g., Mill, op. cit., Ch. 4 [p. 99ff.]; also J. S. Mill, *Utilitarianism* (London, 1962), Ch. 2, pp. 259 ff.
6. Mill, *On Liberty*, op. cit., Ch. 2, p. 34 [p. 62].
7. Ibid., Ch. 3, p. 88 [p. 97].
8. J. S. Mill, *Principles of Political Economy* (London, 1965), Book IV, Ch. 6 (Vol. II, pp. 752 ff.).

that this process of synthesis can be contrived deliberately by any individual moralist acting on his own.

> Truth in the great practical concerns of life is so much a question of the reconciling and combining of opposites that very few have minds sufficiently capacious to make the adjustment with an approach to correctness, and it has to be made by the rough process of a struggle between combatants fighting under hostile banners.[9]

Similarly, brand new ideas do not spring up ready formed in the minds of their proponents; they emerge phoenix-like from "the collision of adverse opinions"[1] in the antagonism of open debate and confrontation.

The second argument concerns not the ideas themselves, but the way they are held. According to Mill, progress is empty and the truth about the good life not worth pursuing, if the views that result are not held in a lively and committed spirit with a full awareness of their meaning and significance for human life and action. When ideas and life-styles clash in open debate, each is put on its mettle, and its adherents are required continually to reassert and therefore to reexamine the content and grounds of their views. No view, however popular, can afford to take its preeminence for granted in an atmosphere of open controversy; each person will take his view seriously and will be made acutely aware in the course of the debate of all its implications for his life and practice. So, if a given creed has anything to offer, ethical confrontation will bring it out; and if it has darker, hidden implications, those will emerge too in the course of earnest and committed debate about its desirability.[2] Without that challenge, the prevailing view, even if it is the soundest view, is likely to take on the character of an empty prejudice or "a few phrases learned by rote."[3] In this condition, a truth is worthless because it does not inform one's action to any significant extent; the valuable kernel of a half-truth lies hidden behind the blandness of its verbal repetition; and a falsehood poses no real provocative challenge to those who might be capable of refuting it.

Further, Mill was convinced that humans themselves benefit, morally and intellectually, from involvement in ethical confrontation. Partly this is a matter of the development of a certain sort of open-mindedness — the open-mindedness that results when each is intellectually alert to the possibility of criticism and cares passionately about its adequate rebuttal. This is not the so-called open-mindedness of the dilettante — the man who is willing to debate and defend an idea whether he believes it or not. As we shall see, Mill is almost as frightened of that attitude as he is of the dead weight of prejudice.[4] He is looking instead

9. Mill, *On Liberty*, op. cit., Ch. 2, p. 58 [p. 78].
1. Ibid., Ch. 2, p. 64 [p. 82].
2. Ibid., Ch. 2, pp. 48–53 [pp. 71–74].
3. Ibid., Ch. 2, p. 48 [p. 71].
4. See Section V, below.

for committed open-mindedness — the openness of a man who is anxious to listen and respond to criticism precisely because he takes his view seriously and is interested in it as a view about the good life or whatever and not just as a verbal habit from which he finds it psychologically difficult to dissociate himself. Partly too it is a matter of the way in which an idea is held and of the effect on a person of full commitment to one view rather than another. Mill seems to be suggesting that, in an environment of confrontation, commitment heightens and alerts the mental faculties, whereas in an atmosphere of conformity we get

> the cases, so frequent in this age of the world as almost to form the majority, in which the creed remains, as it were, outside the mind, incrusting and petrifying it against all other influences addressed to the higher parts of our nature; manifesting its power by not suffering any fresh and living conviction to get in, but itself doing nothing for the mind or heart except standing sentinel over them to keep them vacant.[5]

For these reasons, Mill thinks ethical confrontation is indispensable for genuine moral progress in society. The existence of a plurality of opinions clashing with one another is, he asserted, the only explanation of the progressive character of western civilization to date. But at a time when economic and social forces are making society increasingly homogeneous and the variety of circumstances is diminishing, it becomes even more important not to interfere with what remains of individuality and the clash of ideas that it generates.[6]

So much is this so, that Mill suggests it might be necessary to *manufacture* dissent if it does not offer itself spontaneously. Even in the utopian circumstance of genuine ethical consensus, the lack of intellectual contention and antagonism would be "no trifling drawback" from the universal recognition of the truth.[7] Fortunately, that is not a problem we have to face:

> If there are any persons who contest a received opinion, or who will do so if law or opinion will let them, let us thank them for it, open our minds to listen to them, and rejoice that there is someone to do for us what we otherwise ought, if we have any regard for either the certainty or vitality of our convictions, to do with much greater labour for ourselves.[8]

5. Mill, *On Liberty*, op. cit., Ch. 2, pp. 49–50 [p. 72].
6. Ibid., Ch. 3, pp. 85–8 [pp. 96–99].
7. Ibid., Ch. 2, p. 53[p. 75].
8. Ibid., Ch. 2, p. 55[p. 76].

IV

I do not propose to examine the merits of these arguments. But if there is anything in them at all, then they suggest a striking revaluation of moral offence and distress. Ethical confrontation, we have seen, is a positive good for Mill: it improves people and it promotes progress. But ethical confrontation is not a painless business. It always hurts to be contradicted in debate, if one takes seriously the views one is propounding, and it is distressing to be faced with examples of life-styles which pose a genuine challenge to the validity and grounds of one's own. People are naturally disturbed when they are involved in the collision of opinions. If nobody is disturbed, distressed, or hurt in this way, that is a sign that ethical confrontation is not taking place, and that in turn, as we have seen, is a sign that the intellectual life and progress of our civilization may be grinding to a halt. In those circumstances, we saw that Mill would propose a desperate remedy: we would have to manufacture ethical conflict in order to shake the complacency of accepted views and generate the shock, distress, and disturbance that were missing.

If, on the other hand, widespread moral distress *is* detectable in the community, then far from being a legitimate ground for interference, it is a positive and healthy sign that the processes of ethical confrontation that Mill called for are actually taking place. That a man is morally distressed by another's homosexuality, for example, is for Mill a sign, first, that he takes his own views on sexual ethics seriously, second, that he recognizes now the need to reassert vigorously the grounds of his own convictions, being confronted so dramatically and disturbingly with a case of its denial, and third — if (as is probable) the moral truth about sexual relations is the monopoly neither of his opinion nor its rival — it is a sign that ideas are struggling and clashing with one another in the way that Mill thought most likely to lead to the final emergence of a more balanced and sober truth about human sexuality.

Think what would be entailed by an interpretation which regarded moral distress as sufficient to cross the threshold established by the Harm Principle. What ought to be taken as evidence that freedom of thought and life-style was promoting progress would be invoked instead as a prima facie reason for interfering with that freedom. A sign of vitality would be cited as a necessary condition for legitimately suppressing that vitality. A symptom of progress would be deployed as a justification for acting in a way that would bring progress to a halt. If we assume that Mill took his own arguments seriously, we must say that this cannot have been his view. Since he believed that ethical confrontation was indispensable for moral and social progress, and since he used this as his main argument for individual liberty, it seems odd to suggest that he could have regarded the pain of debate and the distress of moral challenge as reasons for waiving the general ban on interference with personal liberty. Progress through the collision of opinion is the premise of Mill's liberalism. The sensitivity of the opinions involved in these collisions cannot therefore be taken as a basis for arguments justifying the restriction of liberty.

In a recent note, David Gordon has argued that moral distress might count as harm for the purposes of Mill's principle, provided it did not "arise from the holding of false moral views, judged by a correct account of morality."[9] But this account cannot be squared with Mill's arguments either. I shall leave aside the point that this requires the assessor of harm to be already in possession of the moral truth before he can determine which views should be heard in public debate and which life-styles flaunted. For Mill the more important point is that moral distress arising from a correct moral view indicates that the truth is being challenged, the view scrutinized, and therefore the mind of the true believer kept open and alert to the importance of the creed to which he (correctly, on this hypothesis) clings. If moral challenges were to be suppressed because of the sensibilities of those in possession of the truth — indeed if those sensibilities were even to be regarded as a reason for suppression — then the dangers of moral prejudice, intellectual stagnation, and the "incrustation" of the mind, which Mill knew could affect the truth as much as falsehood, would rear their heads again.

For these reasons, the concept of harm in Mill's principle cannot intelligibly be construed in a way that includes moral distress of the kind I have been discussing.

V

If the problem of moral distress is simply the problem of offense and disturbance occasioned by the fact that others hold or practice conceptions of the good that one regards as immoral or depraved, then the points I have just made dispose of it. Sometimes, however, the problem is confused with another one — the problem of the distress occasioned by the *manner* in which a rival conception of the good is expressed. People often say that they are distressed, and some may claim to be harmed, by seeing a life-style they detest *flaunted* or exhibited *aggressively* in front of them. I think Mill's argument has the capacity to deal with this problem also.

The first thing to say is that the good effects of ethical confrontation, on Mill's account, will not accrue unless views are put forward passionately, forcefully, and directly, in a manner that opponents of those views cannot practicably ignore. At the end of Chapter 2 of *On Liberty*, Mill has to deal with the (typically English) suggestion "that the free

9. David Gordon, "Honderich on morality-dependent harm," *Political Studies*, 32 (1984), p. 288.

expression of all opinions should be permitted on condition that the manner be temperate."[1] He is rightly suspicious of any temperateness proviso:

> If the test be offence to those whose opinions are attacked, I think experience testifies that this offence is given whenever the attack is telling and powerful, and that every opponent who pushes them hard, and whom they find it difficult to answer, appears to them, if he shows any strong feeling on the subject, an intemperate opponent.[2]

Intemperance in this sense is as indispensable for progress as the confrontation which it generates, on Mill's account. A "temperate" debate would be one in which views were compared and exchanged in dilettante fashion without any real moral or intellectual engagement on either side.

(In this connection, it is worth noting that when Mill described his father in his *Autobiography*, he cited as a virtue the fact "that he, in a degree once common, but now unusual, threw his feelings into his opinions," and went on:

> Those, who having opinions which they hold to be immensely important, and their contraries to be prodigiously hurtful, have any deep regard for the general good, will necessarily dislike, as a class and in the abstract, those who think wrong what they think right, and right what they think wrong.[3]

It is a very common error to confuse liberalism with the lack of this strong feeling, but Mill insists that vehemence and toleration are perfectly compatible, and that "none but those who do not care about opinions, will confound this with intolerance."[4]

Mill does concede that "the manner of asserting an opinion . . . may be very objectionable and may justly incur severe censure."[5] He has in mind the use of personal invective, sarcasm, vituperative language, and so on. Clearly, these tactics can be distressing, and the distress they occasion adds little to the forcefulness (for Mill's purposes) of the debate or confrontation into which they are introduced. For this reason they are to be condemned and restrained by popular opinion (though Mill is still adamant that "law and authority have no business" in restraining them[6]). He also believes that they are more common tactics

1. Mill, *On Liberty*, op. cit., Ch. 2, p. 64 [p. 82]. Mill's exasperation with this sort of objection is similar to his exasperation with the view (again typically English) that arguments for free discussions should not be "pushed to an extreme"; see ibid., Ch. 2, p. 26 [p. 57].
2. Ibid., Ch. 2, p. 65 [p. 82].
3. J. S. Mill, *Autobiography* (London, 1924), pp. 42–3. I am indebted for this reference to the discussion in Isaiah Berlin, *Four Essays on Liberty* (Oxford, 1969), p. 184 and note. See also Ellis, op. cit., pp. 9–10.
4. Mill, *Autobiography*, op. cit., p. 42.
5. Mill, *On Liberty*, op. cit., Ch. 2, p. 65 [p. 82].
6. Ibid., Ch. 2, pp. 65–6 [pp. 82–84].

on the side of orthodoxy than of heterodoxy and that there is "more need to discourage offensive attacks on infidelity than on religion."[7] For our purposes, the important point is that the distress occasioned by sarcasm and vituperation is not to be regarded as a morality-dependent harm. I can be "harmed" in this sense as much by the sarcastic inculcation of a creed that I am disposed already to believe as by the vituperative objections of an ethical opponent. The harm (if that is what it is) is done by the calculated attack on personality and self-confidence involved in sarcasm and vituperation, not by the attack, however shocking, on the substance of one's views. So Mill's condemnation of this sort of thing, like his later (though, on his own admission, much less well thought out) condemnation of bad manners,[8] adds little to the case for bringing moral distress within the scope of his Harm Principle.

Another suggestion often made in relation to Mill's Harm Principle is that an action may be "harmful" if performed in public even though it would harm no one if it were performed in private. What society generally regards as immorality should be tolerated provided it is practiced in the privacy of one's own bedroom (or wherever) and not brought into the public view. On this account, the public/private distinction is primarily a matter of *geography* rather than a question of the different nature of the moral standards involved.

It is tempting to interpret Mill's distinction between self-regarding and other-regarding actions along similar lines, so that a self-regarding action is paradigmatically an action performed behind closed doors. I think this temptation should be resisted.[9] If moral progress depends, as Mill claims, on struggle and confrontation between opposing views of the good life, the last thing we want is that people should conceal or disguise from others the fact that their opinions or lifestyles are different. The moral, philosophical, and religious confrontation that Mill is calling for must be *public* confrontation between the practicing adherents of rival and antagonistic ethics. Otherwise the benefits to society — not just to the antagonists but also to "the calmer and more dispassionate bystander"[1] — will not be realized. Indeed, one possibility that worries Mill is this — that eccentric, novel, and heretical life-styles might be coerced by public opinion and collective mediocrity back into the purely private lives of those who practice them. In those circumstances, the ideas themselves may survive, but their existence will make little contribution to the general good if, as Mill puts it, "the most active and inquiring intellects find it advisable to keep the general principles and grounds of their convictions within their own breasts."[2] The alternative views will

---

7. Ibid., Ch. 2, p. 66 [p. 83].
8. Ibid., Ch. 5, p. 119 [p. 117] (this passage is discussed at the end of the present section).
9. Ten, op. cit., pp. 40–1.
1. Mill, *On Liberty*, op. cit., Ch. 2, p. 63 [p. 81].
2. Ibid., Ch. 2, p. 40 [p. 66].

never blaze out far and wide, but continue to smoulder in the narrow circles of thinking and studious persons among whom they originate, without ever lighting up the general affairs of mankind with either a true or a deceptive light.[3]

Mill's argument for liberty commits him to the view that such "reticence on the part of heretics" is a social evil, and I think he would regard the modern idea (made popular since the findings of the Wolfenden Report[4]) that we should confine our deviant practices to the privacy of our own bedrooms, and never show them off to our neighbors, with similar disquiet.

When Mill talks, at the beginning of the essay, about a "sphere" of self-regarding action, we must not think of the boundaries of the sphere in quasi-physical terms, as though they were barriers blocking off the awareness of one's action from people liable to be affected by that awareness. (They are not like "transmitter shields" in Bruce Ackerman's "liberal" utopia, allowing anyone to screen out stimuli that he finds distressing.[5] Mill, I think, would be horrified by the suggestion in Ackerman's work that liberalism might involve the physical realization of this intellectual atomism.) Paradoxically, perhaps, the argument for freedom in relation to "self-regarding" actions rests on the hope and the possibility that the progress of moral debate, the struggle between rival views, and therefore (at least indirectly) the course of others' lives, will in fact be affected by those actions.

There is an isolated paragraph in Chapter 5 of *On Liberty* where Mill appears to subscribe to the view that there are some actions, harmless in private, which if done publicly may constitute indecency and therefore be liable to legitimate prohibition.[6] This is a difficult passage to accommodate and one on which Mill, on his own account, found it unnecessary to dwell. He does however make it clear that it is not the deviance or the perceived or actual immorality of the actions in question which makes their public performance indecent; rather it is a matter of the *type* of action that it is. For example, on this view, *all* forms of public copulation might be regarded as indecent, *including* marital sex in the missionary position for the sole and only purpose of procreation, not just sodomy, fellatio, masturbation, etc.[7] So if the spectacle of indecency is to be regarded as harmful, the harm involved is not (straightforwardly) moral distress, in the sense with which we are concerned.

Even so, I find this passage the most difficult to reconcile with the overall tendency of Mill's argument. There is, surely, a debate to be

3. Idem [p. 66].
4. See *Report of the Committee on Homosexual Offences and Prostitution* (London, 1957, Cmnd. 247), esp. para. 62.
5. Bruce Ackerman, *Social Justice in the Liberal State* (New Haven, 1980), pp. 179–80.
6. Mill, *On Liberty*, op. cit., Ch. 5, p. 119 [pp. 117–18].
7. Cf. H. L. A. Hart, *Law, Liberty and Morality* (London, 1963), p. 45.

had about the merits of public lovemaking;[8] and making love in public would be, on Mill's own account, an important contribution to the initiation or the course of such a debate. If copulation in public were banned on the grounds that it is "bad manners" or offends against public decency, it is difficult to see how people could ever get a real sense of the issues involved in this argument, or even of what their own views actually entailed. The danger here, as I see it, is that the very "despotism of custom" which, according to Mill, is the deadliest enemy of individuality and progress, might creep in under the cover of standards of decency to threaten those values all over again.[9]

For this reason, I think the passage we are considering should charitably be overlooked in our reconstruction of Mill's view. If it is not, even the whole basis of his argument for liberty is called into question.[1] At any rate, this isolated passage apart, it is clear that the argument of *On Liberty* does not license the conclusion that putative immorality should be kept from public view.

VI

I have said that Mill is precluded, by his arguments for liberty, from taking moral distress and offence seriously as a form of harm for the purposes of his Harm Principle. In a recent article, Ted Honderich has suggested that this is incompatible with Mill's underlying utilitarianism. "If Mill is Utilitarian with respect to the proper rules for society, how can he be taken to ignore distress when it happens to be the morality-dependent kind?"[2] After all, no one is denying the reality of this distress, nor does our argument depend at all on the view that those concerned are "putting it on" in order to gain some sort of unfair advantage in the utilitarian calculus.[3] The distress is there, on any account, and Honderich is worried by the suggestion that a self-confessed utilitarian might be disposed not to take it seriously. On Honderich's interpretation, Mill *does* include this distress as a form of harm, and dismisses it (to the extent that he does) only on the basis that it is quantitatively inconsiderable.[4]

This last move, however, will not do. Mill describes societies in which the overwhelming majority are revolted by, say, the sexual, religious, or dietary habits of a few.[5] If moral distress counts at all in utilitarian calculation, then there can be no evident or clear-cut case

8. Cf. Williams, op. cit., p. 99.
9. See also Ellis, op. cit., pp. 15 ff.
1. On no account are Mill's views utterly consistent: see, e.g., Ted Honderich's concession, referred to in note 6, p. 325.
2. Honderich, op. cit., p. 513.
3. Cf. the argument about external preferences in Dworkin, "A Right to Pornography?," op. cit., pp. 202 ff.
4. Honderich, op. cit., pp. 507 and 510.
5. See Mill, *On Liberty*, op. cit., Ch. 4, pp. 102–5 [pp. 107–8].

for tolerating this minority deviance. Since Mill believed that there *was* such a case for toleration, no matter how strong and widespread the revulsion, he cannot have held the view that Honderich attributes to him.[6]

Actually, Honderich is mistaken about the character of Mill's utilitarian theory. Mill's utilitarianism is not a Benthamite calculus of pleasures and pains, or of satisfactions and dissatisfactions, of all sorts. The value on which liberty is based is certainly utility, on Mill's account, but, as he insists in his introduction to the essay, "it must be utility in the largest sense, grounded on the permanent interests of man as a progressive being."[7] I take it that this passage refers, not merely to the nature of Mill's utilitarian *computations* (for example, taking a long-run rather than a short-run view, etc.), but to the character of his utilitarian *values*—the fundamental values which he thinks will be promoted by his libertarianism. A considerable part of *On Liberty* is devoted to showing what it is for man to be "a progressive being" and what his interests in such a condition are. These are the interests whose promotion Mill's utilitarianism seeks to maximize.

If we accept the arguments about progress in Chapter 2 of *On Liberty* and spontaneity in Chapter 3, it is not then open to us to say that distress or resentment when one's preconceptions are challenged goes against one's interests as a progressive being. A creature who defined his interests—even in part—in terms of being free from the shock and perturbation of ethical debate and being free from anxiety about the grounds or validity of his opinions would be like the satisfied (and no doubt morally complacent) "fool" mentioned in *Utilitarianism*.[8] Mill is adamant, in the latter work, that there is a distinction between *happiness*, understood as the leading value of his ethical system, and mere contentment or satisfaction.[9] By insisting that distress and uneasiness under the impact of ethical confrontation are negative values for Mill, Honderich is driving the theory back toward the very Benthamism that Mill wanted to repudiate.

It is certainly true that Mill wants to argue, in consequentialist fashion, that the benefits of free discussion and of the open struggle between competing conceptions of the good life outweigh the costs of such confrontation. The costs include the bad effects of people believing falsehoods (Mill concedes, with common sense, that "it is dangerous and noxious when opinions are erroneous"[1]) and the dangers of people practicing life-styles that are actually depraved. They include also the

6. This point appears to have been conceded in Honderich, op. cit., p. 511, where the author states that "if there were more along these lines," there might be a case for saying that Mill discounted morality-dependent harm as irrelevant.
7. Mill, *On Liberty*, op. cit., Ch. 1, p. 14 [p. 49].
8. Mill, *Utilitarianism*, op. cit., Ch. 2, p. 260.
9. Ibid., Ch. 2, pp. 260 ff.
1. Mill, *On Liberty*, op. cit., Ch. 2, p. 53 [p. 75].

tendency for religious and philosophical sectarianism to be "heightened and exacerbated" by the freest discussion.[2] (In certain circumstances, where sectarianism may lead to violence, these costs are so great as to outweigh the benefits of liberty.[3]) But, in Mill's calculations at any rate, the costs of freedom do *not* include the distress occasioned by contradiction or the pain and shock of forceful debate. Those are not experiences which a progressive being has a genuine interest in avoiding and they are therefore not negative values or costs in relation to the permanent interests of man as a progressive being.

SUSAN MOLLER OKIN

[Mill's Feminist Egalitarianism]†

*   *   *

Mill's opposition to the prejudices and beliefs which kept women in a subordinate position in all aspects of social and political life was based on convictions formed very early in his youth, which found expression in many of his works on political and ethical subjects. At the beginning of the work he devoted specifically to these issues, *The Subjection of Women*, he states: "That . . . the legal subordination of one sex to the other . . . is wrong in itself, and now one of the chief hindrances to human improvement . . . [is] an opinion which I have held from the very earliest period when I had formed any opinions at all on social or political matters, and which . . . has been constantly growing stronger by the progress of reflection and the experience of life." Evidence for his continual concern with the position of women is offered by his various biographers and in his letters; he often judged peoples, philosophical systems and periods of history according to their attitudes toward women and their role in society.[1] It will not suffice to confine the following discussion to *The Subjection of Women* alone, since there is in some of his other published works and in his letters, a fuller treatment of some ideas that are rather summarily dealt with in that work. For example, both to guard his own and Harriet Taylor Mill's personal reputations, and in order to avoid endangering the respectability of the incipient movement for women's rights, he played down or omitted his radical ideas about divorce and birth control.[2] Where this occurs, I shall

2. Ibid., Ch. 2, p. 63. [p. 81].
3. This, I take it, is the force of the "corn dealer" example, ibid., Ch. 3, pp. 67–8 [p. 84].
† From Susan Moller Okin, *Women in Western Political Thought*, 197–230. Copyright (c) 1979 by Princeton University Press. Reprinted by permission of Princeton University Press.
1. See, for example, Michael St. John Packe, *The Life of John Stuart Mill*, pp. 90, 294–295; F. A. Hayek, *John Stuart Mill and Harriet Taylor*, pp. 208, 248; Himmelfarb, *On Liberty and Liberalism*, pp. 170, 204–205; *The Subjection of Women*, p. 451.
2. Letter to John Nichol, August 18, 1869, *The Later Letters, Collected Works*, Vol. 17, p. 1634.

make reference to his more explicit discussions of these subjects, and I shall also point out instances in which Harriet Taylor's ideas, as expressed in her own writings on the subject of women, are significantly different from those Mill himself espoused.[3]

Alien though Mill's radical ideas about women were to the mid-nineteenth century climate of opinion in general, it is easy to find stimuli to the development of his feminist convictions amongst several of the groups of thinkers with whom he was in contact during his formative years. The Utilitarians, by whom he was educated, were certainly not unconcerned with the issue. Bentham, for instance, though he thought it would be premature to allow the issue of women's suffrage to distract attention from or endanger his broader purposes, did concede the crucial points that existing differences between the sexes had certainly not been shown to be innate or inevitable ones, and that according to the principle of utility women should have the vote on the same grounds as men.[4] As for his father, John Stuart Mill notes in his *Autobiography* that "he looked forward . . . to a considerable increase of freedom in the relations between the sexes, though without pretending to define exactly what would be, or ought to be, the precise conditions of that freedom."[5] On the subject of female suffrage, however, James Mill, in his *Essay on Government*, had greatly offended the other philosophical radicals by suggesting that women might well be excluded from voting without any bad consequences, since their interests are included in those of the men in their families. A violent controversy was produced in Utilitarian circles, by this single, most unacceptable sentence, from which the young Mill tells us that he and his associates, including Bentham, "most positively dissented."[6] It is clear from his use of the phrase in his subsequent writings about women that Mill was particularly struck by the somewhat exaggerated statement in Macaulay's critical attack on the *Government* essay, that the interests of women were no more identical with those of their husbands than were the interests of subjects with those of their kings.[7] The whole controversy must surely have stimulated John Stuart Mill's concern with feminism. In addition, the Utilitarian's mouthpiece, the *Westminster Review*, had established itself as an early champion of the cause of women's rights. As early as 1824, Mill himself had published in that periodical an article attacking the prevalent custom of regarding mo-

---

3. The two essays on the subject of marriage and divorce which Mill and Harriet Taylor wrote for each other in 1832 are reprinted in Hayek, *John Stuart Mill and Harriet Taylor*, and also in Alice Rossi's edition of their *Essays on Sex Equality*, where the pamphlet *The Enfranchisement of Women*, which was probably, though not certainly, written by Harriet Taylor, is also to be found.
4. Jeremy Bentham, *Plan of Parliamentary Reform*, pp. 463–464, and *Constitutional Code*, pp. 107–109. See Miriam Williford, "Bentham on the Rights of Women."
5. *Autobiography*, p. 107.
6. *Autobiography*, p. 104.
7. See Packe, *The Life of John Stuart Mill*, p. 90.

rality and personal characteristics in completely different lights with reference to the two sexes.[8]

Mill's feminism also derived inspiration from the early French and English Socialists. He mentions meeting William Thompson, an Owenite who had written a lengthy feminist work in the 1820s. He says that he considers it "the signal honour of Owenism and most other forms of Socialism that they assign [to women] equal rights, in all respects, with those of the hitherto dominant sex."[9] We know, also, from his letters, that he was very interested in the ideas of Enfantin and the other Saint-Simonian *missionaires* who came to London in the early 1830s.[1] Tempered though his admiration was by his subsequently justified suspicions of their fanaticism and charlatanry, he continued to recognize the debt owed them by the feminist cause. In his *Autobiography* he writes, "In proclaiming the perfect equality of men and women, and an entirely new order of things in regard to their relations with one another, the St. Simonians, in common with Owen and Fourier, have entitled themselves to the grateful remembrance of future generations."[2]

Another factor which must have tended to confirm Mill's already strongly held feminist convictions was his connection with W. J. Fox and the Unitarian periodical, the *Monthly Repository*. As early as 1823, when Harriet Martineau contributed on the subject of equal education for women, but especially in the 1820s, when Fox was editor, this magazine published articles advocating female suffrage, a more rational attitude toward divorce, and the correction of the countless other injustices in the treatment of women. In his history of the periodical, Francis Mineka says: "Altogether, the *Repository*'s record on the emancipation of women is a distinctly honorable one. For its day, it was far in advance of common opinion; no contemporary periodical so consistently advocated an enlightened policy."[3] Mill wrote for the *Repository* in the early and mid-1830s, and his frequent correspondence with Fox over these years shows that the latter was a distinct spur to his feminist principles.[4]

Finally, we cannot ignore the direct influence on Mill's ideas of the women he met in the intellectual circles in which he moved. Such talented and intelligent, educated and productive women as Harriet Martineau, Sarah Austin, Harriet Grote, Jane Carlyle, and Eliza and Sarah Flower cannot fail to have made their impression on his ideas about their sex and the way it was regarded by contemporary society. Most important of all in this respect, however, was Harriet Taylor.

8. "Periodical Literature 'Edinburgh Review,' " *Westminster Review*, Vol. 1, No. 2, April, 1824.
9. *Principles of Political Economy, Collected Works*, Vol. 2, p. 209.
1. See R. K. Pankhurst, *The Saint-Simonians, Mill and Carlyle*; pp. 3–4, 108–109.
2. *Autobiography*, pp. 167–168; see also letters to Harriet Taylor, February 19, 1849, and January 18, 1855, *Later Letters, Collected Works*, Vol. 14, pp. 9–10, and 298.
3. Francis Mineka, *The Dissidence of Dissent*, p. 296.
4. *The Earlier Letters, Collected Works*, Vol. 12, passim, e.g., pp. 160, 229.

There has been much dispute about the extent of Harriet Taylor's influence on Mill, and the originality of her contribution to his work.[5] This stems from the divergence between, on the one hand, Mill's enraptured statements about her limitless genius and his claims that a great deal of his later work was in fact based on ideas that were hers, so that she played Bentham to his Dumont,[6] and, on the other hand, the decidedly unfavorable impression she made on their contemporaries, and the hardly startling quality of her own extant writings. I am inclined to agree with H. O. Pappe, who concludes his examination of the evidence by saying that it is only Mill's distorted impression of her abilities that suggests that she was endowed with any qualities of genius. However, it is not necessary in the context of Mill's feminist ideas to go deeply into this controversy, for two reasons.

First, Mill has left us with a very clear statement about his wife's effect on his feminist beliefs. He stresses that she was not the source of his convictions about the need for the equality of men and women, and this statement is borne out by his many letters and several publications on the subject which date from before their first meeting. He says, in fact, that it may well have been his strong views on the subject that initially attracted her to him. However, he adds that, in the course of their long relationship and eventual marriage, she had played the part of transforming what had been "little more than an abstract principle" into a real appreciation of the practical, day-to-day effects of women's lack of rights and opportunities. She had also, he says, made him aware of "the mode in which the consequences of the inferior position of women intertwine themselves with all the evils of existing society and with all the difficulties of human improvement."[7] Thus, although there is no doubt that Mill was a convinced feminist independently of the influence of Harriet Taylor, both the existence and the difficult circumstances of their relationship must have increased the

---

5. Until the 1960s, twentieth-century biographers of Mill, such as Ruth Borchard, Hayek and Packe, had tended to accept Mill's estimate of the great extent of Harriet Taylor's intellectual influence on him. This is especially true of Packe, who talks as if Taylor all but wrote all of Mill's major works except the *Logic* (*The Life of John Stuart Mill*, p. 317). In more recent years, however, there has been considerable reaction against this view, from Jack Stillinger, who edited the earlier draft of Mill's *Autobiography*; H. O. Pappe, in *John Stuart Mill and the Harriet Taylor Myth*; and John M. Robson, in *The Improvement of Mankind*. None of these writers disputes that Harriet Taylor was a very important part of Mill's life, and that she certainly provided him with emotional well-being and intellectual companionship without which he may well have been far less productive. What they disagree about with the earlier critics, and with Mill himself, is that the principal ideas of his works were hers, not his. Most recently, Himmelfarb argues that Harriet Taylor was immensely influential, particularly during their married life, but in a way which Himmelfarb considers led Mill astray from his most worthwhile thought. For a more balanced recent view of Taylor's influence, see Virginia Held, "Justice and Harriet Taylor."

6. Letter from J. S. M. to H. T., in Hayek, p. 185. For other examples of Mill's very high praises of her, see, for example, his introduction to *The Enfranchisement of Women*, his *Autobiography*, passim, and the inscription he placed on her tombstone, in Hayek, p. 34.

7. *Autobiography*, p. 244, note; cf. also letter to Paulina Wright Davis, December 11, 1869, *Later Letters*, *Collected Works*, Vol. 17, p. 1670–1671.

strength of his convictions, and of his determination to do what he could to have women's many disabilities remedied.

Secondly, it is impossible to tell which of the ideas that Mill and Harriet Taylor expressed on the subject of women originated in his mind, and which in hers, with the possible exception of those they expressed to each other in two short essays on marriage and divorce, very early in their relationship, and those that appear in the earlier essay, *The Enfranchisement of Women*, but not in *The Subjection of Women*, which Mill wrote after Harriet Taylor's death. From this evidence, one derives the distinct impression that her ideas were somewhat more radical than his. She proposes, for example, that once women have been given full civil and political rights, all marriage laws could be done away with, without harmful results. While Mill was in favor of considerable relaxation of the divorce laws, he never suggested that the contractual basis of marriage be abolished. On most issues, however, it seems that their ideas became very much enmeshed on this subject which was so important to them both. Many of the arguments included in *The Subjection of Women* appeared first in *The Enfranchisement of Women*, but this is not sufficient evidence that they were all originally her ideas, since although the pamphlet was published under her name, Mill refers to it at least once as written by himself. This may, however, have been in order to avoid the publisher's prejudices. Most probably they worked on it together, or at least were in constant touch about the ideas it contained. As Mill himself says, they came from "the fund of thought which had been made common to us both, by our innumerable conversations and discussions on a topic which filled so large a place in our minds."[8]

Thus, to feminist convictions which Mill held from very early in his life were added the influences of a number of groups of thinkers with whom he mixed or at least had considerable contact — the Utilitarians, the early Cooperative Socialists, Saint-Simonians and Fourierists, and the Unitarian radicals. He had come into contact with a number of women whose qualities strongly contradicted contemporary stereotypes of what women were and should be like, and he had a lengthy and intimate relationship with a woman who had directly suffered the effects of discrimination against her sex, particularly in the form of the marriage laws and the denial of educational opportunities. It is, then, not surprising that he should decide to apply his most basic principles to arguing for the emancipation of women.

In *On Liberty*, Mill eschews any appeal to "abstract right, as a thing independent of utility." In *The Subjection of Women*, too, he feels obliged to answer those who might accuse him of advocating "a social

---

8. *Autobiography*, p. 266. I have, however, assumed below that those more radical views expressed in *The Enfranchisement of Women*, which Mill did not repeat in *The Subjection of Women*, were Harriet Taylor's alone.

revolution in the name of an abstract right."[9] At times, however, in spite of this protestation, he does come very near to sounding like a natural rights theorist, rather than a simple utilitarian. He refers, for example, to the injustice of denying to women "the *equal moral right* of all human beings to choose their occupation (short of injury to others) according to their own preferences."[1] Despite a few un-utilitarian "lapses" such as this, however, the basic arguments of the work on women, as of *On Liberty*, are made in the name of utility — that is, in the name of John Stuart Mill's version of utility. The appeal of *The Subjection of Women*, too, is to "utility in the largest sense, grounded on the permanent interests of man as a progressive being."[2]

Mill vehemently rejects the narrow, Benthamite conception of human nature, explicitly in the essay on Bentham,[3] but also implicitly in all his other works. "Human nature," he says in *On Liberty*, "is not a machine to be built after a model . . . but a tree, which requires to grow and develop itself on all sides, according to the tendency of the inward forces which make it a living thing."[4] Whether Mill's totally unmechanistic conception of human nature means that he cannot be regarded as a real utilitarian is a much debated issue. It has been argued that the emphasis he places on the development of the human faculties, rather than simply the pleasures experienced by a given population, takes him so far away from "the greatest happiness of the greatest number" that he cannot be considered a utilitarian in the Benthamite sense. He certainly did not believe that "pushpin is as good as poetry." However, neither did he give up the greatest happiness principle. The basic reason for this is that Mill was convinced that the moral and intellectual advancement of mankind would result in greater happiness for everybody. Believing as he did that the higher pleasures of the intellect yielded far greater happiness than the lower pleasure of the senses,[5] and that consequently, "next to selfishness, the principal cause which makes life unsatisfactory is want of mental cultivation,"[6] he could only conclude that an essential means to the greatest happiness was the opening up to everybody of the joys of poetry and the other higher pleasures. The moral development of humanity, too, would lead to ever greater happiness, because to a moral being virtue was not just a means to

9. *On Liberty*, p. 16 [p. 49]; *The Subjection of Women*, p. 521 [p. 196]. [Page references to this Norton Critical Edition are in brackets, throughout.]
1. *The Subjection of Women*, p. 487 [p. 173].
2. *On Liberty*, p. 16 [p. 49].
3. "Bentham," in *Utilitarianism*, p. 97.
4. *On Liberty*, p. 73 [p. 87].
5. The famous argument about the quality of pleasures is found at the beginning of Chapter 2 of the essay *Utilitarianism*, pp. 258–262. Taken simply as it is presented there, without the unspoken premise that Mill took his own highly intellectual nature as his model of human nature no less than Bentham used his, the argument is quite unsatisfactory. Mill certainly fails to convince us that Socrates really knew what it was like to be a happy pig, any more than Mill himself did.
6. *Utilitarianism*, p. 265.

good action, but a feeling which contributed to his or her own happiness;[7] and also because the decline of selfishness would mean that people would become united in aiming at the greatest happiness of all, rather than just pursuing their own individual pleasures. Thus, Mill's utilitarianism is certainly different from Bentham's, in that Mill did not hope to find the answer to the question "Is the greatest happiness presently being experienced?" simply by asking everyone how they are feeling. As he made clear, particularly in the "Socrates and the pig" passage, he did not consider that people were at all capable of knowing how great and profound their happiness could be, if their full moral and intellectual potential were developed.

There is, undoubtedly, a strong current of intellectual elitism running through Mill's thought. While he had criticized Bentham for basing his concept of human nature on his own narrow and unimaginative person, Mill proceeded to reason in the same way. He assumed that the model for humanity was the intellectual and ascetic aesthete that he himself personified. However, once this bias is acknowledged, it cannot be maintained that he rejected the greatest happiness principle in favor of a "greatest human development" principle. The point is that he was quite convinced that only the cultivated could achieve the greatest happiness available to mankind.

The purpose of this digression from the specific subject of women has been to explore the importance for Mill's version of utilitarianism of his concept of man as a progressive, a morally and intellectually improvable being. In The Subjection of Women and in those parts of his other works in which he argues the need for women's emancipation, the theme of human advancement recurs frequently. This emphasis is most succinctly summarized in a passage in the Principles of Political Economy, where he says: "The ideas and institutions by which the accident of sex is made the groundwork of an inequality of legal rights, and a forced dissimilarity of social functions, must ere long be recognized as the greatest hindrance to moral, social, and even intellectual improvement."[8] There are two other principles that figure very prominently in The Subjection of Women and his other feminist statements — liberty, or the opportunity for self-determination, and justice, in the sense of equal consideration or impartiality. Both of these other concerns, however, are explicitly related to the moral and intellectual advancement of mankind, as well as to the happiness of women themselves.

As is clear from On Liberty, Mill was deeply concerned about the value of individual freedom, regarding it as such an important means to happiness and self-development that it could justifiably be sacrificed only to the extent that is absolutely necessary for the maintenance of

7. Utilitarianism, pp. 289–290.
8. Principles of Political Economy, Collected Works, Vol. 3, p. 765; see also Vol. 2, p. 373, and Later Letters, Collected Works, Vol. 17, pp. 1535, 1801.

security and social cooperation. "After the primary necessities of food and raiment," he asserts, "freedom is the first and strongest want of human nature,"[9] and he recalls the joys of emerging from the tutelage of childhood into the responsibilities of adulthood as indicative of the feeling of added vitality that self-determination can give. Thus, freedom is so essential a part of human well-being that Mill concludes "that the only purpose for which power can be rightfully exercised over any member of a civilized community, against his will, is to prevent harm to others."[1]

Unlike Rousseau, with his rigidly patriarchal conception of freedom, Mill had no doubts about there being ample scope to apply this strongly held value to the contemporary social and legal position of women. Liberty and self-determination are recurrent themes of Mill's arguments against the gross inequality of the marriage laws and the severe discrimination suffered by women in the areas of educational and occupational opportunity. He states that the most direct benefit he envisages resulting from the emancipation of women will be the added happiness of women themselves, resulting from the difference between "a life of subjection to the will of others, and a life of rational freedom."[2] Whereas a woman at the time he wrote had practically no opportunity of any occupation (outside of unskilled labor and a few of the menial service industries) except that of a wife, in a marital relationship in which she was legally bound to obey her husband and had no rights to own property, it was obvious to Mill that an inestimable increase in happiness would result from giving women a real choice of how to spend their lives. He was convinced that "if there is anything vitally important to the happiness of human beings, it is that they should relish their habitual pursuit";[3] thus it was essential that all the careers open to men should be made equally accessible to women. Only then would the choice of whether to marry or not be a meaningful one, rather than the only means of escape from the despised dependency of "old maidhood." It was also essential that those who chose to marry should be granted an equal share in the legal rights and responsibilities of the relationship. Although he did not express his most radical ideas on the subject of marriage in *The Subjection of Women*, he says elsewhere that it should be a free contract in the sense of being dissoluble at the wish of the contracting parties, provided that any children who had resulted from the marriage were well cared for. His dissent from the contemporary view of the binding nature of the marriage contract is summed up in his statement that "surely it is wrong, wrong in every way . . . that there should exist any motives to marriage except the happiness which two persons who love one another feel in associating their exis-

9. *The Subjection of Women*, p. 542 [p. 211].
1. *On Liberty*, p. 15 [p. 48].
2. *The Subjection of Women*, p. 542 [p. 211].
3. *The Subjection of Women*, p. 547 [p. 214].

tence."[4] Any denial of liberty which was not for the sake of protecting some third party from harm was anathema to him.

It was not only, however, for the sake of the added happiness of women themselves that Mill advocates giving them more freedom of choice about how they should spend their lives, but also for the sake of the progress of society as a whole. As he states in *On Liberty*, "the only unfailing and permanent source of improvement is liberty, since by it there are as many possible permanent centres of improvement as there are individuals."[5] The extension of education and the opening up of careers to women, freeing them from the bondage of compulsory domesticity, should also have the beneficial effect of "doubling the mass of mental faculties available for the higher service of humanity."[6]

In addition to this vast increase in available talent, Mill considered that freeing women to become educated and to work at a career would have most valuable effects on men. Both the stimulus of female competition and the companionship of equally educated partners would result in men's greater intellectual development as well. Mill was most impressed by the fact that, since men were becoming less bound up with outdoor pursuits and what were regarded as exclusively masculine activities, their domestic lives were becoming more important, and the influence of their wives was therefore continually increasing. Taking the rather pessimistic point of view that any society or individual which is not improving is deteriorating, he stresses the insidious effects that the constant companionship of an uneducated and frivolous wife can have on a man, even though he might previously have had serious intellectual interests. He asks how it could be considered anything but detrimental to a man's development to be confined for a large proportion of his life with a partner whose mind has been so studiously concentrated on trivia, who is utterly ignorant about matters which should be of the highest concern, and who is bound because of the narrowness of her education to consider the immediate and material interest of her family of greater importance than any public-spirited or intellectual aspirations that her husband might wish to pursue. "With such an influence in every house," Mill asks, "is it any wonder that people in general are kept down in that mediocrity of respectability which is becoming a marked characteristic of modern times?"[7] Rousseau's solution to what he perceived as the unfavorable influence of contemporary women — the segregation of the sexes in the wider world and even within the home — was, needless to say, quite repugnant to Mill. Though women in their current state of subjection and lack of opportunity were in Mill's view acting as a constant force against progress, he was convinced that liberating them would reverse this force.

4. "Early Essay on Marriage and Divorce," *Essays on Sex Equality*, p. 72.
5. *On Liberty*, p. 87 [p. 96].
6. *The Subjection of Women*, p. 525 [p. 199].
7. *The Subjection of Women*, p. 536 [p. 207]; see also p. 540 [p. 209].

Second only to freedom, in the arguments set out in *The Subjection of Women*, is the principle of justice. Just treatment, no less than liberty, is regarded both as essential for the happiness of women themselves and as a necessary condition for the advancement of humanity. Mill's most comprehensive discussion of justice is found in the last chapter of *Utilitarianism*. Here, he deals with the fundamental concept of impartiality, or the requirement that like cases be treated alike, and then goes on to show that the reason different societies have had such different conceptions of what constitutes just treatment is that they have considered different qualities to be grounds for departing from impartiality. * * * In Aristotle's theory of justice, citizens, women, artisans and slaves receive entirely different treatment according to what he perceived as their inherent characteristics and their functions in society. Whereas it is, Mill says, crucial to the idea of justice that "all persons are deemed to have a *right* to equality of treatment, except when some recognized social expediency requires the reverse,"[8] different conceptions of what constitutes social expediency have resulted in acceptance by societies of slavery, caste systems, and many other unequal arrangements now considered completely unjust, as thoroughly justified by the requirements of circumstances. Only when social inequalities have ceased to be considered expedient, have they come to be regarded as not only inexpedient, but also unjust. However, people tend to be "forgetful that they themselves perhaps tolerate other inequalities under an equally mistaken notion of expediency,"[9] and a paradigmatic case of this is the subjection of women. Rousseau, of course, is a perfect example of such thinking. Although the inequality of the sexes "is not felt to jar with modern civilization, any more than domestic slavery among the Greeks jarred with their notion of themselves as a free people,"[1] Mill perceived it as an isolated and anomalous instance of bondage in a world whose guiding principle was human equality. "Marriage," he asserts, "is the only actual bondage known to our law; there remain no legal slaves, except the mistress of every house."[2]

Like entrenched inequalities in the past, however, the unequal position of women was regarded as "natural." "But was there ever any domination which did not appear natural to those who possessed it?" Mill asks.[3] The most cultivated intellects of the ancient world, including Aristotle, were sure that slavery was natural; theorists of absolute monarchy claimed that it was the only natural form of government, conquering races that the right of the stronger was natural, and the feudal nobility that their dominion over their serfs was natural. Since the subjection of women to men is a universal custom, it is not surprising that

8. *Utilitarianism*, p. 320.
9. *Utilitarianism*, p. 320.
1. *The Subjection of Women*, p. 434 [p. 137].
2. *The Subjection of Women*, p. 522 [p. 197].
3. *The Subjection of Women*, p. 440 [p. 141].

society feels so certain of its naturalness. Mill's awareness of the extent
to which nature has been used to legitimize convention is striking. He
comments: "So true is it that unnatural generally means only uncustomary, and that everything which is usual appears natural."[4] However,
since he believed fervently that society in its most desirable form was
the society of equals, it was essential for him to combat the prevalent
claims for the naturalness of the glaring inequality of the sexes. He
looked forward to the day when discrimination on the grounds of sex
would follow that based on nobility of birth into disrepute and oblivion.

In order to build his case for female equality on what he regarded
as the universally accepted principle of just treatment, Mill considered
that he was obliged to demonstrate two things. First, he had to contend
with the assumption that women are inherently inferior. "The objection
with which we are now principally met," he states, "is that women are
not fit for, or not capable of, this, that or the other mental achievement."[5] Consequently, he determined to show, against the strong force
of contemporary opinion, that the reasons which had always been considered ample grounds for treating women differently from men — that
they are naturally inferior, less rational, more emotional — were not
founded on good evidence, and were probably all false. Second, even
when he had demonstrated this to the extent that anyone could at that
time, Mill considered it essential, as a utilitarian, to show that doing
away with the unequal treatment of women would be expedient in the
sense of contributing to the general welfare of society.

In arguing the first of these two claims, Mill had to contend not only
with popular prejudice, but also with the violent reaction which many
intellectuals of the mid-nineteenth century were expressing against
eighteenth-century environmentalism. Many of Mill's contemporaries
considered that French educational theorists of the Enlightenment,
such as Helvétius and Holbach, had attributed excessive importance to
environmental factors in the formation of human character and intellectual capacity. Mill, by contrast, claimed that certainly most, and
probably all, of the existing differences of character and intellect between men and women were due to the very different attitudes of society toward members of the two sexes from their earliest infancy, and
the vastly different types and qualities of education afforded them. In
his fragment on marriage, written about 1832, Mill had vehemently
denied any innate inequality between the sexes apart from that of physical strength — and even this, he said, could be doubted.[6] He was, however, so opposed to dogmatism on any issue that he later modified his
position to the claim that none of the alleged differences between the
mental or moral capacities of the sexes had been proved to be the
inevitable consequences of innate factors, though some of them might

4. *The Subjection of Women*, p. 441 [p. 142].
5. Letter to Alexander Bain, July 14, 1869, *Later Letters, Collected Works*, Vol. 17, p. 1622.
6. *Essays on Sex Equality*, p. 73.

possibly be.[7] His only dogmatic assertion was that nothing was yet certainly known on the subject: "If it be said that the doctrine of the equality of the sexes rests only on theory, it must be remembered that the contrary doctrine has only theory to rest upon."[8]

What "the contrary doctrine" had rested on for millenia, in fact, was a series of assertions about the nature, and natural qualities, of women. Mill points out that these conceptions of the natural woman often differ entirely from one culture to another. In the Orient, women are "by nature" voluptuous, in England, "by nature" cold; in France, they are "naturally" fickle, but in England constant. This in itself is enough to make one question such dogmas. Clearly, women have been assigned different versions of the female role in these different cultures, and their "nature" has been defined accordingly. Thus, Mill argues, it does not get one anywhere in a rational argument to say "that the *nature* of the two sexes adapts them to their present functions and position, and renders these appropriate to them."[9] He asserts emphatically:

> I deny that any one knows or can know, the nature of the two sexes, as long as they have only been seen in their present relation to one another. If men had ever been found in society without women, or women without men, or if there had ever been a society of men and women in which the women were not under the control of the men, something might have been positively known about the mental and moral differences which may be inherent in the nature of each.[1]

Until conditions of equality exist, no one can possibly assess the natural differences between women, distorted as they have been, and men. What is natural to the two sexes can only be found out by allowing both to develop and use their faculties freely. Thus Mill radically dissents from the functionalist definition of women's nature that we have seen prevailing in the works of Aristotle and Rousseau.

In order to analyze the environmental influences on women in contemporary society, Mill returns to his metaphor of human nature as "a tree, which requires to grow and develop itself on all sides." What has been called "the nature of women" is so far from being the result of free development and growth that he likens it to a tree that has been reared with one half in a vapor bath and the other in the snow. It is not natural growth, but "forced repression in some directions, unnatural stimulation in others,"[2] with the aim of pleasing and benefiting men, that have made women into the half-stunted, half-overdeveloped hu-

---

7. In a letter to George Croome Robertson, August 18, 1869, Mill says "it is not certain that the differences spoken of are not partly at least natural ones." *Later Letters, Collected Works*, Vol. 17, p. 1635.
8. *The Subjection of Women*, p. 450 [p. 149].
9. *The Subjection of Women*, pp. 505–506 [pp. 185–86], 451 [p. 149].
1. *The Subjection of Women*, p. 451 [p. 149].
2. *The Subjection of Women*, p. 451 [p. 149].

man beings that they are. In Mill's view, anyone who took the trouble
to consider the very different ways in which contemporary boys and
girls were educated, and their very different assigned tasks in adult life,
could readily explain a great many of the intellectual incapacities and
special moral qualities attributed to women as natural characteristics of
their sex. Those, such as Rousseau, who summarily assessed them as
"naturally" practical and intuitive, capable in small, day-to-day affairs
but lacking in any capacity for rational thought, had only to look at the
way girls were trained to cope with domestic trivia, while boys were
educated in the classics and the sciences. A woman's mistakes were
therefore like those of a self-educated man, who would grasp the
common-sense factors of a situation, some of which might elude the
theorist, but who was likely to suffer from a lack of knowledge of general
principles and of ability to grasp the abstract, conceptual aspect of the
problem.[3] One did not need to look further than the vastly different
environments of the sexes to explain what were almost invariably assumed to be innate differences in their abilities to reason.

Mill was no more prepared to accept as innate the distinctions drawn
in favor of the female character than to accept its allegedly natural
inferiorities. He considered the prevalent nineteenth-century claim that
women are naturally morally superior to men to be just as absurd as
the allegation that they are mentally inferior.[4] Women, like negro
slaves, he says, have had scarcely any opportunity to commit crimes, so
it is not remarkable nor particularly laudable that they have not often
been criminals. Since he believed moral excellence to be "always the
fruit of education and cultivation," to which both sexes were equally
susceptible, he considered that all such "feminine" qualities as unself-
ishness and moral restraint could be explained in terms of women's
particular circumstances of dependence on and accountability to others. He concludes:

> I do not know a more signal instance of the blindness with which
> the world, including the herd of studious men, ignore and pass
> over all the influences of social circumstances, than their silly de-
> preciation of the intellectual, and silly panegyrics on the moral,
> nature of women.[5]

Mill also reacted against the prevailing wisdom, which we have seen
in the writings of Aristotle and Rousseau, that the moral qualities required in women should be different from those required in men. The
piece he had written at the age of eighteen for the *Westminster Review*
had attacked the application of moral standards according to the sex of
the person being judged. It is in order to have their wives entirely

3. *The Subjection of Women*, p. 495 [pp. 149–50].
4. *The Subjection of Women*, pp. 518–519 [pp. 194–95].
5. *The Subjection of Women*, p. 519 [p. 195].

dependent and uncritically devoted to them, he argues, that men have set up an entirely different set of values for them. Thus:

> It is considered meritorious in a man to be independent: to be sufficient to himself; not to be in a constant state of pupillage. In a woman, helplessness, both of mind and of body, is the most admired of attributes. A man is despised, if he be not courageous. In a woman, it is esteemed amiable to be a coward. To be entirely dependent on her husband for every pleasure, and for exemption from every pain; to feel secure, only when under his protection; to be incapable of forming any opinion, or of taking any resolution without his advice and aid; this is amiable, this is delicate, this is feminine: while all who infringe on any of the prerogatives which man thinks proper to reserve to himself; all who can or will be of any use, either to themselves or to the world, otherwise than as the slaves and drudges of their husbands, are called masculine, and other names intended to convey disapprobation.[6]

In contrast to this virtually universal notion of the qualities proper to men and to women, Mill argues in a letter to Thomas Carlyle that in his experience the best people of both sexes have combined the highest so-called "masculine" qualities with the highest of those considered "feminine." He asks, "*Is* there really any distinction between the highest masculine and highest feminine character?"[7] It may not seem remarkable that Mill's conception of morality and excellence was uniform for the two sexes — until one realizes how vast a weight of historical opinion had asserted the opposite. Mill was the first major philosopher since Plato to have argued that goodness was the same in a woman as in a man.

In his attempt to refute the prevailing doctrine that women were innately and irremediably inferior in ability to men, Mill felt greatly hampered by the backward state of psychology. The contemporary preoccupation was with the biological sciences, and there was, he thought, a deplorable lack of attention paid to the influence of environment on the formation of the human character.[8] This had led to far too great a reversal of the Helvétian claim, "l'éducation peut tout," to the point where organic characteristics were now supposed capable of explaining everything. Mill's chief adversary, in his battle to win recognition for the importance of environmental factors in the character-formation of women, was Auguste Comte. The substantial correspondence carried on between the two during 1843 contains an important part of Mill's thinking about this aspect of his case for the emancipation of women.[9] Comte's view was a clear reflection of the confident conviction that

6. *Westminster Review*, Vol. 1, No. 2, April, 1824, p. 526.
7. Letter to Thomas Carlyle, October 5, 1833, *Earlier Letters, Collected Works*, Vol. 12, p. 184.
8. *The Subjection of Women*, pp. 452–453 [pp. 150–51].
9. *Earlier Letters, Collected Works*, Vol. 13, pp. 590–611, and Auguste Comte, *Lettres d'Auguste Comte à John Stuart Mill*, pp. 175–212.

the physical sciences were not just potentially capable of solving all human problems, once their findings were applied by the social sciences, but that they had found practically all the important answers already. Thus Comte was sure that biology was already "able to establish the hierarchy of the sexes, by demonstrating both anatomically and physiologically that, in almost the entire animal kingdom, and especially in our species, the female sex is formed for a state of essential childhood, which renders it necessarily inferior to the corresponding male organism."[1] With a pre-Darwinian confidence in the uniqueness of the human species, he asserts that "the organic condition must certainly prevail, since it is the organism and not the environment that makes us men rather than monkeys or dogs, and which even determines our special type of humanity, to a degree much more circumscribed than has often been believed."[2] Thus, it is not simply for the sake of social expediency that women should be subordinate to men; any other arrangement would be biologically absurd. The causes of all mental characteristics were to be found in the physical organism, the brain, and women, with their physically weaker constitution, must therefore be intellectually inferior to men. Comte granted generously, however, that they were compensated to some extent by being endowed by nature with greater delicacy of feeling and sympathy. They were to be pampered, worshiped, even prayed to, in the society Comte envisaged for the future, but to expect them to be capable of any sort of decision-making or political participation that required reasonable or objective thought, was to go against nature in a way that could only be disastrous both for women and for society as a whole.

Mill, who initially acknowledged the gaps in his knowledge of biology which he was vainly attempting to remedy, adopted a tone that seems extremely humble and conciliatory in contrast to Comte's arrogant confidence in his own convictions.[3] He was simply not prepared to accept, however, the claim that biology had produced any conclusive findings on the subject. He admitted the possibility that it might one day be proved that there are certain physiological differences between the brains of the two sexes, but he stressed in answering Comte that there was, as yet, no definite knowledge of the precise relationship between the physical characteristics of a brain and the intellectual powers of its owner. To rely on such an oversimplification as the contention that men, being bigger than women, have bigger brains and therefore greater mental powers, was to lay oneself open to the charge that big

---

1. *Lettres*, p. 175 (my translation).
2. *Lettres*, p. 199.
3. He reports having read several volumes of the biologist, Gall, during the correspondence. Comte assumes the superior attitude that the only explanation for the divergent opinions of two such great thinkers on such a fundamental subject is that Mill is going through a passing phase, from which he will soon, no doubt, recover. *Lettres*, p. 184.

men are more intelligent than little ones, and whales and elephants more intelligent than either.[4]

Mill was convinced that the sort of reasoning that Comte was engaged in was likely to produce no sound conclusions about the differences between the sexes, as long as the study of the environmental influences on personal development, or ethology, remained so neglected. In *The Subjection of Women* he speaks urgently of the need for the advancement of this science, saying that "of all the difficulties which impede the progress of thought, and the formation of well-grounded opinions on life and social arrangements, the greatest is now the unspeakable ignorance of mankind in respect to the influences which form human character."[5] He was not under any illusions about the difficulty of carrying out such a study, with its problems of isolating causal factors in a sphere in which experimental laboratory conditions are impossible. Despite the difficulties, however, he was convinced that this area of science must not continue to be so neglected, and in the *Logic*, he set out some preliminary ideas for such a science, though he went no further in carrying it into operation.[6] Meanwhile, until that science was well advanced, he argued that none of the intellectual and moral differences between the sexes could reasonably be said to be caused by innate, physiological factors. "No one," he writes bluntly in *The Subjection of Women*, "is thus far entitled to any positive opinion on the subject."[7]

Thus, with knowledge in its limited state, it could certainly not be demonstrated that women were incapable of the same levels of intellectual achievement as men. Such a belief could in no way be regarded as just grounds for keeping them subordinate in society, and denying them all opportunity to show what they could in fact achieve. Further, Mill argues, in many fields women had already achieved a considerable measure of success, despite the weight of circumstance, lack of education, and force of prejudice which worked against them. Though this was to rest the case on very humble grounds, "when we consider how sedulously they are all trained away from, instead of being trained towards, any of the occupations or objects reserved for men,"[8] he cites the achievements of women such as Mme. de Staël and George Sand in the field of literature, and applied his argument most forcefully to the case of politics, in which women had proved their competence at the top executive level. Here one was not confined to speculation about what women might be capable of if suitably educated; what women

---

4. Mill adds, for the benefit of those who are impressed by such statistics, that he knows of a man who has weighed many human brains, the heaviest of which was that of a woman. *The Subjection of Women*, p. 503 [p. 184].
5. *The Subjection of Women*, p. 452 [p. 150].
6. *Logic*, pp. 451–463.
7. *The Subjection of Women*, p. 453 [p. 151].
8. *The Subjection of Women*, p. 489 [p. 175].

had achieved in the political sphere was in itself most persuasive evidence of what they could do. At the top political level, Mill points out, which is practically the only sphere of public affairs to which they have ever been admitted, the great qualities of a proportionately larger number of queens than kings has demonstrated that "exactly where and in proportion as women's capacities for government have been tried, in that proportion have they been found adequate."[9] Citing such examples as Deborah, Joan of Arc, Elizabeth, and Margaret of Austria, he argues that these and other women who have been expert governors or leaders make it quite ridiculous to regard their sex as unfit to participate on all other levels of political life. For their potential in the field has already been demonstrated to be at least equal to that of men.

Of all the spheres of human endeavor, Mill asserts that there are very few in which, however little opportunity they have had to prove themselves, some women at least have not reached a very high level of accomplishment. The fact that they have not, so far, achieved first-class works of genius and originality can, he says, be explained by their lack of the thorough education which is prerequisite to reaching original conclusions once all the first principles in a field are established, by the fact that women are traditionally expected to be always available to minister to the needs of men and children, and therefore seldom have sustained periods in which to concentrate, and by the circumstances of their coming, like the Romans after the Greeks, second to men chronologically in all fields of study and art. For these reasons, he regards what women have achieved as conclusive proof of what they can do, but refuses to treat what they have not so far achieved as conclusive proof of anything at all.

Mill does not consider that he has closed the case for female equality by showing his contemporaries that their grounds for discriminating against women are scientifically undemonstrable, and in many cases contradicted by the facts of history. For, as he points out in the last chapter of *Utilitarianism*, people in general have showed themselves consistently unwilling to admit to the injustice of any social discrimination, until they are convinced that it is also inexpedient. Thus, Mill feels obliged to argue not only that the discriminatory treatment of women has no rational basis in the natures of the sexes, but that it is socially harmful as well, and that to treat women as equals would be beneficial for the happiness and advancement of all. Justice, then, like liberty, is linked in Mill's feminist arguments with the constant theme of the improvement of mankind.

The unjust treatment of women has, Mill argues in *The Subjection of Women*, the detrimental effect that they attempt to gain influence in subversive ways, and to use it for selfish purposes, as happens in other

---

9. *The Subjection of Women*, p. 493 [p. 178].

cases in which legitimate access to power is denied.[1] Under existing conditions within the family, he argues, women are forced to resort to cunning and underhand tactics in order to have their wishes fulfilled, when they and their husbands disagree. There exists no motivation to discuss such issues openly and rationally, since the husband is legally constituted as the family's decision-maker. As far as women's political influence is concerned, Mill is sure that the indirect influence they exert, through their pressure on their enfranchised husbands, is bound to be unconcerned with the welfare of anyone beyond their own immediate families. Thus he, unlike Rousseau, recognizes that the outside world has no hope of winning over the family in the conflict of loyalties that unenfranchised women face. For "their social position allows them no scope for any feelings beyond the family except personal likings & dislikes, & it is assumed that they would be governed entirely by these in their judgment & feeling in political matters."[2] But if they were themselves enfranchised, and thereby given their own legitimate means of influencing the political process, Mill argues, they would in the course of time become far more likely to use these means responsibly and in a more humanitarian spirit. "It is precisely by creating in their minds a concern for the interests which are common to all, those of their country and of human improvement, that the tendency to look upon all questions as personal questions would most effectively be corrected."[3] Convinced by de Tocqueville's impressions of the educative effects of political participation, he is sure that women who were to exercise their political rights would "receive that stimulus to their faculties, and that widening and liberalizing influence over their feelings and sympathies, which the suffrage seldom fails to produce on those who are admitted to it."[4] Thus, by granting women the vote, society would benefit doubly. It would minimize the selfish and narrow influences that many of them already exerted, via their husbands, and it would increase the selflessness and responsibility of the electorate as a whole.

Mill argues, too, that the abolition of the legal inequality of husband and wife would have immeasurable effects on the value of the family as an educative institution. Since he believes that "society in equality is its normal state," and moreover that "the only school of genuine moral sentiment is society between equals,"[5] he considers that the everyday assumption by men of their superiority over women constantly detracts from the value of their own lives as well as those of their wives,

1. *The Subjection of Women*, p. 536 [p. 207], 544 [pp. 211–12].
2. Letter to T. E. Cliffe Leslie, October 5, 1869, *Later Letters, Collected Works*, Vol. 17, p. 1643.
3. Letter to Cliffe Leslie, p. 1643.
4. "Speech of John Stuart Mill, M.P., on the Admission of Women to the Electoral Franchise," p. 12. See also *Representative Government*, pp. 292–293.
5. *The Subjection of Women*, p. 477 [p. 167].

and has very harmful effects on their children. There can be nothing approaching the highest potential of human companionship between two human beings, one of whom is convinced a priori of his greater capacities and value, and of the justice of his always taking precedence over the other. What hope, Mill asks, is there for the moral advancement of society, so long as the domestic atmosphere in which all its members receive their earliest moral education is based on such an unjust distribution of rights and powers? Only when marriage were to become recognized by law and society as a cooperative partnership between equals, might the family at last become, for the children, "a school of sympathy in equality, of living together in love, without power on one side and obedience on the other." Only then could children be prepared for what he regards as the "true virtue of human beings," that is, "fitness to live together as equals."[6]

In spite of these protestations about equality within the family, however, it is in fact because of John Stuart Mill's assumptions and convictions about the family and its traditional roles that his feminism falls short of advocating true equality and freedom for married women. Mill's feminist writings are, implicitly, concerned only with middle- and upper-class women, and it is the bourgeois family that is his model.[7] Though he rejects the legalized inequalities of its patriarchal form, he regards the family itself as "essential for humanity,"[8] and is concerned to reassure his readers that family life has nothing to fear, but rather much to gain, from the complete political and civil equality of the sexes. Though presently "a school of despotism," once justly constituted, it would be "the real school of the virtues of freedom."[9]

Moreover, Mill argues in favor of the traditional division of labor within the family. While he asserts that women should have a real choice of a career or marriage, he assumes that the majority of women are likely to continue to prefer marriage, and that this choice is equivalent to choosing a career. He states:

> Like a man when he chooses a profession, so, when a woman marries, it may in general be understood that she makes choice of the management of a household, and the bringing up of a family, as the first call upon her exertions, during as many years of her life as may be required for the purpose; and that she renounces,

6. *The Subjection of Women*, p. 479 [pp. 167–68].
7. This is clear from the way he argues (*The Subjection of Women*, p. 483) [pp. 170–71] that the husband should earn the family's income (since most working class women then as now had no choice whether to work outside the home or not), as well as from the fact that the general preoccupations of his feminist writings are mainly the concerns of middle-class women, rather than issues such as wages, which he was well aware were far lower for women than men (*Principles of Political Economy*, pp. 394–396).
8. Letter to Emile de Laveleye, September 9, 1869, *Later Letters, Collected Works*, Vol. 17, p. 1638.
9. *The Subjection of Women*, p. 479 [p. 168].

not all other objects and occupations, but all which are not consistent with the requirements of this.[1]

In keeping with this mode of thinking, Mill asserts that there is an
"infinitely closer relationship of a child to its mother than to its father,"[2]
and that "nothing can replace the mother for the education of children."[3] He does not pause to reflect that the qualities of motherhood,
just as much as any of the other existing differences between the sexes,
might be at least partly due to environmental factors, most particularly
to the conditioning that resulted from customary modes of socialization.
Again, in spite of his general rejection of the pressures of opinion, he
calmly accepts that the sexual division of duties within the family is
"already made by consent, or at all events not by law, but by general
custom," and he defends it as "the most suitable division of labour
between the two persons."[4]

In Mill's early essay on marriage and divorce, this position is put
much more dogmatically than later, and in terms which he could not
consistently use in *The Subjection of Women*. This, then, is one area
in which it seems highly likely that the way he stated his views (though
not their substance) was modified by the divergent ideas of Harriet
Taylor. For in 1832, having just asserted that "there is no natural inequality between the sexes," he goes on to say that, in a home where
there are no servants, it is "good and will *naturally* take place . . . that
the mistress of a family shall herself do the work of servants," and "the
mother is the *natural* teacher." He concludes, with little attention to
their own preferences, that "the great occupation of women should be
to beautify life . . . and to diffuse beauty, elegance and grace everywhere," since women are "*naturally*" endowed with greater elegance
and taste.[5]

By the time he wrote *The Subjection of Women*, Mill could no longer
assert that women's domestic role is natural, in so many words, since
in that work he clearly recognizes the invalidity and fraudulence of
identifying the natural with the conventional and then using appeals to
woman's "nature" in order to justify her conventional functions. Despite changes in terminology, however, with "most suitable" and "desirable custom" replacing the appeals to nature, the substance of Mill's
ideas remained unchanged. In those days of primitive contraceptive
techniques, a high rate of infant mortality, and onerous household
chores, it would have been far harder for Mill than it is for us to

1. *The Subjection of Women*, p. 484 [p. 171].
2. Letter to Isabella Beecher Hooker, September 14, 1869, *Later Letters, Collected Works*, Vol.
   17, p. 1640.
3. Letter to Princess Marie Stcherbatov and Associates, December 18, 1868, *Later Letters, Collected Works*, Vol. 17, p. 1528.
4. *The Subjection of Women*, pp. 473–474 [p. 164], 483 [p. 171].
5. *Essays on Sex Equality*, pp. 73–77 (emphasis added).

conceive of the sharing of child rearing and domestic duties. However, it is striking that Mill chose not to question the family and the way it had developed, in any way, or to consider the relationship between the institution of the bourgeois family itself and the contemporary position of women in society. For, clearly, it was no dictate of nature that had led to the formation of the isolated private household, with its "woman's work," and the professional and industrial world of "man's work" outside, and to the vast separation between these two spheres. Mill's assumption of the immutability of the existing family structure, and his failure to discuss its repercussions for the lives of women, constitutes a gap in his feminist thought which the current feminist movement is attempting to remedy.

Mill's acceptance of traditional sex roles within the family places serious limitations on the extent to which he can apply the principles of freedom and equality to married women. First, though he argues in favor of equal property *rights* for married women, these are rights to property inherited or earned by the woman herself, not rights to equal shares in the family income. "The rule," Mill says, "is simple: whatever would be the husband's or wife's if they were not married, should be under their exclusive control during marriage."[6] Clearly, then, the income of the male earner is his, as much after marriage as before, and Mill does not recognize the anomaly that women's work in the home is unpaid labor. Only in *The Enfranchisement of Women* do we find the assertion that it is not only necessary for married women to be able to earn their own subsistence, but that their position in the family would improve significantly "if women both earned, and had the right to possess, a part of the income of the family."[7] Although in *The Subjection of Women* Mill agrees that married women must be able to support themselves, he explicitly rejects the idea that they should actually do so, regarding such a practice as liable to lead to the neglect of the household and children. It seems, therefore, highly likely that the idea stated in the earlier work is Harriet Taylor's, and it is an example where her thought is considerably more in tune than Mill's with present day feminism. She recognizes, as he does not, the importance to women of continuous economic independence, both within the marital relationship, and in case of its disintegration.

Second, Mill's defense of traditional sex roles within the family amounts to a denial of freedom of opportunity and individual expression of talents to that majority of women whom he assumes would always choose to marry. Though he is so much aware that the care of a household is an incessantly preoccupying duty that he cites it as a major reason for women's comparative lack of achievement in many artistic fields, he in fact condones the continuance of this barrier for

6. *The Subjection of Women*, p. 482 [p. 170].
7. *Essays on Sex Equality*, p. 105, text and note.

most women.[8] His refusal to concede that the tiresome details of domestic life should be shared by both sexes, and his failure to question the social institutions that made such sharing practically impossible are striking in the light of the fact that he recognizes that the principal means by which women would come to be recognized as equals was via success in fields formerly monopolized by men. As he writes to Harriet Taylor, the only way of dispelling most people's prejudicial beliefs about women's inferiority is by showing them "more and greater proofs by example of what women can do."[9] If the great majority of women are to remain practically if not legally barred from such achievements, how might these deep-rooted prejudices ever be expected to change?

Here again, *The Enfranchisement of Women* is a more radical document than the work written after Harriet Taylor's death. This essay written in collaboration speaks out more strongly than Mill alone ever did in favor of the married woman's need to have a life and a career of her own, so as not to be "a mere appendage to a man," attached to him "for the purpose of bringing up *his* children, and making *his* home pleasant to him."[1] These were probably aspects of his wife's thought with which Mill did not feel at all comfortable.

John Stuart Mill tried fervently to apply the principles of liberalism to women. He eschewed patriarchy within the family, and the legal and political subordination of women, as anachronisms in the modern age and as gross violations of liberty and justice. However, although a very forward-looking feminist in many respects, he in no way perceived the injustice involved in institutions and practices which allowed a man to have a career and economic independence, *and* a home life and children, but which forced a woman to choose between the two. His refusal to question the traditional family and its demands on women set the limits of his liberal feminism.

---

8. *The Subjection of Women*, pp. 502 [pp. 183–84], 514–515 [p. 192]. He says: "The superintendence of a household . . . requires incessant vigilance, an eye which no detail escapes, and presents questions for consideration and solution, foreseen and unforeseen, at every hour of the day, from which the person responsible for them can hardly ever shake herself free."
9. *Later Letters, Collected Works*, Vol. 14, p. 12.
1. *Essays on Sex Equality*, p. 107.

John Stuart Mill:
A Chronology

1806	Mill born May 20; Napoleon defeats Prussian army at Jena and becomes master of Europe.
1809	Mill's education begins with his learning Greek.
1815	Final defeat of Napoleon; widespread economic distress in Britain with the ending of the war.
1819	James Mill joins the East India Company; in the "Peterloo Massacre," a local militia kills workers who were protesting economic misery.
1823	J. S. Mill joins the East India Company.
1826–?	Mill's "mental crisis."
1829	Passage of Catholic Emancipation Act.
1830	The July Revolution removes the last Bourbon king of France and installs Louis-Philippe; Mill meets Harriet Taylor, wife of John Taylor.
1831	January–May, "The Spirit of the Age" published in the *Examiner*.
1832	The First Reform Act passed.
1836	Mill publishes "Civilization" and his review of *Democracy in America*, vol. 1; James Mill dies.
1838	Mill publishes "Bentham."
1840	Mill publishes "Coleridge" and his review of *Democracy in America*, vol. 2.
1843	Mill publishes *A System of Logic*.
1848	Revolution in France briefly establishes a republican government; Mill publishes *Principles of Political Economy*.
1849	John Taylor dies.
1851	Mill marries Harriet Taylor; Louis Bonaparte seizes power in a coup and is subsequently acclaimed as Emperor Napoleon III.
1858	Mill retires from the East India Company on its dissolution; Harriet dies at Avignon.
1859	Mill publishes *On Liberty*.
1861	Mill publishes *Utilitarianism*.
1862	Mill publishes *Considerations on Representative Government*.

1865	Mill is elected Liberal MP for Westminister.
1867	Second Reform Act passed; Mill tries unsuccessfully to extend suffrage to women.
1868	Mill loses seat at general election.
1869	Mill publishes *The Subjection of Women*.
1870–71	Franco-Prussian War and Paris Commune.
1873	Death of Mill, May 6; posthumous publication of his *Autobiography*.

Selected Bibliography

This is a very small selection of Mill's work and of commentaries on Mill. It is intended essentially for undergraduate use; for more advanced work, *The Collected Works of John Stuart Mill* in thirty-two volumes from the University of Toronto Press (1963–94) is indispensable (cited as CW followed by the volume number). The best bibliographic resource for commentaries is the *Mill Newsletter*, published from 1963 until it was incorporated in the journal *Utilitas* in 1988.

I have annotated the bibliography where Mill's work is concerned, to relate it to the works reprinted here, and where commentaries are concerned, to relate them to the following issues: (1) whether *On Liberty* is at odds with Mill's utilitarian moral philosophy, (2) whether *On Liberty* is at odds with Mill's wider political allegiances, (3) whether Mill's defense of individual liberty is elitist and antidemocratic, (4) the role of Harriet Taylor in forming Mill's later moral and political outlook, and (5) the adequacy of the feminism of *The Subjection of Women*. The first issue in particular has given rise to a large literature on Mill's conception of the "harm" that law and public opinion are supposed to protect us against, whether this is to be analyzed in terms of "interests" and, if so, what those interests are.

I have decided not to add modern, non-Mill-related discussions of the issues raised by Mill's work—the scope and limits of free speech, why the state ought not to be the provider of education, feminism and the family, the nature of spiritual and intellectual authority, the legitimacy of antidrug legislation and of laws that create "victimless crimes," and so on—because the issues are just too numerous. Readers thinking about subjects ranging from the First Amendment to the lawfulness of assisted suicide will find much inspiration in Mill; it is less often that late-twentieth-century discussion sheds much light on Mill.

ESSAYS AND SHORT WORKS BY MILL RELATED TO "THE SPIRIT OF THE AGE," ON LIBERTY, AND THE SUBJECTION OF WOMEN

"On Marriage" (1832–33?), unpublished, printed in CW, vol. 21, 35–49. An early essay on the wickedness of loveless and conventional marriage.

"Tocqueville on Democracy in America [vol. 1]," *London Review* (1835), reprinted in CW, vol. 18, 47–90. This and "Democracy" vol. 2 not only analyze Tocqueville's great book but take to heart Tocqueville's warning that "the tyranny of the majority" can take over the individual's own character. Vol. 2 is markedly less friendly to democratic government than is vol. 1.

"Civilization," *London and Westminster Review* (1836), reprinted in CW, vol. 18, 116–47. This, together with "Bentham" and "Coleridge," expresses the anxiety expressed in "The Spirit of the Age" that the age lacks spiritual authority; like *On Liberty*, it expresses a fear that the age is one of "masses" rather than individuals.

"Bentham," *London and Westminster Review* (1838), reprinted in CW, vol. 10, 75–115. A fierce critique of what Mill believes to be the spiritual thinness and unconcern for character in Bentham's utilitarianism.

"Coleridge," *London and Westminster Review* (1840), reprinted in CW, vol. 10, 117–63. A companion piece to "Bentham"; Coleridge's spiritual vision and his account of what makes for a national spiritual unity are set out as a necessary complement to Bentham's reformism.

"Tocqueville on Democracy in America [vol. 2]," *Edinburgh Review* (1840), reprinted in CW, vol. 18, 153–204. See the note to vol. 1.

"Statement on Marriage" (1851), unpublished, printed in CW, vol. 21, 96–98. Another statement of Mill's distaste for conventional marriage arrangements, written on the occasion of his marriage to Harriet Taylor. It shows the emotions that fueled *The Subjection of Women*.

"Remarks on Mr. Fitzroy's Bill for the More Effectual Prevention of Assaults on Women and Children" (1853), a privately printed pamphlet, reprinted in CW, vol. 21, 99–108. Mill was passionately opposed to the casual way in which the law treated violence within the family. This pamphlet suggests the emotions that lay behind *The Subjection of Women* and *On Liberty*'s insistence that families exist to benefit children, not to gratify their parents.

"The Contagious Diseases Acts" (1871), evidence before the Royal Commission of 1870 on the operation of the Contagious Diseases Acts of 1866 and 1869, reprinted in CW, vol. 21, 349–

71. The act allowed prostitutes in the vicinity of naval yards and army barracks to be arrested and inspected for venereal disease; Mill thought this singled out women unfairly and let their male customers off too lightly.

Wishy, Bernard. *Prefaces to Liberty*. Boston, 1959. Of the many anthologies of Mill's work, this one is particularly valuable because it reprints many more of Mill's ephemeral writings relevant to the essay than are mentioned here.

BOOKS BY MILL

A System of Logic (1843), reprinted in CW, vols. 7–8. Mill's major philosophical treatise; book VI sets out Mill's views on the proper methods of social science; chapter 2 in particular gives an elaborate account of Mill's views on the self-formation of character. Chapter 12 sets out the several branches of utilitarian ethics in a way that makes it at least plausible that *On Liberty* can be given a utilitarian justification.

Principles of Political Economy (1848), reprinted in CW, vols. 2–3. Mill's treatise on economic theory; relevant to *On Liberty* are the long chapter "The Probable Futurity of the Labouring Classes" (book IV, chapter 7), where Mill looks forward to a libertarian socialism brought about by workers who wish to be *self*-managing, and the whole of book V, in which Mill explores the ways in which government action can avoid subverting individual initiative.

Considerations on Representative Government (1861), reprinted in CW, vol. 19. The other face of *On Liberty*; Mill produces an account of liberal democracy in which elements of local participation are balanced by a strikingly elitist and expert-driven national legislature and administration.

Utilitarianism (1862), reprinted in CW, vol. 10. A remarkably short work for the controversy it has aroused; chapter 5 sets out an account of rights that may underlie *On Liberty*. D. G. Brown, John Gray, J. C. Rees, and Alan Ryan have all explored this possibility (see entries below).

Auguste Comte and Positivism (1865), reprinted in CW, vol. 10. Mill used many of Comte's insights in his *Logic* but came to think of his work as "liberticide."

On Socialism [*Chapters on Socialism*] (1879), reprinted with an Introduction by Lewis S. Feuer. Buffalo, 1976.

GENERAL WORKS ON MILL'S LIFE AND THOUGHT

Anschutz, R. P. *The Philosophy of J. S. Mill*. Oxford, 1953. One of the first commentaries to take seriously the connection between Mill's *Logic* and his ethics and to emphasize Harriet Taylor's role in Mill's work.

Bain, Alexander. *John Stuart Mill: A Criticism*. London, 1889. Bain was Mill's disciple, but a critical one. The book is still more than a period piece.

Berger, Fred. *Happiness, Justice and Freedom*, Berkeley, 1984. The best recent commentary on the relationship between Mill's utilitarianism and his defence of freedom. It also includes a good discussion of *The Subjection of Women*.

Britton, Karl. *John Stuart Mill*. Harmondsworth, 1953. A short, clear, and careful account of Mill's entire system.

Carlisle, Janice. *John Stuart Mill and the Writing of Character*. Athens, Ga., 1991. Written by a literary critic, a book that provides an unusual perspective both on how Mill's views about character worked out in his own life and how they illuminate his moral and political theory.

Cumming, Robert Dennon. *Human Nature and History: A Study of the Development of Liberal Political Thought*. Chicago, 1969.

Duncan, Graeme. *Marx and Mill*. Cambridge, 1974. The title suggests the contents; a useful analysis of the consistency of Mill's moral and political theory and a particularly good account of his doubts about democracy.

Hamburger, Joseph. *Intellectuals in Politics: John Stuart Mill and the Philosophic Radicals*. New Haven, 1965. A valuable historical account of the period from 1830 to 1840 during which Mill was in revolt against "Benthamism."

McCloskey, H. J. *John Stuart Mill: A Critical Study*. London, 1971. A short, clear, hostile account of Mill's ethics and politics.

Packe, M. St. J. *The Life of John Stuart Mill*. London, 1954. A rather romantic account of Mill's life, but highly readable and full of useful clues to Mill's development.

Robson, John A. *The Improvement of Mankind: The Social and Political Thought of John Stuart Mill*. London, 1968. An excellent mix of biographical and philosophical analysis; sets Mill's ideas in context in a way few philosophical treatments do.

Ryan, Alan. *The Philosophy of John Stuart Mill*. London, 1970. Argues for the consistency of Mill's utilitarianism and his libertarianism.

Ryan, Alan. *J. S. Mill*. London, 1974. An introduction to all of Mill's work, with chapters on his early reaction against Benthamism as well as on utilitarianism and *On Liberty* and *The Subjection of Women*.

Skorupski, John. *John Stuart Mill*. London, 1992. The best and most up-to-date account of Mill's philosophy of logic and science, but it also contains an excellent analysis of Mill's utilitarianism and liberalism.

Thomas, William. *Mill*. Oxford, 1984. A brief biography and analysis of Mill's leading ideas by a distinguished historian.

Von Hayek, F. A. *John Stuart Mill and Harriet Taylor: Their Correspondence and Subsequent Marriage*. Chicago, 1951. This remains the most valuable source for an understanding of Mill's emotional and intellectual debts to Harriet Taylor.

Wood, John Cunningham. *John Stuart Mill: Critical Assessments*. London, 1987.

WORKS ON "THE SPIRIT OF THE AGE"

Friedman, R. B. "Mill's Theory of Authority." In J. B. Schneewind, ed., *Mill: A Collection of Critical Essays*. London, 1968. The only full-length attempt to reconstruct the theory of intellectual and spiritual authority implicit in "The Spirit of the Age."

Himmelfarb, Gertrude. "Introduction." In her *Essays on Culture and Society*. New York, 1963, vii–xxiv. Himmelfarb is the leading exponent of the doctrine of "the two Mills," one a balanced and pragmatic liberal, the other, overinfluenced by Harriet Taylor, a libertarian radical. This and the next entry make the same case as the extract from *On Liberty and Liberalism* reprinted here (see p. 279).

Himmelfarb, Gertrude. "The Other John Stuart Mill." In her *Victorian Minds*. New York, 1968. See note to the last entry.

WORKS ON *ON LIBERTY*

Anderson, Elizabeth. "J. S. Mill and Experiments in Living." *Ethics* 102 (1991), 1–26. Raises some sharp questions about the plausibility of Mill's belief that such experiments will yield the results he expects.

Archard, David. "Freedom not to be Free: The Case of the Slavery Contract in J. S. Mill's *On Liberty*." *Philosophical Quarterly* 40 (1990), 453–65. Mill handles the case of the man who wishes to see himself into slavery somewhat awkwardly (see pp. 121–22); this is a recent attempt to do the job better.

Arneson, Richard. "Mill versus Paternalism." *Ethics* 90 (1981), 470–89. Defends *On Liberty*'s uncompromising hostility to paternalism but agrees with Archard (see last entry) that Mill's handling of the slavery example is awkward.

Berlin, Isaiah. *Four Essays on Liberty*. Oxford, 1969. In addition to the essay printed here (see p. 253) — the most famous statement of the view that *On Liberty* cannot be squared with utilitarianism — other essays are "Two Concepts of Liberty," "Historical Inevitability," and "Political Ideas in the Twentieth Century." Only "Two Concepts" is directly relevant to Mill.

Brown, D. G. "Mill on Liberty and Morality." *Philosophical Review*, 81 (1972), 133–58. A careful statement of the view that *On Liberty* can be given a utilitarian defense if we follow Mill's analysis of the distinction between the various elements of utilitarian evaluation. See also the entries for Gray, Rees, and Ryan.

Brown, D. G. "Mill on Harm to Others' Interests." *Political Studies* 26 (1978) 395–99. Analyzes and dissents from John Rees's view that it is not mere distress, but harm to our *interests* that Mill is concerned with.

Chopra, Y. N. "Mill's Principle of Liberty." *Philosophy* 69 (1994) 417–41. The most recent attempt to explicate just which interests Mill wants to protect with his "harm principle."

Cooper, Wesley E., et al., eds. *New Essays on John Stuart Mill and Utilitarianism*. Toronto, 1979. Many of these essays are quite narrowly directed toward the subject matter suggested by the title, but David Lyons's "Liberty and Harm to Others," F. R. Berger's "John Stuart Mill on Justice and Fairness," and Jan Narveson's "Rights and Utilitarianism," very usefully discuss Mill's claim that only harm or the threat of harm gives society the right to coerce its individual members.

Cowling, Maurice. *Mill and Liberalism*. Cambridge, 1963. An eccentric but interesting argument to the effect that *On Liberty* is anything but liberal and, particularly, that its purpose is to drive Christianity out of political life in Britain.

Feinberg, Joel. *The Moral Limits of the Criminal Law*. 4 vols. New York, 1984–88. Ranges far beyond Mill, but deepens the discussion of "harm to others" and "offense" as grounds for coercion.

Gray, John H. "John Stuart Mill on Liberty, Utility and Rights." In J. Roland Pennock and John W. Chapman, eds., *Nomos XXIII, Human Rights*. New York, 1981. A shorter version of the argument presented in the next entry.

354   SELECTED BIBLIOGRAPHY

Gray, John H. *Mill on Liberty: A Defence*. London, 1983. An intricate and imaginative development of the argument for the consistency of utilitarianism and liberalism; it deepens both the analysis of utilitarianism and the analysis of Mill's view of our "interests."

Griffiths, A. Phillips, ed. *Of Liberty*. Cambridge, 1983. A set of essays provoked by rather than directly about Mill's essay. David Lloyd-Thomas's essay "Rights, Consequences, and Mill on Liberty" is a useful account of a central difficulty; and Peter Gardner's "Liberty and Compulsory Education" explores an important area of application from a libertarian standpoint more radical than Mill's.

Himmelfarb, Gertrude. *On Liberty and Liberalism*. New York, 1974. A hostile account of *On Liberty* and its impact on our society, arguing that it largely reflects Harriet Taylor's views, that it is a narrow-minded tract in the same style as *The Subjection of Women*, and that its effect has been to undermine civility and social order.

Honderich, Ted. "Mill on Liberty." *Inquiry* 10 (1967), 292–97. An early exploration of the problem of squaring Mill's absolute principle of liberty with his (equally absolute) commitment to utilitarianism.

Honderich, Ted. "The Worth of Mill's *On Liberty*." *Political Studies* 22 (1974), 463–70. Continues the discussion started in the last entry and continued in the next entry.

Honderich, Ted. "On Liberty and Morality-Dependent Harms." *Political Studies* 30 (1982), 504–12. A standing problem in utilitarian is whether to count the distress people feel only because of moral values they hold as a "harm" for utilitarian purposes. Honderich argues that contra Wollheim and Ten, Mill did not rule out all such distress as a candidate for protection.

Letwin, Shirley. *The Pursuit of Certainty*. Cambridge, 1965. A criticism of the rationalism that Letwin sees underlying *On Liberty*, developed along the lines of Michael Oakeshott's *Rationalism in Politics*.

McCloskey, H. J. "Mill's Liberalism." *Philosophical Quarterly* 13 (1963), 143–56. Argues that *On Liberty* is at odds with Mill's utilitarianism.

Rees, John C. "A Re-reading of Mill on Liberty." *Political Studies* 8 (1960), 113–29; reprinted here (see p. 294). See note to his 1985 text.

Rees, John C. *John Stuart Mill's On Liberty*. Oxford, 1985. Contains all Rees's essays on Mill's *On Liberty*, including his 1960 essay, which first stated the argument that it was only harm to *interests* that Mill counted as "harm," and his 1987 essay, which criticizes Himmelfarb's argument for the existence of two mutually incompatible Mills. Students with historical interests will find the essay on "Mill and his Early Critics" fascinating, too.

Rees, John C. "The Thesis of the Two Mills." *Political Studies* 25 (1987), 369–82. See note to his 1985 text.

Ryan, Alan. "Mr. McCloskey on Mill's Liberalism." *Philosophical Quarterly* 14 (1964), 253–60. Response to McCloskey's 1963 essay, making a version of the case put forward in Rees's 1987 essay.

Ryan, Alan. "Mill and the Art of Living." *The Listener* (1965), 620–22. A very brief statement of the view that *On Liberty* is a utilitarian work.

Smith, G. W. "The Logic of J. S. Mill on Freedom." *Political Studies* 28 (1990), 238–52. Argues against Mill's claim that *On Liberty*'s case for freedom is independent of *A System of Logic*'s analysis of freedom of will.

Ten, C. L. "Mill on Self-Regarding Actions." *Philosophy* 43 (1968), 29–37. Argues that the "harm" that law and opinion are intended to prevent must be direct, not mediated by moral attitudes.

Ten, C. L. "Mill and Liberty." *Journal of the History of Ideas* 30 (1973), 47–68. Courteous demolition of Himmelfarb's theory of the "two Mills" and a careful reconstruction of Mill's account of interests.

Ten, C. L. *Mill on Liberty*. Oxford, 1980. Excellent book-length treatment of Mill; friendly to Mill but sceptical of the coherence of his arguments and the consistency of *Utilitarianism* and *On Liberty*.

Waldron, Jeremy. "Mill and the Value of Moral Distress." *Political Studies* 35 (1987), 410–23; reprinted here (see p. 311). Carries the argument about "harm" still further; not only is it not one of our interests to be protected from shock, it is in our interest to be shocked.

Wollheim, Richard. "John Stuart Mill and Isaiah Berlin: The Ends of Life and the Preliminaries of Morality." In Alan Ryan, ed., *The Idea of Freedom*, Oxford, 1972. Argues that Mill's sophisticated utilitarianism supports the arguments of *On Liberty*, contrary to Berlin's essay printed here (see p. 253).

Wollheim, Richard. "John Stuart Mill and the Limits of State Action." *Social Research* 7 (1973), 1–30. Criticizes the interpretations of the idea of "harm" offered by Rees and Ten.

Wolff, Robert Paul. *The Poverty of Liberalism*. Boston, 1965. A short criticism of liberalism in general; attacks Mill's *On Liberty* for excessive individualism.

Wolff, Robert Paul, Barrington Moore Jr., and Herbert Marcuse. *A Critique of Pure Tolerance*. Boston, 1965. See note to last entry.

WORKS ON *THE SUBJECTION OF WOMEN*

Annas, Julia. "Mill and the Subjection of Women." *Philosophy* 52 (1977), 179–94. Argues that more attention should be paid to the essay, but criticizes Mill's acceptance of a domestic role for most women.

Brownmiller, Susan. "Introduction." In J. S. Mill, *The Subjection of Women*, Greenwich, Conn., 1971, 5–11. Short, general introduction to the text.

Caine, Barbara. "John Stuart Mill and the English Women's Movement." *Historical Studies* 18 (1976), 52–62. Lively and interesting account of the (not always admirable) activities of Mill and his stepdaughter Helen Taylor in the various committees for women's suffrage, education, and the repeal of the Contagious Diseases Acts.

Cameron, Barbara. "Mill's Treatment of Women, Workers and Private Property." *Canadian Journal of Political Science* 13 (1981), 775–83. A short essay, following up Hughes's 1980 argument that Mill's radicalism is undermined by his commitment to an economic regime of private property and competition.

Collini, Stefan. "J. S. Mill on the Subjection of Women." *History Today* 34 (1984), 34–39. Lively account of the methodological problems of the essay.

Hughes, Patricia. "The Reality versus the Ideal." *Canadian Journal of Political Science* 12 (1980), 523–42. See note to Cameron.

Jaggar, Alison. *Feminist Politics and Human Nature*. Brighton, 1983. A classical modern restatement of a liberal feminism of a "Millian" kind.

Millet, Kate. "The Debate over Women: Ruskin versus Mill." *Victorian Studies* 14 (1969), 63–82. Another version of Millet's 1970 argument.

Millet, Kate. "Mill versus Ruskin." In her *Sexual Politics*. New York, 1970, 126–51. Perhaps too unkind to Ruskin, but the account that did more than any other to find Mill new readers.

Okin, Susan Moller. *Women in Western Political Thought*. Princeton, 1979. The book covers the field from Plato to Nato; Mill receives modified praise as a genuine egalitarian, but one who was too uncritical of the family.

Rendall, Jane. *The Origins of Modern Feminism*. New York, 1984. Chapter 8 discusses Mill.

Ring, Jennifer. "Mill's *The Subjection of Women*: The Methodological Limits of Liberal Feminism." *Review of Politics* 47 (1984), 27–44. Argues that Mill's feminism is undermined by his subscription to an empiricist philosophy of science that limits his vision of the possibility of social change.

Rossi, Alice. "Sentiment and Intellect." In *Essays on Sex Equality*, Chicago, 1970, 1–63. A general introduction to a collection that includes Harriet Taylor's *The Enfranchisement of Women* as well as *The Subjection of Women*. Explores Harriet Taylor's role in Mill's work, from a friendly perspective.

Shanley, Mary L. "Marital Slavery and Friendship." *Political Theory* 8 (1979), 229–47. A useful, general account of Mill's antipathy to existing marital arrangements and his hope for their replacement by a friendship between equals.

Tulloch, Gail. *Mill and Sexual Equality*. Boulder, Co., 1989. Short, clear, sensible book on the place of Mill's feminism in his wider philosophy; friendly but not uncritical in its approach.

Urbanati, Nadia. "J. S. Mill on Androgyny and Ideal Marriage." *Political Theory* 19 (1991), 627–49. Original and intriguing essay on Mill's attempt to go beyond "masculine" and "feminine" ideals of character.

Index